Industries, Firms, and Jobs

Sociological and Economic Approaches

PLENUM STUDIES IN WORK AND INDUSTRY

Series Editors:
Ivar Berg, *University of Pennsylvania, Philadelphia, Pennsylvania*
and Arne L. Kalleberg, *University of North Carolina, Chapel Hill, North Carolina*

WORK AND INDUSTRY
Structures, Markets, and Processes
Arne L. Kalleberg and Ivar Berg

ENSURING MINORITY SUCCESS IN CORPORATE MANAGEMENT
Edited by Donna E. Thompson and Nancy DiTomaso

INDUSTRIES, FIRMS, AND JOBS
Sociological and Economic Approaches
Edited by George Farkas and Paula England

MATERNAL EMPLOYMENT AND CHILDREN'S DEVELOPMENT
Longitudinal Research
Edited by Adele Eskeles Gottfried and Allan W. Gottfried

WORKERS, MANAGERS, AND TECHNOLOGICAL CHANGE
Emerging Patterns of Labor Relations
Edited by Daniel B. Cornfield

A Continuation Order Plan is available for this series. A continuation order will bring delivery of each new volume immediately upon publication. Volumes are billed only upon actual shipment. For further information please contact the publisher.

Industries, Firms, and Jobs

Sociological and Economic Approaches

Edited by

George Farkas

and

Paula England

University of Texas at Dallas
Richardson, Texas

With a Foreword by

Michael Piore

Massachusetts Institute of Technology
Cambridge, Massachusetts

Plenum Press • New York and London

Library of Congress Cataloging in Publication Data

Industries, firms, and jobs: sociological and economic approaches / edited by
    George Farkas and Paula England.
        p.   cm.—(Plenum studies in work and industry)
    Includes bibliographies and index.
    ISBN 0-306-42865-2
    1. Work. 2. Labor supply. 3. Industry. I. Farkas, George, 1946-   . II. England,
Paula. III. Series.
HD4904.I57   1988   88-14858
331.12—dc19   CIP

© 1988 Plenum Press, New York
A Division of Plenum Publishing Corporation
233 Spring Street, New York, N.Y. 10013

All rights reserved

No part of this book may be reproduced, stored in a retrieval system, or transmitted
in any form or by any means, electronic, mechanical, photocopying, microfilming,
recording, or otherwise, without written permission from the Publisher

Printed in the United States of America

Contributors

Robert T. Averitt, Department of Economics, Smith College, Northampton, Massachusetts

Margaret Barton, Systems Research and Applications Corporation, Arlington, Virginia

E. M. Beck, Department of Sociology, University of Georgia, Athens, Georgia

Ivar Berg, College of Arts and Sciences, University of Pennsylvania, Philadelphia, Pennsylvania

Ronald L. Breiger, Department of Sociology, Cornell University, Ithaca, New York

Glenna S. Colclough, Department of Sociology, University of Alabama-Huntsville, Huntsville, Alabama

William T. Dickens, Department of Economics, University of California, Berkeley, Berkeley, California

Nancy DiTomaso, Rutgers Graduate School of Management, Newark, New Jersey

Paula England, School of Social Sciences, University of Texas-Dallas, Richardson, Texas

George Farkas, School of Social Sciences, University of Texas-Dallas, Richardson, Texas

William Form, Department of Sociology, Ohio State University, Columbus, Ohio

Mark Granovetter, Department of Sociology, State University of New York at Stony Brook, Stony Brook, New York

Randy Hodson, Department of Sociology, Indiana University, Bloomington, Indiana

Jerry A. Jacobs, Department of Sociology, University of Pennsylvania, Philadelphia, Pennsylvania

Arne L. Kalleberg, Department of Sociology, University of North Carolina, Chapel Hill, North Carolina

Robert L. Kaufman, Department of Sociology, Ohio State University, Columbus, Ohio

Kevin Lang, Department of Economics, Boston University, Boston, Massachusetts

Toby L. Parcel, Department of Sociology, Ohio State University, Columbus, Ohio

Leann Tigges, Department of Sociology, University of Georgia, Athens, Georgia

Donald Tomaskovic-Devey, Department of Sociology, North Carolina State University, Raleigh, North Carolina

Michael Wallace, Department of Sociology, Ohio State University, Columbus, Ohio

Oliver E. Williamson, Yale University Law School, New Haven, Connecticut

Foreword

This book is a welcome reassertion of an old tradition of interdisciplinary research. That tradition has tended to atrophy in the last decade, largely because of an enormous expansion of the domain of neoclassical economics. The expansion has fed on two scientific developments: first, human capital theory; second, contract theory. Both developments have taken phenomena critical to the operation of the economy but previously understood in terms of categories separate and distinct from those with which economists generally work and sought to apply the same analytical techniques that we use to understand other economic problems.

Human capital theory has applied conventional techniques to questions of labor supply. It began this endeavor with the supply of trained labor and then expanded to a general theory of labor supply by broadening the analysis to the allocation of time over the individual's life, the interdependencies of supply decisions within the family, and finally to the formation of the family itself. Similarly, contract theory has moved from a theory that explains the existence of closed economic institutions to a theory of their formation and internal operation.

The hallmark of both of these developments is the extension and application of analytical techniques based on purposive maximization under contraints and the interaction of individual decision makers through a competitive market or its analogue.

Some of the chapters in this volume reassert an earlier position, that the behavioral assumptions and analytical techniques of conventional neoclassical economics apply to only a limited range of human experience. Outside that range, one must understand behavior in other terms. This position was hence much more tolerant of interdisciplinary approaches to social problems, but it has been fatally flawed by the fact that the precise domain of the conventional assumptions was never delineated. Thus although the existence of certain limits was widely accepted, the limits themselves were never defined. In the place of a clear definition, the boundary was policed by social processes within the profession itself, and the logical flaw was covered by the ridicule and scorn that were heaped on people who moved economics beyond the "appropriate" boundaries.

A chief victim of this approach was Gary Becker, who is the pioneer in applying economic theory to the family, crime, and altruism, all once considered to lie within the realm of sociology. This no doubt accounts for the tone of the introduction to his book, *Economics of Human Behavior*, that of a hurt outsider, which belies his present position of preeminence among labor economists. It is ironic that Becker shares much in common in this regard with the left-wing radical economists. They were treated with much the same scorn and ridicule, and for much the same reason: they too sought to transgress the traditional boundaries that separated economics from other behavior. But if Becker's sin was to move economics into the realm of sociology, the sin of the radicals was to move sociology into economics. One can wonder whether in the long run, researchers can avoid the question of defining exactly what the boundaries of conventional economic assumptions are.

The chapters in this volume show that, for the time being at least, the social strictures of the past have been overcome and it is again possible for economists to work with sociologists and to explore a range of alternative behavioral assumptions without calling into question one's disciplinary credentials.

Michael Piore

Cambridge, Massachusetts

Preface

What are the links among industrial structure, segmentation, the internal structure of firms, job characteristics, technology, productivity, labor markets, and product markets? These questions cross the borders of sociology and economics. This volume presents articles by sociologists and economists working along this border, and sometimes crossing it. The chapters demonstrate the overlap in the topics explored by sociologists and economists, even while they remind us of the continuing differences between the disciplines. In our concluding essay we delineate these differences, while sketching the terms of a possible integration.

To put this volume in the context of the series of books on Work and Industry of which it is a part, we begin with an essay by the editors of the series, Ivar Berg and Arne Kalleberg. This essay, "Work Structures and Markets," presents a set of analytic categories developed in their book, *Work and Industry: Structures, Markets, and Processes*, which began the series. Kalleberg and Berg propose a multidimensional view that examines such work structures as states, classes, occupations, industries, firms, and unions. They argue that work structures affect and are affected by markets for products, capital, natural resources, and labor. What we see as important in this argument is that, while sociologists and ever more economists may dispute extreme versions of the economic market model, this does not suggest that market forces are unimportant to the understanding of the organization and rewards of work. Indeed, economic reasoning about market forces is necessary to explain new structuralist findings, even while such findings present an anomaly for some parts of the orthodox neoclassical market model.

We thank Ivar Berg and Arne Kalleberg for encouraging us to pursue this project and make it a part of their book series. We are also grateful to the "Problems of the Discipline" grant program of the American Sociological Association for supporting the conference at University of Texas-Dallas for which the chapters by Averitt; Lang and Dickens; Farkas, England, and Barton; Williamson; Granovetter; and Hodson were prepared. The conference, organized by us and an economist, Margaret Barton, provided the rare event of sociologists and economists discussing their differences and prospects for integration face to face. Most of the remaining chapters in this volume were presented at a session of the 1986 American Sociological Association meetings organized by Ivar Berg, to whom we are grateful for suggesting their inclusion in this volume.

We also thank William Lin and our friends at the Han Chu restaurant in Dallas for the wonderful banquet over which a number of the ideas presented here were discussed at the conference.

George Farkas
Paula England

Dallas, Texas

Contents

PART I. INTRODUCTION

Chapter 1

Work Structures and Markets: An Analytic Framework **3**

      Arne L. Kalleberg and Ivar Berg

PART II. ECONOMIC SEGMENTATION RECONSIDERED

PART III. INDUSTRIAL STRUCTURE AND MARKETS

Chapter 5

Structural Effects on Wages: Sociological and Economic Views   93

George Farkas, Paula England, and Margaret Barton

Chapter 6

**Schooling and Capitalism: The Effect of Urban Economic Structure
on the Value of Education 113**

E. M. Beck and Glenna S. Colclough

Chapter 7

**Market Concentration and Structural Power as Sources of Industrial
Productivity**   141

Donald Tomaskovic-Devey

PART IV. FIRMS AND INTERNAL LABOR MARKETS

Chapter 8

The Economics and Sociology of Organization: Promoting a Dialogue . .   159

Oliver E. Williamson

Chapter 9

**The Sociological and Economic Approaches to Labor Market
Analysis: A Social Structural View** 187

Mark Granovetter

Chapter 10

Income Determination in Three Internal Labor Markets 217

Nancy DiTomaso

PART V. THE FUTURE OF WORK

Chapter 13

**The Impact of Technology on Work Organization and Work
Outcomes: A Conceptual Framework and Research Agenda**   303

William Form, Robert L. Kaufman, Toby L. Parcel, and
Michael Wallace

PART VI. SOCIOLOGICAL AND ECONOMIC APPROACHES TO THE
STUDY OF INDUSTRIES, FIRMS, AND JOBS

Chapter 14

Economic and Sociological Views of Industries, Firms, and Jobs   331

Paula England and George Farkas

I
INTRODUCTION

Work Structures and Markets
An Analytic Framework

Arne L. Kalleberg and Ivar Berg

I. INTRODUCTION

Work structures and markets are central foci for sociologists and economists seeking to explain a variety of phenomena related to work and industry. By "work structures" we refer to the arrangements, institutions, and patterns used by social actors to deal with the tasks of production and distribution. They represent the hierarchical orderings of persons and clusters of interests, configurations of norms, and the rights and obligations that characterize the relations among economic actors. Work structures describe the ways in which labor is divided, tasks allocated, and authority distributed; they point to reasons why doctors' work is different from teachers' and why executives are able, with wide degrees of freedom, to hire and fire their employees.

The importance of work structures derives ultimately from their significant consequences for a wide range of social phenomena. For example, "new structuralist" sociologists and "new institutional" economists have shown that many work-related inequalities among individuals are generated by correlates of such work structures as firms, industries, occupations, classes, and unions. Work structures help to define the contexts, and many of the parameters of these contexts, within which people are employed and rewarded. Furthermore, some structural locations are "better" places to work than others because they pay higher salaries and provide greater opportunities for advancement to higher-paying positions. Moreover, it is generally assumed that the overwhelming majority of these work structures exist independently

Arne L. Kalleberg • Department of Sociology, University of North Carolina, Chapel Hill, North Carolina 27514.   Ivar Berg • College of Arts and Sciences, University of Pennsylvania, Philadelphia, Pennsylvania 19104.

of, and are temporally and logically prior to, the involvements of people who work in or otherwise have traffic with them.

Since the economies of industrial societies are complex, empirically well-informed insights are needed from many disciplines—industrial and organizational sociology, labor economics, social history, and political science—in order to account for the origins and correlates of work structures. Unfortunately, disciplinary boundaries have often been major impediments to fuller understanding of work structures, as potentially complementary studies at different levels of analysis have been conducted in isolation from one another. For example, sociologists usually study organizational, occupational, and other *work structures*. In contrast, economists typically focus primarily on *markets* and other macroeconomic forces, and make simplifying assumptions about the nature of the work structures that result from them. Advancing our understanding of the institutional order of the economy requires preliminary *syntheses*, at least, of sociological and economic approaches that take into account the diverse units and levels of analysis involved in the organization and experience of work.

In this chapter, we outline a conceptual framework that provides a "way of looking at" work structures and markets.[1] We argue that (1) work structures are complementary and interrelated in theoretically meaningful and important ways, and (2) societal and historical influences, operating through each of four critically important markets, largely determine the correlates of work structures. We then discuss some key issues raised by a multidimensional view of work structures and markets by the expedient and illustrative use of the other contributions to this volume.

II. SOCIOLOGICAL AND ECONOMIC APPROACHES TO WORK STRUCTURES AND MARKETS

In the 1960s and early 1970s, neoclassical economists and status attainment sociologists[2] showed how people's labor force experiences were shaped by their economically rational choices and interests, marginal productivity, and ability to compete in competitive labor markets. These writers tended to take work structures as "given" in their analyses. Seeking to compensate for the individualism of these approaches, "new institutional" economists and "new structuralist" sociologists[3] in the 1970s and 1980s turned their attention to the structure of the economy itself. In contrast to the first group, these writers did not take work structures as given but rather as objects of inquiry, as "social technologies" invented by human architects more or less planfully.

The "new institutional" economists assume that the social relations be-

---

[1]This chapter is a significantly revised version of Chapter 2 from Kalleberg and Berg (1987). Specifically, this version was "written around" chapters prepared for this volume.

[2]See, for example, the summary of orthodox and neoclassical economic theories in Gordon (1972). The status attainment approach is illustrated by Sewell and Hauser (1975).

[3]For reviews of some of this research, see Baron and Bielby (1980); Kalleberg and Sørensen (1979).

tween employers and employees (whether governed by markets or administrative procedures) are central to an understanding of the workings of the economy. They tend, though, to describe these relations in fairly abstract terms. In Chapter 8 in this volume, for example, Williamson accounts for a wide and diverse set of phenomena by applying a relatively simple and basic principle—that actors seek to economize on costs of their transactions. Thus, firms—"governance structures," not "production functions"—try to economize the costs of their transactions as best they can in view of their bounded rationality. This abstract idea takes us some distance toward an explanation of firms' transactions (such as subcontracting and vertical integration), labor market organization, regulation, and corporate governance. Williamson's model even sheds light on some aspects of family organization.

Research by the "new structuralists" in sociology complements the work of the "new institutional" economists by specifying more precisely the *contexts* within which economic actors make their decisions. At the heart of this parallel effort is the postulate that a variety of economic activities may be considered "rational," depending on the particular context. However, these sociologists vary in the way that they conceptualize the relevant "contexts." In this volume, Granovetter, for example, stresses the role of "weak ties" and other aspects of social networks and contacts in forming the social contexts within which work structures are embedded. Other writers focus on work structures such as industries, firms, occupations, and cities.

In general, economists—both neoclassical (with its twin emphases on marginalism and marginal productivity) and "new institutional" (stressing the minimization of transaction costs)—seek to *reduce* complex realities to more basic processes, thus capturing the "core" or "essence" of human behavior in its various forms and deducing specific structures from these more basic ones. In contrast, the "new structuralists" in sociology are less often guided by assumptions that there are "basic" features of human behavior underlying a wide range of work structures and markets. Rather, they more often seek to *include*, in an inductive fashion, a wide range of concepts in their explanations, in order to provide what they hope is a more accurate and comprehensive description of complex realities and to order their independent, "explanatory" variables without reducing them one to the other. While these distinctions highlight some important differences between economists and sociologists, there are considerable differences among members within each discipline in their assumptions as to whether or not explanations of the institutional order of the economy can be reduced to one or a few work structures.

We label as *univariate structuralists* those sociologists (and economists) who focus on the determinants and consequences of one or another work structure (or market) to the virtual exclusion of others. A diverse group, its members have in common the assumption that the logics associated with their favored structure—which they may or may not conceive to be multidimensional—afford the "one best way" to conceptualize and understand problems related to work and industry.

Other sociologists (and economists) may be classified as *multivariate structuralists*. These writers explicitly posit the existence of *multiple* structures and levels of analysis and seek to *integrate* them in accounting for the nature and consequences of work. This approach offers, we believe, the most fruitful opportunities to integrate sociological and economic approaches, and it is accordingly our main focus in this chapter.

III. A MULTIVARIATE STRUCTURALIST APPROACH

Multivariate structuralists are a diverse group. They differ, for example, in the number of work structures they analyze: Some take into account a large number of work structures and seek to assess their relative impacts on a dependent variable(s)[4]; others hold one or more work structures constant in order to examine the nature and consequences of other work structures.[5] In all cases, the researchers attempt to understand explicitly how the structures they investigate are related to others and how these interrelations affect their conclusions and interpretations of findings.

Six basic and conceptually distinct forms or levels of work organization have drawn the lion's share of the attentions of structural sociologists and institutional economists concerned with stratification:

1. Business organizations (firms and establishments), which differ in their size, market power, and extent of internal labor market development.
2. Industries, or groups of firms producing similar products and/or services, which vary in their degree of concentration, capital intensity, and other features related to the nature of product/service production and distribution.
3. Occupations, or technical activities that are transferable among different firms, which differ in their skill content, resource base, and other attributes reflecting the demand for, and supply of, people who perform particular activities in a societal division of labor (we label as "jobs" the specific tasks within specific firms that are not transferable across organizations).
4. Classes, or control relations between occupants of positions in the firm's structure of power and ownership; these relations reflect differences in the circumstances of employers, managers, and workers.
5. Unions, or organizations that represent workers in their relations with employers; unions may be organized along occupation (craft), class or industry (industrial), and/or firm (enterprise) lines.

[4]See, for example, Kalleberg, Wallace, and Althauser (1981); Kerr, Dunlop, Harbison, and Myers (1973); Sabel (1982).
[5]For example, Form (1973) controls for industry and class in order to study differences produced by country, occupation, and organization. Similarly, Gallie (1978) holds occupation and industry constant in order to study the impacts of nation-state structures, unions, and organizations on the nature of work and the experiences of workers.

6. Nation-states; these structures are important for two reasons: The bureaucracies of modern nation-states employ increasingly larger numbers of people; and the policies of political parties, along with cultural differences among societies, affect the ways in which these work structures are related to markets and to inequalities and other outcomes.

A central assumption underlying this multivariate structuralist approach is that these work structures are *complementary* and related to each other in systematic, which is to say, in theoretically important ways. Business organizations are "basic" units of analysis for studying the institutional order of the economy, since the vast majority of people in industrial societies work in them and they are the main sites of labor (and other) market transactions. Business organizations, in turn, can be aggregated into industries, which are groups of firms that produce similar products. Class groups ("classes *in* themselves")—owners, managers, and workers—are defined within each organization, and there are several kinds of linkages among class positions ("classes *for* themselves") in different firms: For example, craft and industrial unions link workers in different companies, and trade associations and directorial "interlocks" link the agents of owners of different firms. Finally, occupations represent technical activities that are transferable across firms, while jobs are specific tasks within particular organizations.

Multivariate structuralists also argue, as we have noted, that the impacts of these work structures cannot be reduced to one another; each work structure *independently* shapes the nature and consequences of work. Hence, a particular level of analysis—whether organizations, industries, occupations, classes, or similar bodies—is not necessarily the most "appropriate" one for all questions. By contrast, "univariate structuralists" confine their attention to a single level of analysis as follows: Those studying single organizations often do so without considering the industries that form the environments of these organizations and the work structures (such as unions, occupations, or classes) that may span firms; those studying differences among industries often neglect differences in the organization of production within these industries; and those studying occupations often fail to consider differences in the economic organizations within which the occupational activities are performed.

Moreover, multivariate structuralists frequently seek to integrate insights from economics and sociology in order to account for the origins and consequences of work structures. The extension of renewed dialogues between some of the leading members of these disciplines can in part be traced to the growing recognition that neither group can afford to ignore the insights of the other in accounting for differences in inequality and growth rates among the economies of both the less and the more developed nations. In particular, a multivariate structuralist approach is useful for linking the economists' study of markets to the sociologists' focus on work structures and concrete institutions. This approach is useful because multivariate structuralists argue that the origins (or ultimate "causes") of work structures are to be found in economists' *markets* within which exchanges take place *and* in the political and other processes that determine the mix of market and nonmarket initiatives in a society, in an industry, in an occupation, and in firms. As an example, police officers are concerned both with their income returns in narrow economic terms *and* with preserving differences between themselves and other uniformed municipal workers in social or social-psychological terms.

A. Markets

We assume that a central feature of all societies is the need for individuals and groups to exchange goods and services with each other in order to satisfy their wants. This leads them to develop means for conducting transactions that economic agents hope will become conveniently routinized. In industrial societies, these exchanges take place in markets, which can be arrayed along a continuum from more to less competitive or planned; hence, markets are useful constructs for studying work structures even when they do not fit the economic textbook's "perfectly competitive" model. While markets are most visible as mechanisms for the distribution of human resources and opportunities in capitalist systems of production, even the economies of socialist countries depend on markets, since they must compete with other countries in a capitalist world system. In addition, in socialist economies many goods and services may more often be exchanged in "black" markets that, while not legally sanctioned by the state, have been legitimated by long-time practices of their participants as efficient ways to carry out exchanges.

Exchange relations in industrial societies are complex, and so there are many types of markets. Four major types of markets are especially important to work structures. These markets vary in the commodities and capacities being exchanged (labor power, goods and services, money and credit, raw materials and other resources) and in the types of actors (the buyers, sellers, and traders) involved in the exchange. These markets are as follows:

1. Labor markets, the arenas in which workers exchange their labor power, creative capacities (and even their loyalties) with employers in return for wages, status, and other job rewards. Labor markets are intimately related to the institutions and practices that govern the purchase, sale, and pricing of labor services; they are thus the markets wherein labor force inequalities are most directly generated.

2. Product markets, wherein goods and services are bought and sold. In advanced industrial societies, sellers in product markets are generally organizations that range from highly specialized small entrepreneurs to giant corporations selling many different types of products. The buyers in these markets are also diverse, and include individual consumers, other organizations, and governments.

3. Capital markets, wherein the key actors are buyers and sellers (and their agents) of cash, credit, stocks and bonds, and "futures" of different types. The buyers and sellers in these markets are also diverse, and include those individuals or organizations with sufficient resources to participate.

4. Resource markets, which refer to the buyers, sellers, and intermedi-

aries of (a) raw materials such as land, water, fuel, ores, crops, and natural resources; (b) infrastructures (e.g., communities offer resources such as zoning adjustments, tax abatements, access roads, and no- or low-cost water and sewage "hook-ups" to companies in order to attract them to their areas); (c) other organizations (e.g., as in the case of mergers and acquisitions): and (d) ideas (patents, copyrights) and other products of the "knowledge" industry.

A fifth type of market that is becoming increasingly important is the "political market," in which buyers such as interest groups bargain for the help of the state (or the several states in the United States) in a variety of areas, such as tax policies, tariffs, import licenses, public works, defense contracts, loan guarantee programs, and the use of public lands.

B. Markets and Work Structures

The four basic markets can be cross-classified with the six basic work structures, as shown in the matrix in Figure 1. This matrix underscores our theme that it is useful to move away from excessively reductionist thinking and toward more "holistic," synthetic thinking. The cells represent intersections between markets and work structures, and the examples in the cells illustrate phenomena that result from the interplay between markets and structures.

For example, "conglomeration" is an organizational outcome of developments in capital markets; the "oil crisis" in the mid-1970s was a national resource market problem; and "deskilling" was a labor market phenomenon that accompanied the weakening of craft unions' power and growing emphases by employers on jobs as key units in the division of labor. Moreover, the phenomena in the various cells are interdependent: What happens in a partic-

Work Structures

	State	Class	Occupation	Industry	Business organization	Union
Product markets				4		
Capital markets		2			5	
Resource markets	1					
Labor markets			3			6

Examples:
1. Oil crisis
2. Economic concentration
3. Wage contours
4. "Mass" vs. "batch" markets
5. Conglomeration
6. Deskilling

Figure 1. Relations between work structures and markets.

ular cell depends, more or less, on what happens in several other cells. Thus, occupational wage differences in labor markets depend on the labor market activities of unions and on the policies of industries and organizations. They also depend upon developments in product, capital, and resource markets. Conglomeration, as a second example, is affected by the state's actions in capital markets not less than by "raiders'" interests in either diversification, "cash cows," or stock price "run-ups."

The matrix also helps to classify the research by "new institutional" economists and "new structural" sociologists, who differ in their emphases on particular columns, rows, and/or cells of this matrix. Some seek to explain phenomena in a large number of cells: Williamson, for example, seeks to account for institutional structures in *each* of these cells on the basis of a single principle (economizing on transaction costs). Others assume that there are linkages among phenomena in several cells, as do "dual economy" sociologists when they argue that concentration and centralization of product and capital markets—reflected in the unequal power of employers (industries, business organizations)—are "matched" by occupational and union differences in workers' power in labor markets.[6] Still others confine their attention to a single cell or small group of cells, as when "dual labor market" theorists focus on occupational or organizational differences in labor markets.

Many of the strands of research by sociologists and economists on work structures and markets are represented by the other chapters in this volume. We have already noted, for example, that the work by Oliver Williamson illustrates the "new institutional" economic approach. We now turn to a discussion of the other chapters with the aim of showing that they can be profitably located in one or more cells of our matrix. Some of these authors emphasize the interactions (cells) of rows with columns in the matrix, or the relationships between work structures and markets; others focus on the columns, or the interrelations among work structures themselves. Our discussion attempts to illustrate the utility of the matrix as a way of organizing research on work structures and markets as well as to point out some of the connections among the chapters.

IV. THE INTERPLAY BETWEEN MARKETS AND WORK STRUCTURES

A. The Dual Economy

Many "new structuralist" sociologists have turned to dual economy theory in order to understand the dynamics of firms and industries and to account for the organizational bases of stratification. The statement of dual economy theory on which they typically draw was formulated by an economist, Robert T. Averitt (1968). In "The Prospects for Economic Dualism: A

---

[6]See the discussion in Hodson and Kaufman (1982).

Historical Perspective," he reviews some of the background of, and developments since, the publication of his classic work, which applied economic dualism to industrial economies and provided a bridge between the older institutionalists and the "new institutional economists." He argues that a key division in the economy is that between "center" (large, multiproduct) and periphery (small, single-product) firms. The two kinds of firms are linked through dependency and other hierarchical relations: For example, large "parent" organizations often subcontract work to their smaller "satellites" or "children." This polarization or "duality" is a "normal" by-product of the operation of product markets and is a highly developed and enduring feature of industrial economies.

Our matrix is useful for summarizing some key assumptions related to the notion of business dualism. With only a slight amount of recasting, we can interpret Averitt's argument as linking changes in product markets to the creation of duality among firms and industries. Moreover, he recognizes that these developments have consequences for phenomena in other cells. For example, the two kinds of business organizations are associated with different labor market segments: Center firms tend to establish firm internal labor markets, while low-paying, "dead-end" jobs are well adapted to the needs of "periphery" firms. And, industrial differences reflect, in large part, the number and sizes of their constituent organizations as well as the types of unionization found in them. This linkage between business dualism and industries has often been used by "dual economy" sociologists to justify their measurement of dualism by means of industrial variables.

B. Dual Labor Markets

Writers on dual and/or segmented labor markets seek to explain how labor markets become and remain segmented along occupational, job, and organizational lines. As Kevin Lang and William Dickens note in "Neoclassical and Sociological Perspectives on Segmented Labor Markets," the early dual labor market models differed from neoclassical models in their assumptions that jobs are rationed on the basis of nonprice criteria (such as race) and that the motivations, choices, and other social psychological attributes of labor market participants are not exogenous to the economic system. However, they suggest that recent research offers possibilities of integrating these assumptions with the neoclassical approach.

C. Economic Segmentation and Worker Power

The assumption of dual economy theorists that the power of employers is "matched" by the organizational power of employees is based in part on the belief that indicators of employers' power such as market concentration, large size, and capital intensive production technologies also constitute resources for their employees. However, the interplay between the power of employers and employees is more complex than dual economy theories often suggest, and these interrelations need to be examined using a multivariate structural approach that specifies how markets (product, capital, resource, and labor) differentiate work structures such as industries, firms, and unions.

The conditions that contribute to the power of employers and employees are examined by George Farkas, Paula England and Margaret Barton in "Structural Effects on Wages: Sociological and Economic Views." They argue that examining sources of the relative power of employers and employees provides a fruitful way of integrating economic and sociological approaches to economic inequality. In particular, they suggest that differences in the nature of factor and product markets will affect both the size of profits available for distribution and the bargaining strength of employees. Moreover, while they assume that conditions leading to high profits will also tend to enhance employees' bargaining power, such power is also affected by several other work structures.

V. INTERRELATIONS AMONG WORK STRUCTURES

Other authors represented in this volume focus on the consequences of work structures rather than on how these structures derive from the operation of markets. These structuralists tend to examine the "columns" of the matrix, or the interrelations among work structures.

A. Industries

Donald Tomaskovic-Devey, in "Market Concentration and Structural Power as Sources of Industrial Productivity," examines how differences in productivity among industries (both manufacturing and nonmanufacturing) are related to other industrial correlates (such as technology, structural power, and market concentration). These industrial structures, in turn, are outcomes of factors related to product and capital markets. His chapter illustrates a "univariate industry" approach: While he recognizes that industrial correlates are multidimensional, he sets aside the impacts of *other* work structures on productivity. This is problematical since there are good reasons to suspect that industrial differences are only a part of the picture, since there are undoubtedly within-industry differences in productivity: Members of different *occupations* are likely to differ in their productivity, and some *organizations* in an industry, all things considered, will typically be more productive (and hence more successful) than others.

Other authors adopt a multivariate approach to the study of the impacts of industry structures. Leann M. Tigges, in "Dueling Sectors: The Role of Service Industries in the Earnings Process of the Dual Economy," focuses on "what" is produced by an industry and argues that the distinction between transformative and service industries—the second of which is of growing importance in modern societies—is salient for understanding income differences. Consistent with a multivariate structural approach, she argues that the structure of earnings inequality is generated by work structures in addition to industries: *organizational* changes in the "how" of production that have generated a "dual economy" (owing to data limitations, however, she distinguishes between core and periphery capital sectors using data on industries), and changes in how *occupational* activities are rewarded in labor markets. Indeed, "services" may be an occupational as well as an industrial category, suggesting the utility of viewing this sector in "multivariate" terms, i.e., as reflecting intersections of "service" industries *and* occupations.

The importance of the interplay between industries and occupations for explaining labor market behaviors is also a theme in Jerry Jacobs and Ronald Brieger's "Careers, Industries, and Occupations: Industrial Segmentation Reconsidered." They argue that there is only a weak correspondence between industrial sectors (economic dualism among employers) and occupational segments (dualism/segmentation among employees); therefore, each of these work structures needs to be taken into account when examining patterns of mobility produced by the other. Their empirical analysis suggests that mobility is almost as great *between* core and peripheral industries as among industries within the core or within the periphery.

Two additional chapters examine the impact of a key correlate of industries—technology—on occupational characteristics. For example, Randy Hodson, in "Good Jobs and Bad Management: How New Problems Evoke Old Solutions in High-Tech Settings," shows that technological change affects a variety of outcomes (skill change, commitment, and satisfaction) among members of different occupations/classes (workers, engineers, and managers) in 14 "high-tech" companies. Moreover, William Form, Robert L. Kaufman, Toby L. Parcel, and Michael Wallace, in "The Impact of Technology on Work Organization and Work Outcomes: A Conceptual Framework and Research Agenda," speculate on the consequences of technological change for work structures at several levels of social organization. Their framework draws upon the sociological as well as the economic literature and outlines a variety of alternative research designs that can be used to examine the relations among correlates of industries, organizations, and occupations.

B. Firms

Mark Granovetter, in "The Sociological and Economic Approaches to Labor Market Analysis: A Social Structural View," focuses on correlates of *firms* in order to compare (and integrate) sociological and economic approaches to a key labor force behavior—job mobility. He questions the assumption that such behaviors are efficient adaptations to economic problems and doubts whether employees' long tenures imply good job matches and whether low interfirm mobility reflects the efficiency of firm internal labor markets. Rather, he argues, the lower interfirm mobility experienced by members of firm internal labor markets reflects the constraints associated with the social networks and other social structures in which economic behavior is embedded. Consistent with a multivariate structuralist approach, he argues that characteristics of *occupations* and *industries* affect social networks and thus influence rates of mobility within and between firms. For example, incumbents of some occupations are more committed to their occupational activities than others, and are more likely to change firms and pursue their occupations at the expense of their employing organizations. In addition, industrial characteristics that link individual performance to organizational success may limit interfirm mobility: Firms in the airline industry, where mistakes can have grave consequences, are less likely to rely on the external labor market as a source of recruits than are firms in other industries.

Nancy DiTomaso, in "Income Determination in Three Internal Labor Markets," examines the role of internal labor markets in firms in generating interfirm income differences. Consistent with a multivariate structural approach, she argues that other work structures need to be considered in addition to firms in order to explain economic inequality. Hence, within each organization, she looks at earnings differences among members of six nonmanagerial, nonprofessional occupations (technical, craft, operatives, clerical, laborers, service), which she assumes reflect different "labor market segments." Her results suggest that the characteristics of occupations depend on the nature of the firm and the particular demographic group. Secretaries within the manufacturing firm, for example, were paid more than secretaries within the nonmanufacturing firm or the public agency.

C. Cities

A work structure that we have not considered explicitly, but that constitutes an important source of differentiation among the phenomonological structures related to work and industry, is the city or urban area. E. M. Beck and Glenna S. Colclough, in "Schooling and Capitalism: The Effect of Urban Economic Structure on the Value of Education," argue that labor and product markets are segmented by cities, and that differences in the "organization of production of commodities and services" are in part reflected in city differences in occupational and industrial structures. A consequence of these differences, they argue, is to generate inequalities in the economic returns to education among SMSAs (Standard Metropolitan Statistical Areas) that vanish when labor market data are aggregated. However, the SMSA is not equally useful for examining the boundaries of all occupations and industries: Some operate in local labor markets, while other occupations and industries compete in national (and international) markets. We speculate that the economic value of education may be less variable among employees in occupations or industries that operate in national/international labor or product markets than for those who are members of occupations and industries that are bounded by local markets. As the authors themselves suggest, this may account for the great heterogeneity in the returns to education across SMSAs for blacks, women, and the young; members of these groups tend more often to be in local labor markets and to be less mobile than white males.

VI. STUDYING WORK STRUCTURES AND MARKETS: A RESEARCH AGENDA

In this final section, we briefly outline some of the general contours of needed research based on the multivariate approach to work structures and markets that we favor.

A. Disaggregated Studies of Specific Work Structures

A multivariate approach does not imply that "good" studies should incorporate in their explanations *all* work structures, nor that studies including "more" work structures are "better" than those with fewer. Rather, what those in the multivariate structural tradition have in common is that they seek to understand how work structures are related to each other. Disaggregated studies of particular organizations, occupations, industries, class groups, or unions are useful for this purpose, since they enable the researcher to hold some work structures constant in order to analyze the nature and consequences of others (see, for example, Granovetter's argument for the need to disaggregate mobility patterns, and DiTomaso's summary of the advantages of a focus on specific firms).

Disaggregated studies, however, need to pay particular attention to how a given work structure under examination is embedded in the others. Studies of organizations, as an example, need to take account of their industrial and occupational contexts; studies of occupations need to consider differences in how the activity is organized in different firms, and so on. This is often a difficult problem, since a disaggregated case study approach may confound different types of work structures. In DiTomaso's study, for example, the three organizations were selected to represent sectoral "types," and the question accordingly arises concerning to what extent the organizational differences she observed are due to other "parental" or adjacent work structures, such as industries or unions.

B. Segmentation in the Labor Force

We have not touched directly upon gender, race, and age differences, though these are nonetheless very important sources of structural differentiation in the labor force. Men and women, whites and nonwhites, younger and older people, for example, are allocated to different positions in the structure of work and may often be treated differently from others in the same structural position. For example, Beck and Colclough demonstrate that the economic returns to education across cities differ among gender/race groups. And DiTomaso shows that ethnicity and gender are key sources of differentiation within firms. It is necessary to examine systematically the dimensions of industries and occupations that are responsible for these results and, more generally, for segmenting the labor force with respect to patterns of job mobility and earnings determination.

C. Organization-Based Multilevel Research Designs

Though useful for many purposes, the most common way of collecting data in stratification research—from interviews with individuals selected by household sampling frames—is simply inadequate for studying work structures and their consequences. There are several reasons for this: (1) It is difficult, if not impossible, to obtain information on organizational structures from interviews with individual employees; (2) these samples are samples of people, not jobs; and (3) such samples rarely yield more than one or two persons who work in the same organization, thus making it impossible to examine differences among people in the same company. One way to overcome these limitations is to sample organizations, and then to collect data from clusters of individuals within these organizations. This approach not only facilitates the collection of information on organizations, it also enables investigators to study the relative impacts on inequality of organizations, occupations, unions, classes, and the other work structures that constitute the institutional order of the economy.

D. Cross-National Differences

There are ample reasons for suspecting that work structures and markets differ among countries. Nevertheless, we have little hard evidence on such cross-national differences, since the overwhelming preponderance of research on structures and markets has been limited to the United States. Consequently, many of our conclusions about work structures and markets are undoubtedly colored by features that may be specific to the U.S. economy. A fuller understanding of the phenomena suggested by the cells in our matrix demands comparative studies that would enable one to assess the roles of institutional and cultural differences among nations. Only by examining these issues comparatively for a wide range of cultural and societal contexts will we be able to appreciate the cross-national diversity in the correlates and consequences of work structures and markets.

REFERENCES

Averitt, Robert, T. 1968. *The Dual Economy: The Dynamics of American Industry Structure.* New York: W. W. Norton.

Baron, James N., and William T. Bielby. 1980. "Bringing the Firms Back In: Stratification, Segmentation, and the Organization of Work." *American Sociological Review* 45:737–765.

Form, William H. 1973. "The Internal Stratification of the Working Class: System Involvements of Auto Workers in Four Countries." *American Sociological Review* 38:697–711.

Gallie, Duncan. 1978. *In Search of the New Working Class: Automation and Social Integration within the Capitalist Enterprise.* New York: Cambridge University Press.

Gordon, David M. 1972. *Theories of Poverty and Underemployment.* Lexington, MA: D. C. Heath.

Hodson, Randy, and Robert L. Kaufman. 1982. "Economic Dualism: A Critical Review." *American Sociological Review* 47:727–739.

Kalleberg, Arne L., and Ivar Berg. 1987. *Work and Industry: Structures, Markets, and Processes*. New York: Plenum Press.

Kalleberg, Arne L., and Aage B. Sørensen. 1979. "The Sociology of Labor Markets." *Annual Review of Sociology* 5:351–379.

Kalleberg, Arne L., Michael Wallace, and Robert P. Althauser. 1981. "Economic Segmentation, Worker Power, and Income Inequality." *American Journal of Sociology* 87:651–683.

Kerr, Clark, John T. Dunlop, Frederick H. Harbison, and Charles A. Myers. 1973. *Industrialism and Industrial Man*. London: Penguin Press.

Sabel, Charles F. 1982. *Work and Politics*. New York: Cambridge University Press.

Sewell, William H., and Robert M. Hauser. 1975. *Education, Occupation, and Earnings: Achievement in the Early Career*. New York: Academic Press.

II

ECONOMIC SEGMENTATION
RECONSIDERED

Theories of economic segmentation (or dualism) are based on the view that firms or industries can be usefully categorized according to whether they belong to the core (oligopolistic, noncompetitive, large-firm, high-wage) or peripheral (competitive, small-firm, low-wage) sector of the economy. (Sometimes more than two sectors are posited.) The study of firms, industrial organization, and the operation of product markets is thereby linked to the study of labor market employment practices and worker outcomes. Since this linkage is of obvious value for a variety of sociological and economic issues, notions of economic segmentation have been widely discussed within each discipline. Moreover, rather than arising independently within the two disciplines, the evolution of these ideas evidences the sort of interdisciplinary dialogue that is the central theme of this volume. Yet even here, intellectual progress would be facilitated by explicit attempts to bridge the gap between the sociological and economic versions of these ideas. This section's papers make progress in this direction.

Economic dualism or segmentation theory has undergone an intellectual odyssey involving both disciplines. Its modern beginnings can be traced to Robert Averitt's 1968 book, The Dual Economy, a study in the economics of industrial organization. Throughout the 1970s and into the 1980s this viewpoint was attacked by neoclassical economists such as Glen Cain and Michael Wachter, and was kept (barely) alive within economics only by the attention of iconoclasts such as Michael Piore or Marxists such as David Gordon and Richard Edwards. By contrast, "new structuralist" sociologists seized the segmentation notion as the basis of an extensive series of empirical studies. These became far more central to the sociological literature than their antecedents had been within economics. (Sociological studies include works by Beck, Kalleberg, Hodson, Bielby, and Baron, among others.) Now, 20 years after Averitt's book, the work of an energetic group of economists is attempting to reintegrate segmented labor market theory into a newly eclectic neoclassical mainstream.

The three chapters in this section each connect to one of these strands of economic dualism's development. Economist Robert Averitt places his original notion within the historical context of the development of economics as a policy science. He also looks ahead to its future uses. Sociologists Jacobs and Breiger provide a new test of the implications of one portion of the sociological segmentation literature. Economists

Lang and Dickens critically examine both recent sociological studies and the burgeoning mainstream economic literature on segmented labor markets. Central to all three chapters is the question of the existence of labor market segments offering different compensation to identical workers, with a queue forming for the high-wage jobs, whose compensation level persists even in the face of excess supply. That is, labor immobility is observed, in which workers in low-wage jobs are unable to acquire high-wage jobs by partially "bidding down" their wages. The theory and empirics of such sectoral differentation, accompanied by intersectoral immobility, are prominent features of recent research in this area.

In "Prospects for Economic Dualism: A Historical Perspective," Averitt presents dualism as a revisionist approach to the economics of industrial organization. Standard industrial organization analysis categorizes industries according to the extent to which they depart from perfect (price) competition. By contrast, economic dualism is a theory of firms, not industries. The key insight is that small (peripheral) firms generally conform to the expectations of neoclassical theory, whereas large (core) firms do not. Thus, the neoclassical theory of the firm, with its emphasis on maximizing profits under the constraints of revenue and cost curves, applies best to peripheral sector firms. Core firms, which are typically multiproduct and multi-industry, possess considerable market power, only a portion of which is explained by their status as oligopolists. This, combined with their access to the funds necessary for large-scale investment, enables them to pursue a range of strategies and tactics that are simply not available to peripheral firms. Examples include seeking and gaining favorable treatment from the government sector, operating across national boundaries, and manipulating the demand for their product. Accordingly, a nonneoclassical theory of the behavior of large-scale economic institutions is required to understand them.

Averitt notes that dualism has long had greater appeal to sociologists than to mainstream economists. This is because dualism is fundamentally a theory of business hierarchy, and hierarchical notions are basic to sociology but have little place within neoclassical economics. (For further discussion of this point, see Chapter 14 by England and Farkas.) Averitt's emphasis upon the firm rather than the industry as the unit of analysis for segmentation studies is consistent with recent findings and directions within the sociological branch of this literature. Thus, a recent empirical study states: "This paper has demonstrated the utility of conceiving and measuring segmentation in organizational terms. Our analyses show that work arrangements and labor market structures are indeed related to environmental dominance and organizational complexity. However, there is little evidence of discrete sectors of economic activity, particularly along industrial lines" (Baron and Bielby, 1984:471). Thus, sociologists are increasingly turning away from their previous emphasis upon industrial segmentation, and concentrating instead on firm-level analyses. Further evidence for this view is provided by Jacobs and Breiger in Chapter 3.

In "Careers, Industries, and Occupations: Industrial Segmentation Reconsidered," Jacobs and Breiger seek to validate the industrial sectors reported by Tolbert, Horan, and Beck, and/or Bibb and Form by showing that the boundaries of these sectors also define barriers to job mobility. Segmentation based on industrial sectors is valid if job mobility within these sectors is common, while mobility between sectors is uncommon. Such a finding would help explain the failure of market forces to erode the intersectoral wage differentials that are one of the central points of new structuralist studies.

However, Jacobs and Breiger's findings fail to sustain the industry sector view of barriers to mobility, at least for white males, to whom their analysis is limited. Rather, they find that, once one has accounted for the barriers to moving out of one's detailed industry and occupation, uniquely sectoral barriers to mobility are no longer in evidence. These findings suggest generalized sluggishness in mobility between jobs and firms, rather than specific sectoral boundaries constraining mobility. Thus, they are consistent with Averitt's and Baron and Bielby's emphasis upon the firm level of analysis, and support a move away from more aggregated units such as industrial sectors.

A similar point of view underlies the Lang and Dickens chapter, "Neoclassical and Sociological Perspectives on Segmented Labor Markets." In their discussion of "new neoclassical" efficiency wage and related models, they focus on jobs and their embeddedness within firm and industry organizational characteristics. Their stylized facts include the following: First, certain jobs pay above market-clearing wages, so that workers queue up for these jobs, yet the high wages persist in the face of the queues. Second, these wages may be explicable from efficiency wage models in which output depends upon the wage itself. That is, above market-clearing wages maximize profits for some firms. This depends upon the firm's technology; firms with high capital/labor ratios will tend to pay high wages since the need to avoid shirking, absenteeism, and quits is greatest in the presence of large quantities of fixed capital. Such firms tend to lie in the monopoly sector, so there is typically at least a loose correspondance between economic (industrial) sectors and labor market sectors. Third, workers' social-psychological characteristics are endogenous to the job held. This is similar to the view taken by sociologist Melvin Kohn and his co-workers. Lang and Dickens place particular emphasis on the ability of efficiency wages to increase workers' effort and trustworthiness, and to reduce turnover.

The Lang and Dickens chapter is exemplary in that here the dialogue between sociology and economics is fully joined. Referring to the sociological literature as theories of "dual or segmented economy" and to the economic literature as theories of "dual or segmented labor markets," they suggest that both are compatible with the "new neoclassical" view. Within this emerging perspective, the organizational dimensions of technololgy, work, and authority, and the individual social-psychological dimensions of "fairness," the sharing of oligopoly rents, and the elicitation of worker effort are joined to concerns of worker mobility and wage competition in labor markets. Thus, the closing pages of this chapter contain a vision of a truly integrated social/economic theory of firms and workers in which the economists' traditional concern with market forces is fully joined to the sociologists' traditional concern with organizational arrangements and workers' social psychology.

Of course, such a grand design slights or excludes much that some scholars believe to be essential (for example, the class and power structure of society) and in any event is not easily implemented. Accordingly, we recognize that very real disputes still exist among scholars in this field. Indeed, the rather different emphases with which much of the same terrain can be surveyed are illustrated in the chapters by Farkas, England, and Barton, by Granovetter, and by Williamson, all in this volume. Nevertheless, the sociological/economic dialogue has now reached a point where it provides very rich implications for future work. These include the suggestion to disaggregate down to the job level and to place this job within its organizational and market contexts. This must include issues associated with structural effects on workers' behavior and rewards and their link with the organization and technology of production. While economists must correct their tendency to slight such matters, sociologists must learn to explicitly incorporate within their models the very real pressure of competitive market forces whose omnipresence remains the great insight of the neoclassical perspective.

REFERENCES

Baron, James N., and William T. Bielby. 1984. "The Organization of Work in a Segmented Economy." *American Sociological Review* 49:454–473.

2

The Prospects for Economic Dualism
A Historical Perspective

Robert T. Averitt

I. INTRODUCTION

Economics is a policy science. It has been so from the beginning. In the Middle Ages the Church promulgated a doctrine of just price and a prohibition against usury. The enforcement of just price allowed the Church to institute price controls. Country roads were isolated and they carried light traffic by contemporary standards. The infrequent inns on these roads had little competition and could charge what the market would bear. The doctrine of just price was devised to limit the monopoly pricing of such enterprises. The prohibition against usurious rates of interest was an ecclesiastical monetary policy. Unable to regulate the supply of money, the Church pursued the Keynesian option of setting interest rates.

By the 17th century England was a major trading nation, pursuing its international economic interests through the use of royal trading companies like the East India Company. Spain was confiscating gold from the Indians in the New World, then shipping this international currency back to Europe. The English discovered Indian corn and tobacco in their New World territory, but no gold. European armies were heavily peopled with mercenaries, and professional soldiers usually demanded their pay in gold. To lack gold was to suffer a national defense manpower gap. The English adopted two strategies for acquiring gold. The Sir Francis Drake strategy, piracy on the high seas, met with some success. But the second strategy, maintaining a favorable balance of trade with Spain and other nations, offered more long-run promise.

The English Crown's economic advisers adhered to a policy called bul-

Robert T. Averitt • Department of Economics, Smith College, Northampton, Massachusetts 01063.

lionism. The bullionists urged the king to store all of the gold that came into England while actively trading to acquire more foreign gold. This policy of hoarding gold seriously constrained the liquidity of England's trading companies. Sir Thomas Mun, an employee of the East India Company, wrote an influential tract published in 1630 entitled *England's Treasure by Foreign Trade*, perhaps the first systematic economic treatise in the English language (Mun, 1630/1946). Mun argued against government restrictions on the movement of gold because it restrained the ability of traders to increase England's treasure. Mun did agree with the bullionists in their assertion that the nation's wealth is enhanced by an inflow of international money. Mun's argument came to be called mercantilism, but it uses what we would recognize as a monetarist argument to justify unfettered international marketing.

Adam Smith advanced the appeal for free markets even in his opposition to the mercantilist argument. The East India Company and the Hudson's Bay Company were active traders, but they were also state-chartered monopolies. In *The Wealth of Nations*, published in 1776, Smith rejects the notion that economic activity is a zero-sum game. England need not grow wealthy at Spain's expense. A nation's wealth springs from the efforts of its own domestic labor force. It is labor that creates wealth, not foreign trade. If England's wealth is to be maximized, its labor force must be specialized, labor must work with abundant capital, and domestic markets must be freed of government restrictions. Smith saw that trading in markets gave vent to a natural harmony of interests between buyer and seller, allowing both to improve their condition through trading (Smith, 1776/1937). David Ricardo (1817/1911) agreed with Smith and used his seat in Parliament (1819–1823) to argue against the English Corn Laws, a set of statutes that restricted the importation of foreign grain in order to subsidize English farmers.

Sir Thomas Mun was an active international trader during the opening of extensive commerce between Europe and the New World. He developed a trade theory in response to this commercial expansion. By the late 18th and early 19th centuries the expansion of international trade was accompanied by a quickening of domestic economic activity that we refer to as the industrial revolution. James Watt received a patent on his new steam engine in 1776, the same year that Adam Smith published *The Wealth of Nations*. Ricardo developed a sophisticated trade theory based on comparative advantage, but he integrated his international economics with a domestic economic theory. For Smith and Ricardo, writing at the start of the industrial revolution, the key to augmenting labor's productivity was increasing the quantity of capital with which labor worked. The principal source of industrial capital was the savings of individual capitalists, so Smith and Ricardo argued that the wealth of the nation depended upon the distribution of income. When income flows tilted toward capitalists, investment spending and industrial wealth increased. If the gains from economic growth shifted toward the landed gentry, little capital would be accumulated. Of course, this system of thought, now known as classical economics, was partly based upon definitions. If rural landowners saved and invested in industrial capital they became capitalists.

Classical economic theory dominated formal economics for 100 years, roughly from the publication of Adam Smith's *The Wealth of Nations* in 1776 to the introduction of Alfred Marshall's *Principles of Economics* in 1890 (Marshall, 1890/1920). Classical economics was a supply-side theory. With industrialization just beginning, speculation about the nature of demand seemed premature. A poor nation just beginning to move into the process of modern development can easily absorb everything that can be produced, particularly if the international trading system is well developed. Until the 20th century a theory that subjugated demand and the distribution of income to the service of production seemed reasonable. But by 1890 the early signs of genuine affluence were beginning to require an economic analysis of demand just as labor's growing productivity had fostered a theory of supply a century before. Marshall's *Principles* provided an analysis of demand to complement the classical theory of supply. The founding text of neoclassical economics preceded the 20th century by just 10 years.

Neoclassical economics completed the market-justifying job that Mun began in the 17th century. Mun argued that freeing international markets from government interference would increase England's treasure. Smith and Ricardo added that government should avoid regulating virtually all domestic markets as well. All three economists agreed that free markets fostered faster economic growth and economic development. Following William Stanley Jevons (Jevons, 1911), Marshall added the theory of consumer demand. Not only did a market economy encourage growth (even Karl Marx admitted as much), but it also allowed consumers a maximum range of individual choice. The ultimate goal of production, after all, is not just to produce steel mills to produce more steel to be used in producing more steel mills. The ultimate goal of production is consumption. Who is the final authority on consumption? The answer is clear. Individual consumers are the supreme judge of consumption goods. With neoclassical economics the best economy becomes one that maximizes utility for the greatest number for the longest time. The long intellectual march from Church regulation of the economy for the glory of God through state regulation of the economic system for the benefit of the secular kingdom ends with neoclassical economic theory. By 1890 the solitary individual had become the theoretical center of economic analysis in the Western world.

II. THE ENLIGHTENMENT AND ECONOMIC THEORY

The elevation of the individual and the demotion of religious, governmental, and other institutions by economic theory was part of a slow but steady shift in ideology that took place in Western thought during the past three centuries. This sweeping change in social thought, commonly called the *enlightenment*, is characterized by a movement away from theories based upon *hierarchy* in favor of those based on *interchangeability*. The traditional church and state are based on hierarchy. In the Middle Ages the prevailing image of social life was based upon the great chain of being (Lovejoy, 1936). God is at the top of the chain. Man stands just below God, with angels suspended between God and man. Angels look something like men, yet they have the godlike ability to fly on their own. As Billy Graham recently wrote, angels are God's secret messengers to mankind. The great chain of being continues below homo sapiens throughout the animal kingdom until it reaches an end with snakes, the devil's secret messengers.

If one accepts the logic of the great chain of being, and until very recently most residents of the Western world did so, it follows that human life should be organized according to hierarchy as well. In the Church hierarchy the Pope sits at the top, just beneath the angels. The king occupies a similar position in the nation-state. Indeed, the royal doctrine was one of the divine right of kings. The king and the Pope are at the top of their respective hierarchies and everyone else has his or her appointed place. It is the responsibility of all individuals to discover the role that God intended them to play. In the theater of life God wrote many parts, some of them leading roles, others bit parts. But from the highest to the lowest all are essential. Virtue is found in discovering one's role and playing it well (MacIntyre, 1981). The virtuous life is one lived in one's rightful place and lived according to the rules governing that place. The virtuous peasant wife plays her role in the great chain of being no less than the virtuous king. In the good society the great chain of being is unbroken.

Social life, including its economic activities, is choreographed by a dominating social myth when societies are well organized. Until the 17th century life in the Western world was played out in harmony with the great chain of being and its mandate that every person find his or her rightful place and fill that place according to its script. The enlightenment program challenged that myth. In the enlightenment vision interchangeability replaces hierarchy. The fundamental unit of society becomes the sovereign individual, not the tribe or nation. In political life the enlightenment program translates into a call for democracy: one person, one vote. Each vote counts the same as every other vote. No hierarchy here. In social relations an enlightenment-inspired individualism demands an end to social difference. Individuals are to have the same personal rights regardless of sex, color of skin, and national or ethnic origin. Individuals are to be liberated from personal and social differences.

From its beginning modern economic theory has been a full participant in the enlightenment program. In *The Wealth of Nations* Smith argues that individual differences are social products: "The difference of natural talents in different men is, in reality, much less than we are aware of; and the very different genius which appears to distinguish men of different professions, when grown up to maturity, is not upon many occasions so much the cause, as the effect of the division of labor. The difference between the most dissimilar characters, between a philosopher and a common street porter, for example, seems to arise not so much from nature, as from habit, custom, and education" (Smith, 1776/1937:15). By the late 19th century the concept of the individual trader selling his or her labor and buying commodities in markets forms the heart of neoclassical economics. Note that the economic individual has preferences and makes choices but it does not have a sex, skin color, race, or national origin. The pure individual of neoclassical theory cannot be discriminated against because it cannot be put into a social classification. It is the ultimate interchangeable item, the enlightenment ideal.

Clearly markets are a superior form of economic organization in a society running the enlightenment program. In a market society strangers can engage in commercial intercourse free of the inhibitions of social restraint. Of course, even markets demand what Thomas Malthus called "moral restraint." Without this restraint the Mafia is the ultimate market participant. If killing the competition is cost-effective, then murder becomes a competitive tool. As Adam Smith recognized, government must provide a system of justice and secure the national defense in a world divided into nation-states. But the dominant Anglo-American tradition, from Adam Smith through Alfred Marshall, proclaimed that markets foster the welfare of the individual and thus should be given as much latitude as possible.

With the settlement of North America by the English the enlightenment program was planted in very fertile soil. The Spanish and Portuguese dominated Central and South America, bringing with them the ancient regime based on hierarchy. But North America was settled by relatively well-educated bearers of the enlightenment vision. Since the New World contained no ancient barriers to the implementation of a new social program, the United States became the purest exemplar of an enlightenment society. The American Indians did have an established society, but their rudimentary technology and lack of intertribal cohesion sealed their long-term fate. The American nation was soon safe for the American founding fathers and their premise that all men are created equal. In politics the spread of enlightenment principles has been episodic but irresistible. The voting franchise has been progressively expanded from property owners to all free men to men of all races and finally to women and every citizen over the age of 18. The franchise has expanded slowly, but it has never contracted.

The United States has been a pioneer in creating a market-run economy as well. Following Alfred Marshall, economists have long realized that markets do not work well when they are monopolized by a single seller. Even if one fully accepts the neoclassical message that markets are highly efficient, monopolized markets must be recognized as an exception. During the 19th century farmers and tradesmen living in the American West felt that they suffered from the monopoly position of the railroads carrying passengers and freight between the east and west. By 1890 Congress had passed the Sherman Antitrust Act prohibiting restraint of trade by monopolists. Government regulation of monopoly was not inconsistent with the pursuit of the enlightenment program in the economy so long as monopoly was not widespread.

III. ENLIGHTENMENT ECONOMICS CHALLENGED: MONOPOLISTIC COMPETITION AND KEYNES

During the 1930s the enlightenment program as expressed in neoclassical economics encountered its first serious theoretical challenge in the Anglo-American world. The subversion of neoclassical orthodoxy proceeded on two fronts. English economists led by Joan Robinson (1933) and Americans led by Edward Chamberlin (1942) devised theories of monopolistic competition suggesting that modern economies are *not* simply divided into efficiently operating competitive segments and monopolies demanding government regulation. According to the theory of monopolistic competition, elements of monopoly are omnipresent in markets that *appear* to be competitive because they are not dominated by a single seller. The neoclassical conclusions were under serious attack. If the economy is permeated by monopoly elements, perhaps the proper economic role of government is far more extensive than Adam Smith and Alfred Marshall believed.

The widespread acceptance of the theory of monopolistic competition made it clear that the economic portion of the enlightenment program was threatened. But it was the simultaneous introduction of Keynesian economics (Keynes, 1936) that forced the neoclassical paradigm to surrender its total domination of Anglo-American economic thought. John Maynard Keynes was crafty in his assault on neoclassical economics. Ignoring the distinctions between classical and neoclassical economics, he began his seminal book, *The General Theory of Employment, Interest, and Money*, by telling the reader: "I shall argue that the postulates of the classical theory are applicable to a special case only and not to the general case. . . . Moreover, the characteristics of the special case assumed by the classical theory happen not to be those of the economic society in which we actually live, with the result that its teaching is misleading and disastrous if we attempt to apply it to the facts of experience" (Keynes, 1936:3). Thus, Keynes begins by agreeing that the established theory is correct but adding that it is not relevant to an economy having less than full employment.

Keynes was fortunate in having access to a similar theoretical argument made by Thomas Malthus in his *Principles of Political Economy*, published in 1820 (Malthus, 1820/1936). David Ricardo had contended that the workers actually produce goods and the capitalists save and invest in capital equipment making the workers more productive. Dividing the economy into three classes, he asserted that the landowners who lived off rents were the only truly unproductive class. Malthus once resided in a country parsonage supported by landlords. In a famous and extended correspondence with Ricardo he argued that landlords *were* economically useful because they provided demand for the goods produced by workers and capitalists. Since capitalists save part of their income, that is, remove it from the demand for consumption goods, what keeps the effectual demand for consumption goods high enough to make investment profitable? The answer, wrote Malthus, is found in the purchases of those who live off rent. Capitalists and workers, taken together, produce more consumption goods than they buy. There is a tendency toward a periodic glut of such goods. Fortunately for the economy, landlords produce nothing but consume much, thus adding to the market for consumption goods while refraining from augmenting their supply. These unproductive consumers give the market a necessary balance.

By the 1930s the landlord class was quite small and their incomes were diminished, but Keynes could adapt the Malthusian argument to his own purposes. A shortfall in the demand for goods could be corrected in another way. Since money was no longer backed by a commodity such as gold, the central bank could significantly increase the money supply. Keynes made use of his earlier work on money to show that the banking system can create purchasing power in the short run by making new bank loans, thus multiplying any increase in liquidity generated by the central bank. If we assume that prices do not rise as this additional money is introduced into the system, consumers will enjoy a rise in real wealth and purchasing power. Thus, the new source of aggregate demand can emanate from the central bank and the commercial banking system. In the unlikely event that this additional money fails to stimulate a rise in demand because the new liquidity is trapped in the banks or elsewhere, the central government can increase the demand for goods by spending more than its current revenue. The central bank and central government can do in modern times what the landlords did in their day. They can take actions that remove the surplus goods from the market.

How could these surplus goods appear in the first instance? Neoclassical economics assumes that capitalist economies can be seen as nothing more than a series of markets. One of the major advantages offered by markets as a device for conducting economic activity is the self-regulating feature of market exchange. What happens when, for some reason, a glut or surplus of a commodity appears? When markets are allowed to function freely, that is, when government does not interfere with them, a surplus of goods will force a reduction in *price*. This fall in price because of excess inventories has two beneficial effects. It reduces the production of the good in surplus as prices approach and then fall below costs, and it encourages consumers to buy more of the product. The fall in price occasioned by a temporary surplus discourages producers and encourages consumers. The rise in purchases and fall in production will proceed until the quantity demanded by consumers just equals the quantity produced by suppliers. At that point the price of the good will stabilize. Put briefly, when markets are operating correctly there can never be too much or too little of a good, there can only be an incorrect price. The incorrect price will be corrected in the long run, returning the market to equilibrium.

If the economic system is nothing more than a collection of markets, and if all markets are self-regulating or self-equilibrating, how can a general glut appear in a capitalist economy? This was the question that Keynes was forced to answer. Following the general pattern of enlightenment thinking, neoclassical economics uses the interchangeability assumption. All markets are assumed to operate in the same manner. Keynes did not want to make a frontal attack on the economic branch of enlightenment thought. By the 1930s enlightenment assumptions had become common sense. To attack their foundation was to court rejection. Rather, he hoped to show that, while correct in most cases, neoclassical market analysis was not correct in two very important instances. Standard neoclassical conclusions do not apply to money markets because of the peculiar characteristics of money (extreme liquidity and a very low elasticity of substitution) and the fact that the creation of money is monopolized by central banks. And, perhaps more important, Keynes argued that labor markets do not operate in the neoclassical manner.

Like money, labor is a peculiar commodity. It cannot be easily detached from its producer. Once I sell you a car, I can take the money and go about my business. But if I sell you my labor, I must usually remain while the labor power is being used. Keynes makes little use of this very important characteristic of labor, but it *is* used by economic dualists. Instead, Keynes makes two arguments, one empirical and one theoretical. His empirical argument is that real wages (and thus the real price of labor) is a combination of nominal wage rates and the price of goods. Yet when the price of goods rises, nominal wages remaining the same, workers do not withdraw labor from the market. Neoclassical theory would predict that they would do so. Furthermore, workers have no way of bargaining with employers over their real wage since they cannot determine the price of goods. Here Keynes ignores the possibility of indexing wages to the price of goods, a practice that has become common in our time among union workers with COLAs.

The theory of monopolistic competition argued that most markets do not provide consumers with the full efficiency benefits of competition most of the time. Keynes added that a capitalist economy does not predictably provide full employment for the labor force without active government policy. Taken together, the two major 20th-century additions to mainstream economic theory posed a serious threat to the economic version of enlightenment doctrine. One response by economic theorists was to divide economics into two categories, normative and positive. Normative theory attempts to define the economic world as it should be. Positive theory attempts to describe it as it is. This division ensures a place for neoclassical theory in its pure form as normative economics. Even if the world is *not* perfectly competitive, the theory of perfectly competitive markets allows us to measure the world as it is against the world as it ought to be. If markets as we find them are not fully competitive, the gap between markets-as-they-are and markets-as-they-should-be becomes a *policy gap*, a difference that can be at least partially eliminated by government agencies such as the Federal Trade Commission. Neoclassical economics is still useful because it allows us to *measure* the *cost* of monopoly even when for practical or political reasons we can't do much to reduce it.

IV. LABOR AND ECONOMIC THEORY

Labor markets have been the weak link in the great chain of neoclassical theory from the beginning. Keynes wisely inserted his dissent from orthodoxy at this point. It is undeniably true that, if all goods are traded in perfectly competitive markets, price changes will equilibrate the quantity supplied with the quantity demanded. Keynes asserted that labor markets make *quantity* adjustments, not price adjustments, because the price of labor is sticky. When the demand for labor falls because of the falling demand for goods, we may expect most employers to lay off labor before cutting their nominal wages. When the general price level is falling, as happened during the great depression, workers receiving the same nominal wage enjoy a rise in real income. If they were willing to work at the going wage before the fall in prices, they will surely be willing to work at a lower nominal wage with lower prices if the wage decline does not reduce their real standard of living. But Keynes argued that workers are under a money illusion. They confuse nominal wages with real wages. Even if they did not do so, workers are very concerned about the *structure* of wages. Plumbers contend that they should make as much as carpenters. But if the plumbers agree to take a nominal wage cut when prices fall, how can they be sure that carpenters will do the same? The first workers taking a nominal wage cut may prove to be the only workers doing so. If other workers do not follow, the structure of wages shifts against those who are willing to see through the money illusion. The great chain of wages would be altered.

The U.S. policy response to the neoclassical challenge was twofold. During the 1930s a series of agencies was set up to *enforce* competition among American firms selling in the same industry. The Federal Trade Commission and the Anti-Trust Division of the Justice Department remain leaders in that endeavor. In addition, the federal government took the primary responsibility for ensuring the maintenance of full employment in labor markets. Keynes's original notion was that the central government could maintain full employment by using the central bank's power to create and decrease money. According to Keynes, the major problem in labor markets is that workers refuse to take a reduction in nominal wages when prices fall, even though the refusal to do so results in a real wage increase when the demand for goods is falling. Workers maintain a reservation wage in nominal terms, forcing labor markets to resort to a quantity adjustment (rising unemployment) during recessions and depressions.

How can government compensate for this money illusion on the part of labor? Keynes's preferred answer was expansionary monetary policy. If the real price of labor remains stubbornly high during recessions, the central bank must compensate by pushing the real cost of borrowed funds very low. Government can use its monopoly position in money markets to offset the inability of labor markets to undergo a price adjustment. When more money is forced into the economy through the use of open market operations by the central bank, the purchasing power of buyers will grow so long as rising prices do not return the real value of money to its former state. When prices are constant or falling, increasing the nominal money supply increases purchasing power and thus the demand for goods and for labor. When prices do begin to rise because of reflation by the central bank, the real wages of workers subject to the money illusion will be falling, making labor less expensive in real terms. Expansionary monetary policy can move the economy toward full employment so long as nominal wages are slow to adjust to an expanding money supply and rising goods prices.

But what if expansionary monetary policy does not work? What if the expanding money supply is absorbed into a liquidity trap in commercial banks or elsewhere? In that case, Keynes followed Malthus in suggesting expansionary fiscal policy. Business firms and households cannot increase their spending for goods when their incomes are falling. For that reason an initial fall in income tends to multiply as falling private incomes beget reduced expenditures and thus a second round of income declines. This cycle can only be broken by fiscal policy if monetary policy is ineffective. Government can spend that which it has not received in revenue. The credit of the central government does not depend on its income. When those who lend to the government buy government bonds, they are simply exchanging a non-interest-bearing liability of the central bank, money, for an interest-bearing liability of the federal government. Exchanging fiat money for government bonds increases the buyer's yield without increasing the level of risk. So long as the central bank refuses to let the money supply fall, there is an assured market for central government debt at the going rate of interest. During a recession a reduction in tax rates is also salutary for the economy.

Keynes broke the great chain of neoclassical reasoning by refuting its relevance to labor markets. His target was well chosen. His theory finally eroded the conservative resistance to deficit spending by offering an economic message in harmony with democratic political imperatives. Politicians must promise good tidings to their constituents if they are to win election and reelection. Voters are careful calculators of their own costs and benefits. A winning candidate tends to promise the voters an increase in federal benefits (more spending on projects for the district) and lower costs (a general reduction in taxes or at least tax breaks for local interests). To promise a reduction in benefits coupled with a rise in the tax burden is to court defeat. Put differently, the winning election campaign tends to carry a promise of a federal deficit and a rise in the national debt. Keynes argued that at certain times (during recessions) good politics is also good economics. No theory could have been more welcome to the American political community or to economists seeking jobs and influence in the public sector.

V. MARKETS AND DEMOCRATIC POLITICS

A major advantage of markets is that they tend to locate the cost of any action in the same place as the benefits of that action. If I decide to spend some of my limited income on a new automobile, I am at the same time deciding not to spend that money on other goods. The real cost of the automobile consists of the foregone opportunity to purchase that which I would have bought had I not decided on a new car. I benefit from the car and I bear the opportunity cost of having purchased it. True, if the good that I purchase has positive or negative externalities, I do not bear the full cost or possibly reap the full benefits of my decision. Where externalities of production or consumption are very strong, markets do not work well in the cost–benefit sense. But most markets do localize most of the costs and benefits most of the time.

The same cannot be said of government spending and taxing. We often hear that government spending is for the common good. For example, national defense expenditures are used to defend the nation that we share in common. Even so, those who *receive* these public expenditures are twice blessed. They receive the spending as income while also enjoying the benefits provided for all citizens. All public spending benefits some more than others even when the spending serves a cause that everyone deems worthy. The cost of government is also uneven. One does not buy public services with taxes. The obligation to pay taxes does not carry with it the right to government services beyond those offered citizens who have no tax liability. In brief, government offers economic benefits and imposes financial costs, but it deliberately severs the direct connection between the two. Since the level of federal benefits enjoyed by individuals and voting districts bears no necessary relationship to the local cost of those benefits, politicians feel compelled to promise a shift of benefits toward, and of costs away from, the voters that they seek to charm.

The geographic separation of political costs and benefits is important, but it is not the only way that politicians weaken the discipline of cost–benefit analysis. Costs are also separated from benefits in time. Federal borrowing allows the benefits of government spending to be concentrated in the present while pushing the costs into the future. The current generation may enjoy the benefits of government programs even when they crowd out private investment and thus retard the economy's ability to produce goods efficiently in the future. The temporal separation of benefits and costs in favor of the present is most effective when the U.S. government borrows from foreigners, leaving a legacy of foreign debt for those who follow. When the government benefits of today take the form of transfer payments and not public sector investment, little if any improvement is shifted to the generations that must pay the cost of servicing the foreign debt.

Anglo-American economic theory and practice have experienced a pendulum swing from the 17th century to the present. Economic theory has been, and essentially remains, an argument about the economic role of the private and public sectors. Beginning with Sir Thomas Mun and picking up momentum through the writings of Adam Smith and Alfred Marshall, mercantilist, classical, and neoclassical economics has argued in favor of a market-oriented economy with government restricted to those areas where the market does not work well. Joan Robinson, Edward Chamberlin, John Maynard Keynes, and a host of 20th-century economists have argued against the interchangeability assumptions of the classical economists in favor of a stronger role for government in economic affairs.

The antimarket argument has taken three primary forms. First, the theory of monopolistic competition states that markets are rarely free of monopoly. Only government supervision can minimize the monopoly element in a market economy. Second, Keynes and the Keynesians contend that a market economy is inherently unstable and thus periodic bouts of unemployment and reduced output are inevitable unless government acts as a stabilizing force. Finally, the theory of externalities suggests that a market system often does not locate costs and benefits in the same place. If so, government should intervene to encourage the production of those goods that are subject to positive externalities (for example, health and education) while discouraging the generation of negative externalities like environmental pollution.

VI. CONTEMPORARY POLITICAL ECONOMY

The liberating message of the enlightenment is that social systems need not be based on a specific kind of immutable hierarchy. Human life must constantly grapple with the *physical* constraints of existence, but within those constraints we are free to choose from an extensive menu of *social* devices. As John Stuart Mill observed over a century ago, "We cannot alter the ultimate properties either of matter or mind, but can only employ these properties more or less successfully, to bring about the events in which we are interested. It is not so with the Distribution of Wealth. That is a matter of human institution solely. The things once there, mankind, individually and collectively, can do with them as they like" (Mill, 1878:250).

In our own time the enlightenment program is available in two political versions. The reading favored by those on the political left has recently been systematized by John Rawls (1971) in *A Theory of Justice*. Rawls argues that a just enlightenment society is one that seeks an equality of social and economic *result*. True, some of us are born with greater talent, energy, and beauty than others. These differential qualities are part of the physical constraints of social life. But natural inequalities need not be reinforced by social inequalities. According to Rawls, a just society is one that is arranged to *minimize* the social consequences of injustices inherent in the physical world. Self-perpetuating social and economic elites are not a result of natural inequalities. Elites form in societies that allow cumulative causation to direct society's rewards toward those having an initial social advantage. Success breeds success, just as failure gives birth to failure. The price of a society free of entrenched dominating elites is eternal vigilance. The enlightenment ideal of interchangeable individuals can be preserved only by constantly redistributing resources toward those having the lowest social and economic position.

Those on the political right read the enlightenment message differently. They agree that social life can be designed as we wish so long as it allows us to meet our physical requirements. But as Robert Nozick (1974) points out in *Anarchy, State, and Utopia*, the enlightenment dream of individual interchangeability need not extend to economic *results*. The recognition that hierarchy is not a social imperative certainly does not require that a just society seek to achieve an equality of individual economic accomplishment. For conservatives the essence of a just society is the preservation of the right of each citizen to formulate a life-plan and to pursue that plan. True contentment is found in the *seeking* of goals freely formulated and persistently pursued. It is the hunt that provides the greatest pleasure, not the kill. So long as the poor and the disadvantaged are free to dream and to pursue their dreams without state-sanctioned interference, the enlightenment ideals can be achieved. It is the equality of opportunity to struggle in one's own way and on one's own individual terms that provides the key to personal happiness.

Until the 1930s the mainstream of economic thought tended to favor the conservative version of enlightenment doctrine. Neoclassical economics can be seen as an elaborate analytical justification of an economic system based on competitive markets. Economic competition creates winners and losers. A market system will not provide an outcome resembling Rawls's equality of result. But competitive markets do tend to move the economy toward the largest output produced at the lowest cost. If we agree that more useful goods and services are better than fewer goods and services, we must admit that a competitive economy is an excellent device for meeting the challenge of expanding *production*. Admittedly, the economic system that maximizes production will probably leave a pronounced inequality of income as its residue. A market system sacrifices an *equality* of consumption in favor of an *abundance* of production.

During the New Deal years of the 1930s most economists began to advocate the increasingly popular liberal solution known as a mixed economy. Under this doctrine the private sector of the economy continues to be regulated by markets, but the public sector expands its responsibility for redistributing income downward using progressive income taxes and regressive government expenditures. In addition, a variety of government agencies provide regulation for those industries where competition does not work well because of natural monopoly or for other reasons. This liberal segmentation of the economy into two distinct parts, public and private, allows the public sector to pursue the egalitarian goal of equality of economic result, while seeking the advantages of competitive markets in the private sector. This public/private split allows the economics profession to simultaneously advocate the opposing goals of competitive production and egalitarian consumption. The study of economics has become in large part a never-ending debate about the proper relationship between the public and private parts of the economy. To be liberal is to argue for a bit more emphasis on public control; to be conservative is to suggest a marginal expansion of the private sector's domain.

VII. THE THEORY OF ECONOMIC DUALISM

How does economic dualism fit into all of this? To answer that question we must outline the essence of economic dualism. In *The Dual Economy* I took an institutionalist perspective. Everyone agrees that the public sector of the U.S. economy is organized differently from the private sector. The public sector operates according to the logic of democratic politics, while business seeks monetary profits. But within the private sector neoclassical economic theory treats all business firms, large and small, as belonging to the same organizational family. I dissented from that view. I argued that small business firms do act in roughly the way that neoclassical theory says they do. Large firms do not do so. Large firms achieved their prominence using a different technology from small firms (large batch and mass production as opposed to unit output). Unit output is craft-oriented, while large batch and mass production usually requires more capital equipment. The superior size of large firms is accompanied by a substantial share of at least one market in a key industry. Joseph Bowring recently summarized the difference as follows: "Core firms are qualitatively different from periphery firms. While size is required for core membership, size is not a proxy for efficiency. Size creates access to a realm of large-scale investments required to compete across the range of tactics employed by core firms and thus is required for and creates an element of market power. Large size together with significant market share held jointly with other large firms in an industry or industries requiring such investment, is required for the market power associated with core firm status" (Bowring, 1986:185).

Standard industrial organization analysis posits four types of *industries* based upon their competitive mode. The first two types, perfect competition and monopolistic competition, ensure that long-run profits will not exceed the minimum level necessary to maintain the existing industry capacity. William Baumol and others have recently suggested that profits may not be excessive even in industries dominated by a single firm so long as markets in the industry are "contestable," that is, when entry into and exit out of the industry are easy (Baumol, Panzar, and Willig, 1982). The theory of contestable markets emphasizes the importance of freedom of entry in determining whether or not long-run profits will exceed the minimum necessary to assure a maintenance of current industry capacity. Thus, the term *monopolistic competition* refers to a monopoly in an industry that other capitalists can enter with relative ease. Oligopoly and monopoly, the remaining industry structures, are based upon restricted entry into the industry allowing long-run profits to exceed the level necessary to maintain a constant long-run output.

By contrast, economic dualism is a theory of *firms*, not industries. Dualism divides firms into two fundamental types, center (or core) and periphery. Dualism organizes industries according to their technology, not by the price competitiveness of their participating firms. Most core firms operate in more than one industry. Thus, the traditional theory of industrial organization misreads the actual organization of the business economy. Concentrating on industries, not firms, standard theory is really a theory of the product. The cost curves and revenue curves that price theory calls "the theory of the firm" is really nothing more than a theory of the product. Since virtually all large firms are multiproduct producers, they escape the standard theoretical construct.

VIII. ECONOMIC DUALISM AND THE POLITICS OF ECONOMICS

Clearly theories of dualism are antithetical to the business firm interchangeability assumptions of classical and neoclassical theory. Just as Malthus made the first economic argument that we recognize as Keynesian in spirit, I shall contend that the publication of my book, *The Dual Economy* (Averitt, 1968), followed in three years by *Internal Labor Markets and Manpower Analysis* by Peter Doeringer and Michael Piore (1971), introduced economic dualism as applied to industrial economies. Writing about his own predecessor, Keynes observed: "Malthus, indeed, had venhemently opposed Ricardo's doctrine that it was impossible for effective demand to be deficient; but vainly. For, since Malthus was unable to explain clearly (apart from an appeal to the facts of common observation) how and why effective demand could be deficient or excessive, he failed to furnish an alternative construction; and Ricardo conquered England as completely as the Holy Inquisition conquered Spain" (Keynes, 1936:32). It might not miss the mark by very much to say about *The Dual Economy* what Keynes says about Malthus's *Principles of Political Economy*. It was unable to explain dualism clearly apart from an appeal to the facts of common observation. Twenty years ago the Keynesian revolution seemed contained within Paul Samuelson's brilliant neoclassical synthesis (Samuelson, 1947), the fight against monopolistic competition and oligopoly seemed to have benefited the careers of lawyers as much as consumers, and the pollution of the environment seemed a manageable problem susceptible to well-conceived effluent taxes. During the first half of the 19th century Ricardo engaged in an extensive public debate with Malthus over their respective theories. By contrast, *The Dual Economy* was not reviewed by the *Journal of Economic Literature* (the book review publication of the American Economic Association) or by any other major economic quarterly. Nevertheless, the book is still in print 18 years after its original publication.

In writing *The Dual Economy* I adopted a version of the strategy used by Keynes. Keynes asserted that the standard theory of employment was not wrong, it was simply partial. I approached neoclassical theory in roughly the same way. I did not quibble with the accepted theory of demand, although I did suggest in a later paper (Averitt, 1975) that consumption was structured and not interchangeable. I argued that the theory of the firm underlying the economist's supply curves is roughly correct for that part of the economy that I called the periphery. It does not fit the center or core sector of the economy very well.

I made two fundamental criticisms of the neoclassical theory of the firm. First, it is really a theory of the *product* and not a theory of the firm. Small firms in the periphery economy tend to be single-product or few-products suppliers, so the theory applies to this sector reasonably well. Large firms do not rely upon the production of a single product, so their activities are better explained by a theory that emphasizes the behavior of large economic institutions. Second, I noted that the traditional theory of the firm does not have a useful long-run component, or, to put the matter differently, the long-run is seen as nothing more than a series of short runs. I realize that Keynes said that in the long run we are all dead, but large business firms do not expect to die, not even in the long run. After outlining the differences between the periphery and center sectors of the private economy, I proceeded to discuss the implications of economic dualism for labor unions and for government.

While the mainstream economic journals were greeting *The Dual Economy* with what might pass for a conspiracy of silence, the book did catch the attention of several radical economists and numerous business historians. It was quickly translated into Japanese, and it inspired an international conference on dualism complete with television interviews in Torino, Italy. Statistical work began attempting to confirm or deny the existence of economic dualism in the United States. The statistical work by economists tended to confirm dualism. The dual labor market thesis was also a bit slow in catching the attention of economists, but it is now gaining considerable scholarly momentum. A very important paper in the September 1985 volume of the *American Economic Review* reports: "Our results provide strong support for two of the basic tenets of dual market theory: there are two distinct sectors of the labor market with different wage-setting mechanisms, and there is a queue for primary sector jobs. . . . It is relatively straight-forward to develop a model in which a high fixed cost/low variable cost technology is used in the 'stable' demand sector and a low fixed cost/high variable cost technology is used to accommodate fluctuations in demand" (Dickens and Lang, 1985a: 801). The authors, William T. Dickens and Kevin Lang, note that those with whom they discussed their preliminary results had strong reactions tending to deify or execute the messenger.

Clearly economic dualism is on the upswing in economics after a slow start fostered by a cool mainstream reception. Michael Piore and Charles Sabel published *The Second Industrial Divide* in 1984, suggesting that in the United States the mass production (center) economy is in crisis while craft production (periphery) may have a strong future. They examine economic dualism in an increasingly integrated international economy. Joseph Bowring's book confirming the dual economy was published by the Princeton University Press in 1986. One of the most recent, and most interesting, papers on dualism was produced by Jeremy Bulow and Lawrence H. Summers at the National Bureau of Economic Research in Cambridge, Massachusetts (Bulow and Summers, 1985). They develop an economic theory of sloth using dual labor market theory.

Building upon the recent interest in implicit contracts between workers and employers, Bulow and Summers drop the neoclassical assumption of homogeneous work effort. They postulate that worker shirking is a major problem for the primary sector, where job-specific skills are important, but much less of a problem in the secondary job market, where labor does tend to be interchangeable in terms of the work skills required. Labor that shirks in the secondary sector can be laid off with little cost to the firm, but in the primary job market a promotion ladder and pay incentives are needed to sustain the maximum in work effort. Since firms in the core economy cannot monitor key workers perfectly, they create wage differentials unrelated to skill differentials in order to make workers value their jobs. In the primary job market high wages are substituted for supervision so long as the marginal cost of wage premiums is below the cost of additional supervision.

Several implications of the Bulow and Summers paper are interesting.

Lester Thurow (1985) and other economists have suggested that the United States should develop international economic policies that encourage high value-added firms in the United States because these firms provide good high-wage jobs. Japan has done so for the past 20 years. Industrial policy makes little sense within the neoclassical paradigm, but it may make sense in the context of dual labor markets. Disputing the classical theory of comparative advantage first championed by David Ricardo, Bulow and Summers find, "It is apparent that as long as the domestic primary sector is 'nearly competitive,' allowing free trade will reduce national economy welfare" (Bulow and Summers, 1985:22). High-wage jobs support an expanded middle class. When free trade severely reduces the number of high-wage jobs in an industrial economy, making both human and physical capital redundant, the income and social loss may exceed the comparatively small gains going to consumers in the form of cheaper imported goods. If the foreign exchange value of the dollar can be properly adjusted, it may be possible to retain high-wage U.S. jobs without tariffs or import quotas. Bulow and Summers also construct a dual labor market model that explains discrimination and voluntary unemployment (or "wait unemployment" as workers queue for primary sector jobs).

IX. THE FUTURE OF ECONOMIC DUALISM

A major test of any economic theory is its ability to remain relatively simple while explaining a wide range of economic observations. Economic dualism, including dual labor market theory, is proving more adept at meeting this exacting standard with every additional publication on the topic. Malthus found his vindication in the work of Keynes over 100 years after he published his book advocating public works financed by deficit spending. The pioneer economic dualists have been more fortunate. We have not had to wait in obscurity for more than a century. Economic dualism as applied to advanced economies is attracting a large and growing following among professional economists and sociologists less than 20 years after its introduction.

While most economists aspiring toward mainstream careers seemed initially reluctant to pursue research into economic dualism, the concept caught the interest of sociologists rather quickly. The implied idea that poverty attached to the job and not to the individual, and that a modern industrial system needed low-pay, dead-end jobs to function well, seemed to spur the sociological imagination. Human capital theory was never as persuasive in sociological circles as in economic ones. Economists, having fully absorbed the enlightenment assumption of interchangeability, found the image of individuals absorbing discrete doses of capital and receiving a return on that capital compelling. Seen in this way, capital is really quite homogeneous, essentially the same in both human and material form. Economists also have a pronounced fondness for econometrics, a preference that may increase their tendency to assume an interchangeability of goods and of markets. As Lester

Thurow notes: "In short, untestable and unprovable theoretical models of reality became even more dominant than they were before econometrics was developed. This was bound to reinforce the position of the price-auction model, since that model of the world dominates both the learning and teaching of economists" (Thurow, 1983:118). Sociologists are comfortable with a broad range of statistical techniques. As might be expected, sociologists testing the dualism hypothesis soon discovered that various statistical tests using different data bases tended to yield conflicting results. Nevertheless, the theory of economic dualism has survived sociological testing quite well.

It is probably not an oversimplification to say that radical economists on the left and sociologists kept economic dualism alive in the academy until economists closer to the mainstream could discover it. Those who are relatively new to the theory seem taken aback by the hostility that it generates in an older generation of economists. They should not be surprised. Keynesian economics was sanitized and partially folded back into the neoclassical mold by Paul Samuelson in the United States (1947) and Professor Hicks (1939) in England. Keynes's general theory, published in 1936, did not become official U.S. economic policy until President Kennedy endorsed it in a speech at Yale in 1962. Since Adam Smith, economists have been wedded to the interchangeability assumption. Conservatives have identified the interchangeability of markets and of firms and of individual decision making with equality of opportunity, democracy, and freedom. The theory of economic dualism, with its rejection of business interchangeability, suggests that even when there is easy entry and exit into virtually all industries, the business sector cannot be left to its own devices by the state unless society is willing to tolerate an ongoing inequality of economic result that has little to do with workers' individual choices. Under the current arrangement the economy needs its peripheral firms and its peripheral workers. That message is not a comfortable one for economic conservatives or for liberals who wish to minimize the economic interaction between the public and private sectors.

In the end, economic theory follows the pull of economic policy. Putting the matter humorously, Senator Hollings from South Carolina says that an economist is a person who sees something working in practice and wonders if it will work in theory. It was easy for the United States to champion free trade, comparative advantage, and open markets so long as the United States seemed to have a comparative advantage in the world's core economy. We must not forget that the theory of free trade and comparative advantage was formulated in England when she was the world's industrial leader. If the United States continues to witness a deterioration of its own place atop the industrial hierarchy, theories that emphasize hierarchy are likely to become increasingly acceptable. Nations, like individuals, are unaware of power relationships when they are powerful. But once the powerful begin to sense a loss of their power the importance of hierarchy is suddenly revealed.

Theories of dualism are based upon a notion of business hierarchy. They will become more compelling to Americans to the extent that Japan and our other industrial competitors in the world gain in international trade. That

Bulow and Summers use dual labor markets to argue against free trade and comparative advantage is interesting and revealing. It was no accident that radical economists were the first to accept economic dualism. The phrase "commanding heights of the economy" is popularly identified with Lenin. We will know that the American century is truly over when mainstream Japanese economists begin to extol the virtues of comparative advantage and free trade.

Sociologists have long been impressed with the importance of hierarchy and social stratification. For them the notion that advanced economies exhibit dualism was no surprise. The interchangeable individualism of neoclassical theory has always seemed exceedingly artificial and unfruitful to most sociologists. If the economic mainstream is beginning to move in a direction that sociologists find more recognizable, should economists and sociologists join their efforts and construct an interdisciplinary new structuralism? I would urge cooperation but not a merger. Academic disciplines are informed by their special histories and theoretical proclivities. Since academic positions are necessarily hierarchical, it is difficult for new ideas outside the mainstream of a profession to get a hearing. Perhaps two mainstreams that run close together are better than one large current carrying all theoretical debris swiftly in one direction. I believe that the separation of economics and sociology has served economic dualism well, and it may well be of service to the new heresies that we must forever explore to remain relevant in a constantly changing social and economic universe.

REFERENCES

Averitt, Robert T. 1968. *The Dual Economy: The Dynamics of American Industry Structure*. New York: W. W. Norton.

Averitt, Robert T. 1975. "Time's Structure, Man's Strategy: The American Experience." Pp. 13–35 in *Evolution of International Management Structures*, edited by Harold F. Williamson. Newark, DE: University of Delaware Press.

Baumol, William, John C. Panzar, and Robert D. Willig. 1982. *Contestable Markets and the Theory of Industry Structure*. New York: Harcourt Brace Jovanovich.

Bowring, Joseph. 1986. *Competition in a Dual Economy*. Princeton, NJ: Princeton University Press.

Bulow, Jeremy I., and Lawrence H. Summers. 1985. "A Theory of Dual Labor Markets with Application to Industrial Policy, Discrimination and Keynesian Unemployment." *National Bureau of Economic Research, Inc., Working Paper Series*. Working Paper No. 1666.

Chamberlin, Edward. 1942. *The Theory of Monopolistic Competition*. Cambridge, MA: Harvard University Press.

Dickens, William T., and Kevin Lang. 1985a. "A Test of Dual Labor Market Theory." *American Economic Review* 75:792–803.

Doeringer, Peter B., and Michael J. Piore. 1971. *Internal Labor Markets and Manpower Analysis*. Lexington, MA: D. C. Heath.

Hicks, John Richard. 1939. *Value and Capital*. Oxford: Clarendon Press.

Jevons, William Stanley. 1911. *The Theory of Political Economy*. London: Macmillan.

Keynes, John Maynard. 1936. *The General Theory of Employment, Interest, and Money*. New York: Harcourt, Brace.

Lovejoy, Arthur O. 1936. *The Great Chain of Being*. Cambridge, MA: Harvard University Press.

MacIntyre, Alasdair. 1981. *After Virtue*. Notre Dame, IN: University of Notre Dame Press.

Malthus, Thomas R. 1936. *The Principles of Political Economy*. London: University of London. (Originally published 1820)

Marshall, Alfred. 1920. *Principles of Economics*. 8th ed. London: Macmillan. (Originally published 1890)

Mill, John Stuart. 1878. *Principles of Political Economy*. London: Longmans, Green, Reader, and Dyer.

Mun, Sir Thomas. 1946. "England's Treasure by Foreign Trade." Pp. 6–27 in *Masterworks of Economics*. Vol. I, edited by Leonard Dalton Abbott. (Originally published 1630)

Nozick, Robert. 1974. *Anarchy, State, and Utopia*. New York: Basic Books.

Piore, Michael J., and Charles Sabel. 1984. *The Second Industrial Divide*. New York: Basic Books.

Rawls, John. 1971. *A Theory of Justice*. Cambridge, MA: Harvard University Press.

Ricardo, David. 1911. *The Principles of Political Economy and Taxation*. London: J. M. Dent. (Originally published 1817)

Robinson, Joan. 1933. *The Economics of Imperfect Competition*. London: Macmillan.

Samuelson, Paul. 1947. *Foundations of Economic Analysis*. Cambridge, MA: Harvard University Press.

Smith, Adam. 1937. *The Wealth of Nations*, edited by Edwin Cannan. New York: Modern Library. (Originally published 1776)

Thurow, Lester C. 1983. *Dangerous Currents: The State of Economics*. New York: Random House.

Thurow, Lester C. 1985. *The Zero-Sum Society*. New York: Simon & Schuster.

3

Careers, Industries, and Occupations
Industrial Segmentation Reconsidered

Jerry A. Jacobs and Ronald L. Breiger

I. INTRODUCTION

Two strands of structuralism have become prominent in stratification research in recent years. The first is the focus on labor market structures as mediating contexts for the determination of socioeconomic rewards. Baron and Bielby have introduced the phrase "the new structuralism" in urging the centrality of organizations in the analysis of social stratification (Baron and Bielby, 1980; see also Kalleberg and Berg, 1987). They delineated a series of levels for structuralist analysis, ranging from the job to the firm to the industrial sector. At the most aggregated level of this continuum, researchers have identified economic sectors that influence the distribution of social rewards (Beck, Horan, and Tolbert, 1978; Berg, 1981; Bibb and Form, 1977; Tolbert, Horan, and Beck, 1980). Other important structural research has focused on the effects of local labor markets on the income determination process (Parcel and Mueller, 1983), the sex segregation of occupations (Jacobs, 1983a; Reskin, 1984; Rosenfeld, 1983), and demographic constraints on careers within corporate settings (Rosenbaum, 1984; Stewman and Konda, 1983). Two reviews summarize much of this structural research (Baron, 1984; Kalleberg and Sorenson, 1979).

Another important line of structuralist inquiry has been the renewed focus on the structure of the mobility table. The emergence of log-linear analysis has facilitated the examination of the configuration of relationships in mobility tables. A recent spate of developments in the analysis of mobility tables (Breiger, 1981; Clogg, 1981; Duncan, 1979; Goodman, 1981; Hauser,

Jerry A. Jacobs • Department of Sociology, University of Pennsylvania, Philadelphia, Pennsylvania 19104.   Ronald L. Breiger • Department of Sociology, Cornell University, Ithaca, New York 14853.

1978; Hout, 1983; Logan, 1983; Yamaguchi, 1983) has made this one of the most lively foci of sociological advance in recent years. Mobility tables have reclaimed their place alongside regression models of status attainment in the study of social mobility.

Surprisingly, no efforts have been made to date to combine these two strands of structuralist analysis. There have been no attempts to apply the formidable range of mobility table techniques to the problems introduced by the new structuralism in stratification. Perhaps the most surprising hiatus is the absence of applications of log-linear mobility table techniques to the analysis of industrial sector models. Tolbert (1982) may be considered an exception to this generalization, but flaws in Tolbert's approached discussed below preclude drawing conclusions regarding mobility patterns from his research (see also Jacobs, 1983b).

This chapter will begin to bridge this gap by applying mobility table analysis to hypotheses regarding industrial segmentation. We use the terms *segments* and *segmentation* to refer to all models that divide labor markets according to industry position in a discrete fashion. We view the two-sector model as a special case of a multiple segments approach.

II. MOBILITY AND LABOR MARKET SEGMENTATION THEORY

The industrial sectors employed by Tolbert *et al.* (1980) and Bibb and Form (1977) are derived from a factor-analytic examination of many dimensions of industrial organization, such as size, market concentration, and profitability. These models divide the economy into a core and a periphery. The core consists of industries dominated by large firms with substantial market power that organize jobs along elaborate career ladders, also referred to as internal labor markets. The periphery, on the other hand, is the competitive sector, with relatively small, unstable firms without elaborate career ladders. The advocates of the core-periphery model have argued that income, income growth with experience, returns to education, and career mobility are influenced by sectoral location.

Mobility is an important assumption underlying any hypothesis regarding labor market segmentation. Sectors have not been defined on the basis of mobility patterns, yet particular mobility patterns are nonetheless implied by these theories. The dual economy thesis has been employed to provide at least a partial explanation of the inequality among workers. The argument has been proposed that workers of equal background and ability receive different amounts of rewards because of their location in different economic sectors (Tolbert *et al.*, 1980). It is clear that if there is frequent mobility between sectors, then the inequality between sectors that proponents identify can be reduced by movement out of the secondary sector. The maintenance of structural inequality of this nature requires some barriers to mobility. This assumption has been emphasized by economists critical of the segmentation perspective (Cain, 1976). Economists, assuming competitive markets, have argued that even if independent sectors were to arise, they could not maintain themselves because the workings of competitive labor markets would undermine the distinction between the sectors through either eroding the wage and other reward differences between sectors or through sorting the best workers into the preferred sector. But the economist's assumption is the sociologist's empirical issue. We propose to examine the degree of career mobility that actually occurs between economic sectors.

The immobility required by a sectoral model must be located at sector boundaries. The mere inertia of remaining in a job in a particular firm or industry should not be taken as evidence of immobilty between sectors. (See a related discussion by Farkas, England, and Barton, Chapter 5 in this volume.) If this inertia were the only constraint on career mobility, then all effects would be located at the firm or industry level, not at the sector level. This is why it is important to distinguish sector effects on mobility from detailed industry (and occupation) effects, as we detail below.

A degree of immobility is clearly an essential component of any theory of industrial sectors. It is equally central to theories that delineate multiple segments, rather than two principal sectors. The question we raise, then, is: What are the segments in an industrial mobility table? Where are sector or segment boundaries located, and how many such boundaries are there? To what extent does labor market segmentation overlap or coincide with the sectoral division of the economy?

Evidence on the degree of immobility between sectors or segments has been equivocal (Jacobs, 1983b; Kalleberg and Griffin, 1980; Rosenfeld, 1983). Criticisms have also been directed to tests of industrial sector immobility (Jacobs, 1983b). Jacobs shows that Tolbert's (1982) analysis takes detailed industry immobility as evidence of sectoral immobility. When this effect is removed, the degree of immobility between sectors is far less than the degree of immobility between white-collar and blue-collar occupations. As attractive as many find the industrial dualism perspective, one must conclude that to date the evidence on intersectoral immobility is inconclusive.

There is no general agreement on the appropriate division of the economy into sectors. Various industrial sector and segmentation schemes have been proposed (Bibb and Form, 1977; Hodson, 1978; Tolbert et al., 1980). This discussion will focus primarily on the Tolbert-Horan-Beck model; results obtained with the Bibb-Form industrial sector model will be presented for comparison.

Critics of the dual economy model have argued that it oversimplifies reality by incorporating many conflicting dimensions of inequality in a single dichotomy (Kaufman, Hodson, and Fligstein, 1981; see also Wallace and Kalleberg, 1981). Kaufman et al. (1981) have proposed a multisector model that they argue avoids this difficulty. A multisector model can be tested in the same way that a dualistic model can be tested. We consider one such partition, derived from an attempt to fit an industrial mobility table rather than from a theory of industrial segmentation.

In addition to industrial segmentation models, another approach to labor market segmentation has focused on occupational distinctions (Fox and Hesse-Biber, 1984; Piore, 1975). Segmentation models that delineate an upper and lower primary market and an upper and lower secondary market are, in essence, models of occupational stratification, rather than models of industrial segmentation (with which they are sometimes confused). These models of occupational labor market segmentation may also be tested as partitions of an occupational mobility table, as proposed below.

III. INDUSTRIAL SEGMENTS AS PARTITIONS OF A MOBILITY TABLE

We propose a specific test with respect to career mobility for an industrial segmentation model. We suggest that a labor market segmentation model presupposes easy movement within segments and immobility between segments. The two aspects to the notion of segmentation are important to distinguish: (1) internal homogeneity and (2) identifiable boundaries.

Easy movement within segments is an essential element in a segmentation model. If it were difficult to move within segments, then there would be segments within segments. There may be inertia at the level of the individual job, or industry-specific skills that make interindustry mobility difficult. But, removing these factors from the picture, sectors or segments should be internally homogeneous. If one cannot find relatively homogeneous areas of movement in an industrial mobility table, one is left with a stratified system, not a segmented system. In this case, effects such as inertia and job-, firm-, industry-, and occupation-specific skills may be responsible for posing mobility barriers and for maintaining wage differences. This is distinct from the implications of a sectoral model. Internally homogeneous sectors, net of these detailed effects, are required for sectors to produce a common effect on all incumbents.

Immobility between segments is equally crucial to a segmentation model. As suggested above, without immobility at segment boundaries, the competitive market would erase inequality between segments. The boundaries of segments must constitute hurdles that inhibit mobility. For segments or sectors to have an independent effect, net of the detailed industry and occupation effects described above, mobility barriers must be located at sector or segment boundaries. The task for mobility research is identifying these boundaries.

The requirements of labor market segmentation theory correspond closely with statistical for models for collapsing categories in mobility tables. Breiger (1981) has argued that the question of the number of categories employed in the analysis ought to be a central issue for mobility table analysis, rather than taken as an unexamined starting point, as is so often the case. He argued that one should test theoretical propositions regarding the number and nature of classes against specific empirical criteria. He proposed a model of intracategory homogeneity and intercategory ordering as a method for collapsing large tables into a relatively small number of segments (or classes). Goodman (1981) has proposed an alternative model of partitioning mobility tables. Breiger's model is less restrictive than the model Goodman proposes, as Hout has demonstrated (1983). The advantage of the Breiger approach is that, where Goodman's criterion is too strong to fit any large mobility table, Brieger's model has been shown to fit large tables effectively.

What is suggested above is that industrial sectors (or segments) constitute a partition of an industrial mobility table. The segments must be internally homogeneous, with statistical independence or quasi-independence characterizing the structure of the segments. Quasi-independence is an approach to mobility tables that tests for statistical independence on all off-diagonal rows of a mobility table. Quasi-independence is particularly appropriate when there are theoretical reasons for controlling for industry persistence, i.e., the tendency of persons not to change major industry categories, as is the case here (see below). We can test whether an observed table of career mobility between industries can be characterized by a model that assumes easy mobility within segments and barriers to mobility between segments—that is, whether such a model constitutes a good approximation of the data. A similar test can be applied to an occupational mobility table to test occupation-based segmentation models.

IV. PARCELING OUT INDUSTRIAL PERSISTENCE

Jacobs (1983b) presented evidence suggesting that the manual versus nonmanual distinction constitutes more of a barrier to career mobility than the core-periphery industrial sector dichotomy. This analysis rested on the distinction between stayers and movers. Jacobs showed that Tolbert's (1982) finding of immobility between sectors was in part the result of stayers, those individuals remaining in the same detailed industries. When industry stayers are removed, there is a relatively weak pattern of immobility between sectors, while a sizable collar-color barrier remains even after occupation stayers are removed. These results suggest that the sector effect Tolbert reported is more appropriately viewed as an inertial effect, the tendency of many people to stay where they are. One would find such inertia in any partition of industries or occupations, including a random division of detailed industries.

Immobility between segments, then, must rest on more than persistence in the same industries. While focusing on movers constitutes a hurdle for tests of immobility between segments, it facilitates the test of internal homogeneity. Since persistence in the same industry is a well-known feature of careers, it would be unlikely to find a broad classification that met the criterion of internal homogeneity without distinguishing between stayers and movers.

Removing stayers from the analysis may be viewed as a nested process that may or may not correspond to removing the diagonal from the mobility table. One may remove detailed industry stayers, which will leave some entries on the diagonal when the row and columns of the table are major industry categories. Removing major industry stayers is equivalent to removing the diagonal entries from the analysis, as is done in quasi-independence models. One may also remove industry segment stayers or industry sector stayers. The thrust of this approach is to consider the stayer–mover distinction as a substantive one that may or may not correspond to constraining diagonal cell entries.

V. PARCELING OUT OCCUPATIONAL PERSISTENCE

We further propose that industry mobility tests must factor out occupational persistence. Existence evidence suggests the importance of occupational persistence in influencing career mobility (Blau and Duncan, 1967; Featherman and Hauser, 1978). To some extent, persistence in occupations may account for the appearance of immobility between industries. For example, one reason it is difficult to move from construction to finance may be that few occupations are common to both industries. Since one may not be able to change industries without changing occupations, the social distance between industries may simply reflect the relative difficulty of changing occupations. In occupations that overlap between these industries, mobility may not be especially difficult. A thorough test of industry immobility models must factor out occupational persistence: It should be clear that immobility between industries does not simply reflect occupational effects. Occupational stayers can be thought of in a nested way to include detailed occupation stayers, major occupation stayers, occupational class stayers, and manual versus nonmanual occupation stayers. In our analysis we begin with the stayers included, and remove them layer by layer in order to isolate the effects of persistence at each level of analysis.

Here again we treat the removal of stayers in a way that does not correspond to constraining diagonal cells to zero. In this case, removing occupational stayers involves removing from the analysis those who are stayers on a variable not explicitly treated in the industry mobility table. The number of cells in the industrial mobility table remains the same, but the sample size is reduced.

VI. PARCELING OUT OCCUPATIONAL MOBILITY EFFECTS

A final step in factoring out extraneous effects involves screening out occupational mobility effects. As is well known to students of mobility, occupational effects go beyond excessive persistence on the diagonal. Movement between occupational categories becomes more difficult the more distance between them in the occupational hierarchy. Thus, beyond the direct matter of persistence in the same detailed occupation, one suspects that immobility between industries may be the result of the occupational distance between those industries.

In order to control for occupational mobility, we examine the structure of an industrial mobility table within cells of an occupational mobility table. Thus, if 14 major industry categories are the units of analysis for industry, and 4 broad occupational classes are the units of analysis for occupation, we would propose to examine 14 by 14 industry tables within the cells of a 4 by 4 occupational mobility table. In doing so, we can examine the pattern of industry mobility among specific groups of occupation movers as well as among occupation stayers.

Once the relationship between industrial and occupational mobility table is conceived of in this way, interesting hypotheses can be put forward. For example, we hypothesize that industrial barriers to mobility are weakest for occupationally downwardly mobile individuals. In contrast, we expect the strongest industry effects to be found among those who are occupationally immobile—that is, those who are "stayers" in the occupational mobility table.

In sum, the analysis will examine whether an industrial mobility can be partitioned into discrete labor market segments. We first examine whether industrial sector models proposed in the literature can serve as partitions of an industrial mobility table. Subsequently, we consider a five-category industrial segmentation model. We test whether this partition of a major industry mobility table into segments based on patterns of homogeneity and immobility characterizes the data. The partitioning analysis is performed on a series of industry mobility tables sequentially removing effects of industrial persistence, occupational persistence, and occupational mobility. We compare these results to those obtained by removing industry effects from an occupational mobility table. This comparison is useful in showing that our results are not artifacts of the procedures employed, and for assessing the relative importance of occupation and industry in constraining career mobility.

VII. DATA AND METHODS

Data from the second Occupational Change in a Generation (OCG2) survey are employed in this analysis. These data have been frequently analyzed in studies of occupational mobility (Featherman and Hauser, 1978; Hout, 1983). The two Occupational Change in a Generation data sets have become benchmarks against which models of the American occupational structure are to be measured.

We focus on the career mobility of employed white men in 1973. With OCG2 data, career mobility refers to movement from first industry to current industry, or first occupation to current occupation. Following the procedures indicated by Featherman and Hauser, the sample was weighted to estimate the white experienced civilian labor force. For purposes of estimates of statistical significance, the sample was divided by the average sample weight. In addition, since the sample was not a pure random sample, the actual sample size was reduced by a factor of 0.75 to reflect the efficiency of the sample design. The rationale for this handling of the sample is detailed in Featherman and Hauser (1978).

Hauser and Featherman treat similar issues regarding industrial mobility in an earlier study (1977). Our sample differs from that employed in Hauser and Featherman's examination of industrial mobility in several ways: (1) We are analyzing the OCG2 (1973) data, not the original OCG data (1962); (2) while Hauser and Featherman restrict their sample to men over 24 to minimize the extent of correspondence between origin and destination industry, we include men under 24 and address the issue of persistence directly; (3) while Hauser and Featherman exclude men with foreign-born fathers to facilitate intergenerational analysis, we include them, since we are concerned only with intragenerational mobility. Agriculture is excluded in the analyses because of the unique patterns of farm occupational mobility and also because industrial and occupational definitions overlap so greatly in this area.

Including only whites, we obtain a weighted sample of 21,445. Missing or incomplete information on industry or occupation reduced the weighted sample to 16,848. Excluding farming reduces the sample to 14,670. (Fractional weighted cell entries are rounded to the nearest decimal for the purpose of the statistical analysis.) The decision to restrict the analysis to white males reflects the need for very large numbers of cases in our analysis. This restriction is unfortunate, since the interactions of race and gender with segmentation are important.

The analysis will focus on a 15 by 15 industry mobility table. Each of the 14 major industry categories, except agriculture, is included. Two of the 14 are divided into 2: manufacturing, durable goods and manufacturing, nondurable goods both are divided into a core-sector component and a periphery-sector component, following the Tolbert-Horan-Beck scheme. Separating these categories allows us to test the mobility patterns of the Tolbert-Horan-Beck model. We compare these results to those obtained dividing industries as suggested by the Bibb-Form core-periphery model.

A series of other models were considered. Results are presented for a five-category industrial segmentation model, which consists of (1) finance, (2) administration, (3) services, (4) secondary goods, and (5) primary goods. Table 1 lists the industrial categories that form the rows and columns of the industrial mobility table, and indicates which categories are grouped together for the different models.

Industrial persistence is defined as individuals staying in the same industry between first job and current job. Industrial persistence may be measured at the detailed industry level, at the major industry level, or at the segment or sector level. Occupational persistence is similarly defined as persistence in the same (detailed or major) occupation between first and current job. Persistence

Table 1. Modified Major Industry Categories

Category	Tolbert-Horan-Beck placement[a]	5-category model placement[b]
1. Mining	Core	5
2. Construction	Core	5
3. Manufacturing, durable goods (lumber, furniture, misc.)	Periphery	4
4. Manufacturing, durable goods (stone, metal, machinery, transport equipment, ordnance)	Core	4
5. Manufacturing, nondurable goods (food, tobacco, textiles, leather, nonspecified)	Periphery	4
6. Manufacturing, nondurable goods (paper, printing, chemicals, petroleum, coal, rubber)	Core	4
7. Transportation, communications, utilities	Core	5
8. Wholesale trade	Core	4
9. Retail trade	Periphery	3
10. Finance, insurance, and real estate	Core	1
11. Business and repair services	Periphery	2
12. Personal services	Periphery	3
13. Entertainment and recreation services	Periphery	3
14. Professional and related services	Core	2
15. Public administration	Core	2

[a]Tolbert-Horan-Beck models include agriculture in the periphery, but the present analysis excludes agriculture.
[b]The substantive titles for the 5 categories are (1) finance, (2) administration, (3) services, (4) secondary goods, (5) primary goods.

here plays the same role that inheritance plays in intergenerational mobility analysis.

In order to control for occupational mobility, industry mobility is examined within a 4 by 4 occupational mobility table. The four categories are (1) upper white-collar, including professionals and managers; (2) lower white-collar, including clerical and sales workers; (3) upper blue-collar, including craft and operative positions; and (4) lower blue-collar, including laborers and service workers.

We will perform a parallel set of analyses removing industrial persistence effects from occupational mobility tables. First, 15 by 15 occupational mobility tables will be examined. These categories correspond with Blau and Duncan's (1967) 17 occupational strata, with the two farm categories removed. Then we examine the effect of sequentially removing industrial effects on two additional models of the occupational mobility table: Breiger's (1981) eight-class model (here seven classes, owing to the removal of farming) and Fox and Hesse-Biber's (1984) four-category model of occupational strata (which corresponds to the four occupational class model outlined above).

VIII. RESULTS

The search for industry sectors begins with the analysis of the 15-category industry mobility table. Table 2 presents analyses of models of the 15 by 15 table that partition this table into discrete industry segments. Independence and quasi-independence models are presented for comparison. The columns refer to the models examined; the rows reflect the successive elimination of various groups of "stayers." Both the likelihood ratio chi-squared (L2) and the index of dissimilarity (D), which indicates the proportion of misclassified cases, are presented. The categories included in the Tolbert-Horan-Beck core-periphery model and the 5-category segmentation model are indicated in Table 1.

We will begin with a discussion of independence and quasi-independence, proceeding down the columns of results in Table 1. We will thus consider in turn the effect of removing each group of stayers from the model under consideration. The first row of Table 2 indicates that there is a strong relationship between the major industry of first job and the major industry of current job (L2 = 11,025.7, df = 196). This relationship is not surprising, and it is well documented in the literature (Featherman and Hauser, 1978). Much, but not all, of the relationship between major industries over time is a matter of persistence in the same detailed (Census 3-digit) industry. When detailed industry stayers are removed from the table, (row 2 of Table 2), the relationship between major industry categories over time is substantially reduced but not completely eliminated (L2 = 1,127.5, df = 196), a nearly 90% reduction in the L2 statistic.

Rows 3, 4, and 5 of Table 2 remove detailed, major, and occupational-class stayers in turn (but leave in detailed industry stayers in the first column). The successive removal of occupational stayers diminishes but does not eliminate the relationship between origin and destination industry.

Nor does persistence in major industry categories account for the remainder of the career–industry relationship. The quasi-independence models, which represent the removal of the major industry stayers, are depicted in the second column of Table 2. This model does not fit the data for the entire sample (L2 = 546.7, df = 181), indicating that there is a significant relationship between industries off the main diagonal. Row 2 of Table 2 removes detailed industry stayers. Removing detailed industry stayers is redundant for the quasi-independence models, and so the last three tests of the first and second rows are identical.

One of the most important pattern of findings in Table 2 emerges as one moves down the second column. In the quasi-independence model, the successive removal of detailed occupation, major occupation, and occupational-class stayers in turn nearly eliminates the observed industry relationship. What remains is an L2 of 222.1 with 181 degrees of freedom, a statistically significant relation but with little punch left.

The results of Table 1 strongly indicate that intragenerational industrial

Table 2. Tests of Industrial Segmentation Models for Tolbert-Horan-Beck 15 Industrial Categories

	Independence (df = 196) L2 (D)	Quasi-independence (df = 181) L2 (D)	Tolbert-Horan-Beck core-periphery[a] (df = 154) L2 (D)	5-segment model[a] (df = 86) L2 (D)
1. Entire sample (n = 14,670)	11,025.7 (29.9)	546.7 (7.5)	436.5 (7.6)	143.5 (3.3)
2. Detailed industry changers (n = 10,510)	1,127.5 (11.6)	546.7 (7.5)	436.5 (7.6)	143.5 (3.3)
3. Detailed occupation changers (n = 11,428)	4,611.3 (20.7)	394.7 (7.7)	328.6 (6.8)	116.1 (3.1)
4. 10 major occupation changers (n = 9,004)	2,678.0 (18.0)	311.4 (5.4)	251.1 (6.5)	101.5 (n.s.) (3.5)
5. 4 occupational class changers (n = 6,653)	1,807.7 (17.4)	222.1 (5.4)	178.4 (n.s.) (6.1)	85.3 (n.s.) (3.6)

[a]See Table 1 for list of industry categories included in each model.

mobility must be understood in the context of industrial and occupational persistence. That is, a large proportion of the relationship between first industry and current major industry is accounted for by persistence in detailed industries, with about a 90% reduction in L2. Nonetheless, detailed industry changers are disproportionately likely to end up in the same major industry. When all major industry persistence is accounted for, the remaining industry relationship is reduced by about half.

Much of the balance of the relationship between the industry of a man's first job and later job is accounted for by occupational persistence. Detailed occupational persistence accounts for more than one-quarter of the balance, major occupational persistence another 20%, and broad occupational class amost another 30%. Thus, the great majority of the relationship between industries over time is accounted for by industrial and broad occupational persistence. *The removal of the inertial or barrier effects between more detailed industry units, combined with the removal of occupational effects, leaves little immobility between major industries to be explained.*

Given this weak relationship in need of explanation, let us turn to the two segmentation models we are considering to see how they fare. The first substantive model considered is the Tolbert-Horan-Beck core-periphery model. All of the industries they incorporate in the core are grouped together into one labor market segment; the balance are assigned to the periphery. The Tolbert-Horan-Beck model does not produce an adequate partitioning of the industrial mobility table when the entire sample is included. A Breiger test of quasi-independence for the Tolbert-Horan-Beck model does not fit the data when the entire sample is included (L2 = 436.5, df = 154), indicating that these two economic sectors do not represent two discrete and internally homogeneous labor market segments. However, this model fits better and better the more stayers are removed from the analysis. When we reach row 5, the model finally fits the data (χ^2 = 178.4, with 154 df). This represents a statistical improvement over quasi-independence (43.7 L2 with a use of 27 degrees of freedom). The Tolbert *et al.* dual sector model fits the data when sufficient persistence effects are accounted for. Thus, there is support for the Tolbert model, but the degree of immobility it explains is quite modest.

The five-industry segment model fares better than the Tolbert model on each row of Table 2. (The categories included in each segment are presented in Table 1.) When the entire sample is included, the Breiger quasi-independence test of this industrial segmentation model considerably improves the fit to the data over the Tolbert model, but it is nonetheless rejected for the entire sample (L2 = 143.5, df = 86).

The five-segment model fits the data when major occupational stayers are removed (row 4 of Table 2). This model represents a statistically significant improvement over the dual sectors model (the L2 improvement equals 149.6 using 68 degrees of freedom). The five-segment model represents an improved fit compared to the Tolbert-Beck-Horan model even when occupational class stayers are removed (93.1 L2 with 68 df), although one might argue that this comparison represents a case of overfitting the data.

Thus, in Table 2 there are results that support a variety of viewpoints. *The strongest pattern in these results is that the bulk of the relationship in a career industry mobility table are accounted for by persistence in occupation and industry categories.* The remaining relationships are definitely secondary. Substantively, this indicates that more attention should be paid to immobility at the industry, occupation, and perhaps firm level, rather than the more aggregated level of segment or sector. *Nonetheless, there is limited support for a sectoral model, which does fit the data after successive layers of stayers are removed from the analysis. However, a five-segment model consistently outperforms the dual sector model.*

Table 3 describes the 15 modified major industry classifications employed for the Bibb-Form model. The Bibb-Form model divides nondurable manufacturing differently than does the Tolbert-Horan-Beck model, and thus a test of this model requires us to reclassify the detailed industries. We obtain a 15 by 15 industry mobility table, as before, but with modified categories. The Bibb-Form model groups paper products and printing with apparel, textiles, tobacco, and food processing in the periphery, whereas the Tolbert-Horan-Beck model groups paper and printing with chemicals, petroleum, coal, and rubber manufacturing in the core of the economy. The detailed industries included in categories 6 and 7 of the 15 modified major industry divisions differ between Tables 1 and 3, and the core-periphery placement of several of the other categories also differs.

Table 3.   Alternative Modified Major Industry Categories

Category	Bibb-Form placement	5-category model placement[a]
1. Mining	Core	5
2. Construction	Core	5
3. Manufacturing, durable goods (lumber, furniture, misc.)	Core	4
4. Manufacturing, durable goods (stone, metal, machinery, transport equipment, ordnance)	Core	4
5. Manufacturing, nondurable goods (food, tobacco, textiles, apparel, paper, printing, leather, misc.)	Periphery	4
6. Manufacturing, nondurable goods (chemicals, petroleum, rubber)	Core	4
7. Transportation, communications, utilities	Core	5
8. Wholesale trade	Periphery	4
9. Retail trade	Periphery	3
10. Finance, insurance, and real estate	Periphery	1
11. Business and repair services	Periphery	2
12. Personal services	Periphery	3
13. Entertainment and recreation services	Periphery	3
14. Professional and related services	Periphery	2
15. Public administration	Core	2

[a]The substantive titles for the 5 categories are (1) finance, (2) administration, (3) services, (4) secondary goods, (5) primary goods.

Table 4. Tests of Industrial Segmentation Models for Bibb-Form 15 Industry Categories

	Independence (df = 196) L2 (D)	Quasi-independence (df = 181) L2 (D)	Bibb-Form core-periphery[a] (df = 154) L2 (D)	5-segment model[a] (df = 86) L2 (D)
1. Entire sample (n = 14,670)	10,878.0 (29.6)	550.2 (8.6)	378.8 (7.0)	153.4 (3.5)
2. Detailed industry changers (n = 10,510)	1,110.7 (11.4)	550.2 (8.6)	378.8 (7.0)	153.4 (3.5)
3. Detailed occupation changers (n = 11,428)	4,520.1 (20.4)	408.8 (7.7)	297.7 (6.3)	122.9 (3.2)
4. 10 major occupation changers (n = 9,004)	2,608.8 (17.7)	336.0 (7.5)	246.6 (6.2)	105.3 (n.s.) (3.4)
5. 4 occupational class changers (n = 6,653)	1,771.8 (17.1)	240.0 (7.4)	198.9 (6.5)	87.5 (n.s.) (3.4)

[a]See Table 3 for list of industry categories included in each model.

Table 4 repeats the analysis presented in Table 2 using the Bibb-Form 15 industry categories as the units of analysis. The results in Table 4 generally follow those in Table 2. The Bibb-Form model does not quite fit, even when occupation class stayers are removed from the analysis. While the Tolbert-Horan-Beck model does succeed, the differences between these schema in terms of statistical fit are quite small. The five-industry segment model again fits once major occupation stayers are removed, and constitutes a significant improvement in fit over the Bibb-Form model.

Table 5 presents tests of a broader examination of occupational influences, returning to the Tolbert-Horan-Beck 15 industry categories. Whereas Table 2 and 4 considered only occupational immobility effects, Table 5 considers whether off-diagonal occupational distance is responsible for the remainder of the industrial immobility. Table 5, then, considers the relationship between occupational mobility and industrial mobility. Occupational mobility is operationalized in a 4 by 4 occupational class mobility table, industrial mobility in a 15 by 15 mobility table. Thus, the tests presented in Table 5 are for a 4 by 4 by 15 by 15 occupation by occupation by industry by industry table.

The first row of Table 5 indicates that the model of independence is an extremely poor approximation of this table. Quasi-independence (with respect to the 15 industry categories) is a substantially improvement but still does not adequately characterize the data. However, a model that incorpo-

Table 5. Tests of Models for Occupation by Occupation by Industry by Industry Table

	Categories	Model	Statistics
		A. $4 \times 4 \times 15 \times 15$ table ($n = 14,760$)	
1.	Multiway table $4 \times 4 \times 15 \times 15$	Independence	$L2 = 29,569.5$ $df = 3,565$
2.	Multiway table $4 \times 4 \times 15 \times 15$	Quasi-independence	$L2 = 10,915.3$ $df = 3,325$
3.	Multiway table $4 \times 4 \times 15 \times 15$	Fit occupations $(1–2)(1–3)(1–4)(2–3)(2–4)$	$L2 = 3,253.4$ $df = 3,148$
4.	Multiway table $4 \times 4 \times 15 \times 15$	Fit industries $(1–3)(1–4)(2–3)(2–4)(3–4)$	$L2 = 3,920.1$ $df = 2,976$
		B. 15×15 tables, grouping occupation by occupation cells	
5.	Above the diagonal	Quasi-independence	$L2 = 242.4$ $df = 181$ ($n = 2,302$)
6.	Below the diagonal	Quasi-independence	$L2 = 225.5$ $df = 181$ ($n = 4,459$)
7.	Cells $(1,2)+(1,3)+(1,4)$*	Quasi-independence	$L2 = 196.9$ $df = 181$ ($n = 690$)
8.	Cells $(2,3)+(2,4)+(3,4)$*	Quasi-independence	$L2 = 233.4$ $df = 181$ ($n = 1,612$)
9.	Cells $(2,1)+(3,1)+(3,2)$*	Quasi-independence	$L2 = 193.7$ $df = 181$ ($n = 2,736$)
10.	Cells $(4,1)+(4,2)+(4,3)$*	Quasi-independence	$L2 = 172.9$ $df = 181$ ($n = 1,723$)

[a]In lines 7–10, models are applied to the specified combination of cells.

rates the occupational relationships and tests quasi-independence for the industry relationships fits the data (L2 = 3,253.4, df = 3,148). This model takes as given the relationship between first occupation and current occupation (1, 2), the relationship between first occupation and both origin and destination industry (1, 3) and (1, 4), and the relationship between destination occupation and origin and destination industry (2, 3) and (2, 4). Thus, all two-way relationships are fitted, with the exception of the industry–industry relationship (3, 4). This model indicates that, once one has accounted for the occupational relationships in this table, the career industry mobility table is quasi-independent.

Substantively, this indicates that there is no industrial immobility left to explain once one takes occupational mobility and the relationship between occupational mobility and industry mobility into account. Thus, there are no sector effects left to explain.

A potential difficulty with the results in Table 5 is that there are so many cells (3,600) in the table examined here that the results may be artifacts of the small number of cases per cell (3.95). To try to minimize this problem, we collapsed several of the occupation cells into one to obtain a denser table for analysis. We tested the quasi-independence model for a single 15 by 15 industry table for all of the 6 occupation cells above the diagonal in Table 5, and again for the 6 cells below the diagonal. Quasi-independence does not fit these tables. A subsequent test divided the above-diagonal cells into two groups of three, and divided the below-diagonal cells into two groups of three. All four of these groups fit the data. The large number of cases (690, 1,612, 2,736, and 1,723) with only 181 degrees of freedom indicates that the results are not artifacts of the relatively sparse number of cases per cell. We conclude that the industrial quasi-independence is a substantive conclusion rather than a statistical artifact.

The preceding analysis examines the industry effects that remain after occupational effects are removed. Now let us reverse this analysis to see how strong career occupation relationships are once industry effects are removed. Row 4 in Table 5 repeats the analysis of row 5 but tests the strength of occupational effects after controlling for industry effects. In row 4 a model was tested that fit the relationship of first and current industry (3, 4) and all the industry–occupation effects (1, 3) (1, 4) (2, 3) (2, 4) but left the occupation relationship (1, 2) quasi-independent. This model does not fit the data, whereas the model fitting the occupation relationships (row 3) does.

This comparison suggests two conclusions. First, the finding of quasi-independence for industries is not an artifact, since the same procedure does not result in a finding of quasi-independence for occupations. *Second, the strength of the occupation relationship, net of industry effects, is clearly stronger than the industry relationship, net of occupational effects.*

Table 6 examines the same industry–occupation relation in a slightly different fashion. Table 6 reports an examination of the 15 by 15 industry table for each of the 16 occupational cells separately. Table 6 indicates that for 14 of the 16 cells, the model of quasi-independence fits. For only two cells, (1, 1)

Table 6.   Quasi-Independence Models for OCG2 Men, for 15 by 15 Industry
Mobility Tables, within 4 by 4 Occupational Mobility Table

		Occupational class, 1973			
		Upper white-collar	Lower white-collar	Upper blue-collar	Lower blue-collar
Occupational class, first job	Upper white-collar	$n = 2,623$ $L2 = 302.4$ $df = 181$	$n = 328$ $L2 = 153.7$ $df = 155$	$n = 288$ $L2 = 154.6$ $df = 168$	$n = 74$ $L2 = 79.2$ $df = 111$
	Lower white-collar	$n = 1,098$ $L2 = 152.5$ $df = 181$	$n = 326$ $L2 = 155.0$ $df = 15$	$n = 748$ $L2 = 110.2$ $df = 168$	$n = 259$ $L2 = 240.5$ $df = 168$
	Upper blue-collar	$n = 1,067$ $L2 = 136.0$ $df = 181$	$n = 571$ $L2 = 143.6$ $df = 168$	$n = 3,959$ $L2 = 243.5$ $df = 181$	$n = 605$ $L2 = 144.3$ $df = 181$
	Lower blue-collar	$n = 345$ $L2 = 132.3$ $df = 168$	$n = 222$ $L2 = 150.8$ $df = 168$	$n = 1,156$ $L2 = 154.4$ $df = 181$	$n = 545$ $L2 = 179.2$ $df = 155$

	Entire sample			3-digit occupation changers
1. Cell (1,1)	$(n = 2,623)$			$(n = 1,318)$
Independence			$L2 = 1,207.5$	$df = 196$
Quasi-independence			$L2 = 216.3$	$df = 181$
Core-periphery model	$L2 = 239.6$	$df = 154$	$L2 = 192.3$	$df = 154$
Segmentation model	$L2 = 109.9$	$df = 85$	$L2 = 96.6$	$df = 81$
2. Cell (3,3)	$(n = 3,959)$			$(n = 2,725)$
Independence			$L2 = 760.3$	$df = 196$
Quasi-independence			$L2 = 166.9$	$df = 181$
Core-periphery model	$L2 = 192.3$	$df = 154$	$L2 = 140.1$	$df = 154$
Segmentation model	$L2 = 77.8$	$df = 83$	$L2 = 69.7$	$df = 83$

and (3, 3) does quasi-independence fail to fit. Thus, as we saw in Table 5, the more one controls for occupational effects, the less off-diagonal industrial relationship is observed. We also note in Table 6 that, as hypothesized, occupationally downwardly mobile individuals are not constrained by their industry of origin. As it turns out, neither are occupationally upwardly mobile individuals. The concentration of industry effects is evident for individuals who remain in the same broad occupational class.

Table 6 reports tests of partitions of these two recalcitrant cells. The segmentation model fits the upper blue-collar cell and barely misses fitting the upper white-collar cell. The Tolbert-Horan-Beck model dies not fit the industry table adequately when the entire sample (of these two cells) is included. However, when detailed occupation stayers are removed, the industrial segmentation model fits the upper white-collar cell, while quasi-independence fits the upper blue-collar cell. (Removing detailed occupation stayers is not redundant: Quasi-independence blanks out major industry stayers, not occupation stayers.)

The above results suggest that industry effects may consist primarily of persistence in major industry categories, once occupational effects are removed from the analysis. Rather than clustering into two main sectors or five main segments, industry mobility effects are very weak after successive occupational effects are removed.

We finally considered the effects of removing industrial effects on a 15 by 15 occupational mobility table, reversing the control variable as we did in Table 5. The results of this analysis are presented in Table 7. Strong occupation effects persist after successive waves of industrial persistence effects are removed. Independence and quasi-independence fail in all cases, as does the four broad occupational segmentation model.

An interesting pattern of effects is evident for the Breiger seven-class model. Breiger (1981) has noted that his occupational class model does not fit career mobility tables. However, his seven-class model does fit once industrial persistence effects are removed.

A final point should be made regarding the results in Table 7. We have noted that the procedure of removing successive groups of industry stayers can be viewed as a nested process: All three-digit industry stayers are removed once all major industry stayers are removed, and so on. The succes-

Table 7.   Tests of Occupational Class Models

	Independence (df = 196) L2 (D)	Quasi-independence (df = 181) L2 (D)	Breiger 7 nonfarm class model (df = 53) L2 (D)	4-segment model (df = 107) L2 (D)
1. Entire sample (n = 14,669)	10,538.4 (31.9)	2,756.4 (20.9)	106.0 (3.2)	473.8 (7.2)
2. Detailed occupation changers (n = 11,835)	4,095.9 (23.3)	2,756.4 (20.9)	106.0 (3.2)	473.8 (7.2)
3. Detailed industry changers (n = 10,510)	3,695.0 (23.1)	1,769.6 (18.3)	68.8(n.s.) (2.5)	156.8 (4.5)
4. Major industry changers (n = 9,045)	2,757.7 (21.7)	1,525.7 (18.1)	69.8(n.s.) (2.7)	150.3 (4.7)
5. Industry segment changers[a] (n = 7,046)	2,931.0 (25.4)	1,910.7 (21.7)	78.9 (3.3)	729.1 (9.9)
5. Industry sector changers[a] (n = 3,740)	1,430.8 (23.3)	1,014.8 (21.1)	115.3 (5.4)	410.2 (10.5)

[a]See Table 1 for list of industry categories included in each model.

sion of steps almost invariably improves the fit of the table, indicating that immobility is greater for the group of stayers than for the balance of the sample.

Yet the removal of industrial segment and industrial sector stayers does not improve the fit of the occupational tables. The chi-squared statistics rise for the last two rows of Table 7, contrary to the general pattern of declining figures as one moves down the table. This curious pattern suggests that occupational effects are weaker within these segments than between them, that the relationships within the occupational table are not concentrated within these sectors or segments. This final twist of the occupational data again suggests that the segmentation and dual-sector models are not the most appropriate categories for understanding career mobility patterns.

IX. DISCUSSION

Once occupational mobility is controlled for, few industry effects remain besides persistence on the diagonal. The overwhelming majority of the relationships in a career industry mobility table are accounted for by detailed industry persistence, major industry persistence, and occupational persistence. As indicated in the analysis in Table 5, the balance is accounted for by occupational mobility effects and occupation by industry interactions.

Evidence that economic sectors define barriers to mobility is weak. This correspondence between labor market segments and economic segments is observed only when industry effects verge on disappearing altogether—namely, when all of the extraneous persistence effects are removed from the analysis. (We should add a cautionary note that there might be less mobility for blacks and women. But see Jacobs, 1983b, for contrary evidence.) In all cases, a more variegated segmentation model outperforms a dual sector model. In sharp contrast, occupational effects persist more strongly when industry effects are removed.

However, immobility between major industries may be sufficient to sustain wage inequalities between economic sectors over time. Quasi-independence, of course, is not independence. The evidence of immobility between industries, even after occupational effects are removed, is indisputable. Whether this immobility is the result of different skills acquired, different geographical locations of different industries, or other factors cannot be shown from the present analysis. Quasi-independence may account for the wage effects Tolbert et al. (1980) and others have obtained. The degree of immobility required to sustain wage disparities across industries is a matter that we cannot pursue here. However, since immobility appears to be more a matter of industry rather than of sector effects, we would expect wage inequality equations that are operationalized at the industry level to pick up more inequality than those operationalized at the industrial sector level.

Thus, the thrust of our argument is that we should not confuse micro-level structural effects with macrolevel ones. The mobility and wage effects that are attributable to industry and occupation should not be attributed to segments or sectors. Once one has accounted for such effects, we find little or no sectoral barriers to mobility remaining.

The movement of new structuralist analysis has been toward firms and away from aggregated units of analysis such as industrial sectors. Our results would tend to support this trend. While we have not employed data on firms in this analysis, we do find that smaller units of analysis outperform larger ones. We expect that characteristics of firms are particularly important determinants of income and mobility, and that behavior at the firm level is likely to be responsible for much of the more aggregated relationships we have observed.

Another important part of this picture not examined here is the influence of geography on mobility. Some industries are concentrated in particular localities, so the significance of industrial effects may be highlighted in local markets. This question will have to be addressed in a multivariate context, taking into account regional as well as occupation and industry patterns.

Three programmatic notes are in order. This chapter underscores the utility of partitioning models in addressing substantive concerns. Second, this chapter indicates the importance of considering mobility in a multidimensional context, as Logan (1983) has argued. Results that are implied by particular models of a mobility table may disappear when other variables, here simply occupation, are controlled. Third, this chapter highlights the utility of a multilevel view of social structure outlined by Baron and Bielby (1980) and Kalleberg and Berg (1987).

ACKNOWLEDGMENTS

An earlier version of this paper was presented at the American Sociological Association Meetings, New York, August 1986. We gratefully acknowledge the comments of Ross M. Stolzenberg, Fred Block, Samuel H. Preston, and the editors of this volume on an earlier draft of this paper.

REFERENCES

Baron, James. 1984. "Organizational Perspectives on Stratification." *Annual Review of Sociology* 10.
Baron, James, and William Bielby. 1980. "Bringing the Firms Back In: Stratification, Segmentation and the Organization of Work." *American Sociological Review* 45:737–765.
Beck, E. M., Patrick M. Horan, and Charles M. Tolbert, III. 1978. "Stratification in a Dual Economy: A Sectoral Model of Earnings Determination." *American Sociological Review* 43:704–720.
Berg, Ivar, ed. 1981. *Sociological Perspectives on Labor Markets.* New York: Academic Press.
Bibb, Robert, and William Form. 1977. "The Effects of Industrial, Occupational and Sex Stratification on Wages in Blue Collar Markets." *Social Forces* 55:974–996.
Blau, Peter, and Otis D. Duncan. 1967. *The American Occupational Structure.* New York: Wiley.
Breiger, R. 1981. "The Social Class Structure of Occupational Mobility." *American Journal of Sociology* 87:578–611.

Cain, Glen G. 1976. "The Challenge of Segmented Labor Market Theories to Orthodox Theory: A Survey." *Journal of Economic Literature* 14:1215–1257.

Clogg, Clifford C. 1981. "Latent Structure Models of Mobility." *American Journal of Sociology* 86:836–868.

Duncan, Otis D. 1979. "How Destination Depends on Origin in the Occupational Mobility Table." *American Journal of Sociology* 84:793–803.

Featherman, David L., and Robert M. Hauser. 1978. *Opportunity and Change*. New York: Academic Press.

Fox, Mary F., and Sharlene Hesse-Biber. 1984. *Women at Work*. Palo Alto: Mayfield.

Goodman, L. 1981. "Criteria for Determining Whether Certain Categories in a Cross-Classification Table Should Be Combined, with Special Reference to Occupational Categories in an Occupational Mobility Table." *American Journal of Sociology* 87:612–650.

Hauser, Robert M. 1978. "A Structural Model of the Mobility Table." *Social Forces* 56:919–953.

Hauser, Robert M., and David L. Featherman. 1977. *The Process of Stratification*. New York: Academic Press.

Hodson, Randy D. 1978. "Labor in the Monopoly, Competitive, and State Sectors of Production." *Politics and Society* 8:429–480.

Hout, Michael. 1983. *Mobility Tables*. Beverly Hills: Sage.

Jacobs, Jerry A. 1983a. The Sex Segregation of Occupations and Women's Career Patterns. Doctoral dissertation, Department of Sociology, Harvard University.

Jacobs, Jerry A. 1983b. "Industrial Sector and Career Mobility Reconsidered." *American Sociological Review* 47:415–421.

Kalleberg, Arne L., and Ivar Berg, 1987. *Work and Industry: Structures, Markets, and Processes*. New York: Plenum Press.

Kalleberg, Arne L., and L. J. Griffin. 1980. "Class, Occupation, and Inequality in Job Rewards." *American Journal of Sociology* 85:731–768.

Kalleberg, Arne L., and Aage B. Sorensen. 1979. "The Sociology of Labor Markets." *Annual Review of Sociology* 5:351–379.

Kaufman, R., R. D. Hodson, and N. D. Fligstein. 1981. "Defrocking Dualism: A New Approach to Defining Industrial Sectors." *Social Science Research* 10:1–31.

Logan, John A. 1983. "A Multivariate Model for Mobility Tables." *American Journal of Sociology* 89:324–349.

Parcel, Toby, and Charles Mueller. 1983. *Ascription and Labor Markets: Race and Sex Differences in Earnings*. New York: Academic Press.

Piore, Michael. 1975. "Notes for a Theory of Labor Market Segmentation." Pp. 125–150 in *Labor Market Segmentation*, edited by R. Edwards, M. Reich and D. Gordon. Lexington, MA: D. C. Heath.

Reskin, Barbara, ed. 1984. *Sex Segregation in the Workplace: Trends, Explanations, Remedies*. Washington, D.C.: National Academy of Sciences Press.

Rosenbaum, James E. 1984. *Career Mobility in a Corporate Hierarchy*. New York: Academic Press.

Rosenfeld, Rachel. 1983. "Sex Segregation and Sectors: An Analysis of Gender Differences in Returns from Employer Changes." *American Sociological Review* 48:637–656.

Stewman, Shelby, and S. L. Konda. 1983. "Careers and Organizational Labor Markets: Demographic Models of Organizational Behavior." *American Journal of Sociology* 88:637–685.

Tolbert, Charles M., III 1982. "Industrial Segmentation and Men's Career Mobility," *American Sociological Review* 47:457–477.

Tolbert, Charles, Patrick Horan, and E. M. Beck. 1980. "The Structure of Economic Segmentation: A Dual Economy Approach." *American Journal of Sociology* 85:1096–1116.

Wallace, Michael, and Arne L. Kalleberg. 1981. "Economic Organization of Firms and Labor Market Consequences: Toward a Specification of Dual economy theory." Pp. 77–118 in *Sociological Perspectives on Labor Markets*, edited by Ivar Berg. New York: Academic Press.

Yamaguchi, Kazuo. 1983. "The Structure of Intergenerational Occupational Mobility: Generality and Specificity in Resources, Channels and Barriers." *American Journal of Sociology* 88:718–745.

4

Neoclassical and Sociological Perspectives on Segmented Labor Markets

Kevin Lang and William T. Dickens

I. INTRODUCTION

Segmented labor market models gained popularity in economics during the late 1960s and early 1970s but fell fairly rapidly into disrepute following criticisms by Cain (1976) and Wachter (1974). At about this time, sociologists, drawing on the work of Averitt (1968) of segmented labor market theorists, developed a theory of a dual or segmented economy.[1] The sociological theory is portrayed as corrective of the labor-supply-side and individualistic orientation of human capital and status attainment theory.

In this chapter, we argue that neoclassical theory has been misrepresented in the literature on segmented economy and that tests designed to distinguish between "structural" and "neoclassical" models are inadequate for that task. Moreover, we maintain that dual labor market and dual economy theorists have concentrated on the aspects of the theory that represent the least significant departure from neoclassical economics. In fact, following a

[1]Throughout this paper we use the following nomenclature: We use "dual or segmented *labor markets*" when we refer to the economic literature, "dual or segmented *economy*" when we refer to the sociological literature, and "dual or segmented markets" when we refer to both literatures simultaneously. Neoclassical economists should be viewed as distinct from the Marxists and institutionalists who, together, constitute the schools of economic thought from which dual labor market theory developed.

Kevin Lang • Department of Economics, Boston University, Boston, Massachusetts 02215. **William T. Dickens** • Department of Economics, University of California, Berkeley, Berkeley, California 94720.

research heuristic of their own, neoclassical economists have developed elements of a segmented labor market model that is in many ways similar to the segmented economy theories found in sociology. We sketch this model and argue that the neoclassical model gives a precise meaning to the concept of *dual* or *segmented* labor markets but does not suggest that a classification system for job characteristics must rely on a single dimension.

II. NEOCLASSICAL WAGE DETERMINATION[2]

Sociological critics (e.g. Berg, 1981; Bibb and Form, 1977; Horan, Beck, and Tolbert, 1980; Sorenson and Kalleberg, 1981) have sometimes characterized the neoclassical model of wage determination as supply-driven. According to this view, neoclassical economics ascribes productivity to the worker rather than to the job or to some combination of job and worker. Wage differences are said to be explained by individual characteristics rather than by the characteristics of the jobs the individuals hold. From this perspective, dual economy and dual labor market theory are perceived as reminding economists of their long-standing interest in demand as well as supply.

While these critics are certainly correct in their view that economists have paid excessive attention to the human capital model of earnings determination, neoclassical economists have developed quite sophisticated models in which individuals' productivities vary according to their job and have concerned themselves with the process whereby workers and jobs are matched. In developing such models, neoclassical economists clearly take account of both supply and demand. It is no more surprising to the neoclassical labor economist than to the dual labor market theorist that their graduate students will earn more as professional economists in consulting firms than as dishwashers in restaurants.

In this section, we describe the neoclassical model of wage determination under pure competition when there is perfect information and when jobs and workers are heterogeneous. The model has a fairly extensive modern history; even if we ignore the obligatory reference to Adam Smith, the essentials of the model were developed in the early 1950s (Roy, 1950, 1951; Tinbergen, 1951, 1956). More recent work (Heckman and Sedlacek, 1985; Rosen, 1974; Sattinger, 1979, 1980; Thaler and Rosen, 1975) has built on this tradition.

In this model, the wage paid to workers in any particular job will depend on personal attributes that affect productivity and on characteristics of the job that affect its desirability. The relation between personal attributes and wages varies among jobs. Since information is assumed to be perfect, workers know what wage they will receive in any job if they have a certain combination of attributes and the job has a particular combination of characteristics. Certain attributes (e.g., height) are, of course, not easily altered, but others such as

---

[2]This section is based heavily on Kahn and Lang (1988). A related analysis of the market for occpuational safety is described in Kahn (1986).

education are somewhat under the control of the individual. It is these personal attributes and job characteristics that are the primary subject of economic analysis.

Let us consider an individual's decision about how much education to obtain. Since education is costly, individuals require higher earnings in order to compensate them for obtaining additional education. Figure 1 shows "indifference curves" for two different workers. The indifference curves represent combinations of schooling and earnings that leave that worker equally well off. Indifference curves that are higher and to the left are preferred since they represent higher earnings for a constant level of education (or the same earnings for less education). Of course, individuals care about aspects of a job other than the education it requires and the wages it pays. Myriad factors such as location, safety, and job pace affect the way workers view jobs. Those readers who feel comfortable imagining tangencies of n-dimensional surfaces are encouraged to recognize the immediate applicability to the more general problem. For simplicity, we consider the case where jobs and workers have only two characteristics, which, for purposes of concreteness, we term *wages* and *education*.

Figure 1 also shows the combinations of wages and schooling that are available to the individuals. Each individual chooses the point along the wage/schooling locus (or hedonic wage equation) that puts him or her on the highest indifference curve. By comparing the slopes of the two sets of indifference curves at points at which they are depicted as crossing, it can be seen that individual B requires less compensation for obtaining education than does individual A. This may reflect any of several possibilities. For example,

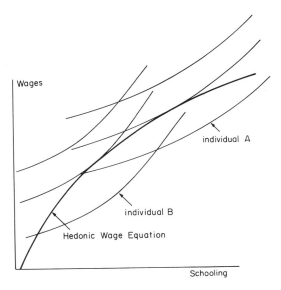

Figure 1. Indifference curves for two different workers.

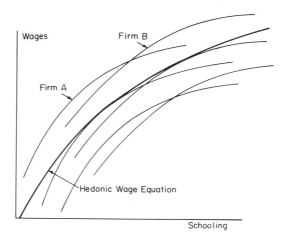

Figure 2. Isoprofit curves for two different firms.

perhaps B enjoys education more or has more financial resources with which
to finance education and therefore, relative to A, chooses a combination of
wages and schooling that involves higher wages and more schooling.

Figure 2 shows a similar decision for two different firms for a particular
type of job. In each firm, workers' productivities depend on how much education they have received. However, education contributes more to productivity in firm B than in firm A. Figure 2 shows isoprofit curves for each firm,
representing combinations of wages and education that leave the firm with
the same profit. Isoprofit curves are more desirable to the firm as one moves
down and to the right, representing combinations involving more education
and lower wages. Firms have a decision problem that is analogous to that of
workers. They recognize that they must pay higher wages in order to get
workers with higher levels of education. Firms in which education increases
productivity to a greater extent will be willing to spend more on hiring more
educated workers. They choose the wage/education combination given by
the point along the hedonic wage equation (HWE) that is just tangent to the
isoprofit curve, representing the highest level of profit attainable by the firm.

The final element of the theory is the determination of the HWE. The
HWE adjusts until the number of workers with each level of education is
exactly equal to the number demanded. The result, shown in Figure 3, is that
firms in which education is particularly valuable are matched with workers
who require relatively little compensation for getting education. The HWE
represents the market relation between education and wages.[3]

[3]More formally, the firm chooses the number of workers to hire and the level of education to
require of them in order to maximize profits given by

$$\text{profits} = f(L, E, u) - w(E)L \tag{1}$$

where without loss of generality the price of output has been normalized to equal 1, f is the
production function net of any capital costs, L is the number of workers hired, E is their level of

The HWE is a standard wage equation of the type estimated in human capital models. We have derived it using a human capital theoretic explanation of the role of education, which assumes that education increases productivity. However, we could equally have assumed that education serves as a signal of innate ability and that innate ability is more valuable in certain jobs than in others. The human capital interpretation is not essential to the model. In the light of sociological critiques of the human capital model, it is, however, important to note that the wage equation does not ignore "demand" factors. Instead, the HWE is the market equilibrium locus resulting from the joint action of supply and demand when workers and jobs are heterogen-

---

education, w is the wage they receive, and u is a parameter measuring the contribution of education to productivity in the firm.

Similarly, workers choose their level of education in order to maximize their appropriately discounted lifetime earnings net of education costs

$$\text{net earnings} = w(E) - c(E,e) \tag{2}$$

where c is the appropriately amortized cost of education and e represents the ease of obtaining schooling for the individual.

It can be shown that the firm's demand depends on u and the slope of the HWE (the w function) and that, similarly, the level of education chosen by the worker depends on e and the slope of the HWE:

$$E^d = E^d(w',u) \tag{3}$$

$$E^s = E^s(w',e) \tag{4}$$

where superscripts denote supply and demand, and w', the slope of the HWE, serves the role of price in standard supply or demand equations.

The competitive market matches workers with high values of e with firms with high values of u. This matching process can be described by a function relating e to u:

$$e = f(u) \qquad f'>0 \tag{5}$$

To derive the HWE, we proceed as follows: First, solve (3) and (4) for u and e as functions of w' and E:

$$e = e(w',E) \tag{6}$$

$$u = u(w',E). \tag{7}$$

The next step is to substitute (6) and (7) into (5) to obtain

$$e(w',E) = f(u(w',E)) \tag{8}$$

and then solve for w' as a function of E

$$w' = w'(E) \tag{9}$$

Finally, (9) can be integrated to obtain the hedonic wage equation

$$w = w(E) \tag{10}$$

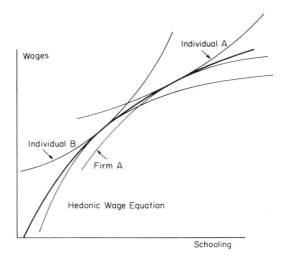

Figure 3. Determination of the HWE.

eous. In fact, given the manner in which the model has been developed, it is not evident whether education should be considered a characteristic of the worker or of the job. It is, in fact, neither or both, depending on one's semantic choice, since it is a characteristic of the worker/job match.[4]

In particular, this model does not ignore marginal productivity theory. However, the theory's assumptions are hidden in the equilibrium requirement that the quantity supplied equal the quantity demanded. Firms simultaneously choose the number of workers to hire and the level of education. In equilibrium, the number of workers hired by the firm will be such that the wage exactly equals the value of the marginal product of the type of worker hired.

There are several limitations to the model that should be noted. In particular, it is a model of a perfectly competitive labor market. Thus, it ignores the role of unions and monopsony.[5] Economists have generally used quite different models to describe wage setting in the presence of unions and do not apply the competitive model described here.

In addition, the model assumes perfect information, which makes the assumption of perfect matching of workers and firms sensible. More realistically, the matching process should be modeled as one involving search and imperfect, costly information. However, it seems unlikely that allowing

[4]The fact that the wage equation can be interpreted as the equilibrium outcome of the interaction of supply and demand does not mean that this fact was clearly recognized in the seminal work of Becker (1971) and Mincer (1974). To the extent that the development of the human capital model ignored demand factors, the sociological criticism of the theoretical work is justified.
[5]Monopsony refers to a market with only one buyer. In a labor market a monopsony exists when one firm or a group of firms acting together are the sole source of employment for a particular group of workers.

for search would alter the model significantly. A model can be constructed in which at each level of education, there is a distribution of wages available. In this model, when choosing their level of education, workers maximize their expected net wage (or expected utility) given optimal search behavior. Workers with low costs of schooling get more education, set higher reservation wages, and tend to end up in firms in which education contributes significantly to productivity. Thus, while the matching process in a search model is not perfect, the broad outlines of the perfect information model continue to hold.

Simple search theory (dating at least from Stigler's (1962) seminal piece) allows workers to receive different wages for the same job; the extension to heterogeneous jobs is obvious. Models in which there is uncertainty about the quality of the job match have also been incorporated into the economic model (Jovanovic, 1979a,b). It should, therefore, be evident from this description that the major departure of dual labor market theory from neoclassical theory is not that workers receive different wages depending on the job they obtain. There are, however, significant differences between the neoclassical and dual labor market models. These are addressed in the next section.

III. THE CHALLENGE OF SEGMENTED LABOR MARKET THEORIES TO ORTHODOX THEORY

Aside from a difference of methodology, which has been emphasized by Woodbury (1979) and Piore (1983), the dual labor market models of the late 1960s and early 1970s departed from the standard neoclassical model in three significant ways.

First, they introduced non-price rationing for good jobs. Unlike neoclassical labor economists, dual labor market theorists maintained that some individuals who were qualified for and wanted certain types of jobs at the going wage could not obtain them. In the standard economic model such people would bid down the wages in the desired jobs until supply equated demand—the available jobs would be rationed by the price mechanism. In addition, difficulties of access were thought by dual labor market theorists to be systematic. Women, blacks, and other minorities faced barriers that inhibited them from obtaining desirable jobs.

A number of authors (Bluestone, 1970; Hodson and Kaufman, 1982; Kalleberg and Sorenson, 1979; Leigh, 1976; Rosenberg, 1980; Schiller, 1977; Tolbert, 1982), including some dual labor market theorists, have interpreted the view that there were two sectors of the labor market with little or no mobility between them as a significant departure from human capital theory. However, lack of mobility between "sectors" is fully compatible with the neoclassical model as long as the initial worker–job matches are optimal. Further, mobility between sectors does not demonstrate the absence of non-price rationing.

A very simple neoclassical model in which workers acquire firm-, occupa-

tion-, industry-, or sector-specific skills is consistent with no mobility whatsoever among firms, occupations, industries, or sectors, respectively. Of
course, more realistic models allow for some mobility, but limited mobility is a
direct consequence of the existence of such skills. Thus, much of the literature
on internal labor markets and mobility chains is fully compatible with the
neoclassical model. On the other hand, if qualified blacks had to work in bad
jobs for a few years before obtaining good jobs but equally qualified whites
could obtain good jobs immediately, there would be mobility between the
sectors. In fact, we might find that blacks were more likely than whites to
leave the "secondary" sector. However, the non-price rationing of good jobs
would be inconsistent with standard models, despite the presence of mobility.

The second departure of dual labor market theories from neoclassical
theory is the argument that the same product is often produced using two
distinct technologies. While the assumptions of neoclassical economics do not
preclude the existence of multiple solutions to the firm's maximization problem, in general, standard convexity assumptions provide structure to neoclassical models and ensure a unique maximum.

We will argue in section V that both of these aspects of dual labor market
theory have been incorporated into neoclassical economics by recent developments. These developments have occurred largely without explicit reference
to dual labor market theory. We conclude that they were never really incompatible with neoclassical theory, although at the time they were viewed as
significant departures.

Instead, we agree with Piore (1974) and Wachter (1974) that the major
innovation of dual labor market theory was the attempt to make certain social-
psychological qualities endogenous to the economic system. Thus Doeringer
and Piore (1971) argue that the development of stable work habits depends on
the type of job that workers obtain. In his later work (1980b), Piore defines
labor market sectors in terms of the types of reasoning they require and
promote. Thus, in the upper tier of the primary sector, we find a wide range
of related work tasks; this enhances the worker's ability to achieve an abstract
understanding of the work and is, thus, conducive to abstract understanding
and learning. In the lower tier of the primary sector, the range of tasks is
narrower and thus supports concrete more than abstract learning and understanding. Finally, work is organized in the secondary sector so that understanding is not required and, hence, inhibits abstract understanding. Dickens
(1979) relates sector of employment to Kohlberg's stages of development and
to Melvin Kohn's studies of work and personality.

It is important to note that Piore is not involved in psychological reduc-
tionism. Although the cognitive processes developed prior to employment,
particularly in schools where training may depend on the social stratum from
which the student is drawn, affect the initial placement of workers, the relation between job placement and cognitive processes is seen as reciprocal. The
role of labor market stratum in determining cognitive processes is equally
important. Thus, the work is not antisociological but instead has natural links

to sociological work on how social structure influences the way in which the individual comes to understand his place in society, a concern which has traditions dating at least to Marx, Durkheim, and Simmel and which continues to interest modern researchers such as Thom (1983). Indeed, the issues addressed by Piore are also discussed in Durkheim's *Division of Labor in Society*.

Wachter suggests that endogenous tastes are not antithetical to neoclassical economics. We see little value in an extended debate on the philosophy of economics, but it appears to us that if neoclassical economics has any core tenets, they are that individuals have preferences that are exogenous to the economic system and are unchanging or only slowly changing over time and that they use available information efficiently to maximize their welfare given these preferences. Thus, endogenous work habits and cognitive processes represent a significant departure from that model. It is unfortunate that this is also the aspect of dual labor market theory that has received the least attention.

We have not discussed the internal labor market as a significant contribution of dual labor market theory. This is in part a matter of definition. While some of the most significant contributions to our understanding of internal labor markets are from dual labor market theorists (particularly, Doeringer and Piore, 1971), we perceive their work as complementing rather than contradicting ongoing neoclassical work, a view shared by Cain (1976). Neoclassical economists recognized that the presence of firm-specific human capital created a bilateral monopoly with incentives for long-term employment relations but an indeterminate wage profile over the course of that relation. Essentially any wage profile that gave both firm and worker incentives to maintain the employment relation and paid the (appropriately discounted) competitive wage over the life of the relation would be consistent with neoclassical theory. The internal labor market contribution considered how that indeterminancy is resolved.

IV. THE SOCIOLOGICAL RESPONSE

On the whole, the sociological literature on dual economy has not been concerned with the issues outlined above. To a certain degree, this reflects the fact that sociologists have drawn on a tradition derived from Averitt's (1968) work on dual economy and have relied only loosely on the dual labor market literature. With the possible exceptions of Bluestone (1970) and Edwards (1975), there is general agreement that, while the core or monopoly sector of the dual economy contains a preponderance of primary jobs, dual economy and dual labor markets represent different sources of division in the economy. Piore's work (1980a,b) on these linkages seems to have been largely overlooked.

Thus, the sociological literature on dual or segmented economy has taken as its starting point the existence of monopoly rents in the core sector. Wages in the monopoly sector may be higher because workers are able to capture part of these rents or because monopoly firms use their ability to pay to purchase worker cooperation. The need to assure worker loyalty is greater in large organizations, and thus, purchasing loyalty through higher wages is particularly useful in the monopoly sector. The literature on segmented economy (Kalleberg, Wallace, and Althauser, 1981) argues that the sources of worker power are more complex than suggested by dual economy theorists, but retains the emphasis on worker power. The dual and segmented economy models therefore explicitly reject the assumption of a perfectly competitive labor market, which is crucial to the neoclassical model described in the previous section. In a perfectly competitive labor market, workers would be unable to capture rents that firms accrue in the product market. Moreover, "ability to pay" does not affect wage rates in a competitive market. Employers' ability to pay is irrelevant because competition among workers guarantees that all employers will pay the same wage for equivalent workers in jobs that are equally unpleasant. An employer who offered a wage below the market equilibrium wage would be unable to hire any workers. No employer would want to pay more (even if he or she could) since profits could be increased by paying only the going wage.

To an economist, the dual economy approach implies that there will be a queue (excess supply of workers) and thus non-price rationing for jobs in the monopoly sector since wages in that sector are above their market-clearing level. Wages in the state sector are presumed to be patterned on monopoly sector wages; consequently, there should be a queue for state sector jobs as well. We do not wish to imply that the only prediction of the dual economy literature is that wages are higher in the core sector. On the contrary, the dual economy literature contains a number of hypotheses regarding the relation between worker attributes and sector of employment. For example, in the core sector, education is expected to play a larger role because of the greater reliance on credentials in large organizations. However, to a large extent these predictions can be interpreted either as resulting from the absence of market clearing, as in the case of discrimination (since employers can choose workers from the excess supply who correspond to the type of worker they desire), or as being hypotheses regarding where the firm will locate along the HWE and thus fully compatible with the neoclassical model. Thus, on the whole, again economic and sociological perspectives do not conflict but rather address different issues.

Thus, from an economist's perspective the primary departure of segmented economy theory from neoclassical theory is the rejection of market clearing in the model of wage determination. Dual labor market theory also rejects market clearing; however, unlike most dual labor market models (for exceptions see Doeringer and Piore, 1971; Piore 1975), dual economy theory provides a theoretical basis for the existence of queues and labor market segmentation that is derived from the ability of workers to capture monopoly rents.

On the other hand, dual economy theory has not taken up the two other departures from neoclassical theory that we discussed in the previous section.

Unlike dual labor market theory, dual economy theory has tended to treat entire industries as being in the core or periphery and thus has not dealt with the use of differing technologies to produce the same output. Also, it has not addressed the relation involving cognition, socialization, and sector of employment with which dual labor market theory has been concerned.

Although the major departure from neoclassical theory of sociological theories of segmentation is the rejection of market clearing, the dual economy literature has concentrated on the issue of whether characteristics of the employer influence the wage received by the worker. A frequent practice in the segmented economy literature has been to test the model by regressing wages on firm and/or industry characteristics as well as worker characteristics (Hodson, 1984; Kalleberg *et al.*, 1981; Wallace and Kalleberg, 1981). The fact that, in general, industry and/or firm characteristics enter the equation significantly is presented as evidence contradicting the human capital model.

There are two problems with this approach. First, the neoclassical model of section II implies that firm or industry characteristics will generally enter the wage equation with significant coefficients even when worker/job match characteristics or worker attributes are included, because inevitably not all characteristics are included and the functional form is only approximate. Second, if the dual market approach is correct, ordinary least squares is not a legitimate estimator for the wage equation. We discuss these problems in turn.

In the neoclassical model, it is perfectly legitimate to express the wage equation entirely in terms of worker characteristics, entirely in terms of firm characteristics or in terms of the worker/job match as in the HWE. To express the wage equation solely in terms of the worker's characteristics, note that from Figures 1 and 3, the level of education the worker obtains will depend entirely on his or her attributes. Therefore, instead of expressing wages as a function of worker/job match characteristics, it is possible to express the wage as a function of worker attributes. Similarly, wages can be expressed as a function of firm attributes.[6] Thus, to reiterate, even if one interprets standard wage equations as expressing the wage solely in terms of worker attributes, it does not follow that they have ignored the importance of "demand."

More significantly, since the model can be expressed as a function of any of the three types of characteristics, it is likely that when firm (or industry) characteristics are included in the equation along with worker characteristics, both will turn out to be significant. Since any functional form for the wage equation is inevitably an approximation to the "true" functional form, the error term in the wage equation with only worker characteristics will almost definitely be correlated with firm characteristics. Only if the wage equation were specified exactly and all relevant worker characteristics were measured

[6]More formally, from equation (9), w' is a function of E. Therefore, it is possible to substitute for w' in the demand equation and solve for E as a function of e. Kahn and Lang (1988) refer to this as the quasi-reduced form demand equation. Having derived E as a function of e, it is possible to substitute for E in the HWE and derive w as a function of e. By a similar process, it is possible to express the wage solely in terms of firm characteristics.

perfectly would this not be true. Otherwise, firm or industry characteristics will be correlated with unmeasured characteristics such as job safety or the quality of worker hired.

Dickens and Katz (1986, 1987) address the issue of why there are significant inter-industry wage differences. They suggest three possibilities: (1) that the model outlined in section II is accurate but that there are interindustry wage differentials resulting from temporary disequilibria, (2) that the model outlined in section II is accurate and that interindustry wage differentials reflect unmeasured job match characteristics, and (3) that the neoclassical model outlined in section II is inaccurate. They provide evidence that interindustry wage differentials have persisted over extended periods of time and thus conclude that the temporary disequilibrium hypothesis can be rejected. They also marshall evidence that interindustry differentials persist even after careful statistical controls for a large number of job match characteristics, and that interindustry differentials are strongly correlated across occupations. Thus, they conclude that the neoclassical model outlined in section II is probably inaccurate.

However, as noted above, the standard neoclassical model implies that firm or industry characteristics enter the wage equation containing individual characteristics because they are correlated with the error term. In contrast, the dual economy model suggests that these characteristics belong in the equation in their own right. Therefore, this conclusion ultimately rests either on conjectures about how large interindustry wage differentials can be or on auxiliary hypotheses such as how correlated over time and across occupations and nations interindustry wage differentials should be. Thus, including industry or firm characteristics in the wage equation at best provides a weak test of the neoclassical model.

Moreover, if the segmented market model is correct, it is not legitimate to interpret the OLS coefficients of a single wage equation with industry dummies or characteristics as measuring the amount of monopoly rents captured by workers. As noted above, the dual economy hypothesis implies that there are queues for good jobs. Since there is an excess supply of workers for these jobs, firms will choose the "best" available workers from the queue. These workers will be those whose wages are unusually low given their productivity. Since it is inevitable that we do not measure all determinants of wages, the expected value of the contribution of unmeasured characteristics to the wage (in other words, the error term) in those jobs is negative rather than zero as required for ordinary least squares. Thus, in general, ordinary least squares will overestimate the importance of industry dummies or characteristics.

This criticism is, if anything, more compelling when applied to tests that have divided the sample into sectors and tested for the existence of separate equations explaining the determination of wages for each sector (Beck, Horan, and Tolbert, 1978; Hodson, 1978, 1984; Horan *et al.*, 1980; Osterman, 1975; Zucker and Rosenstein, 1981). The endogeneity of sector of employment is particularly important because, as Cain (1976) has pointed out, if workers are divided into two sectors, a large sector composed mainly of workers with high wages and a small sector composed mainly of workers with low wages, we will estimate that the returns to education and experience are lower in the "low-wage sector" even if in fact there are not two distinct sectors. The estimated return to education will be biased downward in both sectors by the truncation of the wage, but the bias will be more serious in the smaller sector since the fraction of "missing" observations is larger. This statistical problem can be avoided only by explicitly modeling the assignment of workers to sectors. There is an extensive literature on consistent estimation of models with this sort of selection problem (see Maddala, 1983, for an excellent review).

A second difficulty arises because, with the exception of Dickens and Lang (1984/1985, 1985, 1987, 1988), all estimates of sectoral models assume that the sector of employment is known. Yet as Zucker and Rosenstein (1981) make clear, the correlations among classification schemes that divide industries into a core and periphery sector are relatively weak, ranging from 57% to 83% agreement for the four taxonomies they study. The degree of disagreement is striking when one considers that if each study had assigned people to sectors randomly but in the same proportions as in the actual studies, the level of agreement would have ranged from 40% to 50%.

Without doubt, part of the disagreement is due to underlying theoretical differences. However, much of the disagreement simply reflects the difficulties entailed in moving from the theoretical conception to the empirical application. It simply is not possible to use industry of employment to establish sector of employment with any degree of certainty.

The appropriate solution is to model sector of employment as unknown *a priori* and to let the estimation technique determine the sector of employment. The appropriate statistical technique is described in Dickens and Lang (1984/1985): "endogenous switching with unknown regimes." To estimate this model, the research specifies two or more equations that describe the wage determination process in each sector as a function of human capital and other variables. The researcher also specifies an equation describing the process by which people are assigned to the two sectors as a function of human capital and ascriptive criteria. The model is estimated by maximum likelihood. In effect, the model assigns a probability of being in each sector to each person on the basis of ascriptive and human capital variables. Simultaneously, it estimates the return to human capital and other variables in each sector. This "endogenous switching model with unknown regimes" stands at the opposite end of the spectrum from the "exogenous switching models with known regimes" that have been used in the dual economy literature. The latter assume that industry of employment provides complete information about sector of employment while the former makes no use of industry information to assign workers to sectors. (If one wished to compromise between the two approaches, one could modify the technique developed by Dickens and Lang to take account of industry information without assuming that sector of employment is known perfectly.)

In sum, the segmented economy literature distinguishes itself from the neoclassical model primarily by rejecting the assumption that wages adjust to clear labor markets. As will be discussed below, there has been a resurgence of interest in such models in neoclassical economics as well. However, while both economists and sociologists have concerned themselves with testing the segmented markets model by establishing whether firm or industry characteristics enter a wage equation significantly, this does not really address the issue of market clearing. Moreover, the estimation techniques used in these "tests" are inappropriate for the dual market model.

V. TESTING FOR QUEUES

Since both the dual labor market and dual economy models differentiate themselves from the neoclassical model by rejecting the existence of market clearing, the most direct way to distinguish between segmented market models and the standard neoclassical model is to test for the existence of queues.

The most straightforward manner in which to consider whether or not there are queues for jobs is to examine the effect of interindustry wage differentials on quit rates. If workers in high-wage industries are, in fact, receiving rents, we would expect them to have lower quit rates. This prediction is confirmed by a number of studies. However, interpretation of this result is hindered by an inadequate theory of why quits occur. Moreover, if high-ability workers tend to invest more heavily in firm-specific capital, they will simultaneously have higher wages and lower quit rates.

Farber (1983) presents the most sophisticated approach to studying queues in his examination of queues for union jobs. He points out that it is necessary to model the process whereby individuals are allocated to each sector. Allocation is the outcome of two decisions. First, workers must decide whether or not to seek union employment. Since the nonunion sector is assumed to be competitive, those workers who desire nonunion jobs at the going wage rate enter the nonunion sector. However, not all workers who desire union jobs obtain them. Instead, the union wage premium results in a queue (excess supply of workers) for union jobs. Workers obtain union jobs only if an employer chooses them from the queue. Thus, the probability of being allocated to the union sector is the probability of wanting a union job multiplied by the probability of obtaining a union job given that the worker desires one. If there is not an excess supply of labor for union jobs, the latter probability is one, and the model reduces to one in which only the probability of wanting a union job equation needs to be estimated. Thus, the no-queue model is nested in the queue model, and it is possible to test for the existence of queues. Farber's work is facilitated by the presence of a measure of whether or not the workers desire union jobs.[7]

Dickens and Lang (1984/1985, 1985, 1988) use a somewhat different ap-

---

[7]Nevertheless, Abowd and Farber (1982) demonstrate that it is possible to test for the existence of queues even in the absence of such a measure.

proach in the context of a dual labor market model. They point out that if workers were free to choose their sector of employment, they would tend to enter the sector in which their earnings, adjusted for the value of nonwage characteristics of employment, were highest. Using the endogenous switching model with unknown regimes discussed above, they find that for an equal wage differential between the sectors, nonwhites are more likely to be employed in the secondary sector. There are two possible conclusions—either nonwhites place a lower value on the nonwage characteristics of the primary sector or nonwhites find it more difficult to obtain primary employment. Auxiliary evidence[8] tends to contradict the first conclusion. Therefore, it appears that nonwhites face nonprice discrimination, which implies the absence of market clearing.

VI. NOTES FOR A NEOCLASSICAL MODEL OF LABOR MARKET STRATIFICATION

We have presented evidence in support of the view that there is an excess supply of labor for certain types of jobs. Since one of the major departures of segmented market theory from earlier neoclassical theory is the existence of queues, it is important to consider the extent to which queues are compatible with more recent developments in neoclassical theory. The major conclusion of this section will be that recent neoclassical theorists have produced the elements of a model that, on those topics that have traditionally concerned neoclassical economists, captures the major departures of dual labor market theory from neoclassical theory. In addition, this theory helps clarify the relation between dual economy theory and dual labor market theory. Moreover, there is considerable convergence between the neoclassical and sociological models. The major difference is that, in the recent neoclassical theory, nonmeritocratic stratification can occur even when all markets are competitive.

For the last decade, some of the most important work in economics has concerned itself with developing a microeconomic foundation for macroeconomics. Within economics there has been a split between a microeconomic model, which assumes general equilibrium with market clearing, and a Keynesian macroeconomic model, which many would argue is based on the failure of market clearing. Two schools of thought have arisen in response to this dichotomy. One of these has attempted to explain macroeconomic phenomena in terms of a market-clearing model, and the other

---

[8]Blacks are more likely to support unions in representation elections (Dickens, 1983; Farber and Saks, 1980), are less likely to quit a job (Viscusi, 1979), and have greater demand for occupational safety than equivalent whites (Kahn, 1983). Primary jobs are generally believed to be more heavily unionized, to provide more stable employment, and to be safer than secondary jobs. Thus, it is doubtful that blacks prefer the nonpecuniary features of secondary employment to a greater extent than whites.

has attempted to develop microeconomic models to explain the absence of market clearing (see Solow, 1979b, for a discussion of this debate).

The latter school has developed a number of related models that fall under the general rubric of efficiency wage models. In order to describe efficiency wage models, it is easiest to make the simplifying assumption that all workers and jobs are homogeneous (though this assumption is not necessary to the models). In this model, each firm chooses the amount of labor it employs in order to maximize profits. In the standard model, the derivative of profits with respect to the wage is just the negative of the amount of labor employed. In other words, as wages increase, profits fall. Therefore, the firm would like to set the wage as low as possible, and it would never pay more than the minimum necessary to obtain the quantity (and, in a more general model, quality) of workers it desires.

Under the various efficiency wage models, raising wages can increase profits. In most efficiency wage models, this results from the fact that output depends on the wage. As a consequence, in efficiency wage models, firms do not necessarily choose the lowest possible wage; instead they choose the wage that maximizes their profits. If the wage that maximizes profits is above the market-clearing wage, some workers will be unemployed. In the standard model, unemployed workers would bid down any wages above the market-clearing level. However, in efficiency wage models, since the wage has been chosen to maximize profits, lowering the wage would actually lower profits. Consequently, there can be an excess supply of labor.

Katz (1986) and Yellen (1984) provide extensive reviews of the various efficiency wage models. We provide only a brief summary here. In most efficiency wage models, output is assumed to depend on the wage and not just on the quantity of labor employed, as in more standard models. Wages may affect output in a number of ways—through worker morale (Akerlof, 1982; Solow, 1979a), through differences in the quality of workers hired that are unobservable by the firm (Weiss, 1980), by reducing quits, or by reducing shirking, stealing, and cheating (Bowles, 1985; Calvo, 1979; Shapiro and Stiglitz, 1984; Stoft, 1982). In the models in which higher wages reduce the probability of workers' cheating, shirking, or quitting, the higher wage makes it costly for workers to lose their jobs and thus provides a disincentive to behavior that might cause them to be fired. In the morale models, the higher wage might be thought of as changing workers' preferences, but in the other models, preferences are clearly constant, and workers change their behavior only because incentives have been modified. The latter fit more easily into the neoclassical paradigm of profit-maximizing firms and utility-maximizing workers with constant preferences.

The motivations for paying high wages are similar to those found in the segmented economy literature. However, it should be noted that none of the models above relies on the existence of monopoly rents or "ability to pay" that is central to the segmented economy literature. Instead, in most efficiency wage models, the queues exist despite pure competition in the product market. One version of the efficiency wage model, however, is quite close to the most prevalent model in the dual economy literature. Dickens (1986) argues that firms may pay higher wages in order to deter workers from taking collective action such as forming a union. The need to pay union-deterring wages is greatest when the potential rents captured by the union are large owing either to the firm's monopoly power in the product market or to the presence of fixed capital.

Although the efficiency wage models were developed to explain what many economists perceive as the failure of the wage to adjust to clear the labor market, they have obvious application to the development of a formal neoclassical model of labor market segmentation. If the costs of monitoring workers or the costs of worker malfeasance differ among industries, the wage levels that maximize profits will differ among industries. If there is a set of firms that pay efficiency wages and a set of firms that do not pay efficiency wages, then there will be two sectors of the labor market. One will have high wages and an excess supply of labor. The other will have low wages and behave according to the standard competitive model. Such models are developed informally in Dickens and Lang (1984/1985) and Yellen (1984) and formally in Jones (1985) and Bulow and Summers (1986).

The above discussion suggests a clear relation between the dual economy and dual labor market classifications. The primary sector consists of all jobs for which there is structural and equilibrium excess supply even in equilibrium. Thus, the queues are structural rather than transitory. Jobs in the monopoly or core sector tend to be in the primary sector because, in general, the existence of a large amount of fixed capital or monopoly rents is conducive to the formation of a union. In addition, some versions of the efficiency wage model imply that firms that earn rents will pay high wages because workers' conceptions of fair pay depends on the ability of firms to pay. Also, such firms may pay high wages to deter unionization since the potential gains from unionization are greater in the presence of rents. Furthermore, monopoly sector firms tend to have high capital/labor ratios. Many efficiency wage models suggest that firms with high capital/labor ratios will pay high wages since the need to avoid shirking, absenteeism, and quits is greatest in the presence of large quantities of fixed capital. Thus, monopoly sector firms tend to pay efficiency or union-deterring wages. However, some firms that are not in the monopoly sector may find it beneficial to pay efficiency wages that exceed market-clearing levels to at least some of their workers. Consequently, the primary labor market is considerably more extensive than the monopoly sector.

Unfortunately, the efficiency wage model described above does not provide a completely satisfactory neoclassical model of dual labor markets. The major difficulty is that it suggests that unemployment consists of people queuing for jobs in the primary labor market. Since primary jobs tend to be stable, this contradicts evidence that much unemployment consists of frequent long spells of unemployment interrupted by short spells of employment and certainly conflicts with a perspective designed to explain persistent poverty and unemployment among certain disadvantaged groups.

The answer to this problem lies in a model that is described informally in Piore (1975) and developed independently in a neoclassical model of contestable markets under uncertainty by Appelbaum and Lim (1985). In that model, there is uncertain demand for industry output. Output may be produced using either of two technologies, a low variable-cost/high fixed-cost technology, which requires investment prior to the realization of the state of demand, or a high variable-cost/low fixed-cost technology, which does not require prior investment. Firms will invest in the low variable-cost technology in order to satisfy relatively certain demand. When demand is high, they will produce additional output using the high variable-cost technology. The proportion of demand that is satisfied using the low variable-cost technology will depend on the relative costs of the two technologies, on the cost of storing the good, and on the variability of demand. If demand is perfectly stable or if the high variable-cost technology is much more expensive than the low variable-cost technology and the good is storable, all output will be produced using the low variable-cost technology. On the other hand, if demand is highly unstable, the good is not storable, and the cost difference is small, almost all demand will be produced using the high variable-cost technology. In most industries some output will be produced using the low variable-cost technology, but this output will be supplemented in boom periods through the use of the high variable-cost technology.

It is worth noting that it is possible that high demand/high variable-cost technology production may take place in the same firms that also use the low variable-cost technology, or in firms that "specialize" in high variable-cost technology. For example, consider an old-fashioned luncheonette that sells ice cream. For the luncheonette the marginal cost of supplying the relatively stable day-to-day demand for ice cream is low. However, every once in a while, there is an unusually hot day and the demand for ice cream increases. The increased demand for ice cream might be accommodated by setting up an additional stand outside the luncheonette, or pushcart operators who sell hot chestnuts in the winter might rapidly convert their carts to handle ice cream. Factors such as the nature of the technology and access to short-term labor markets and ice cream suppliers would determine whether one or both of these solutions would be used.

The Appelbaum/Lim contestable markets model provides a very different model of economic dualism than the one based on a division of firms into those in the monopoly and competitive sectors. Moreover, as Piore (1975) argued, it is clear that not only can different firms within an industry use different technologies, but even within firms, different technologies may be used to produce the same output.

It is easy to see why primary sector jobs would tend to be located in firms using low variable-cost technologies. As Bulow and Summers (1986) point out, when jobs become unstable, the wage required to deter cheating increases since workers expect to receive that wage over a shorter period of time. When the efficiency wage required to avoid worker malfeasance becomes sufficiently large, firms will prefer to use other means, such as direct monitoring of workers' behavior. Thus, firms facing stable demand will tend to pay efficiency wages, while firms facing unstable demand will tend to use direct monitoring. This link between sector and method of worker regulation is reminiscent of Edwards (1979).

Of course, the link between stable demand and primary labor market jobs will not be perfect. In some stable jobs, the cost of direct monitoring will be sufficiently low that it will be preferable to paying efficiency wages, while, in some unstable jobs, the cost of monitoring may be sufficiently high to justify the use of efficiency wages despite the instability. Thus, while job stability, the use of low variable-cost technology, and high wages will tend to be linked, none of the pairwise correlations will be perfect.

In addition, economic theory suggests that a number of other factors are likely to be correlated with job stability, including investment in on-the-job training and the use of pensions and job ladders. Thus, there are a number of job characteristics that we would expect to be correlated.

In this way, the neoclassical approach to dual labor market theory casts light on the usefulness of factor-analytic approaches to testing the model. A number of papers (Buchele, 1976; Gordon, 1971; Hodson and Kaufman, 1981; Horan, Tolbert, and Beck, 1981; Kaufman, Hodson, and Fligstein, 1981; Oster, 1979; Tolbert, Horan, and Beck, 1980) have interpreted dual economy theory or dual labor market theory as maintaining that all jobs can be classified on the basis of a single bimodal factor. They either have attempted to test these models by techniques such as factor-analyzing job or industry characteristics to see whether they can be classified using a single bimodally distributed factor, or have criticized dual economy theory for not recognizing the greater dimensionality of segmentation (Kalleberg et al., 1981; Wallace and Kalleberg, 1981). In the light of the neoclassical model, this approach is generally misguided. Nothing in the model suggests that a single factor should be sufficient to classify jobs. It does suggest that one important factor should link wages, stability, and technology.

However, dual labor market theory does not imply that the dual labor market is the only basis on which jobs can be classified. For instance, if in the list of job characteristics we were to include outdoor work in winter, western region, commuting distance, commuting method, whether or not most workers in the firm were born in the state or unionized, a factor analysis would probably uncover an additional factor that might be termed "sun belt." The presence of this second factor would in no way disprove dual labor market theory. The model implies that certain characteristics should be correlated, not that no other characteristics are.

One of the weaknesses of dual labor market theory has been that it has generally been presented as a classification scheme designed to describe certain empirical regularities. Without an underlying theoretical base, it is difficult to maintain that one classification scheme is superior to another. Thus, if a study finds that the variation in wages that can be explained by a 4-, or 16-, or 64-sector model is significantly greater than that which can be achieved with a 2-sector model, it is tempting to conclude that the dual labor market model has been rejected. Drawing this conclusion is inappropriate for two reasons—first, because dual labor market theory does not suggest that the only determinant of wages is sector of employment and, second, because dual labor market theory should not be regarded principally as a classification system.

VII. SOME CONCLUDING REMARKS

Although dual labor market theory has been largely atheoretical, the neoclassical model we sketched in the last section is not the first attempt to provide it with a theoretical underpinning. In fact, we perceive that model as being a relatively faithful neoclassical rendering of ideas presented by Doeringer and Piore (1971) and Piore (1975, 1980a,b). The fact that it is possible to present a neoclassical version of these ideas suggests that they were never all that incompatible with neoclassical economics.

Similarly, we believe that dual economy theory should also be perceived as being compatible with neoclassical economics. The sociological work in this area addresses the problems of eliciting worker effort that, from a different perspective, are the concern of efficiency wage and agency (Becker and Stigler, 1974; Lazear, 1979, 1981) models in economics. There is clear potential for cross-fertilization of the economic and organizational (e.g., Baron and Bielby 1980, 1982, 1984; Stolzenberg, 1978) perspectives. From an economic perspective, the sociological literature has paid undue attention to the role of monopoly rents and insufficient attention to other economic conditions that foster or inhibit the growth of different administrative mechanisms.

Nevertheless, in the light of our analysis, we cannot avoid a certain disappointment that sociologists have not concerned themselves more with the most significant departure of dual labor market theory from neoclassical economics—the attempt to incorporate social-psychological feedback into the system. Whether a model that dropped the assumption of perfect rationality to incorporate the Piagetian concepts of Piore (1980b) or a model that allowed tastes to be endogenous would still be neoclassical is largely a matter of definition. We are, however, inclined to agree with Piore (1974) that exogeneity of tastes and perfect rationality are essential to the neoclassical model and that dropping these assumptions would give rise to a model that differed significantly from existing theory. In neoclassical economics, the individual is a completely formed entity from birth. His or her utility function is exogenous to the economic system, and since all individuals are fully rational with unlimited cognitive capacity, cognition is independent of the organization of work. It is in this area that the dual labor market model presents the greatest challenge to neoclassical economics.

Moreover, sociologists have more training and experience with this type of model. Perhaps sociologists have neglected dual labor market theory's tentative steps toward integrating these sociological notions with labor market theory because of the weakness of the economists' efforts in this direction.

We expect that this is one direction of inquiry in which sociologists could make substantial contributions to theories of labor markets.

ACKNOWLEDGMENTS

We are grateful to Sam Gilmore, Shulamit Kahn, Ken Small, David Smith, and Gary Thom for helpful comments and criticisms, and to the National Science Foundation for research support under grant number SES8606139. Any errors of fact or interpretation are, of course, entirely our responsibility.

REFERENCES

Abowd, John M., and Henry S. Farber. 1982. "Job Queues and the Union Status of Workers." *Industrial and Labor Relations Review* 35:354–367.

Akerlof, George A. 1982. "Labor Contracts as Partial Gift Exchange." *Quarterly Journal of Economics* 87:543–569.

Appelbaum, Eli, and Chin Lim. 1985. "Contestable Markets Under Uncertainty." *Rand Journal of Economics* 16:28–40.

Averitt, Robert T. 1968. *The Dual Economy*. New York: Norton.

Baron, James N., and William T. Bielby. 1980. "Bringing the Firms Back In: Stratification, Segmentation, and the Organization of Work." *American Sociological Review* 45:737–765.

Baron, James N., and William T. Bielby. 1982. "Workers and Machines: Dimensions and Determinants of Technical Relations in the Workplace." *American Sociological Review* 47:175–188.

Baron, James N., and William T. Bielby. 1984. "The Organization of Work in a Segmented Economy." *American Sociological Review* 49:454–473.

Beck, E. M., Patrick M. Horan, and Charles M. Tolbert. 1978. "Stratification in a Dual Economy: A Sectoral Model of Earnings Determination." *American Sociological Review* 43:704–720.

Becker, Gary S. 1971. *Human Capital: A Theoretical and Empirical Analysis with Special Reference to Education*, 2nd ed. New York: Columbia University Press.

Becker, Gary S., and George J. Stigler. 1974. "Law Enforcement, Malfeasance, and the Compensation of Enforcers." *Journal of Legal Studies* 3:1–18.

Berg, Ivar. 1981. "Sociological and Institutional Perspectives on Labor Markets." Pp. 1–7 in *Sociological Perspectives on Labor Markets*, edited by Ivar Berg. New York: Academic Press.

Bibb, Robert, and William H. Form. 1977. "The Effects of Industrial, Occupational and Sex Stratification on Wages in Blue-Collar Markets." *Social Forces* 55:974–996.

Bluestone, Barry. 1970. "The Tripartite Economy: Labor Markets and the Working Poor." *Poverty and Human Resources Abstracts* 5:15–35.

Bowles, Samuel. 1985. "The Production Process in a Competitive Economy: Walrasian, Neo-Hobbesian and Marxian Models." *American Economic Review* 75:16–36.

Buchele, Robert. 1976. Jobs and Workers: A Labor Market Segmentation Perspective on the Work Experience of Young Men. Unpublished doctoral dissertation, Harvard University.

Bulow, Jeremy I., and Lawrence H. Summers. 1986. "A Theory of Dual Labor Markets with Application to Industrial Policy, Discrimination and Keynesian Unemployment," *Journal of Labor Economics* 4:376–414.

Cain, Glenn. 1976. "The Challenge of Segmented Labor Market Theories to Orthodox Theory." *Journal of Economic Literature* 14:1215–1257.

Calvo, Guillermo. 1979. "Quasi-Walrasian Theories of Unemployment." *American Economic Review* 69:102–107.

Dickens, William T. 1979. "Work and Personality: A Structural Interpretation of the Class-Values Relation." Not published.

Dickens, William T. 1983. "The Effect of Company Campaigns on Certification Elections: Law and Reality Once Again." *Industrial and Labor Relations Review* 36:560–575.

Dickens, William T. 1986. "Wages, Employment and the Threat of Collective Action by Workers." NBER Working Paper No. 1856.

Dickens, William T., and Lawrence Katz. 1986. Occupational and Industry Wage Structures and Modern Theories of Wage Determination. Mimeo.

Dickens, William T., and Lawrence Katz. 1987. "Industry Characteristics and Interindustry Wage Differences." Pp. 48–89 in Unemployment and the Structure of Labor Markets, edited by Kevin Lang and Jonathan S. Leonard. Oxford: Basil Blackwell.

Dickens, William T., and Kevin Lang. 1985. "A Test of Dual Labor Market Theory." American Economic Review 75:792–805. (Previously NBER working paper No. 1314, 1984)

Dickens, William T., and Kevin Lang. 1985. "Testing Dual Labor Market Theory: A Reconsideration of the Evidence." NBER working paper No. 1670.

Dickens, William T., and Kevin Lang. 1988. "Labor Market Segmentation and the Union Wage Premium." Review of Economics and Statistics, forthcoming.

Dickens, William T., and Kevin Lang. 1987. "Where Have All the Good Jobs Gone? Deindustrialization and Theories of Dual Labor Markets," Pp. 90–102 in Unemployment and the Structure of Labor Markets, edited by Kevin Lang and Jonathan S. Leonard. Oxford: Basil Blackwell.

Doeringer, Peter B., and Michael J. Piore. 1971. Internal Labor Markets and Manpower Analysis. Lexington, MA: D. C. Heath.

Edwards, Richard. 1975. "The Social Relations of Production in the Firm and Labor Market Structure." Pp. 3–26 in Labor Market Segmentation, edited by Richard Edwards, Michael Reich, and David M. Gordon. Lexington, MA: D. C. Heath.

Edwards, Richard. 1979. Contested Terrain. New York: Basic Books.

Farber, Henry S. 1983. "The Determination of the Union Status of Workers." Econometrica 51:1417–1438.

Farber, Henry S., and Daniel H. Saks. 1980. "Why Workers Want Unions: The Role of Relative Wages and Job Characteristics." Journal of Political Economy 88:346–369.

Gordon, David M. 1971. Class, Productivity and the Ghetto. Unpublished doctoral dissertation, Harvard University.

Heckman, James J., and Guilherme Sedlacek. 1985. "Heterogeneity, Aggregation, and Market Wage Functions: An Empirical Model of Self-Selection in the Labor Market." Journal of Political Economy 93:1077–1125.

Hodson, Randy. 1978. "Labor in the Monopoly, Competitive and State Sectors of Production." Politics and Society 8:429–480.

Hodson, Randy. 1984. "Companies, Industries, and the Measurement of Economic Segmentation." American Sociological Review 49:335–348.

Hodson, Randy, and Robert L. Kaufman. 1981. "Circularity in the Dual Economy: Comment on Tolbert, Horan, and Beck." American Journal of Sociology 86:881–887.

Hodson, Randy, and Robert L. Kaufman. 1982. "Economic Dualism: A Critical Review." American Sociological Review 47:727–739.

Horan, Patrick M., E. M. Beck, and Charles M. Tolbert. 1980. "The Market Homogeneity Assumption: On the Theoretical Foundations of Empirical Knowledge." Social Science Quarterly 61:278–291.

Horan, Patrick M., Charles M. Tolbert, and E. M. Beck. 1981. "The Circle Has No Close." American Journal of Sociology 86:887–894.

Jones, Stephen R. G. 1985. Minimum Wage Legislation in a Dual Market. Mimeo, University of British Columbia.

Jovanovic, Boyan. 1979a. "Job Matching and the Theory of Turnover." Journal of Political Economy 87:972–991.

Jovanovic, Boyan. 1979b. "Firm-specific Capital and Turnover." Journal of Political Economy 87:1246–1260.

Kahn, Shulamit. 1983. Occupational Safety and Worker Preferences. Unpublished doctoral dissertation, Massachusetts Institute of Technology.

Kahn, Shulamit. 1986. "Economic Estimates of the Value of Life." Technology and Society 5:24–29.

Kahn, Shulamit, and Kevin Lang. 1988. Efficient Estimation of Structural Hedonic Systems. *International Economic Review*, forthcoming.

Kalleberg, Arne, and Aage B. Sorenson. 1979. "The Sociology of Labor Markets." *Annual Review of Sociology* 5:351–379.

Kalleberg, Arne, Michael Wallace, and Robert P. Althauser. 1981. "Economic Segmentation, Worker Power, and Income Inequality." *American Journal of Sociology* 87:651–683.

Katz, Lawrence F. 1986. "Efficiency Wage Theories: A Partial Evaluation." Pp. 235–276 in *NBER Macroeconomics Annual, 1986*, Cambridge, MA: M.I.T. Press.

Kaufman, Robert L., Randy Hodson, and Neil D. Fligstein. 1981. "Defrocking Dualism: A New Approach to Defining Industrial Sectors." *Social Science Research* 10:1–31.

Lazear, Edward. 1979. "Why Is There Mandatory Retirement?" *Journal of Political Economy* 87:261–284.

Lazear, Edward. 1981. "Agency, Earnings Profiles, Productivity, and Hours Restrictions." *American Economic Review* 71:606–620.

Leigh, Duane. 1976. "Occupational Advancement in the Late 1960s: An Indirect Test of the Dual Labor Market Hypothesis." *Journal of Human Resources* 11:155–171.

Maddala, G. S. 1983. *Limited-Dependent and Qualitative Variables in Econometrics*. New York: Cambridge University Press.

Mincer, Jacob. 1974. *Schooling, Experience and Earnings*. New York: National Bureau of Economic Research.

Oster, Gerry. 1979. "A Factor Analytic Test of the Theory of the Dual Economy." *Review of Economics and Statistics* 61:33–51.

Osterman, Paul. 1975. "An Empirical Study of Labor Market Segmentation." *Industrial and Labor Relations Review* 28:508–523.

Piore, Michael J. 1974. "Comment on Wachter." *Brookings Papers on Economic Activity* 3:684–688.

Piore, Michael J. 1975. "Notes for a Theory of Labor Market Stratification" Pp. 129–150 in *Labor Market Segmentation*, edited by Richard C. Edwards, Michael Reich, and David M. Gordon. Lexington, MA: D. C. Heath.

Piore, Michael J. 1980a. "Dualism as a Response to Flux and Uncertainty." Pp. 23–54 in *Dualism and Discontinuity in Industrial Societies*, edited by Suzanne Berger and Michael J. Piore. New York: Cambridge University Press.

Piore, Michael J. 1980b. "The Technological Foundations of Dualism." Pp. 55–81 in *Dualism and Discontinuity in Industrial Societies*, edited by Suzanne Berger and Michael J. Piore. New York: Cambridge University Press.

Piore, Michael J. 1983. "Labor Market Segmentation: To What Paradigm Does It Belong?" *American Economic Review Papers and Proceedings* 73:249–253.

Rosen, Sherwin. 1974. "Hedonic Prices and Implicit Markets: Product Differentiation in Pure Competition." *Journal of Political Economy* 82:34–55.

Rosenberg, Samuel. 1980. "Male Occupational Standing and the Dual Labor Market." *Industrial Relations* 19:34–49.

Roy, A. D. 1950. "The Distribution of Earnings and of Individual Output." *Economic Journal* 60:135–146.

Roy, A. D. 1951. "Some Thoughts on the Distribution of Earnings." *Oxford Economic Papers* 3:135–146.

Sattinger, Michael. 1979. "Differential Rents and the Distribution of Earnings." *Oxford Economic Papers* 31:60–71.

Sattinger, Michael. 1980. *Capital and the Distribution of Labor Earnings*. Amsterdam: North-Holland.

Schiller, Bradley R. 1977. "Relative Earnings Mobility in the United States." *American Economic Review* 67:926–941.

Shapiro, Carl, and Joseph E. Stiglitz. 1985. "Equilibrium Unemployment as a Worker Discipline Device." *American Economic Review* 74:433–444.

Solow, Robert. 1979a. "Another Possible Source of Wage Stickiness." *Journal of Macro Economics* 1:79–82.

Solow, Robert. 1979b. "Alternative Approaches to Macroeconomic Theory: A Partial View." *Canadian Journal of Economics* 12:339–354.

Sorenson, Aage B., and Arne L. Kalleberg. 1981. "An Outline of a Theory of the Matching of Persons to Jobs." Pp. 49–74 in *Sociological Perspectives on Labor Markets,* edited by Ivar Berg. New York: Academic Press.

Stigler, George J. 1962. "Information in the Labor Market." *Journal of Political Economy* 70:94–105.

Stoft, Steve. 1982. Cheat Threat Theory: An Explanation of Involuntary Unemployment. Mimeo, Boston University.

Stolzenberg, Ross M. 1978. "Bringing the Boss Back In: Employer Size, Employee Schooling, and Socioeconomic Achievement." *American Sociological Review* 43:813–828.

Thaler, Richard H., and Sherwin Rosen. 1976. "The Value of Saving a Life: Evidence from the Labor Market." Pp. 265–298 in *Household Production and Consumption,* edited by Nestor Terleckyj. New York: Columbia University Press.

Thom, Gary B. 1983. *The Human Nature of Social Discontent.* Totowa, NJ: Rowman & Allenheld.

Tinbergen, Jan. 1951. "Some Remarks on the Distribution of Labour Incomes." *International Economics Papers* 1:195–207.

Tinbergen, Jan. 1956. "On the Theory of Income Distribution." *Weltwirtschaftliches Archiv* 77:155–173.

Tolbert, Charles M. 1982. "Industrial Segmentation and Men's Career Mobility." *American Sociological Review* 47:457–477.

Tolbert, Charles M., Patrick M. Horan, and E. M. Beck. 1980. "The Structure of American Economic Segmentation: A Dual Economy Approach." *American Journal of Sociology* 85:1095–1116.

Viscusi, W. Kip. 1979. *Employment Hazards: An Investigation of Market Performance.* Cambridge, MA: Harvard University Press.

Wachter, Michael L. 1974. "Primary and Secondary Labor Markets: A Critique of the Dual Approach." *Brookings Papers on Economic Activity* 3:637–680.

Wallace, Michael, and Arne L. Kalleberg. 1981. "Economic Organization of Firms and Labor Market Consequences: Toward a Specification of Dual Economy Theory." Pp. 77–117 in *Sociological Perspectives on Labor Markets,* edited by Ivar Berg. New York: Academic Press.

Weiss, Andrew. 1980. "Job Queues and Layoffs in Labor Markets with Flexible Wage Expectations." *Journal of Political Economy* 88:526–538.

Woodbury, S. A. 1979. "Methodological Controversy in Labor Economics." *Journal of Economic Issues* 13:933–955.

Yellen, Janet L. 1984. "Efficiency Wage Models of Unemployment." *American Economic Review Papers and Proceedings* 74:200–205.

Zucker, Lynne G., and Carolyn Rosenstein. 1981. "Taxonomies of Institutional Structure: Dual Economy Reconsidered." *American Sociological Review* 46:869–884.

III

INDUSTRIAL STRUCTURE AND MARKETS

The chapters in this section analyze the effects of industrial structure on three outcomes: wages, returns to human capital, and productivity. Taken together, they demonstrate the continued relevance of the "new structuralist" emphasis on the characteristics of firms and industries, the need to expand or revise aspects of economists' market model, and the continued importance of market forces in these processes.

In "Structural Effects on Wages: Sociological and Economic Views," Farkas, England, and Barton present a theoretical explanation for recent empirical findings about net effects of industrial and firm characteristics on wages. The chapter argues that wages are higher where workers have more bargaining power and/or firms are more profitable. The bargaining power of workers is greater in the presence of unions, a threat of costly malfeasance or sabotage, class consciousness, and less elastic labor demand.

Theorizing over the possibility that the threat of malfeasance or sabotage enhances workers' power represents a situation where the views of economists and sociologists are beginning to converge. Sociologists have focused on this causal mechanism to explain the effects of capital intensity on wages, since working with expensive machinery provides workers with an informal collective threat. Economists have focused less on the collective aspects of this threat but have developed the theory of efficiency wages to explain why employers may gain by paying above market wages in situations where motivating "good" behavior through such "efficiency wages" is cheaper than elaborate surveillance. (Efficiency wages are discussed in greater detail by Lang and Dickens in this volume.)

A novel feature of the discussion by Farkas et al. is its use of the Hicks-Marshall laws of economics to account for a number of empirical findings by structuralist sociologists. The Hicks-Marshall laws focus on the determinants of variation in the elasticity of labor demand. This elasticity refers to the tilt of the demand curve, and thus to how many fewer workers will be employed if the wage rate is bargained upward. One of these laws states that the elasticity of labor demand is higher whenever the elasticity of demand for the good or service produced with this labor is higher. An implication of this is that employers with a monopoly in their product market have a less elastic demand for labor. This follows from the empirical tendency of oligopolists to *behave like monopolists, and the fact that a monopolist faces the entire industry's product market, which is less elastic than the demand for a single competitive firm's product. Thus, opportunities for workers to bargain over the oligopoly "rent" are enhanced by the low elasticity of labor demand, which makes the trade-off between jobs and wages less severe. Another Hicks-Marshall law states that labor demand is more elastic when labor is a higher proportion of production costs. Since labor's proportion of costs will be lower where production is capital-intensive, this helps explain why employee bargaining is more successful in capital-intensive industries. The chapter uses a variety of such arguments to explain a range of findings on effects of industrial and firm characteristics upon wages.*

One irony of this thesis is that economic theory is used to explain why certain characteristics of industries and firms have the effects on wages that sociologists have observed, yet it argues that the persistence of these effects is inconsistent with the neoclassical market model. This is because mobility between sectors and wage competition between firms should erode wage differentials between sectors. If one sector pays higher wages than another for workers of equivalent human capital and tastes, then many workers will try to move to the higher wage sector. This should allow the higher wage sector to lower wages and/or require the lower wage sector to raise wages until the wage levels in the two sectors equalize. The mystery is why this process does not happen to a greater extent. The chapter examines the factors that prevent or at least slow such mobility, and thus perpetuate structural effects on wages. These factors include the costs of job search and implicit contracts, which are increasingly incorporated into economists' theories. They also include factors that sociologists have emphasized, such as informal networks of job contacts, feedback effects from discrimination to supply-side behavior, and the influence of one's job upon tastes and habits. These factors challenge economists' view that preferences are exogenous to market processes, and suggest the need for a model incorporating the reciprocal effects of preferences, habits, and demand-side structures. (For a similar view, but with a greater emphasis on the ability of efficiency wage theory to render new structuralist views compatible with a revised but still essentially neoclassical economic theory, see Chapter 4 by Lang and Dickens.)

In "Schooling and Capitalism: The Effect of Urban Economic Structure on the Value of Education," Beck and Colclough examine how the industrial structure of urban areas affects the (percentage) rate of return to workers' education. Earlier structuralist research found differences in earnings and in rates of return to education between "core" and "peripheral" industries. This chapter takes the investigation of structural effects one step further by examining how the industrial mix of employment in an SMSA affects rates of return to schooling.

The analysis proceeds in two stages. First, regression analyses are performed within each race/gender group in each urban area. The estimated rates of return from these first analyses then become dependent variables in a second set of analyses where SMSAs are the cases. To capture economic structure, each urban area is scored on five factors that become the independent variables of interest: ratio of capital to labor, business sales activity, oligopoly concentration, business profitability, and the relative influence of the government as an employer. Other "labor-supply-side" variables are included as controls. This second analysis assesses the net effects of urban economic structure on rates of return to education for specific race/gender groups.

Major conclusions include the following: (1) Urban industrial structures have a significant effect on the economic value of educational credentials. (2) These effects are larger for blacks than for whites. (3) The value of college training is more strongly affected by the industrial structure of an urban economy than is the value of lower levels of schooling. (4) Urban economic characteristics that increase rates of return for both black and white male college graduates—a large financial sector and a restricted sales sector—are the same characteristics that disadvantage comparably educated white women. (Unfortunately, there were too few black females for separate analysis.)

Beck and Colclough point out that these interurban differences in returns to education are examples of the uneven development that Marxists and some other sociologists have argued to be intrinsic to capitalism. These same regional differences in wages and rates of return are viewed by neoclassical economists as transitional disequilibria that will eventually erode as a consequence of the geographical mobility of capital and labor. Analyses such as this one serve to specify those local characteristics leading to systematic deviations from the homogeneous rates of return predicted by neoclassical theory. Further research along these lines can lead to integration of economic and sociological theories of regional differences by identifying both market forces and the factors that prevent or slow these processes. Future research in this area might usefully be based on overtime data, perhaps via a cross-section–time-series design permitting tests of the regional convergence predicted by neoclassical theory, as well as investigation of any deviations from such convergence.

In the final chapter in this section, Tomaskovic-Devey explores "Market Concentration and Structural Power as Sources of Industrial Productivity." He observes that sociologists seldom study productivity, a claim also made by Granovetter (Chapter 9, this volume), and a point that underscores the need for sociologists to pay more attention to the incentives market forces provide for productivity. Tomaskovic-Devey conceptualizes productivity as value created by either the production or the sale of commodities. Thus, he defines a firm as more productive if it produces more efficiently, but also if it receives a higher price for its product. This is an unconventional definition, since it does not take productivity to be determined solely by the technology of production and the quantity and quality of labor and capital, as emphasized by marginal productivity theory. Rather, what Tomaskovic-Devey calls productivity is also affected by the ability of firms within particular industries to raise prices. In one sense this accords with the standard economic view that oligopoly in product markets may raise product prices. However, neoclassical theory minimizes the role of oligopoly. The definition has the effect of combining the firm's "physical" productive efficiency with its product market situation.

Tomaskovic-Devey's presentation also departs from standard economic views in that he sees oligopoly power in product markets as only one of the types of power facilitating the control of pricing. He proposes a more sociological notion of structural power as well. One index of such power is "industrial centrality," the volume of sales by the industry to all other industries (but not to final consumers) as a ratio of all interindustry sales in the economy. Industries that are more central in this sense of "downstream dependence" on them are hypothesized to be more powerful in price setting. The second index of an industry's structural power is "interindustry sales." This is a measure of the proportion of the industry's output sold to other industries rather than to final consumers. Following Ronald Burt, Tomaskovic-Devey suggests that industrial consumers are more effectively organized than are households, the final consumers of goods. The more organized consumers are, the more difficulty producers will have keeping prices high. Thus, interindustry sales should have a negative effect on productivity.

Tomaskovic-Devey's empirical work takes manufacturing industries as the unit of analysis. The dependent variable, productivity, is measured as value added per full-time equivalent employee. He finds that capital investment has a positive effect on productivity, as predicted by marginal productivity theory. Interestingly, a control variable, the percent black of the work force, has a positive effect on productivity. One possible interpretation of this finding is that industries hiring more blacks have higher profits because they exploit blacks by paying them less. Alternative hypotheses to explain this finding should be explored in future research, making use of the rich integrative literature from sociology and economics on discrimination.

As expected, Tomaskovic-Devey finds that oligopolistic industries show higher productivity. The more sociological notions of power also have significant effects, as predicted; industries facing more disorganized consumers (households instead of industries) and industries on whom other industrial buyers are more dependent for sales are found to be more productive.

This latter finding identifies another area where sociological and economic viewpoints might be usefully applied: Under what conditions do individuals form groups for collective action? The fields of public choice and parts of the new institutionalism in economics explore such questions about political action. They posit that the costs of collective participation will be weighed against the expected gains by each individual. For example, they might explain Tomaskovic-Devey's finding by the fact that it is more costly to organize millions of households, each of which can gain only a tiny amount from keeping one industry's price down, than to organize an industry of firms that routinely buy the products of another industry. Yet this line of argument might be usefully augmented by the sociological perspective offered by Granovetter in Chapter 9. The access one has to informal networks through one's job affects not only the cost of collective action but also the emotional attachments, trust, and group loyalties that result. Exploration of how these factors combine to predict the circumstances under which collective action will be undertaken is an area currently under active consideration by both sociologists and economists.

The three chapters in this section exemplify an important theme of this volume: the need to examine both the phenomena predicted by market models, and systematic deviations from such predictions. These chapters do not ignore neoclassical economic predictions, yet they carry the agenda of the new structuralism in sociology forward by looking for systematic deviations from these predictions. The chapter by Farkas et al. seeks to provide a theoretical framework for understanding wage determination by market and nonmarket forces, the first project tackled by new structuralist research. The other chapters carry the empirical project of the new structuralism into two heretofore neglected topics—industrial productivity and regional differences.

5

Structural Effects on Wages

Sociological and Economic Views

George Farkas, Paula England, and Margaret Barton

I. INTRODUCTION

The "new structuralism" in sociology has shown that characteristics of firms and industries affect the wages of those who work in them, even after adjusting for differences in employees' human capital. Similar findings appear in the economic literature. This chapter draws from both economics and sociology to propose a conceptual framework with which to explain these structural effects. Our orienting assumption is that, net of human capital, workplace wage levels are determined by (a) employees' bargaining power and (b) the size of the after-cost (economic) profit available for distribution as wages. We wish to understand how structural characteristics of firms and industries affect these variables, and to use this understanding to explain recent empirical findings by structuralist sociologists.

The impetus for empirical studies of structural effects came from notions of economic segmentation introduced by institutionalist and Marxist economists (Averitt, 1968; Bluestone, Murphy, and Stevenson, 1973; Edwards, 1975; Gordon, 1972; Vietorisz and Harrison, 1970). These heterodox economists also borrowed from the orthodox economic model. However, they departed from this neoclassical model in rejecting its prediction that market forces will erode net structural effects. Building on this foundation, sociologists have undertaken empirical work designed to estimate the hypothesized structural effects (Baron and Bielby, 1980; Beck, Horan, and Tolbert, 1978; Hodson, 1978, 1983, 1984; Kalleberg, Wallace, and Althauser, 1981; Tolbert, Horan, and Beck, 1980; Zucker and Rosenstein, 1981). These investi-

George Farkas and Paula England • School of Social Sciences, University of Texas-Dallas, Richardson, Texas 75083-0688.   Margaret Barton • Systems Research and Applications Corporation, Arlington, Virginia 22201.

gators hypothesize a multitude of causal mechanisms. Our goal is to clarify the resulting issues and propose a unified framework to explain existing findings. Throughout the chapter we use the term *structural effects* to refer to additive effects of firms' or industries' characteristics on wages, net of human capital.

II. POWER

The framework we propose rests on two propositions. First, wages will be higher where employees have more bargaining power. Second, such bargaining power will be more effective in the presence of higher levels of economic profit. Economists refer to "market power" whenever perfect competition—many buyers and sellers in a particular market—is lacking. Either there is only one seller (a monopolist) or one buyer (a monopsonist). If monopoly can be maintained, theory says that profits will be higher than under competition. This excess profit is called a "rent," "supranormal profit," or "excess profit," and is an instance of "economic profit" (see Hirshleifer, 1984:177, 216). If the monopolist is a firm selling a product, it is expected to sell less, but at a higher profit (per unit) than under competition. Similarly, if the monopolistic seller is selling labor (for example, if all the workers available to work in a particular occupation belong to a single union), wages will be higher than under competition.

Within economics there is debate over the consequences of economic concentration. Since true monopolies are almost nonexistent, the main issue concerns whether oligopoly (a few sellers, rather than a single seller) also leads to excess profits. In theory this should occur only in the presence of formal or informal collusion in price setting. There is a large literature on the conditions facilitating such collusion (Scherer, 1980). Yet, despite theoretical uncertainty, a host of studies find higher profitability in product markets that are oligopolistic, i.e., in product markets that have a large share of sales concentrated within a small number of firms (Scherer, 1980: 267–282; Weiss, 1974). Some researchers believe that these higher profits are indeed "supranormal"; others argue that they merely result from a natural tendency of more efficient companies to achieve greater market share (Scherer, 1980:280–295). That is, such accounting profits may reflect production efficiency rather than market power.[1]

---

[1] A recent economic literature on "contestable markets" has extended this skepticism about inferring market power wherever there are only a small number of (dominant) sellers. These economists argue that were profits to become supranormal within a particular industry, new firms would be motivated to enter the industry and would bid such excess profits away (Baumol, 1982; Baumol, Panzar, and Willig, 1982, 1986). This is a rather extreme view that relies on the existence of perfect capital markets to preclude the barriers to entry that new firms would otherwise experience. We believe it more realistic to assume that where market entrance requires a large capital investment, owing to economies of scale or the benefits of capital intensive production, this will pose a substantial barrier to entry (Averitt, 1968).

In addition to product market power, we are also concerned with the "monopoly power" labor can achieve through unionization. If all workers with a particular skill belonged to a single union, this union could be regarded as a monopolistic seller of labor. And even where this situation is only loosely approximated, some of its gains may be realized directly through collective bargaining and indirectly through "emulation" or "threat" effects on nonunion firms seeking to avoid unionization. Yet, just as the monopolistic firm fears that consumers will substitute away from its product in response to a price hike, the union monopoly leaves workers vulnerable to the firm's substituting production away from their workers (via automation, moving production, hiring nonunion labor, or outsourcing), or even going out of business. Nonetheless, the economic, social, and legal costs or restrictions employers face in substituting away from union labor lead to some monopoly power for unions.

Sociologists have not typically followed economists' practice of conceptualizing power in terms of a comparison of the outcome in question with that expected under perfect competition. Rather, sociological exchange theorists talk of a power disparity when one party to an exchange can achieve more of what it wants (more utility) than the other. Since economists disbelieve the possibility of interpersonal utility comparisons, they avoid this way of stating the issue. However, where empirical work is concerned, sociologists and economists approaches can be reconciled even though their conceptualizations of power differ. The determinants of employees' bargaining power can be assessed with regression analyses in which wages are the dependent variable and individual, job, firm, and industry characteristics the independent variables. Such calculations have become a standard feature of the empirical literature in both sociology and economics.

III. EMPLOYEES' BARGAINING POWER

In this section we consider factors affecting the bargaining power of employees, drawing on the discussions of economists and sociologists. We use these ideas to examine the effect of firm and industry characteristics on such bargaining power, and hence on wages. Where effects of these structural characteristics have been explicitly tested in the literature, we review the empirical findings and provide our interpretation.

A. Unions

That the presence of unions increases workers' bargaining power is beyond dispute. Consistent with this view, empirical studies find net positive wage effects of union membership or of employment in highly unionized firms or industries (Flanagan, Smith, and Ehrenberg, 1984:553–570; Freeman and Medoff, 1984:43–60; Hodson, 1983, 1984; Hodson and England, 1986; Kalleberg et al., 1981).

It is instructive to examine the similarities and differences between the situation of a monopoly seller facing its customers and a union facing the employer of its workers. The situations are similar in that the monopoly firm is free to set its price as high as it likes, with only the danger of selling less product as impediment (where the magnitude of this effect is determined by the price elasticity of consumer demand). Similarly, the union may hold out for a high wage, with only the danger of job loss as impediment (where the magnitude of this effect is determined by the price elasticity of the employer's demand for its workers). However, as pointed out by Freeman and Medoff (1984:6), the situations are different in that the monopolistic firm is happy to sell fewer units if greater profit is thereby achieved, whereas the union must be concerned with job loss as well as wage gains. In this sense, the "monopoly power" of a union is less than that of a monopolistic firm in a product market, and the exercise of this power may depend upon the firm's price elasticity of labor demand. This is one instance of a more general set of effects usually referred to as the Hicks-Marshall laws. These play a central role in the neoclassical understanding of the determinants of employee bargaining power.

B. The Hicks-Marshall Laws

The bargaining strength of any group of employees is influenced by the nature of the trade-off between their employment and wage rate. This trade-off arises because labor demand curves tilt downward. Thus, other things being equal, employees who bargain for a higher wage will find that fewer positions are available, and their own jobs may even be in jeopardy. The key to employee bargaining power is the extent of this tilt.

Let wage rates be graphed on the vertical axis, and the number of workers employed by the firm or industry on the horizontal axis. Consider two employers' demand curves of differing slope. In the case of the one with the less steep slope, a small increase in wage rates leads the employer to cut way back on employment; fear of this outcome weakens the employees' bargaining position. In contrast, where an increase in wage rates leads to very little decrease in the quantity of labor demanded, workers are in a stronger position to press for increases. The tilt of the demand curve shows what is called the own-wage elasticity of labor demand. In the former case—a less steep slope—labor demand is said to be more elastic; in the latter case it is less elastic.[2]

We suggest that the lower this elasticity of labor demand, the greater the bargaining power of the workers. In the extreme case of completely inelastic labor demand, the firm or industry will hire the same amount of labor no matter what its cost. In this situation, workers have no reason to fear that

[2]Strictly speaking, this elasticity is defined as the percentage change in employment resulting from a 1% increase in the wage rate. Thus, if the demand curve were a straight line (constant slope), the elasticity would vary along the curve. Nonetheless, at any one point, a steeper slope indicates a less elastic curve.

wage increases might lead to unemployment. On the other hand, where labor demand is very elastic, even a small increase in the price of labor will lead to large employment reductions. This likelihood may dissuade workers from pressing hard for wage gains.

An important caveat is that, strictly speaking, we should expect this reasoning about workers' bargaining power to apply only to unionized work settings, where the employer is unable to deal with the workers on an individual basis (see the examples provided by Flanagan *et al.*, 1984:93–94). However, similar effects may be observed in nonunion firms as long as there is a credible threat of unionization or of the loss of workers to union firms (Freeman and Medoff, 1984).

If workers' bargaining power is inversely related to the elasticity of demand for their labor, then an examination of the determinants of this elasticity will reveal structural conditions that provide workers with resources for bargaining. This will advance the "resource perspective" called for by sociologists Hodson and Kaufman (1982). In economics, the four determinants of this elasticity are known as the Hicks-Marshall laws. As originally stated by Marshall (1923:518–538) and refined by Hicks (1966:241–247), the laws state that the elasticity of demand for a category of labor is higher (1) when the price elasticity of demand for the product being produced is high, (2) when other factors of production can be easily substituted for the category of labor in question, (3) when the supply curves of other factors of production are highly elastic (that is, when the employment of other factors of production can be increased without substantially increasing their price), and (4) when the cost of employing the category of labor is a large share of the total cost of production[3] (Flanagan *et al.*, 1984:88).

Law 1: Demand Elasticity in the Product Market. The first Hicks-Marshall law draws attention to the firm's or industry's position in the market for the good or service it produces. When the price elasticity of demand for its product is high, the firm or industry's attempt to raise prices leads to a large decrease in the quantity it is able to sell. Under this market pressure, it can ill afford wage increases in comparison with firms selling a product with a lower price elasticity. In this latter case, the firm or industry can pass along cost increases as price increases without suffering as large a decline in sales.

This leads to one reason that theorists of the "dual economy" have emphasized the ability of the oligopolistic sector of the economy to pay high wages. Consider first a firm that is a monopolist in its product market. It is well known that the price elasticity of consumer demand for the product of a particular firm within an industry is greater than the price elasticity of consumer demand for the output of the entire industry. This is because, in response to a price increase, buyers can more easily substitute the product of a competing firm than they can substitute the product of an entirely different

---

[3]This law does not always hold (Hicks, 1966). It is reversed in the special case where it is easy for employers to substitute capital or another kind of labor for the presently employed workers, but there is a low price elasticity of demand.

industry. Thus, when a firm is a monopolist in its product market, the firm faces a product demand curve that is less elastic than it would be under competition. This is because the firm faces the curve for the entire industry. According to the first Hicks-Marshall law, such firms have less elastic labor demand curves. Thus, workers in monopolistic firms occupy an improved bargaining position in comparison with that of workers employed by firms whose products are competitively priced.

To the extent that oligopolists behave like monopolists in exerting some degree of control over product prices, oligopolistic firms and industries will also exhibit less elastic labor demand, so that their workers will be afforded a better bargaining position than would obtain were the industry fully competitive. This suggests a positive effect of oligopoly (market concentration) on wages. Most studies show that, after controls for individual characteristics, concentrated industries do pay higher wages (Dalton and Ford, 1977; Ehrenberg, 1979; Hodson, 1984; Kalleberg *et al.*, 1981; Kwoka, 1983; Long and Link, 1983; Mellow, 1982; Tolbert *et al.*, 1980). However, after controls for productivity, capital intensity, or economic scale, the net effects of oligopoly often fail to be significant (Hodson, 1984; Hodson and England, 1986). Yet, since measures of economic scale, capital intensity, and accounting profit may themselves serve as proxies for oligopoly power, the effects of oligopoly may be obscured by overpartialing in these latter analyses.

Tests of whether unionization is particularly successful in raising wages within oligopolistic industries have also yielded conflicting findings. The first Hicks-Marshall law suggests that unions might have greater success in concentrated industries as a consequence of the less elastic demand curves faced by the firms in such industries, and thus that unionization and market concentration would exhibit a positive interaction in their joint effects upon wage rates. Yet, contrary to this prediction, several analyses have found a negative interaction (Kalleberg *et al.*, 1981; Lewis, 1963; Weiss, 1966). This may be explained by the fact that oligopolists are able to coordinate an industry-wide response to unionization and strikes as well as using their supranormal profits to withstand such union activities. Hodson (1984) emphasizes these negative effects of industry concentration on workers' gains.

The first law also helps explain the finding that industries selling more of their product to the government tend to pay higher wages (Bluestone, 1974; Hodson, 1984). Since the government's product demand is less price-sensitive than that of other consumers, such industries exhibit less elastic labor demand, so that their workers enjoy a stronger bargaining position.

Law 2: Substitutability of Other Factors. The second Hicks-Marshall law states that as a particular category of labor becomes more expensive, the employer has an increased incentive to substitute alternative means of production. The easier this is, the higher the wage elasticity of demand, and the more difficulty workers will experience bargaining for wage increases.

One obvious substitution is nonunion for union labor. Since this possibility seriously erodes union bargaining power, unions typically press for legislation raising the cost of such substitution. Examples include the minimum wage, requirements that union wages be paid on federally financed construction projects, restrictions on worker replacement during strikes, restrictions on plant closings, and immigration restrictions. Limiting firms' abilities to substitute other labor for union labor makes the labor demand curve for union workers less elastic, and means that fewer union jobs will be lost in response to a wage gain.

Another potential substitution is capital for more expensive labor. Such capital–labor substitution is easiest where the jobs require little skill and are highly repetitive. Since it is more difficult to substitute capital for skilled workers, the labor demand curve is more inelastic for high-skilled than for low-skilled workers. This may be one reason that unions had their earliest successes organizing skilled workers.

Finally, there is outsourcing. Here the firm no longer produces a particular component but buys more cheaply from another domestic or foreign producer. The decision to retain control of production, but to move it to another plant, has a similar effect on union power. The greatest labor cost savings are typically obtained by foreign production, where wages may be quite low. Of course, this possibility also makes the labor demand curve more elastic; an increase in wages leads to larger job loss when production can be moved elsewhere. Such outsourcing or runaway plants are more easily achieved in firms and industries characterized by conglomerate domination. However, Hodson (1984) fails to find a significant net effect of such domination on wage rates. Better measures of firm and industry variation in these substitution possibilities would improve the empirical work in this area.

Law 3: The Elasticity of Supply of Other Factors. The ease of substitution discussed above depends upon both the technical relationships of production and governmental regulation. By contrast, the third Hicks-Marshall law refers to market conditions determining the price *elasticity* of supply of the other factors of production. The more elastic this supply, the larger the quantity of these inputs the employers can purchase without substantially driving up their price. The third law states that the more elastic the supply of alternative factors of production, the more elastic the demand curve for labor. And, as we have already observed, the more elastic the demand for labor, the less bargaining power workers have.

The process might work as follows. A firm or industry substitutes a little capital for labor, with plans to substitute further if all goes well. However, if the increased demand for these capital goods begins to bid up their price, such substitution becomes less economic, and fewer jobs are lost. If, on the other hand, the price of these goods fails to rise because their supply is very elastic, greater substitution occurs and more jobs are lost. A similar argument applies to labor–labor substitution and outsourcing.

This mechanism of effect has been largely ignored in empirical work. This is not surprising; supply elasticities for factors of production that compete with current workers may vary dramatically across firms, industries, and their geographic locations, yet they are difficult to measure on a firm- or industry-specific basis. Further, it may be crucially important whether the firm or industry seeks to buy a large enough share of the entire market to drive up a factor's price. If not, its supply may be completely elastic to the firm or industry. In the former case, economists speak of "supply bottle-necks" or "capacity constraints" leading to price inflation. Some empirical progress may be attained by focusing on those firms or industries that are constrained to produce in particular local areas. Examples include certain services, construction, trucking, the maritime industry, and mining. Such geographic specificity may lead to less elastic supplies of competing produc-tion factors. Empirical study of the magnitude of such effects would be a useful addition to the structural research agenda.

Law 4: The Share of Labor in Total Costs. The fourth Hicks-Marshall law states that the demand curve for labor is more elastic the greater is this factor's share of total costs. Thus, a wage increase can be expected to have greater impact on the number of workers a firm is willing to hire where labor costs are 90% of total costs than where they are just 10% of total costs. Product prices will rise more in the former case, and, as the quantity of goods sold falls dramatically, so too will employment. Since labor's proportion of costs is lower where production is particularly capital-intensive, and this lower pro-portion of costs raises workers' bargaining power, this fourth law helps ex-plain why wages are higher in capital-intensive industries (Averitt, 1968:139; Hodson, 1984; Kalleberg *et al.*, 1981).

C. "Sabotage" and "Shirking"

Hodson and Kaufman (1982) and Hodson (1984) suggest that capital intensity affects wages at least partly because of the implicit bargaining power gained by workers able to sabotage expensive machinery. Their sociological argument is similar to one version of the recently developed economic theory of "efficiency wages" (Bulow and Summers, 1986; Katz, 1986). The theory refers to above-competitive wages that, for some firms, may more than repay their additional cost.

One version of the theory, the "shirking model," focuses on the potential costs of workers' malfeasance (such as shoddy work or sabotage) combined with the costs of detecting such malfeasance. Even with minimal surveillance, workers know that there is some probability of losing their jobs for malfea-sance. If they are paid more than they could make elsewhere, they will have a motivation to avoid malfeasance so as to avoid the wage drop that would attend being fired if they were caught misbehaving. Where the costs of mal-feasance or the costs of detecting it are especially high, it may be cheaper to reduce shirking through raising the wage level than to spend money on the technology or personnel that would permit more thorough surveillance. If the costs of detection or the damage to productivity resulting from worker mal-feasance are greater where production is capital-intensive, this model shares with Hodson's and Kaufman's sabotage model the prediction that wages will be higher in capital-intensive firms or industries as a result of employees' implicit bargaining power.

The evidence on whether capital intensity affects wages is equivocal. The capital intensity of one's industry has been found to affect men's (but not women's) wages (Hodson, 1984; Hodson and England, 1986; Kalleberg *et al.*, 1981). Yet Hodson (1984) did not find a relationship between firms' capital intensity and wages.

D. Class Consciousness and Economies of Scale in Organizing Workers

One sociological thesis dates back to Marx, who suggested that workers in large firms will be more alienated and identify less with management (Averitt, 1968:129; Hodson and Kaufman, 1982). The resulting heightened class consciousness, combined with the economies of scale for union organizing provided by large plants, may help explain the positive effect of plant size on earnings (Freeman and Medoff, 1984; Hodson, 1984; Kalleberg *et al.*, 1981).

IV. THE SIZE OF THE PIE

Much of the writing on economic segmentation has emphasized variables associated with high levels of economic profit (whether derived from productivity or market power) that make higher wages possible. Variables that may serve as proxies for firms' or industries' capacity to earn economic profit include reported (accounting) rate of profit, market concentration, productivity, the capital intensity of production, plant size, and foreign holdings or dividends (Shepherd, 1970, 1979). In this section we summarize those variables and causal mechanisms whose effect on wages is best justified via their influence in raising economic profit at either the firm or industry level.

Reported (accounting) rates of profit represent one attempt to operationalize the economic-profit mechanism for wage increases. Three studies find that industries' average profit rates are positively associated with wages (Hodson, 1984; Hodson and England, 1986; Pugel, 1980), even after controlling labor quality. Yet one analysis (Hodson, 1984) found no net effects of either industrial- or firm-level profits on wages. Since each of these studies employs accounting rates of profit rather than true measures of economic profit, measurement error may have biased these estimates toward zero. (See Hirshleifer, 1984:177, on the distinction between accounting and economic profit.)

Foreign investment has also been hypothesized to exert a positive effect on wages because of its elevation of profit levels. Controlling for individual characteristics, Hodson (1984) reports a positive effect at the industrial level for men but not women and no effect for either sex at the plant level. In contrast, Hodson and England (1986) find a positive effect at the industrial level for a related measure of foreign dividends for women, but not for men. Thus, the findings are inconsistent; however, since all were estimated controlling for accounting profitability, it is possible that overpartialing has obscured a real effect.

If one wishes to measure supranormal profit, market concentration at the industry level may provide a more reliable proxy than reported (accounting) rates of profit. Indeed, a long line of economic studies show higher rates of profit in oligopolistic industries (Scherer, 1980:267–282; Weiss, 1974). Among sociologists, Kalleberg *et al.* (1981) find a positive effect of market concentration on wages when not controlling productivity or profits, whereas studies controlling these variables find insignificant effects (Hodson, 1983, 1984; Hodson and England, 1986). Since it is improper to control these variables that measure the mechanism through which industrial concentration has its effects, we are inclined to believe the positive effects. Most economists' studies have found evidence of higher wages in concentrated industries, controlling for human capital (Dalton and Ford, 1977; Ehrenberg, 1979; Kwoka, 1983; Long and Link, 1983; Mellow, 1982). The exception is Weiss's (1966) study, which found effects of concentration to disappear when workers' characteristics were controlled.

The size of an establishment's work force has been shown to be positively associated with wage rates (Freeman and Medoff, 1984; Hodson, 1984; Kalleberg *et al.*, 1981). This may be due to larger firms' generating greater class consciousness, greater economies of scale in union organizing, or union "threat" effects, subjects that have been treated above. However, it may also be due to economies of scale in production, leading to profits that can be shared with employees. Hodson (1984) finds that the industry average number of workers employed per establishment exerts no net effect on wages. Since we would expect economies of scale to work at the plant or firm rather than industry level, this finding does not contradict our reasoning.

The capital intensity of production has also been argued to increase wages via its effects on productivity and thus economic profit. Several studies find positive effects of industry averages of capital intensity on men's wages (Hodson, 1984; Hodson and England, 1986; Kalleberg *et al.*, 1981). Surprisingly, however, Hodson (1984) found no wage effect of establishment-level capital intensity once worker characteristics were controlled. Since the productivity argument should operate at the plant level, this finding casts some doubt on the effect.

"Economic scale" has also been seen as a proxy for economic profit and hypothesized to positively affect wages. Hodson (1984) operationalizes this with both firm- and industry-level measures of sales, assets, net worth, and employment. However, he finds no significant (net) effects. Similar results are reported by Kalleberg *et al.* (1981) and Hodson and England (1986).

A final explanation of structural effects via profitability comes from the recently developed theory of "efficiency wages" mentioned above. All versions of this theory share the notion that paying above competitive wages may raise profits by raising revenues more than costs. One version holds that above-competitive wages increase workers' morale and, hence, their productivity. Akerlof (1982, 1984) refers to this as a "sociological" model because the mechanism linking wages and productivity involves norms of fairness affecting group morale. If employers in all sectors benefited from efficiency wages to an equal extent, the notion would have little relevance to the explanation of structural effects on wages. But it is possible that workers' norms of fairness include the notion that firms should pay higher wages when they have a greater "ability to pay," i.e., when they have higher profit levels. In this case, firms with higher profit levels will gain more in workers' morale and productivity from sharing these profits with workers than will other firms (Katz, 1986). Though the theory is still only in a formative stage, it does offer one possible explanation of how profitability might affect wages even in the absence of substantial employee bargaining power.

V. NEOCLASSICAL THEORY AND STRUCTURAL EFFECTS

In the "purest" of neoclassical models, with perfect competition in factor and product markets, structural effects on wages, net of human capital, could not persist. This is not to say that interfirm or interindustry variation in variables such as capital intensity or wages is anomalous for neoclassical theory. It is not. Thus, zero-order relationships between structural characteristics of firms or industries and wages are consistent with neoclassical theory. However, the continued finding of such effects, net of human capital, is anomalous. As Beck *et al.* put it, referring to models of individuals' wage rates:

> Neoclassical theories of social structure include both individual participants in the socioeconomic attainment process and a structural context. . . . The structural context, however, is such that when it is assumed to be working according to theoretical specifications, it need not be included in the analyses. Like Adam Smith's "invisible hand" the competitive structure presumed by neoclassical theory guarantees that differential placement in the socioeconomic order is accomplished in a manner such that this placement is a reflection of a worker's basic value to the system. (Beck *et al.*, 1978)

This view (that the anomaly consists of the presence of these structural effects, net of human capital) led economists Dickens and Lang (1985) to refer to the anomaly as the "rationing of primary or core jobs." In this section we explain why neoclassical economists believe that such effects do not and could not persist. Then, in the following section, we go on to consider why structural effects do persist, neoclassical arguments notwithstanding.

A. Compensating Differentials and Unmeasured Human Capital

How do neoclassical economists respond to evidence that structural characteristics of firms and industries affect wages, net of human capital? One approach is to argue that statistical estimates of such structural effects are baised because they fail to control for (a) forms of human capital other than the commonly measured years of education and experience, and (b) nonpecuniary amenities of jobs. Broadly construed, human capital theory implies that markets will reward all kinds of human capital, not just that gained in formal schooling or years of job experience. Further, economists' theory of compensating differentials posits that workers seek to maximize utility, not just earnings, and will trade a portion of their earnings for a more pleasant job. Thus, other things equal, higher wages must be offered if firms are to procure labor in jobs the marginal worker finds unpleasant. If the structural locations alleged to positively affect wages contain workers with higher unmeasured human capital or jobs requiring compensating differentials, then the alleged structural effects may be spurious. (For an example of this neoclassical critique of structuralist interpretations, see Cain, 1976.) Sociologists Kalleberg *et al.* (1981) and Hodson (1984) employ the neoclassical notion of compensating differentials when they suggest that larger plants may offer higher wages because such settings are alienating and unpleasant. But the new structuralist tradition espoused by these authors implicitly argues that certain structural locations are disadvantageous after both earnings and all nonpecuniary job conditions are accounted for. It is the existence and persistence of such *uncompensated differentials* that is claimed by structuralists but inconsistent with the neoclassical view.[4] The question then arises—why do neoclassical economists believe structural effects cannot persist?

B. Structural Effects Involving Employees' Bargaining Power

We begin with those structural effects that act via their effect upon employee bargaining power. Consider first the Hicks-Marshall laws regarding characteristics of firms and industries that lower the elasticity of labor demand. Such characteristics include oligopoly in the product market, the difficulty of substituting other factors of production for current workers, and labor accounting for a low proportion of the costs of production. We argued that workers are in a more favorable bargaining position when the demand for labor is less elastic. Yet in the absence of a union or other monopoly in the labor market, such effects on wages are rejected by the strict neoclassical view.

This is because, in a competitive labor market, firms don't "bargain" over wages with employees, they merely pay the marketwide wage for employees with a given set of preferences and human capital characteristics. Thus, all firms pay the same wage, determined by the intersection of marketwide demand and supply curves for labor of a given type. It is the point of intersection, not the slopes of these curves, that matters. Any firm attempting to pay lower than this wage will find no takers. Any firm offering to pay above this wage is not maximizing profit, and if it persists, it may be driven out of business because of its above-market costs of production.

There is another way of expressing this neoclassical argument. Assume for simplicity that all workers are homogeneous, and suppose a sector is paying an above-market wage. These higher wages will quickly be "bid away" by market forces because many workers in other firms will begin

[4]In the presence of compensating differentials, unbiased estimation of structural effects requires data on job conditions that workers regard as nonpecuniary compensations or disamenities. Few data sets have such measures. This is one reason that neoclassical "purists" doubt the usefulness of those empirical analyses that have claimed to find structural effects.

applying for jobs in the higher-wage sector. The excess of supply over demand for workers at the above-market wage will lead the wage in this sector to fall until it is equivalent to that in the other sector.

However, in the presence of union monopoly power able to raise wages above a competitive level, neoclassical theory states that such effects will be larger in firms or industries with a less elastic demand for labor (Flanagan *et al.*, 1984:93; Freeman and Medoff, 1984:50). This raises the broader question of what neoclassical theory says about the effect of unions on wages. Here there are two views. The first is that unions raise wages because they exert a simple monopoly effect thanks to governmental intervention (via the National Labor Relations Act and other statutes) in what would otherwise be free markets (Freeman and Medoff, 1984:6).

In this first view of unions, the government has given unions more power than they would have in a "free market" by legally obligating employers to permit union elections, to bargain collectively with the certified union, and to refrain from paying a premium to nonunion members of a bargaining unit. Of course, these requirements are not perfectly enforced (Freeman and Medoff, 1984:221–245), but they have some effect. An extension of this view is that where unionization represents a particularly credible threat, this implicit threat itself may raise wages (Dickens, 1986). Freeman and Medoff (1984:151–154) argue that the greater threat of unionization in large firms explains the large firm/small firm wage gap among nonunion workers.

The second neoclassical view on unions is more complicated. It builds on the observation that a union's "monopoly" power cannot raise wages (without putting firms out of business) unless the union organizes the industry-wide labor market, or unless unionized firms have monopoly power in their product markets. Monopoly in product markets leads to excess profits, which can be used for wages without driving the firm to bankruptcy. Thus, Freeman and Medoff observe:

> The fact that union monopoly power is likely to be important only when unionized firms either completely dominate a market or operate in a noncompetitive market has created an interesting intellectual anomaly. Some economists of a strong free-enterprise bent, who one might expect to be strongly opposed to unions, are in fact rather indifferent. They believe that markets are competitive enough to give unions little or no power to extract monopoly wage gains. (Freeman and Medoff, 1984:7)

This conclusion follows *a fortiori* for economists who believe that neither oligopolistic nor even monopolistic industries earn excess profits since there is always a sufficient threat of market entry by new competitors to keep profits close to a competitive level (see footnote 1). Thus, to the extent that neoclassical theory permits the consideration of "employee bargaining power" and union wage effects, these rest on monopoly-like conditions in labor and/or product markets. Further, true believers in the theory expect that such noncompetitive conditions are difficult to sustain, so that effects of monopoly are typically both transient and weak.

Neoclassical economists have a further reason for doubting the persistence of structural effects that operate via employee bargaining power. The argument is based on the sorting of workers across jobs. Assume the existence of some structural positions characterized by heightened bargaining power of workers so that wages are bid up. Employers would prefer workers with greater human capital, since such workers will likely be more productive, even in jobs requiring lower skill levels. But generally they can't get better workers "free." However, if, for exogenous reasons, they are going to have to pay a higher wage, they can use it to attract better workers. Over time, through new hires, employers who are forced to pay a higher wage for structural reasons will have the opportunity to employ those with higher human capital. In these situations, employers can get better workers "free." The result will be to reduce *net* structural effects on wages toward zero, since these effects represent higher wages, *net of human capital*. Of course, discrimination may prevent some highly qualified workers from moving into the high-wage jobs. Yet in the strict neoclassical model, race and sex discrimination in hiring will also erode in competitive labor markets because it actually costs employers something to discriminate. (For an explanation of why neoclassical economists believe discrimination should erode in competitive markets, see Arrow, 1972; England and Farkas, 1986:130–131; England and Mc-Creary, 1987.) Thus, in the strict neoclassical view, structural effects on wages cannot exist net of workers' human capital.

C. Structural Effects via Profits

The neoclassical arguments in this section parallel those just described. The structuralist contention is that more profitable sectors pay higher wages for labor of equivalent quality than do other sectors. The most basic neoclassical objection to this is that economic profit rates between sectors cannot differ in the long run. If they did, investment in the less profitable sectors would decline and eventually cease. Further, competitive product markets imply that no sectors should be able to maintain supranormal profits.

Even where sectors did differ in profitability, the neoclassical view holds that intersectoral wage differentials will be bid away. Thus, if firms are profit maximizers, more profitable firms have little motivation to offer higher wages than are offered by the less profitable. Competition in labor markets should bid away any intersectoral wage differentials as workers in the lower paid sectors attempt to move into the higher-paid sectors.

Finally, even if sectors did differ in their wage levels for jobs of similar skill requirements (perhaps because some sectors found it more profitable to pay "efficiency wages"), the resulting sorting by human capital would still result in no wage differentials *net of human capital*.[5] That is, employers who

---

[5] The one case in which this would not occur is where there is an efficiency wage resulting from employee's norms that make morale a function of how well wages *for a given level of human capital* reflect the ability of the firm to pay. But strict versions of neoclassical theory do not admit that firms will differ in economic profit (and hence "ability to pay"), and they are more likely to see implicit contracts than efficiency wages as a solution to the problem of morale. (For discussion of implicit contracts, see England and Farkas, 1986, Chap. 6. For a comparison of implicit contract and efficiency wage theory, see Katz, 1986.)

pay higher wages will win out in the competition for the best workers, and workers with higher human capital will win out in the competition for high-wage jobs. Over time, the net result will be a nearly perfect correlation between human capital and wages. In sum, the neoclassical view predicts the absence of structural effects on wages.

VI. WHY STRUCTURAL EFFECTS PERSIST

Despite the doubts of neoclassical economists, evidence of structural effects on wages abounds. We have reviewed the effects variable by variable above. But more global findings are relevant as well. For example, Tolbert *et al.* (1980) reduced a number of industrial variables to one factor and found large effects on earnings, net of human capital. In a similar vein, economists' empirical work has found large interindustry differences in wages after controlling for occupation and human capital (see Katz, 1986, for a review). Since it is interindustry worker mobility that neoclassical theory credits with eroding net structural effects on wages, the existence of barriers to such mobility is a key issue. Thus, sociologist Tolbert (1980, 1982) has recognized the importance of such intersectoral immobility for the validity of the new structuralist view.

What factors impede mobility? The literature on segmentation has emphasized statistical or other forms of racial and sexual discrimination (Dickens and Lang, 1985; Gordon, 1972). Sufficient evidence of such discrimination exists to raise the question as to why, contrary to the neoclassical expectation, it has not entirely eroded. We believe that one important reason involves "feedback effects" from discrimination to nonmarket behavior that create new discrimination before the "old regime of discrimination" has been eroded by competitive forces (see England and Farkas, 1986: Chap. 6 and 7; England and McCreary, 1987, for an elaboration.) Thus, discrimination provides at least one explanation of imperfect labor market sorting, and the associated persistence of structural effects.

However, discrimination alone cannot account for the full range of empirical findings. Numerous authors (Beck *et al.* 1978; Hodson, 1984; Hodson and England, 1986; Kalleberg *et al.*, 1981; Tolbert *et al.*, 1980) find industrial and firm effects on earnings net of controls for race, sex, or both. Thus, discrimination aside, we require an explanation of the finding of structural effects within race and sex groups (Coverman, 1986; Hodson and England, 1986). That is, we need to understand sluggish labor market mobility that exists for reasons other than discrimination.

One explanation of such limited mobility focuses on the costs of information. Workers are often unaware of the wage rates available elsewhere. Neoclassical economics long assumed perfect information and rationality. More recently, the assumption of perfect information has been modified. Building on the observation that information is costly to transmit or acquire (Stigler, 1961, 1962), "search theories" of employment see workers and employers making benefit-cost calculations regarding the dissemination and collection of labor market information (Lippman and McCall, 1976; Spence, 1974). This viewpoint implies more restricted mobility than would occur if information were costless. Further, mobility between low- and high-paying jobs sometimes entails the costs of geographical migration. These include the psychic costs of loss of attachment to community and kin.

In a related vein, sociologists have focused on how personal networks control access to job-related information and economic opportunity (Granovetter, 1974, 1985, see also Chapter 9, this volume). This perspective goes beyond search theory in seeing personal networks as more than merely mechanisms for transmitting information. Rather, such networks also control economic opportunity itself. They affect not just who knows which jobs are available, but also the loyalties and trust that determine who will in fact be offered such jobs. Thus, in Granovetter's (1985) phrase, economic activity is "embedded in local structures of social relations." This elucidates the way structures of social relations modify the assumption of "free mobility, contingent on information costs," which is central to the atomistic economic view.

Another limitation on the mobility of workers arises from the existence of firm-specific human capital, and associated implicit contracts and internal labor markets. Investment in firm-specific human capital (on-the-job training that is specific to the particular firm) limits the ability of employers to respond to a wage hike by replacing current workers with those possessing greater skill. That such investment leads to internal labor markets has long been recognized by institutionalist economists (Doeringer and Piore, 1971; Dunlop, 1958). However, related and expanded ideas have been more widely accepted among neoclassical economists under the rubric of "implicit contract theory," and "principal-agent theory" (England and Farkas, 1986; Farkas and England, 1985; Okun, 1981; Pratt and Zeckhauser, 1985; Stiglitz, 1984). Important here is the observation that employers may structure wage-experience profiles to depart from marginal revenue product profiles over the expected duration of worker tenure with the firm. That is, employers may pay workers less than their marginal revenue product in their early years, and more than this product in later years. (Empirical evidence in support of this view includes Lazear, 1979; Medoff and Abraham, 1980, 1981.) From the employer's perspective, low wages in the early years help recoup the costs of training, while higher wages in later years provide an incentive for effort at all experience levels, induce long time-horizon workers to self-select themselves into employment, and discourage already trained workers from quitting.

This view also profoundly undermines the older neoclassical view in which "market forces" constantly erode net wage differentials between sectors. For the world of implicit contracts and internal labor markets more nearly resembles one of lifetime employment. Consequently, the competitive forces that serve to sort workers by their general human capital operate at the single time-point of entry to a firm. It is at this point that employers offering greater lifetime earnings will be motivated to choose those workers with the greatest productive potential. This means that the competitive forces in labor markets are focused upon a few discrete moments within the individuals' job life cycle, those moments when they enter a firm. But when competitive forces operate only upon these discrete moments, they can no longer bear the weight of emphasis insisted upon within neoclassical theory. In combination, discrimination, search costs, personal networks, and the contractual features of internal labor markets explain the imperfect sorting of workers posited by structural sociologists.

VII. CONCLUSION

We have proposed a framework for understanding why characteristics of firms and industries affect employees' earnings, net of human capital. Many of the structural effects observed in past research can be interpreted to operate through employees' bargaining power and/or the profitability of their firms or industries. We have argued that employees' bargaining power is greater in the presence of unions (or a threat of unionization), less elastic labor demand, a threat of undetected and costly malfeasance or sabotage, and class consciousness. This bargaining power will be even more effective in more profitable firms and industries.

There is some evidence for all these contentions, although findings are sometimes equivocal. A number of hypothesized structural effects have been rejected owing to lack of significant coefficients in regression analyses that enter variables to many hypotheses at once. A better method of testing hypotheses would consider the causal order of variables implied by each hypothesis and would estimate the appropriate structural and reduced-form equations. Inappropriate controls for intervening variables have likely led to overpartialing in past research. Yet, taken as a whole, structural variables do appear to affect earnings, net of human capital.

We have also examined neoclassical economists' reasons for ignoring such structural effects. Their theory easily accommodates firms and industries that vary according to capital intensity, plant size, unionization, wages, or other characteristics. The theory assumes that employers prefer more productive workers even in low-skill jobs, and since workers prefer higher wages, there is a sorting process in which the better workers come to occupy the higher-paying jobs. This sorting should proceed until structural effects no longer exist net of human capital. Such sorting does occur to a certain extent, yet it is apparently not sufficient to completely erase the structural effects.

We suggested several explanations for the sluggishness of those labor market adjustments that could be expected to erode structural effects. These include feedback effects from market discrimination, information and other costs of job search, and informal networks of job contacts. We have also emphasized that mobility is limited because of the related features of internal labor market and implicit contracts which imply that all the competitive forces that should accomplish the sorting of workers by human capital have their effects concentrated at the points when employees enter firms rather than diffused continuously throughout the employment life cycle. This view suggests that labor markets are constantly in a state of moving disequilibrium, in which firm or industrial conditions create upward or downward wage pressures, which lead, at a slower rate, to worker re-sorting by human capital. Typically, this re-sorting is still incomplete when structural conditions shift again.

Disequilibrium is undoubtedly not limited to markets for labor. This raises the larger issue of what determines the distribution of structural job slots. That is, what determines the relative number of firms and industries at various points along distributions of characteristics that affect whether they will offer high or low wages? While interfirm and interindustry differences on these same characteristics are no anomaly for neoclassical theory, persistent firm and industry differences in economic profit rates *are* anomalous for neoclassical theory. If sectors with supranormal profits do persist for significant periods, we need to understand why product and capital market adjustments are too sluggish to fully erode them. Both sociologists and economists might profitably attend to the varied sources of persistent disequilibria. For economists, this requires greater attention to empirical evidence inconsistent with neoclassical theory. For sociologists, it requires an understanding of market forces that *would* erode structural effects were it not for the systemic features whose effects we seek to understand. Both fields would benefit from the development of a coherent structural theory that takes both market forces and disequilibria into account.

REFERENCES

Akerlof, George A. 1982. "Labor Contracts as Partial Gift Exchange." *Quarterly Journal of Economics* 87:543–569.

Akerlof, George A. 1984. "Gift Exchange and Efficiency Wages: Four Views." *American Economic Review* 74:79–83.

Arrow, Kenneth. 1972. "Models of Job Discrimination" and "Some Mathematical Models of Race in the Labor Market." Pp. 83–102 and pp. 187–204 in *Racial Discrimination in Economic Life*, edited by A. Pascal. Lexington, MA: D. C. Heath.

Averitt, Robert T. 1968. *The Dual Economy.* New York: McGraw-Hill.

Baron, James N., and William T. Bielby. 1980. "Bringing the Firm Back In: Stratification, Segmentation, and the Organization of Work." *American Sociological Review* 45:737–755.

Baumol, William J. 1982. "Contestable Markets: An Uprising in the Theory of Industry Structure." *American Economic Review* 72:1–15.

Baumol, William J., John C. Panzar, and Robert D. Willig. 1982. *Contestable Markets and the Theory of Industry Structure.* San Diego: Harcourt Brace Jovanovich.

Baumol, William J., John C. Panzar, and Robert D. Willig. 1986. "On the Theory of Perfectly Contestable Markets." Pp. 339–372 in *New Developments in the Analysis of Market Structure*, edited by J. E. Stiglitz and G. F. Mathewson. Cambridge, MA: M.I.T. Press.

Beck, E. M., Patrick M. Horan, and Charles M. Tolbert II. 1978. "Stratification in a Dual Economy." *American Sociological Review* 43:704–720.

Bluestone, Barry. 1974. *The Personal Income Distribution: Individual and Institutional Determinants.* Doctoral dissertation, Department of Economics, University of Michigan.

Bluestone, Barry, William M. Murphy, and Mary Stevenson. 1973. *Low Wages and the Working Poor.* Ann Arbor, MI: Institute of Labor and Industrial Relations.

Bulow, Jeremy I., and Lawrence H. Summers. 1986. "A Theory of Dual Labors Markets with Application to Industrial Policy, Discrimination, and Keynesian Unemployment." *Journal of Labor Economics* 4:376–414.

Cain, Glen G. 1976. "The Challenge of Segmented Labor Market Theories to Orthodox Theory: A Survey." *Journal of Economic Literature* 14:1215–1257.

Coverman, Shelly. 1986. "Segmentation and Sex Differences in Earnings." Pp. 139–172 in *Research in Social Stratification and Mobility,* edited by Robert V. Robinson. Greenwich, CT: JAI Press.

Dalton, James A., and E. J. Ford. 1977. "Concentration and Labor Earnings in Manufacturing and Utilities." *Industrial and Labor Relations Review* 31:45–60.

Dickens, William T. 1986. "Wages, Employment, and the Threat of Collective Action by Workers." National Bureau of Economic Research, Working Paper No. 1856, Cambridge, MA.

Dickens, William T., and Kevin Lang. 1985. "A Test of Dual Labor Market Theory." *American Economic Review* 75:792–805.

Doeringer, Peter, and Michael Piore. 1971. *Internal Labor Markets and Manpower Analysis.* Lexington, MA: D. C. Heath.

Dunlop, John T. 1958. *Industrial Relations Systems.* New York: Holt, Rinehart & Winston.

Edwards, Richard C. 1975. *Contested Terrain.* New York: Basic Books.

Ehrenberg, Ronald. 1979. *The Regulatory Process and Labor Earnings.* New York: Academic Press.

England, Paula, and George Farkas. 1986. *Households, Employment, and Gender: A Social, Economic, and Demographic View.* New York: Aldine.

England, Paula, and Lori McCreary. 1987. "Gender Inequality in Paid Employment." Pp. 286–320 in *Analyzing Gender,* edited by B. Hess and M. Ferree. Beverly Hills: Sage.

Farkas, George, and Paula England. 1985. "Integrating the Sociology and Economics of Employment, Compensation, and Unemployment." Pp. 119–146 in *Research in the Sociology of Work,* vol. 3, edited by Richard Simpson and Ida Harper Simpson. Greenwich, CT: JAI Press.

Flanagan, Robert J., Robert S. Smith, and Ronald G. Ehrenberg. 1984. *Labor Economics and Labor Relations.* Glenview, IL.: Scott, Foresman.

Freeman, Richard B., and James L. Medoff. 1984. *What Do Unions Do?* New York: Basic Books.

Gordon, David M. 1972. *Theories of Poverty and Unemployment.* Lexington, MA: D. C. Heath.

Granovetter, Mark. 1974. *Getting a Job.* Cambridge, MA: Harvard University Press.

Granovetter, Mark. 1985. "Economic Action and Social Structure: The Problem of Embeddedness." *American Journal of Sociology* 91:481–510.

Hicks, John R. 1966. *The Theory of Wages,* 2nd ed. New York: St. Martin's Press.

Hirshleifer, Jack. 1984. *Price. Theory and Applications.* Englewood Cliffs, NJ: Prentice-Hall.

Hodson, Randy. 1978. "Labor in the Monopoly, Competitive and State Sectors of Production." *Politics and Society* 8:429–480.

Hodson, Randy. 1983. *Worker's Earnings and Corporate Economic Structure.* New York: Academic Press.

Hodson, Randy. 1984. "Companies, Industries, and the Measurement of Economic Segmentation." *American Sociological Review* 49:335–348.

Hodson, Randy, and Paula England. 1986. "Industrial Structure and Sex Differences in Earnings." *Industrial Relations* 25:16–32.

Hodson, Randy, and Robert L. Kaufman. 1982. "Economic Dualism: A Critical Review." *American Sociological Review* 47:727–739.

Kalleberg, Arne, Michael Wallace, and Robert Althauser. 1981. "Economic Segmentation, Worker Power, and Income Inequality." *American Journal of Sociology* 87:651–683.

Katz, Lawrence. 1986. "Efficiency Wage Theories: A Partial Evaluation." In *Macroeconomic Annual.* Cambridge, MA: National Bureau of Economic Research.

Kwoka, John E. 1983. "Monopoly, Plant, and Union Effects on Worker Wages." *Industrial and Labor Relations Review* 36:251–257.

Lazear, Edward. 1979. "Why is there Mandatory Retirement?" *Journal of Political Economy* 87:1261–1284.

Lewis, H. G. 1963. *Unionism and Relative Wages in the United States*. Chicago: University of Chicago Press.

Lippman, Steven, and John J. McCall. 1976. "The Economics of Job Search: A Survey." *Economic Inquiry* 14:155–189.

Long, J. E., and Link, A. N. 1983. "The Impact of Market Structure on Wages, Fringe Benefits, and Turnover." *Industrial and Labor Relations Review* 36:239–50.

Marshall, Alfred. 1923. *Principles of Economics*, 8th ed. London: Macmillan.

Medoff, James, and Katherine Abraham. 1980. "Experience, Performance, and Earnings." *Quarterly Journal of Economics* 95:703–736.

Medoff, James, and Katherine Abraham. 1981. "Are Those Paid More Really More Productive? The Case of Experience." *Journal of Human Resources* 16:186–216.

Mellow, W. 1982. "Employer Size and Wages." *Research in Economics and Statistics* 64:495–501.

Okun, Arthur. 1981. *Prices and Quantities: A Macroeconomic Analysis*. Washington, D.C.: Brookings.

Pugel, T. 1980. "Profitability, Concentration and the Interindustry Variation in Wages." *Review of Economics and Statistics* 62:248–253.

Pratt, John W., and Richard J. Zeckhauser. 1985. *Principals and Agents: The Structure of Business*. Boston: Harvard Business School Press.

Scherer, F. M. 1980. *Industrial Market Structure and Economic Performance*, rev. ed. Chicago: Rand McNally.

Shepherd, William. 1970. *Market Power and Economic Welfare*. New York: Random House.

Shepherd, William. 1979. *The Economics of Industrial Organization*. Englewood Cliffs, NJ: Prentice-Hall.

Spence, A. Michael. 1974. *Market Signaling*. Cambridge, MA: Harvard University Press.

Stigler, George. 1961. "The Economics of Information." *Journal of Political Economy* 69:213–225.

Stigler, George. 1962. "Information in the Labor Market." *Journal of Political Economy* 70, Suppl. 70.

Stiglitz, Joseph. 1984. "Theories of Wage Rigidity." National Bureau of Economic Research Working Paper No. 1442, Cambridge, MA.

Tolbert, Charles. 1980. *Occupational Mobility in a Dual Economy*. Doctoral dissertation, Department of Sociology, University of Georgia.

Tolbert, Charles. 1982. "Industrial Segmentation and Men's Career Mobility." *American Sociological Review* 47 (August):457–477.

Tolbert, Charles, II, Patrick Horan, and E. M. Beck. 1980. "The Structure of Economic Segmentation: A Dual Economy Approach." *American Journal of Sociology* 85:1095–1116.

Vietorisz, T., and B. Harrison. 1970. *The Economic Development of Harlem*. New York: Praeger.

Weiss, Leonard W. 1966. "Concentration and Labor Earnings." *American Economic Review* 56:96–117.

Weiss, Leonard W. 1974. "The Concentration-Profits Relationship and Antitrust." Pp. 201–220 in *Industrial Concentration*, edited by H. Goldschmidt, H. Michael Mann, and J. Fred Weston. Boston: Little, Brown.

Zucker, Lynne G., and Carolyn Rosenstein. 1981. "Taxonomies of Institutional Structure: Dual Economy Reconsidered." *American Sociological Review* 46:869–884.

6

Schooling and Capitalism
The Effect of Urban Economic Structure on the Value of Education

E. M. Beck and Glenna S. Colclough

I. INTRODUCTION

Given the assumption that industrial capitalism relies on "achievement" criteria to rationally allocate workers to jobs, there exists a fundamental belief in the American ideology of education—the notion that schooling is the key to occupational and financial success. This belief is evidenced by individuals when in ever-growing numbers they "invest" in higher education, and by public policies that seek to control poverty and other social ills by increasing access to education and training programs. This belief constitutes the essence of an implied social contract between the economic and educational institutions in American society. The experience of the past decades has shown, however, that these promised payoffs to schooling are neither guaranteed, homogeneous, nor universal.

Research has documented repeatedly that the dollar value of education depends, in part, on the labor supply characteristics of workers such as their age, gender, race, and social class (Blau and Ferber, 1986; Geschwender, 1978; Wright, 1978). However, it is becoming equally clear that the value of this implied social contract is affected not only by labor supply factors but, perhaps more importantly, by the organization of production of commodities and services.

This research explores this relationship by demonstrating that (1) the economic value of schooling varies across large urban economies in the

E. M. Beck • Department of Sociology, University of Georgia, Athens, Georgia 30602.   Glenna S. Colclough • Department of Sociology, University of Alabama-Huntsville, Huntsville, Alabama 35899.

United States, (2) supply- and demand-side factors of the organization of production within these economies affect the value of education,[1] and (3) the effects of the urban economy on schooling are not homogeneous across race and gender classes of labor. Thus, we show that the value of the schooling-reward contract is conditioned by specific configurations of the organization of production within major urban economies.

II. THE LINKAGE BETWEEN EDUCATION AND CAPITALISM

The historical relationship of education and economic institutions in this country has been interpreted in a variety of ways. A recent approach by revisionist historians proposes that the educational reform movement in America evolved in response to the changing needs of a developing capitalist economy (Bowles and Gintis, 1976; Katz, 1973; Spring, 1972). According to this view, the system of education was initiated to assimilate a cultural and behaviorally diverse population to meet labor shortages in the expanding industrial economy of the 19th century. Revisionists argue that by the early 20th-century education was being shaped and guided by professional educators and spokesmen of the business community whose views mirrored the interests of the owners and managers of capital wealth. As schools served the needs of the factory system of commodity production, they became increasingly like factories themselves for sorting, molding, and refining the next generation's labor force to fit the skill and attitudinal requirements of the evolving industrial order. The organizational similarities between the structure of education and the factory system of production were accompanied by a functional relationship between the industrial order and schooling processes (Bowles and Gintis, 1976).

Early 20th-century transformations of the organization of production produced dramatic changes in the mix of jobs in the technical division of labor; new jobs were created, old ones were modified, and others became obsolete. Since education is one of the mechanisms for screening and allocating labor into slots in this distribution, transforming the mix of jobs shifted the demand for differing types of education. The proliferation of a wide variety of higher educational institutions, as well as the growth of differentiated curricular programs in secondary schools, represents an attempt by American education to meet this changing demand for skills.

Though the linkage between education and economic institutions is accepted widely by varying schools of thought in the social sciences, theorists disagree on what exactly schooling provides for entrants into the labor market. Traditional theories, such as human capital approaches in economics and structural-functionalist schools in sociology, argue that schooling conveys skills and knowledge that are offered in the labor market in return for wages.

---

[1]Throughout this chapter we use the terms *demand* and *supply* in a nontechnical sense as loose handles for categories of variables affecting labor market earnings.

More skeptical theorists, such as Lester Thurow (1972), argue that when making hiring decisions, employers use education as a screening device to indicate the "trainability" of potential employees. Thus, employers are purchasing the potential for learning, rather than learning itself.

Clearly, though, stronger educational credentials have become an increasingly necessary ticket for admission into the arena where privileged positions within the technical division of labor are awarded, and the lack of such credentials poses a formidable barrier restricting access to that market arena. Whether these credentials represent needed training for new jobs or jobs whose skills have been upgraded (Bell, 1973), or increasingly higher credentials are demanded by employers to maintain class inequalities among a more well-educated public (Collins, 1977), is a debatable point. However, it has become clear that higher education is a prerequisite for economic success, though it certainly does not ensure it.

The allocation of higher educational credentials demonstrates another linkage between economic and educational systems in American society. Like commodities and services that are distributed through economic markets, educational credentials are for the most part allocated through economic markets as well. Beyond secondary school, in this country, access to higher education is a privilege—not a guaranteed right. To a certain extent, this privilege is based on various measures of academic merit, but more fundamentally such opportunities rest on economic and cultural capital. These constraints serve not only to stratify those who can go to college from those who cannot but also to stratify students according to the type, quality, and prestige of the institution they attend. Finally, through labor markets the value of educational credentials are assigned. However, this value is a product not only of the stratified supply of labor but also of the differentiated demand for labor. Such differentiation can be understood as resulting from the uneven development of American capitalist economy.

A. Uneven Development of Urban Economies

Industrial capitalism has not developed linearly nor at a uniform rate (Castells, 1980; Gordon, Edwards, and Reich, 1982; Smith, 1984; Sweezy, 1972). Different stages of capitalist development have required varying mixes of the factors of production and varying strategies for maintaining control over the labor process (Smith, 1984). The culmination of this uneven rate of economic progression has been the creation of advancing and lagging local economies that are characterized by visible differences in their organization of production, and in the structure and composition of their labor force (Noyelle, 1983; Perry and Watkins, 1982; Scott and Storper, 1986; Watkins and Perry, 1977).

This lack of geographically uniform development is viewed by neoclassical economists as a transitional imbalance resulting from regional differences in the costs of the factors of production that, in the long run, would be expected to be reduced through the mobility of capital and labor. On the other hand, uneven development as described by radical economists and Marxists is seen as a structural, not transitional, feature of industrial capitalism, and may even be a necessary condition for capitalism's continued existence (Markusen, 1980; Scott and Storper, 1986). Whether this uneven development is slowly frictional or structural, regional differences in the organization of production are clearly apparent and persistent even in our advanced capitalist economy.

Gordon (1978), Harvey (1973), and Thompson (1965) have noted that the historical growth and organization of urban economies has been intimately linked to, and dependent upon, the overall development of industrial capitalism in the United States. Empirically, the early research of Aurousseau (1921), Duncan and Reiss (1956), Harris (1943), McKenzie (1933), and Ogburn (1937), as well as the more contemporary work of Berry and Kasarda (1977) and Hadden and Borgatta (1965), convincingly documents city differences in the structure of production. This intercity variation can be seen as but a fragment of the more general trend of the "uneven" development of modern capitalism.

B. Uneven Development and the Value of Schooling

Given the various linkages between education and the economy elaborated above, we believe that the value of schooling is also linked to the uneven development of advanced capitalism. If the staggered growth of capitalism produces advancing and lagging urban economies, and if there is a correspondence between the functional organization of capitalism and the demand for schooling, as we argue, it would follow that the value of schooling will vary among local economies owing to regional differences in their organization of production. Indeed, Hanushek's (1973) investigation of regions in the United States, Harrison's (1972) analysis of intercity employment, and Fossett and Galle's (1980) analysis of large urban areas in America lend credence to this broad thesis and make further empirical investigation worth pursuing.[2]

While this research is largely exploratory, previous research provides some general expectations for our findings. For example, segmentation literature has shown that returns to schooling (at least for white males) are greater in "core" rather than in "peripheral" industries, suggesting that economies dominated with "core-type" characteristics—industries with large assets and profits, capital-intensive, oligopolistic product-markets—may enhance the value of schooling for this group. Though the characteristics of economies are measured on the level of industry, the job structures that derive from the industrial base should produce differences in the value of schooling by gender, if not race as well, because these structures are highly segregated by

---

[2]While these analyses are enlightening and suggestive, they cannot be taken as conclusive because of limited regional variation, restrictive definitions of the organization of production, and incompletely specified theoretical models.

gender and race. Low-wage jobs in labor markets that to a degree correspond to "periphery" industrial sectors are often filled by women and other minority workers, thus likely producing lower values of education of these groups. The state sector has been very important in providing employment opportunities for minorities; thus, the presence of this sector should enhance the value of schooling for such groups. Finally, the "labor queue" approach supports the notion of variation in the value of schooling as a result of labor demand and supply characteristics. The effects of these and other aspects of urban economies on the value of schooling are to be explored in the analysis.

III. THE VALUE OF SCHOOLING: DEFINITION AND MEASUREMENT[3]

There is a well-established empirical association between the years of schooling completed and annual earnings, both in time series and cross-sectional research, and in both aggregate and microlevel analyses. This correlation does not, however, reflect a simple causal process even within homogeneous classes of labor, but one in which education has played a critical role in affecting a host of intervening factors, which in turn affect the pecuniary rewards from participation in the marketplace. As illustrated in Figure 1, schooling has been shown to affect the degree of labor force attachment and employability, job placement and work performance, the opportunities for promotion, risks of unemployment, attitudes and values toward work and supervision, as well as entering into the wage-setting process itself (Haveman and Wolfe, 1984).

As the model in Figure 1 suggests, to gain a full understanding of how schooling affects earnings, and hence to determine the value of schooling itself, investigations would explore all of the subtle, as well as obvious, ways by which schooling influences the mechanisms determining the allocation of labor income. Such a comprehensive and detailed endeavor is, however, beyond the scope of this analysis and may be well beyond the purview of any single piece of research. Yet while we will not identify and estimate each of the separate direct and indirect linkages by which schooling affects income from labor, we can estimate the *overall* value of schooling, net of age-related factors, by taking advantage of an expanded variant of the microlevel earnings equation proposed by Rosenzweig (1976).

In this model a worker's annual earnings is expressed as an exponential function of the linear and quadratic effects of schooling and age, and their

[3]Our definition of the "value" of schooling is restricted to the annual earnings value of education. This definition does not consider the value of schooling in terms of lifetime earnings; neither does it consider nonearnings pecuniary rewards such as having an attractive fringe benefit bundle, nor does it consider nonpecuniary job payoffs such as working conditions or prestige. And finally, it does not include the host of nonmarket payoffs to schooling. (See Haveman and Wolfe, 1984, for a discussion of the broader value of education in American society.)

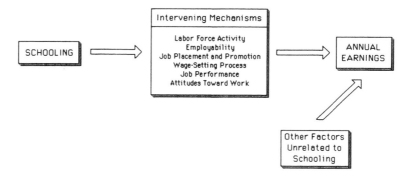

Figure 1. Effect of schooling on earnings within a local economy.

linear and quadratic interactions. This specification is attractive because it allows for (1) a nonlinear earnings-age profile, (2) a nonlinear effect of schooling on earnings, and (3) by including the age–schooling interaction terms, for the value of education to be contingent upon the age of the worker, a cohort effect. Expressing this worker-level earnings specification in its log-linear form, we have

$$\text{Ln EARNINGS}_i = \beta_0 + \beta_1 \text{SCH}_i + \beta_2 \text{AGE}_i + \beta_3 \text{SCH}_i^2 + \beta_4 \text{AGE}_i^2 \\ + \beta_5(\text{SCH}_i \times \text{AGE}_i) + \beta_6(\text{SCH}_i \times \text{AGE}_i)^2 + u_i \quad (1)$$

where SCH_i and AGE_i are the years of schooling and age of the ith worker, and u_i is a random disturbance.[4]

Given this specification the *overall value of schooling can be defined as the partial derivative of earnings (log) with respect to schooling* because this represents the amount of change in earnings (log) expected given change in schooling attainment:

$$\text{VALUE} = \partial(\text{Ln EARNINGS})/\partial(\text{SCH}) \\ = \beta_1 + 2\beta_3\text{SCH} + \beta_5\text{AGE} + 2\beta_6(\text{SCH} \times \text{AGE}^2) \quad (2)$$

This partial derivative shows that the "value" of schooling is a function not only of the coefficients of the earnings determination equation [1] but also of the levels of schooling and age themselves. That is, the adopted specification [1], and consequently its partial derivative [2], permits the value of education to vary by the age of the worker as well as by the level of schooling attained. As a result of this theoretical specification, it is necessary to specify at what particular age and level of schooling the partial derivative [2] is to be evaluated in order to obtain a single estimate of the value of schooling. Once

---

[4]This model can be considered the reduced-form of a vastly more complex model in which schooling is exogenous to the various intervening mechanisms producing labor income, as illustrated in Figure 1.

these are set, the value of education can be obtained by estimating the earnings determination model [1], substituting the appropriate coefficients into Eq. [2], and solving for the value of education at the predetermined levels of schooling and age. Conceptually, this value represents the *total effect* of schooling on earnings, not separating out the many ways in which schooling affects earnings, as shown in Figure 1.[5] Empirically, this specification of value of schooling denotes a *percentage* return to education, and not the dollar return.

Allowing for variation in age and schooling levels is important for several reasons. First, the age and schooling structures of urban areas are not always homogeneous. For example, high-growth "boomtowns" may attract high numbers of younger well-educated workers, while declining areas may age as younger workers with less investment in the community relocate elsewhere. On a microlevel, these variations are important, as well. The importance of education has been shown to diminish over the employment experience of individuals. Also the value of one year of high school, for example, is not the same as for one year of college, and these values may vary from one cohort to another.

If Eq. [1] is estimated and Eq. [2] evaluated within multiple urban economies differing in their organization of production, estimates of the value of education under varying conditions of urban economic structure will be obtained. Once these estimates are derived, the "value" of schooling can be expressed as a function of a set of aggregate indicator variables capturing both the demand and supply sides of the organization of production of the urban economy:

$$\text{VALUE}_i^{jk} = \pi_0^{jk} + \sum_{r=1} \pi_{1r}^{jk} \text{DEMAND}_{ir} + \sum_{s=1} \pi_{2s}^{jk} \text{SUPPLY}_{is} + e_i^{jk} \tag{3}$$

where VALUE_i^{jk} is the estimated value of schooling for workers in the ith urban economy evaluated at the jth level of schooling and kth age, DEMAND_{ir} is the rth demand-side dimension of the organization of production in the ith economy, SUPPLY_{is} is the sth supply-side component of the ith urban area, and e_i^{jk} is a random disturbance.[6] The π^{jk}'s are effect parameters to be estimated.

It is these π parameters that are of major interest because each reflects the relative influence of a structural factor on the *overall* value of schooling, when that schooling is evaluated at the predetermined levels of education and age. If the value of schooling is independent of the structure of the urban economy, the parameters of Eq. [3] will be statistically insignificant. On the other hand, if the null hypothesis that $\pi_{r,s} = 0$ can be rejected, there will be evi-

[5]Defining the value of schooling, based on a micro-level earnings model where the direct effects of schooling were determined, was also attempted. Results from such a model proved far too complex to draw meaningful conclusions.

[6]We assume that the random disturbance in Eq. [3] is linearly independent of the disturbance term in Eq. [1].

dence that the organization of the urban economy affects the value of schooling and mediates the implied social contract specifying the payoffs to education.

In sum, in order to investigate the relationship between the structure of the urban economy and the value of schooling, a three-step procedure is necessary: (1) estimate the microlevel earnings, Eq. [1], within each urban economy, (2) substitute the estimated coefficients into the partial derivative, Eq. [2], thereby obtaining an estimate of the value of schooling within each urban economy, and finally, (3) employ these computed values of education as the dependent variable in a regression model expressing the value of schooling as a function of the "demand" and "supply" sides of the urban economy (see Figure 2 and Eq. [3]).

To estimate the value of schooling within each urban economy we use data from the 1976 Bureau of the Census Survey of Income and Education (SIE). In content and structure the SIE survey instrument is similar to the March Supplement of the Current Population Survey, with detailed labor force participation, employment, and earnings data being collected for the 1975 calendar year. The SIE contains the necessary geographical codes that allow for the selection of workers within 119 uniquely identifiable Standard Metropolitan Statistical Areas (SMSAs). From these urban areas we selected persons who were 18 years old or older in 1975 and who were employed full time or part time in a civilian job in 1975, or those who were not working in 1975 but were looking for employment and who had been employed in a civilian job lasting two weeks or more in the period 1971–1975. After other nonwhite minorities were eliminated, 79,971 observations remained: 40,719 white males, 30,073 white females, 4,531 black males, and 4,648 black females. During preliminary analyses it was found that statistical results for the black females were unstable and characterized by marked outliers; for this reason black females were deleted from our analyses and we report only the results for black males, white females, and white males.

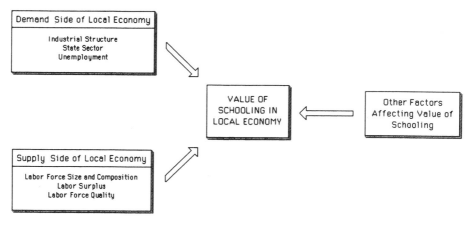

Figure 2. Determinants of the value of schooling within a local economy.

Table 1. Intercity Dispersion in the Value of Schooling (Interquartile Range)

Class of labor	Schooling evaluated at	Age evaluated at (years)				
		25	30	35	40	45
White males[a]	8 years	0.1509	0.1137	0.0831	0.0849	0.0783
	12 years	0.0738	0.0613	0.0544	0.0451	0.0450
	16 years	0.0890	0.0931	0.0851	0.0836	0.0781
Black males[b]	8 years	0.3654	0.2746	0.2575	0.1769	0.1154
	12 years	0.2096	0.1569	0.1343	0.1093	0.1449
	16 years	0.3313	0.2802	0.2651	0.2325	0.2621
White females[c]	8 years	0.2318	0.1963	0.1753	0.1572	0.1477
	12 years	0.1152	0.0928	0.0922	0.0756	0.0718
	16 years	0.1712	0.1721	0.2104	0.1933	0.1828

[a]Based on 119 urban economies.
[b]Based on 76 urban economies.
[c]Based on 119 urban economies.

These remaining 75,323 observations were grouped by SMSA, and the earnings determination equation, Eq. [1], was estimated separately by SMSA for each of the three race-gender classes of labor, using least squares with the appropriate SIE sampling weights.[7] Next, within each SMSA the value of schooling was computed by substituting the appropriate SMSA-specific coefficients into Eq. [2]. We chose to evaluate Eq. [2] at five different ages (25, 30, 35, 40, and 45 years) and three levels of schooling (8, 12, and 16 years) so we could explore the possibility that the effects of urban economies differ depending upon worker's age and educational credentials. By following these procedures we were thus able to obtain estimates of the value of schooling at the elementary, high school, and college levels for typical workers 25 to 45 years old within each of the SMSA-level urban economies. The results of this step in the analyses are summarized in Table 1.

Table 1 contains descriptive measures of interurban variation in the value of schooling. The entry in each cell of Table 1 is the interquartile range of the value of schooling computed across the urban economies for workers differing in race, gender, age, and educational attainment. The data summarized in Table 1 suggest three conclusions. First, there tends to be greater intercity variation in the value of schooling for younger workers than for older ones. Second, there is a characteristic U-shaped curve showing greater intercity variation in the value of schooling for those with either above-average or below-average levels of education.[8] And last, the value of schooling has greater intercity variation for black than for white workers, and greater variation

---

[7]For white workers there were sufficient number of sample observations to estimate the earnings equation, Eq.[1], within all 119 urban economies. Unfortunately, 43 SMSAs did not contain a sufficient number of black males for estimation. Thus, for white male and female labor, initial analysis was based on 119 urban economies, while for black males, initial analysis was based on 76 urban economies. A listing of all urban economies included in this study is available from the first author.

for female than for male labor. Put another way, *the value of education for white male workers is more homogeneously uniform across urban economies than is the value of schooling for black males or white females. Yet even for white males, there is considerable variation in the value of schooling from one urban economy to another across the United States.*[9]

IV. THE STRUCTURE OF URBAN ECONOMIES: DEFINITION AND MEASUREMENT

A variety of simplifying schemes have been proposed for defining the socioeconomic organization of urban areas. Much early ecological research sought to develop a taxonomy of city types based on the functional specialization of the ecological community. The work of Aurousseau (1921), Bean, Poston, and Winsborough, (1972), Duncan and Reiss (1956), Harris (1943), McKenzie (1933), and Ogburn (1937) falls into this category. Recently taxonomical approaches have fallen into disfavor in preference to single-indicator measures of industrial structure. The proportion of the urban labor force

---

[8]Median schooling completed for all race-gender classes of labor was 12 years.

[9]To establish that the value of schooling varies among urban economies, a necessary condition to make subsequent analysis meaningful, we first estimated a model in which annual earnings (log) is expressed as a nonlinear function of schooling, age, urban community, and their interactions:

$$Ln\ Earnings_{ij} = \beta_0 + \Sigma\beta_{1j}SMSA_{ij} + \beta_2SCH_{ij} + \beta_3AGE_{ij} + \beta_4SCH_{ij}^2 + \beta_5AGE_{ij}^2$$
$$+ \beta_6(SCH_{ij} \times AGE_{ij}) + \beta_7(SCH_{ij} \times AGE_{ij})^2 + u_{ij} \tag{1a}$$

where $SMSA_{ij}$ is a binary variable indicating that the ith worker is located in the jth urban economy. This specification allows each urban area to have a different mean level of earnings (log) but constrains the effects of schooling and age to be constant across urban areas.

Next we estimated a less restrictive model in which the linear and quadratic terms for schooling, and the schooling–age interactions, may vary among the urban economies, i.e.,

$$Ln\ Earnings_{ij} = \beta_0 + \Sigma\beta_{1j}SMSA_{ij} + \beta_2SCH_{ij} + \beta_3AGE_{ij} + \beta_4SCH_{ij}^2 + \beta_5AGE_{ij}^2$$
$$+ \beta_6(SCH_{ij} \times AGE_{ij}) + \beta_7(SCH_{ij} \times AGE_{ij})^2$$
$$+ \Sigma\beta_{8j}(SCH_{ij} \times SMSA_{ij}) + \Sigma\beta_{9j}(SCH_{ij}^2 \times SMSA_{ij})$$
$$+ \Sigma\beta_{10j}(SCH_{ij} \times AGE_{ij} \times SMSA_{ij})$$
$$+ \Sigma\beta_{11j}(SCH_{ij}^2 \times AGE_{ij}^2 \times SMSA_{ij}) + u_{ij} \tag{2a}$$

This model relaxes some of the constraints present in model [1a] by permitting the value of schooling to vary among the urban places. If the value of schooling does *not* vary by urban area, model [2a] will not produce a significant increase in goodness-of-fit relative to model [1a], and the interaction terms involving the urban areas in model [2a] will be statistically zero.

Table 2 presents the results of contrasting models [1a] and [2a] for white male, white female, and black male labor. These F ratios demonstrate that model [2a] produces a statistically significant increase in goodness-of-fit over model [1a], and all except one of the interaction terms involving schooling and the urban areas are statistically different from zero for these subgroups of urban workers. These F ratios provide empirical evidence that the value of schooling does vary among the urban economies in this study.

Table 2.   *F* Ratios for Models [1a] and [2a]

Interactions with urban area	White		Black males
	Males	Females	
Contrasting models [1a] and [2a][a]	2.84[c]	1.58[c]	1.54[c]
Specific Interaction terms[b]			
Schooling × SMSA	3.45[c]	1.39[c]	1.62[c]
Schooling² × SMSA	2.45[c]	1.81[c]	1.09
Schooling × Age × SMSA	2.63[c]	1.66[c]	1.98[c]
Schooling² × Age² × SMSA	2.85[c]	1.47[c]	1.49[c]

[a]Tests null hypothesis that model [2a] fits the data no better than model [1a].
[b]Tests null hypothesis that the specific interaction term is zero.
[c]Statistically significant at the 0.01 level.

employed in manufacturing has been very widely used (e.g., Betz, 1972; Fossett and Galle, 1980; Jiobu and Marshall, 1971). The percent of employment in oligopolistic industries (e.g., Bloomquist and Summers, 1982) and similarly employment in the "core" sector of the economy (e.g., Bibb, 1982) have been proposed as relevant measures. Parcel (1979) adopts average wages in manufacturing as her indicator of structure, while others have even used city size as an implicit proxy for a host of other characteristics (e.g., Lane 1968; Mueller, 1974).

Rather than adopt either the taxonomical approach or one of the single-indicator tactics, we view the structure of urban production as being composed of multiple components, a strategy similar to that employed by Horan and Tolbert (1984), Parcel and Mueller (1983), and others. Although there is little consensus as to the number of such components of urban economic structure, it is important to consider elements of both demand and supply sides of the urban economy.

On the demand side we chose indicators of the size of the urban economy's capital market, the importance of the service sector, the extent of oligopolistic concentration, the penetration of the labor market by the state sector, and local demand for labor.

Through the use of industrial data published by the Bureau of the Census, the Bureau of Labor Statistics, and the Internal Revenue Service, eight indicators of structure were selected initially (see Table 3) and analyzed using an iterated principal factors model.[10] That analysis suggested that the indicators could be reduced to four factors with eigenvalues of sufficient magnitude to justify inclusion. An oblique (promax) rotation produced four clearly iden-

[10]The dimensionality of the data could have been reduced through principal components analysis, a common procedure for eliminating collinearity among a set of redundant regressors. While such a procedure will yield orthogonal components, it factors the total variance among the regressors and may not produce conceptually meaningful solutions. For the problem presented here, iterated principal factors analysis is to be prefered.

Table 3. Definitions of Variables Used in Factor Analysis

Variable	Definition
Labor demand	Mean weeks of unemployment for the Experienced Civilian Labor Force (ECLF). Source: estmated from the SIE
Business size	Weighted average industry assets for corporations and partnerships. Source: Internal Revenue Service
Business profits	Weighted average industry net income of corporations, partnerships, and proprietorships. Source: Internal Revenue Service
Rate of profit	Weighted average profits per dollar of sales for corporations, partnerships, and proprietorships. Source: Internal Revenue Service
Capital to labor	Weighted average industry ratio of total assets to total employee compensation for corporations and partnerships. Source: Bureau of Economic Analysis and Internal Revenue Service
Oligopoly power	Weighted average 4-firm sales concentration ratio for nonagricultural profit-making industries. Source: Shepherd, 1969
Product-demand sensitivity	Weighted average percent of industry workers who were employed less than full time year-round. Source: Bureau of Labor Statistics
Business activity	Weighted average industry dollar sales. Source: Internal Revenue Service

tifiable and conceptually meaningful components of urban production: (1) ratio of capital to labor—a measure that reflects primarily the size of the local banking and financial sector, the capital market; (2) business sales activity—an indicator of the size of the local sales service sector; (3) oligopoly concentration—a measure strongly correlated with the extent of durable manufacturing in the local economy; and (4) business profitability—a measure that is most positively associated with the size of the professional service sector.[11] In addition to these variables, we also included a measure of the relative influence of the state as an employer within the urban economy as a demand-side factor. O'Connor (1973) has stressed the importance of the state in organizing and structuring market activities, and others have noted the importance of the state sector especially in providing opportunities for minorities.

To assess the supply side of the urban economy, five indicators were chosen: (1) labor force size, in log form; (2) minority representation in the labor force; (3) average schooling completed, a measure of labor force quality; (4) aggregate labor surplus; and (5) the average price of all labor in the urban work force.[12] The measures of these indicators are presented in Table 4.

And finally, to complete the model we included a binary variable indicat-

---

[11]The four components are correlated, but their redundancy is not so strong as to preclude meaningful interpretation. The strongest correlation (−0.379) is between the components of oligopoly power and business sales volume. There is a modest correlation between business volume and capital intensity (0.293) and between business volume and labor demand (−0.242).

[12]Izraeli (1983) has shown that the cost of living affects the returns to education. By using the median hourly wage of the urban economy's work force as a rough proxy for the cost of living, we will be controlling for this factor in our analyses.

Table 4. Definitions of Labor Force Variables

SMSA variable	Definition
Labor force size	Log of the number of workers in the experienced civilian labor force (ECLF). *Source:* estimated from the SIE
Minority composition	Percent of the ECLF in that is black or Spanish-speaking. *Source:* estimated from the SIE
Labor force quality	Mean years of schooling completed by the ECLF. *Source:* estimated from the SIE
Labor surplus	Mean weeks not in the labor force for the ECLF. *Source:* estimated from the SIE
Price of labor	Median imputed hourly wages of the ECLF. *Source:* estimated from the SIE
State sector	Percent of the ECLF employed in local, state, or federal government. *Source:* estimated from the SIE
Located in the South	Binary variable scored unity if the SMSA was located in Alabama, Florida, Georgia, Kentucky, Louisiana, Mississippi, North Carolina, South Carolina, Tennessee, Texas, or Virginia

ing whether the urban economy is located in the South.[13] This is to capture any salient effects due to the South's historically unique position within the evolution of the structure of production in the United States, and does not represent either a clearly demand-side or supply-side factor of the urban economy.

V. EFFECTS OF THE URBAN ECONOMY ON THE VALUE OF SCHOOLING

To determine whether the structure of the urban economy affects the value of schooling, we estimated, using a Weighted Least Squares solution, the multiple correlation between supply- and demand-side variables and the value of schooling at three different levels of education (8, 12, and 16 years) and at five different ages of workers (25, 30, 35, 40, and 45 years).[14] The

[13]The "South" included SMSAs in Alabama, Florida, Georgia, Kentucky, Louisiana, Mississippi, North Carolina, South Carolina, Tennessee, Texas, and Virginia.

[14]These multiple correlations were obtained by regressing the estimated value of schooling on the supply- and demand-side urban economy variables. The regressions were estimated by Weighted Least Squares where the weight is the reciprocal of the Mean Square Error (MSE) for the within-urban area worker-level regression; that is, the weight factor associated with the jth urban economy is

$$W_j = 1/(MSE_j)$$

where MSE_j is the Mean Square Error from the worker-level earnings regression, Eq.[1], estimated within the jth urban economy. The effect of this weighting is to reduce the importance of those urban economies in which the worker-level earnings regression is estimated with large error.

Table 5.   Multiple Correlations between Structure of Urban Economy
and Value of Schooling (Adjusted for Degrees of Freedom)[a]

Class of labor	Schooling evaluated at	Age evaluated at (years)				
		25	30	35	40	45
White male[b]	8 years	0.000	0.000	0.000	0.000	0.000
	12 years	0.117	0.259[e]	0.328[f]	0.309[f]	0.203
	16 years	0.397[g]	0.439[g]	0.448[g]	0.415[g]	0.300[f]
Black male[c]	8 years	0.582[g]	0.532[g]	0.431[f]	0.265	0.000
	12 years	0.420[f]	0.371[f]	0.213	0.088	0.265
	16 years	0.644[g]	0.618[g]	0.436[f]	0.221	0.240
White female[d]	8 years	0.000	0.000	0.000	0.000	0.000
	12 years	0.000	0.103	0.249[e]	0.301[f]	0.312[f]
	16 years	0.298[f]	0.319[f]	0.355[g]	0.388[g]	0.365[g]

[a]Weighted Least Squares Solution. See text.
[b]Based on 119 urban economies.
[c]Based on 76 urban economies.
[d]Based on 119 urban economies.
[e]Significant at the 0.10 level.
[f]Significant at the 0.05 level.
[g]Significant at the 0.01 level.

multiple correlation coefficients, adjusted for degrees of freedom, are reported in Table 5.

As can be seen in Table 5, the structure of the urban economy affects the
value of schooling for all classes of labor, at each of the different levels of
schooling, and at each of the various workers' ages. Yet these effects are
neither homogeneous nor universal. For white males and females, the organization of the urban economy influences the value of schooling in all age
cohorts that have above-average educations, but it has its most conspicuous
influence on the value of schooling for established workers 30, 35, and 40
years old.

Regarding black workers, we find a substantially different pattern. The
effects of urban structure are more important in affecting the value of schooling for the best- and worst-educated black males, those with either 8 years or
16 years of schooling, than in affecting the value of education for black males
with average levels of schooling. Furthermore, the multiple correlations in
Table 5 indicate that urban structure is a more salient factor for black male
workers in the youngest age cohorts than for those workers over the age of
35.

The results reported in Table 5 warrant four general conclusions: (1)
There is significant evidence that the demand and supply sides of the urban
economy play a role in determining the economic value of educational credentials; (2) the saliency of the urban economy varies according to the age,
gender, and race of the worker, with economic structure being more important for black workers than white workers; (3) the value of college training
appears to be particularly strongly affected by the organization of the urban
economy; and (4) the urban economy has its strongest impact on the value of

schooling for white workers well established in the labor force, those over age 30, and younger black male workers, those under age 30.

In order to isolate how the supply- and demand-side components of the urban economy affect the value of schooling, we regressed, again using a Weighted Least Squares solution, the value of education estimated at 8, 12, and 16 years of schooling, on the multiple indicators of urban economic structure.[15] In our initial analyses, regressions were computed separately by region (South vs. non-South) to estimate the magnitude of any regional interactions. No compelling evidence was found of regional interactions for either white males or females; thus, later regressions were based on pooling nonsouthern and southern urban economies. For black males, however, we found significant regional interactions; therefore, subsequent regressions were estimated separably for black males in nonsouthern and southern urban economies.

A. The Value of Schooling for White Male Labor

Table 6 reports the WLS regression results for the model predicting the value of schooling for white male workers 35 years old.[16] As can be seen in the last two rows of the table, the effect of urban structure on the value of schooling becomes more salient as educational attainment rises; that is, the organization of the urban economy has little or no influence on the value of elementary school education, but it has a modest effect on the payoffs to a high school diploma and a stronger influence on the value of college credentials. This reveals a process of earnings allocation in which the structure of the urban economy plays a minor role in affecting how much education is worth for those prime-age white males with less than average schooling, yet becomes an increasingly significant factor in determining the earnings value of schooling once beyond high school. In other words, the kind of urban economy in which one works is of greater consequence to the white college-trained male than to his school dropout counterpart.

The specific coefficients in Table 6 show that both supply- and demand-side factors play an important role in determining the value of education once beyond the elementary level, with supply-side factors being markedly more important in affecting the value of high school credentials and demand-side

[15]After all inital analyses were completed, we analyzed the residuals from each regression. Using both Cook's "D" and the Studentized residuals we found large outliers in some solutions (a residual with a Cook's D $\geq$ 0.4 and a Studentized value re $\geq$ |2.0|). In order to avoid misleading results, we deleted the outliers before final analyses. For white males, no deletions were necessary. For white females, one urban economy was dropped: Worchester, MA. For black males, three were deleted: Albuquerque, NM, Baton Rouge, LA, and Jersey City, NJ. These deletions resulted in the white male analysis being based on 119 urban economies, the white female regressions being based on 118 economies, and the black male regressions being based on 73 economies, 27 southern and 46 nonsouthern.

[16]We chose to evaluate the value of schooling for white males at age 35 because the results reported in Table 5 indicate that urban structure has its largest effect at that age for white males. For similar reasons, the value of schooling for white females was evaluated at age 40 and the value of black males at age 25.

Table 6. Effects of the Organization of the Urban Economy on the Value of Schooling for White Male Labor (Weighted Least Squares Solution)[a]

| | Value of schooling evaluated at | | | | | |
| | 8 years | | 12 years | | 16 years | |
Urban structure	Metric	Standardized[b]	Metric	Standardized	Metric	Standardized
Labor demand factors						
Capital market sector	0.004	0.040	0.015[d]	0.351[e]	0.026[e]	0.457[e]
Oligopoly manufacturing	0.003	0.025	−0.008	−0.157	−0.012[d]	−0.277[d]
Sales sector	0.028[e]	0.275[c]	−0.001	−0.027	−0.030[e]	−0.503[e]
Professional services sector	0.008	0.083	0.008	0.176	0.007	0.125
State sector employment	−0.001	−0.041	0.001	0.081	0.003[e]	0.190
Labor demand	0.008	0.070	0.006	0.115	0.004	0.055
Labor supply factors						
Labor force size (log)	−0.016	−0.121	−0.005	−0.093	0.005	0.064
Minority composition	−0.001	−0.137	−0.001[c]	−0.205[e]	−0.000	−0.077
Labor force quality	−0.023	−0.130	−0.028[d]	−0.354[d]	−0.033[d]	−0.310[d]
Labor surplus	−0.013	−0.138	−0.012[d]	−0.288[d]	−0.012[e]	−0.200[c]
Price of labor	−0.009	−0.045	−0.013	−0.142	−0.016	−0.137
Region						
South	0.013	0.053	−0.007	−0.062	−0.026	−0.182
$R^2 \times 100$	9.69		19.85[d]		28.17[e]	
Adjusted $R^2 \times 100$	0.00		10.78		20.04	

[a]Evaluated at age 35 years, see text. $N = 119$ urban economies.
[b]Standardized regression coefficients.
[c]Significant at the 0.10 level.
[d]Significant at the 0.05 level.
[e]Significant at the 0.01 level.

factors being more important for college graduates. On the supply side, the quality of the economy's labor force and the amount of labor surplus are particularly important in affecting the value of high school and college educations; not surprisingly, the value of schooling is less in those economies with a highly educated labor force and those with labor excesses.

As noted above, demand-side factors are relatively more important than the structure of the labor force in affecting the value of a college education for these white males. In particular we find that the value of college credentials is enhanced in those urban economies with large capital markets, a relatively small retail sales sector, and, to a lesser degree, relatively little oligopolistic manufacturing. This reflects the greater demand for college training in urban areas where the economic base is grounded firmly in the financial sector.

Finally, as the magnitudes of the coefficients in Table 6 attest, we could find little evidence that the size of the professional service and state sectors, the level of labor demand, the size of the labor force, its racial composition, or the price of labor have any effect on the value of schooling for prime-age white males.

B. The Value of Schooling for White Female Labor

Table 7 presents the regression coefficients for white female labor age 40. Here the overall pattern is quite similar to that reported for white males: urban economic structure has no effect on the value of an elementary school education, a modest influence on the value of a high school diploma, and a strong effect on the payoffs to college credentials. Also similar to what we found for white males, the results in Table 7 suggest that the demand side is the more salient feature of the urban economy; in fact, supply-side factors have virtually no influence on the value of schooling for white females, regardless of their educational attainments. While these findings show that the broad pattern for females is similar to that found for white males, the effects of specific components of the urban economy differ between genders.

On the demand side, females with average or above-average schooling have their credentials most highly rewarded in urban economies with a large sales sector but a relatively small capital market. This is consistent with the notion that job opportunities for these white females are greater in the sales sector of the urban economy than in the financial sector. This situation being directly opposite to that found for white males, it is clear that arrangements of the urban economy that maximally benefit white male college graduates, a large financial sector and a restricted sales sector, are the same arrangements where comparably educated females are at a most serious competitive disadvantage.

We also found that a relatively weak demand for labor tends to increase the payoffs to college education for white females (see Table 7). This is consistent with Thurow's argument that education is used by employers as a screening device. But it suggests that the extent of such screening varies with the demand for labor, or how far down employers must go on the labor

Table 7. Effects of the Organization of the Urban Economy on the Value of Schooling for White Female Labor[a] (Weighted Least Squares Solution)

	Value of schooling evaluated at					
	8 years		12 years		16 years	
Urban structure	Metric	Standardized[b]	Metric	Standardized	Metric	Standardized
Labor demand factors						
Capital market sector	0.021	0.135	−0.015c	−0.212c	−0.051e	−0.343e
Oligopoly manufacturing	−0.029	−0.163	−0.002	−0.025	0.025	0.145
Sales sector	−0.016	−0.098	−0.037e	0.504e	0.090e	0.584e
Professional services sector	−0.004	−0.022	−0.005	−0.062	−0.006	−0.036
State sector employment	−0.000	−0.005	0.003	0.146	0.006	0.144
Labor demand	0.028	0.148	−0.007	−0.077	−0.041d	−0.277d
Labor supply factors						
Labor force size (log)	0.018	0.082	−0.009	−0.095	−0.036c	−0.176c
Minority composition	0.002	0.129	−0.000	−0.003	−0.002	−0.136
Labor force quality	−0.034	−0.119	−0.034c	−0.255c	−0.034	−0.121
Labor surplus	0.015	0.101	0.007	0.102	−0.001	−0.008
Price of labor	−0.010	−0.029	0.030	0.193	0.069	0.215
Region						
South	−0.049	−0.127	−0.020	−0.112	0.009	0.025
$R^2 \times 100$	6.59		19.76d		24.67e	
Adjusted $R^2 \times 100$	0.00		10.58		16.06	

[a]Evaluated at age 40 years, see text. N = 118 urban economies.
[b]Standardized regression coefficients.
[c]Significant at the 0.10 level.
[d]Significant at the 0.05 level.
[e]Significant at the 0.01 level.

queue. For example, when the demand for labor is strong, employers must go further down on the queue to less preferable workers, and white women will be hired regardless of their educational credentials. Although we do not have data in this research to test this, we suspect that the occupations to which women are typically allocated also minimize the need for educational screening. It should be noted, however, that no such comparable effect was found for white males, and an opposite effect was found for black males.

C. The Value of Schooling for Black Male Labor

The WLS metric regressions for the value of schooling for black male workers age 25 are reported in Table 8, while the standardized coefficients are given in Table 9. For black males there is a more complex pattern of relationships than was reported for either white males or females because economic structure interacts with region to determine the value of schooling for young black male workers.

Comparing the coefficients in the last row of Table 8 shows that, in general, the effects of the urban economy are markedly more pronounced in the South than in the non-South, especially at the high school and college levels. More particularly it is the demand side of the urban economy that is more important in determining the value of schooling in the South, while outside this region the demand side has virtually no effect.

Of those demand factors, Tables 8 and 9 show that in the South an average or above-average level of schooling has greater value in urban economies with a large capital market, a restricted sales sector, and a relatively small proportion of the labor force employed in oligopolistic manufacturing. Since this is the same pattern than was reported for white males, it appears that being in a financially orientated economy benefits male workers of either race since the value of their schooling increases with the size of the financial sector. But it must be recalled that this pattern exists for white males without regard to region, whereas for black males the relationship holds only in southern urban economies; outside the South the size of the financial sector has no effect on the value of schooling for young black males.

A further comparison of the results for white males with those for black males reveals another interesting relationship: Aggregate labor demand affects positively the value of black educations within southern urban economies but has no significant effect on the value of schooling for white males or black males outside the South. Again, a possible explanation for this involves the differential effect that changes in labor demand have on black and white labor queues.

Results reported in Table 8 suggest that under favorable conditions of high labor demand, the "benefits" of college training increase for black males. This could be due to a queuing effect such that when labor demand is strong, southern employers hire and reward blacks, but only those with superior schooling; that is, the benefits of "good" economic conditions, with its attendant high demand for labor, do not "trickle down" proportionately to poorly

Table 8. Metric Effects of the Organization of the Urban Economy on the Value of Schooling for Black Male Labor By Region[a] (Weighted Least Squares Solution)

| | Value of schooling evaluated at | | | | | |
| | 8 years | | 12 years | | 16 years | |
Urban structure	South	Non-South	South	Non-South	South	Non-South
Labor demand factors						
Capital market sector	0.113[b]	0.158	0.221[d]	0.104	0.329[d]	0.050
Oligopoly manufacturing	−0.185[b]	−0.029	−0.241[d]	0.008	−0.297[c]	0.045
Sales sector	−0.058	−0.296	−0.143[d]	−0.133	−0.227[c]	0.029
Professional services sector	−0.021	0.307[c]	−0.032	0.103[b]	−0.045	−0.101
State sector employment	0.031	0.004	0.020	−0.003	0.010	−0.001
Labor demand	0.017	−0.095	0.085[b]	0.003	0.152[b]	0.089
Labor supply factors						
Labor force size (log)	0.136[b]	0.200[b]	0.027	0.105[c]	−0.083	0.010
Minority composition	−0.002	0.006	−0.005	−0.002	−0.008	−0.009
Labor force quality	−0.187	−0.301	−0.087	−0.172	0.014	−0.043
Labor surplus	−0.039	0.038	−0.106[d]	0.028	−0.174[d]	0.019
Price of labor	−0.144	−0.569[c]	0.088	−0.113	0.320	0.343[d]
$R^2 \times 100$	64.49[b]	43.21[c]	83.93[d]	31.53	78.73[d]	50.06[d]
Adjusted $R^2 \times 100$	38.46	24.83	72.15	9.37	63.13	33.91

[a] Evaluated at age 25 years, see text. N = 27 urban economies for the South and N = 46 urban economies for the non-South. Underlined figures indicate significant regional variation in effects.
[b] Significant at the 0.10 level.
[c] Significant at the 0.05 level.
[d] Significant at the 0.01 level.

Table 9. Standardized Effects of the Organization of the Urban Economy on the Value of Schooling for Black Male Labor By Region[a] (Weighted Least Squares Solution)

	Value of schooling evaluated at					
	8 years		12 years		16 years	
Urban structure	South	Non-South	South	Non-South	South	Non-South
Labor demand factors						
Capital market sector	0.477[b]	0.312	0.884[d]	0.498	0.776[d]	0.186
Oligopoly manufacturing	-0.719[b]	-0.034	-0.888[d]	0.022	-0.645[c]	0.099
Sales sector	-0.217	-0.500	-0.504[d]	-0.548	-0.473[c]	0.094
Professional services sector	-0.081	0.479[c]	-0.122	0.390	-0.090	-0.300
State sector employment	0.451	-0.037	0.283	-0.057	0.082	-0.018
Labor demand	0.064	-0.180	0.304[b]	-0.014	0.322[b]	0.319
Labor supply factors						
Labor force size (log)	0.398[b]	0.343[b]	0.074	0.439[c]	-0.135	0.034
Minority composition	-0.128	0.074	-0.264	-0.049	-0.240	-0.216
Labor force quality	-0.408	-0.242	-0.179	-0.336	0.017	-0.065
Labor surplus	-0.201	0.063	-0.526[d]	0.116	-0.507[d]	0.061
Price of labor	-0.198	-0.498[c]	0.115	-0.241	0.246	0.567[d]
$R^2 \times 100$	64.49[b]	43.21[c]	83.93[d]	31.53	78.73[d]	50.06[d]
Adjusted $R^2 \times 100$	38.46	24.83	72.15	9.37	63.13	33.91

[a]Evaluated at age 25 years, see text. $N = 27$ urban economies for the South and $N = 46$ urban economies for the non-South. Underlined figures indicate significant regional variation in effects.
[b]Significant at the 0.10 level.
[c]Significant at the 0.05 level.
[d]Significant at the 0.01 level.

educated black workers in the South. For white males and black males outside the South, the demand for labor has no discernible effect on the value of their schooling. It seems, then, that the value of their educations are insulated from secular changes in labor demand; it is possible that this is due to higher rates of labor unionization in nonsouthern urban economies and/or lower levels of statistical discrimination against these groups.

Outside the South the structure of the urban economy has much less influence on the value of black education regardless of the level of schooling, and what little influence there is appears to be due more to two labor supply factors—the size of the labor force and the average price of labor (see Table 9).

In sum, these regression results show that the shape of the urban economy affects the value of black schooling, but the strength of this effect is contingent upon regional location, with the value of schooling being tied more directly to the economy's structure in the South than in the non-South.

D. Summary of Empirical Analyses

As reported in Table 1, there is substantial interurban variation in the earnings value of schooling. In general, this variation is greater for females than males, greater for blacks than whites, and greater for the young than the old. Second, there is greater interurban variation in the value of the lowest and highest educational credentials (elementary school and college) than in the value of high school education. All of this suggests that interurban migration would have the greatest effect on the value of education for minority workers, especially for those with either above- or below-average levels of schooling.

In fact, the greater ability (or fewer constraints) on mobility for white males, as well as the types of industries seeking these workers, may be a reason for the more limited variation in the value of schooling for this group. These data suggest that minorities, black males and women, are more confined to "local" labor markets for employment. Advantaged white males are more highly sought by employers whose offers must be competitive—thus homogenizing the value of schooling for this group. White males are then operating in more of a national or regional labor market, while minorities operate in a more circumspect local market. Among minorities, the greater goodness-of-fit for their models in predicting schooling value from urban economic characteristics also suggests this interpretation.

The regression results reported in Tables 5–9 are supportive of the thesis that intercity differences in the organization of production are an important factor in explaining regional variation in the economic value of schooling. It has been shown that the payoff to education is, at least in part, a function of a complex set of interactions involving the organization of the urban economy, the race and gender class of labor, and workers' level of education. Urban economic structure affects the social contract specifying returns to schooling for every class of labor, but this effect varies dramatically contingent upon age, race, gender, and schooling achieved.

For white male and female workers who are well established in the labor force, urban structure, especially the demand side of the city's economy, affects the value of schooling for average and above-average educated workers, with this influence being more pronounced for the college-educated. The size of the city's capital market and sales sectors have significant effects on the payoffs to schooling for both white males and females, but the direction of these effects depends radically on gender. The value of schooling for females is diminished under the same structural conditions that enhance the rewards for males, that is, an expanding capital market and a relatively small sales sector. Thus, the structural conditions that maximize the rewards of schooling for highly educated white males are, for the most part, the same conditions under which highly educated white females find their college credentials *least* valued. We could find little evidence that the size of professional service sector, the state sector, the geographical region, the labor force size, the racial composition, or the average cost of labor had any particularly noteworthy direct effects on the value of schooling for either white males or white females.

The regression analysis for young black male workers revealed a complex web of relationships that involved regional interactions. While the general pattern for black males paralleled that of white males, their educations being more positively rewarded in economies with strong capital markets and weak sales sectors, this comparability existed only for blacks in southern urban economies. Outside the South, the structure of the urban economy, especially the demand side, had far less influence on the value of their schooling. Or, put another way, unidentified factors other than the shape of the economy are more important in affecting the value of young black male schooling outside the South.

Though not all of our expectations were supported by this analysis, our notions concerning differences at least for gender groups were confirmed. It appears that sex segregation along industrial and occupational lines (possibly between primary and secondary labor markets) are producing inequalities in percentage returns to schooling among gender groups. For example, service sector jobs, such as those in retail trade, have provided employment opportunities for women that are not found in the banking and financial sector, other than low-level clerical positions (secretaries and bank tellers). Again, the dominance in urban economies of the retail sector enhances, while the banking and financial sector diminishes, the value of schooling for women. Racial segregation did not appear as salient since both black and white males seemed to lose or benefit from similar urban economic structures.

Also the theory of job competition and labor queuing seems useful for interpreting our findings. White males, presumably on the top of the labor queue, appear least affected by local economic structure. But those lower down (black males and females) are greatly affected by local conditions. The demand for labor seems to affect the use of schooling as a screening device. But our findings suggest that this is only for minorities since these groups are lower on the labor queue.

VI. CONCLUSIONS

The institutionalized system of education serves the needs of advanced capitalism by providing a differentiated work force appropriate for graded positions in the technical division of labor, and by rationalizing this hierarchical social order through invidious distinctions based on educational credentials. This linkage between economic structure and education suggests that the economic consequences of schooling structures and processes are not invariant with respect to changes in the technical division of labor or, more broadly, the organization of production.

Taking the uneven development of regional economies as a point of departure, we argued that advanced capitalism has created advancing and lagging urban economies that differ in their organization of production. Since the value of schooling is not invariant, but conforms to changes in the broad contours of the industrial order, we expected to find the value of schooling differing among urban labor markets. Thus, we posited a model of earnings determination in which there are complex interactions between the economic value of schooling and the structure of the urban economy. Our empirical results are supportive of this model. Urban structure does affect the economic returns to schooling, thereby mediating the social contract that specifies the reward value of education.

Although significant evidence for our main hypothesis has been reported, most obviously for those workers with college training, it is clear that the structure of the urban economy does not explain all the interurban variations in the value of schooling. For black male labor, urban structure explains about 80% of the variance in the value of college for black graduates in the South and about 50% of the variance in the value of college training outside the South. Yet for white male and female labor the model is notably less successful; urban structure explains only about one-fourth of the regional variation in the value of their college training.

There are two possible explanations for this lack of robustness for white labor: (1) The most salient dimensions of urban structure have not been successfully tapped, or our operationalizations are seriously flawed, and (2) there is a lack of variation in the value of schooling for white males. With regard to the first explanation, it is quite possible that the oligopolistic market segment of the urban economy where whites (especially males) are more likely employed contains constraints on wages (such as unions or bureaucratic rules) that blunt the effects of the supply and demand factors evaluated in this model. These factors that "fix" wages but could not be included in this analysis may homogenize the value of schooling for whites across urban economies. The second explanation, however, seems more plausible. The limited variation in the value of schooling among white males probably results from their greater geographical mobility, which allows them to participate in more regional or national labor markets rather than being confined to the local labor markets as minorities may be.

This research indicates a strong but complex relationship between the value of schooling and the organization of industrial capitalism within urban economies in America. The value of schooling has been shown to vary as a result of both supply and demand factors of urban labor markets, further explicating the linkage between educational and economic institutions in our society. Further, this research suggests that the commonly accepted meritocratic ideology concerning the allocation of economic rewards in this country may be more illusory than real. If the same schooling credentials yield different economic rewards depending on the areal economic structure and on the race and gender of those in the labor market, then clearly merit is less important in the competition for success than we would like to believe.

ACKNOWLEDGMENTS

This research was partially supported by Grant SES-8025390, "Urban Wages and Employment: A Labor Market Approach," from the National Science Foundation to E. M. Beck. We are indebted to Paula England for her insightful criticisms and valuable suggestions made on an earlier draft of this chapter.

REFERENCES

Aurousseau, Marcel. 1921. "The Distribution of Population: A Constructive Problem." *Geographical Review* 11:569–572.
Bean, Frank D., Dudley Poston, and Halliman Winsborough. 1972. "Size, Functional Specialization, and the Classification of Cities." *Social Science Quarterly* 53:20–32.
Bell, Daniel. 1973. *The Coming of Post-Industrial Society.* New York: Basic Books.
Berry, Brian J. L., and John D. Kasarda. 1977. *Contemporary Urban Ecology.* New York: Macmillian.
Betz, D. Michael. 1972. "The City as a System Generating income inequality." *Social Forces* 51:192–198.
Bibb, Robert. 1982. "The industrial Composition of Local Labor Markets: Sex Stratification and the intermetropolitan Structure of Blue-Collar Earnings." Unpublished paper, Department of Sociology and Anthropology, Vanderbilt University.
Blau, Francine D., and Mariann A. Ferber. 1986. *The Economics of Women, Men, and Work.* Englewood Cliffs, NJ: Prentice-Hall.
Bloomquist, Leonard E., and Gene F. Summers. 1982. "Organization of Production and Community Income Distributions." *American Sociological Review* 47:325–338.
Bowles, Samuel, and Herbert Gintis. 1976. *Schooling in Capitalist America.* New York: Basic Books.
Castells, Manuel. 1978. *The Economic Crisis and American Society.* Princeton: Princeton University Press.
Collins, Randall. 1977. "Functional and Conflict Theories of Educational Stratification." Pp. 118–136 in *Power and ideology in Education,* edited by J. Karabel and A. H. Halsey. New York: Oxford University Press.
Duncan, Otis Dudley, and Albert J. Reiss, Jr. 1956. *Social Characteristics of Urban and Rural Communities, 1950.* New York: Wiley.
Fossett, Mark, and Omer R. Galle. 1980. "Community Context and the Structure of Earnings Attainment: A Comparative Investigation of Structure and Process in American Metropolitan Communities." Paper No. 2.004, Texas Population Research Center, University of Texas, Austin.
Geschwender, James A. 1978. *Racial Stratification in America.* Dubuque, IA: Wm. C. Brown.
Gordon, David M. 1978. "Capitalist Development and the History of American Cities." Pp. 25–63

in *Marxism and the Metropolis: New Perspectives in Urban Political Economy,* edited by William K. Tabb and Larry Sawyers. New York: Oxford University Press.

Gordon, David M., Richard Edwards, and Michael Reich. 1982. *Segmented Work, Divided Workers: The Historical Transformation of Labor in the United States.* Cambridge: Cambridge University Press.

Hadden, Jeffrey K., and Edgar F. Borgatta. 1965. *American Cities: Their Social Characteristics.* Chicago: Rand McNally.

Hanushek, Eric A. 1973. "Regional Differences in the Structure of Earnings." *Review of Economics and Statistics* 55:204–213.

Harris, Chauncy D. 1943. "A Functional Classification of Cities in the United States." *Geographical Review* 33:86–99.

Harrison, Bennett. 1972. *Education, Training, and the Urban Ghetto.* Baltimore: Johns Hopkins University Press.

Harvey, David. 1973. *Social Justice and the City.* Baltimore: Johns Hopkins University Press.

Haveman, Robert H., and Barbara L. Wolfe. 1984. "Education, Productivity, and Well-Being: On Defining and Measuring the Economic Characteristics of Schooling." Pp. 19–55 in *Education and Economic Productivity,* edited by Edwin Dean. Cambridge: Ballinger.

Horan, Patrick M., and Charles M. Tolbert II. 1984. *The Organization of Work in Rural and Urban Labor Markets.* Boulder, CO: Westview Press.

Izraeli, Oded. 1983. "The Effect of Variations in the Cost of Living and City Size on the Rate of Return to Schooling." *Quarterly Review of Economics and Business* 2:93–108.

Jiobu, Robert M., and Harvey H. Marshall. 1971. "Urban Structure and the Differentiation between Blacks and Whites." *American Sociological Review* 36:638–649.

Katz, Michael. 1973. *Class, Bureaucracy, and Schools.* New York: Praeger.

Lane, Angela. 1968. "Occupational Mobility in Six Cities." *American Sociological Review* 33:740–749.

Markusen, Ann R. 1980. "Regionalism and the Capitalist State." Pp. 31–52 in *Urban and Regional Planning in an Age of Austerity,* edited by Pierre Clavel, John Forester, and William W. Goldsmith. New York: Pergamon Press.

McKenzie, R. D. 1933. *The Metropolitan Community.* New York: McGraw-Hill.

Mueller, Charles W. 1974. "City Effects on Socioeconomic Achievements: The Case of Large Cities." *American Sociological Review* 47:325–338.

Noyelle, Thierry J. 1983. "The implications of industry Restructuring for Spatial Organization in the United States." Pp. 113–133 in *Regional Analysis and the New international Division of Labor,* edited by Frank Moulaert and Patricia W. Salinas. Boston: Kluwer-Nijhoff.

O'Conner, James. 1973. *The Fiscal Crisis of the State.* New York: St. Martin's Press.

Ogburn, William F. 1937. *Social Characteristics of Cities.* Chicago: International City Managers Association.

Parcel, Toby L. 1979. "Race, Regional Labor Markets, and Earnings." *American Sociological Review* 44:262–279.

Parcel, Toby L., and Charles W. Mueller. 1983. *Ascription and Labor Markets: Race and Sex Differences in Earnings.* New York: Academic Press.

Perry, David C., and Alfred J. Watkins. 1982. "Contemporary Dimensions of Uneven Urban Development." Pp. 115–142 in *City, Class and Capital,* edited by Michael Harloe and Elizabeth Lebas. New York: Holmes & Meier.

Rosenzweig, Mark R. 1976. "Nonlinear Earnings Functions, Age, and Experience: A Nondogmatic Reply and Some Additional Evidence." *Journal of Human Resources* 11:23–27.

Scott, Allen J., and Michael Storper. 1986. "Industrial Change and Territorial Organization: A Summing Up." Pp. 301–311 in *Production, Work, Territory: The Geographical Anatomy of Industrial Capitalism,* edited by Allen J. Scott and Michael Storper. Boston: Allen and Unwin.

Shepherd, William G. 1969. "Market Power and Racial Discrimination in White-Collar Employment." *Antitrust Bulletin* 14:141–161.

Smith, Neil. 1984. *Uneven Development: Nature, Capital, and the Production of Space.* New York: Basil Blackwell.

Spring, Joel. 1972. *Education and the Rise of the Corporate State.* Boston: Beacon Press.

Sweezy, Paul M. 1972. *Modern Capitalism and Other Essays*. New York: Monthly Review Press.
Thompson, Wilbur R. 1965. *A Preface to Urban Economics*. Baltimore: Johns Hopkins University Press.
Thurow, Lester. 1972. "Education and Economic Equality." *Public interest* 28:66–81.
Watkins, Alfred J., and David C. Perry. 1977. "Regional Change and the Impact of Uneven Urban Development." Pp. 19–54 in *The Rise of the Sunbelt Cities*, edited by David C. Perry and Alfred J. Watkins. Beverly Hills: Sage.
Wright, Erik Olin. 1978. "Race, Class, and Income inequality." *American Journal of Sociology* 83:1368–1397.

7

Market Concentration and Structural Power as Sources of Industrial Productivity

Donald Tomaskovic-Devey

I. INTRODUCTION

This is a discussion about productivity variation among U.S. industries. Sociologists rarely study productivity, and when they do, it is most often in the terms and using the theories of economists (e.g., Galle, Wiswell, and Burr, 1985). The most common notion of productivity is that it reflects the effort of productive actors in organizational settings (i.e., firms), particularly the quality of labor and the extent of capital investment. This chapter argues that variations in productivity must be understood in terms of the power that producers have to set prices as well. In effect, I am extending the intraorganizational analysis of productivity as the efficiency with which products are created to an interorganizational sensibility that value is determined by the power of sellers in product markets. The degree of market concentration for a product, the structural power of producers (i.e., industry) in the larger economy, and the concentration of consumers will all effect the price for which a product can be sold.

This chapter develops the conceptual apparatus necessary for understanding industry level variations in productivity as value produced. The more widespread notion that productivity is the efficiency with which objects are produced I find fairly limited. Productivity understood not as objects produced but as value extracted from markets is much more interesting. This notion of productivity as value produced by the *production and sale of* goods

Donald Tomaskovic-Devey • Department of Sociology, North Carolina State University, Raleigh, North Carolina 27695-8107.

and services represents both the creation of the wealth of an economy and the first step in the distribution of that wealth within the society. Who gets what shares of the economic pie is intimately linked to this creation of wealth commonly thought of as productivity. If firms accumulate wealth through their productivity, then the distribution of income in a society begins with the value received through commodity markets at the level of firm and industry. To the extent that some firms or industries are in the position to realize higher value for their products, then individuals associated with those organizations (both capital and labor) are in the position to receive larger shares of the societal wealth. The observation that concentrated markets lead to higher rates of profits for capital (Burt, 1983; O'Connor, 1973; Scherer, 1970) and potentially higher wages for labor (Hodson, 1984; Kalleberg, Wallace, and Althauser, 1981; O'Connor, 1973) is best understood in terms of the ability of organizations in the market to extract a larger share of the societal wealth from the national economy and redistribute it to participants (both capital and labor) within those organizations.

II. UNDERSTANDING PRODUCTIVITY

A. Marginal Productivity Theory

In neoclassical economic theory, productivity is generally conceptualized as a physical output. The rate at which individuals produce some object is their productivity. If they can produce more objects in an hour, their productivity has gone up. The specific notion in human capital theory (Becker, 1964, 1971a,b; Mincer, 1974) is that better workers (ones with more human capital) with better tools (ones with more physical capital) will have higher productivity. This is at face value a reasonable proposition.

In most studies productivity is measured in dollar terms, that is, as value received for an object net of input costs (valued added) or for a given level of productivity (wages). For example, the paper by Galle et al. (1985) measured productivity as Value Added/Total Labor Hours for each industry. They use the same measurement of productivity as the U.S. Department of Labor, and current recommendations on the measurement of productivity are variants of this measure (Panel to Review Productivity Statistics, 1979). Research on the level of organizational or industrial productivity tends to focus on the value created during the production process. Industry variation in productivity is generally measured by economists as value added per unit of labor input (Denison, 1974; Gallop and Jorgenson, 1980; Kendrick, 1973; Kunze, 1979; Waldorf, 1973). These economists pay a great deal of attention to the respective roles of capital and labor in creating value, reflecting the focus of American marginal productivity theory on the efficiency of use of factors of production (land, labor, and capital) and the equity of distribution of that value back to its sources (i.e., rent, wages, and profits). Human capital researchers (e.g. Corcoran and Duncan, 1979; Mincer, 1974), when examining individual-level labor quality, generally evaluate hourly wage as a reflection of workplace productivity.

Social scientists can use wages as a measure of productivity when they are willing to assume that market forces operate to guarantee that people are compensated for what they produce. Sociologists are generally uncomfortable with the market assumptions that many economists tend to take for granted. While wage differences may reflect differences in individual level productivity, they will also be the product of power and status relationships in the workplace (Blau and Duncan, 1967; Tomaskovic-Devey, 1986; Treiman and Hartmann, 1981; Wright and Perrone, 1977).

Value added per worker per hour is, on the one hand, a better measure of productivity than wages. It is not confounded by distributional struggles within the labor process and between management and capital. These struggles are obscured or even ignored in microeconomic marginal productivity theory's focus on factors of production and the equitable distribution of value to inputs. Value added is not, however, a purely physical measure of productivity. If productivity is conceptualized as objects/labor hour, and measured as value added/labor hour, then we must clarify the relationship between objects produced and value added. Value added is the market price of those objects minus the cost of materials used in producing them. Thus, this measure of productivity is not merely physical but social as well. Productivity, measured as value added per labor hour, is the combination of physical productivity (both volume and quality of production) and the value consumers are willing to pay for a commodity.

The interpretation of the measure hinges, then, on the relationship between the object (a commodity) and its market price. What determines the price that a firm or industry can charge for its product? In neoclassical economic theory firms have no control over the price of goods; rather, the market determines prices and the firm adjusts factors of production (land, labor, and capital) to influence profitability. However, under the assumption of competitive markets, price should reflect the value embodied in the physical product during the production process. That is, price should fairly compensate for the value produced by the three factors of production. If prices are too high, other firms will enter the market and reduce the price to the level of value produced. If the market price for a commodity is too low, firms will produce less or stop producing, reducing supply and so bringing price back in line with the value produced. In competitive product markets, then, the price of an object (its value) is functionally identical to the physical notion of productivity.

1. Degree of Market Competition

The assumption of product market competition is no longer universally held within economics (Averitt, 1968; Scherer, 1970), although it is still prevalent within most microeconomic theorizing. The absence of market competition is still seen as a temporary anomaly to be destroyed by new firms entering concentrated markets to exploit the high profits available in the low-competition markets. The historical record, of course, shows that market concentration is not an anomaly; rather, it is a central feature of modern industrial societies (Baran & Sweezy, 1966; O'Connor, 1973).

It is clear that industries vary a great deal in the competitiveness of their markets and their structural power within the economy. Firms within structurally more powerful industries may be able to extract higher market values for their products than firms in more competitive and less powerful industries. What do the economic and sociology liteartures tell us about the relationship between price and economic structure?

The most obvious example of market price as influenced by market structure is embodied in the dual economy literature (Averitt, 1968; Gailbraith, 1967; O'Connor, 1973) in which firms in concentrated industries are able to extract higher prices for their goods from the marketplace. These monopolistic or, more commonly, oligopolistic industries can be expected to have high value added per object produced not merely because of their internal productivity but also because they can raise prices and so extract value from consumers because of the low or absent level of product competition. These monopoly rents are then translated into both higher profits for their owners and higher wages for their work forces than in more competitive industries (O'Connor, 1973). When productivity is measured as value added per labor hour, it seems reasonable to predict that more concentrated industries should have higher productivity net of both labor force characteristics and the amount of physical capital available.

2. Structural Power

A more recent and less well known approach to industry stratification can be found in the work of the late Luca Perrone (1984). Perrone argued that the success of strikes by unions is dependent upon the "disruptive potential" that workers have. Disruptive potential, he argued, is a function of the "structural power" (or "positional power") of the industry in which the strike activity occurs. By disruptive potential he means the effect of strike activity not only on the firm or industry in question but also upon all other economic actors that depend upon the products of that industry for their production process. Thus, activities within industries vary in their consequences for other sectors of the economy as a function of the industry's "structural power" within a national economy. Although Perrone (1984) limited his argument to the "disruptive potential" of strikes, it is reasonably generalizable to all activity within an industry. Industries will vary in their "positional power" as a function of the dependence of downstream sectors of the economy upon that industry's products. While that power may accrue to strikers, I do not see a logical reason why it should not be available to managers when setting prices as well. It would seem a reasonable extension of Perrone's (1984) theoretical work that the "structural power" of an industry should have an impact on its realized productivity, net of human and physical capital characteristics and the degree of concentration in the industry.

Ronald Burt's recent work (1983; Burt, Christman, and Kilburn, 1980) has suggested that corporate profits are constrained not only by the degree of product market concentration but also by the degree of concentration a firm (or industry) faces among its consumers. Some consumers (e.g., General Motors) may be able to dictate the price and product to a relatively dispersed set of suppliers. The notion that consumers are more or less concentrated complements Perrone's (1984) description of structural power. Downstream dependence and the ability to dictate prices because consumers are relatively unorganized seem to be flip sides of the same coin. Burt's emphasis on profits is probably misplaced. All of his arguments refer to value realized on the market (i.e., productivity as value added), of which profits is one distributional outcome.

B. Race

A recent paper by Galle et al. (1985) examined the relationship between racial composition and productivity for manufacturing industries. The study reviewed human capital theory (Becker, 1964, 1971a,b; Mincer 1974), dual labor market theory (Doeringer and Piore, 1971), and industrial segmentation theory (Beck, Horan, and Tolbert, 1978; Bibb and Form, 1977; Bluestone, 1968; Bluestone, Murphy, and Stevenson, 1973; Hodson, 1978; Kaufman, 1980). It concluded that, while they differ on some explanations of the wage determination process, each perspective generally predicts a negative relationship between percent black and industrial productivity. One empirical exception to this consensus is Hodson's (1984) finding that black employment was proportionally greater in the core and oligopoly sectors of the economy, where most researchers expect to find generally high productivity.

In their empirical examination of the relationship between productivity and proportion black in the labor force, Galle et al. (1985) held physical capital investment (capital expenditure/production worker) and human capital quality (mean education and mean age of work force) constant. They found for both 1960 and 1970 that percent black was *positively* associated with industrial productivity in their universe of manufacturing industries.

This suggests, contrary to most human capital explanations of the individual-level wage gaps between blacks and whites, that blacks may be generally *more* productive than whites given the same tools and other human capital characteristics. While this may be the case, the Galle et al. (1985) paper does not purport to demonstrate this, and only suggests it in the mildest of language. Yet their empirical finding indicates that, at least for manufacturing industries, racial composition of the labor force may effect productivity and should be treated as a control variable.

C. Summary

This discussion suggests that productivity has both a social and a physical component. The physical component, stressed by human capital and marginal productivity theory, should be determined by the quality of the work force and its tools. Specifically, industries with higher investments in physical capital should exhibit higher physical productivity. Similarly, industries whose work forces have relatively high investments in general human capital (education or experience) or specific human capital (from tenure in a firm), or are composed of groups with more continuous employment histories (i.e., white males) should exhibit higher productivity. The translation of physical productivity into social productivity—that is, objects produced into value realized in a commodity market—should be governed by other forces. The "structural power" of an industry conceptualized as the degree of dependence of other industries, and the society in general, upon its output, and the concentration of commodity and consumer markets, should both effect the actual value earned by the firm for the products it sells. This discussion is schematically illustrated in Figure 1.

D. A Theoretical Aside on the Role of the Firm

The discussion up to this point and the empirical analysis to follow use industry as the unit of analysis. In fact, the theory depicted in Figure 1 operates on two levels of analysis. The first, which has to do with physical production, is on the level of the firm. It is on this level that actual physical products or services are produced. In keeping with marginal productivity theory, it is the firm that creates the mix of capital investment and various types of labor that actually leads to production. Thus, physical production is conceptualized as a firm- (or more properly establishment-) level phenomenon.

The market forces that affect productivity as value realized (price) are, however, industry-level (product market) phenomena. All firms in an industry can be assumed to share the level of competition in that particular market. This does not mean that all firms are equally productive. Intraindustry productivity should vary as a function of the physical productivity of the firms discussed above. The use of industry-level data analysis in the next section

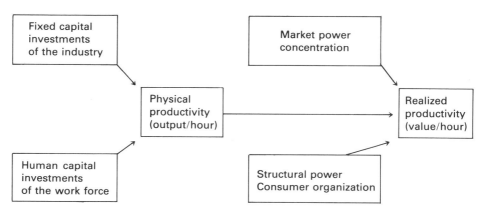

Figure 1. A conceptual diagram of the determinants of industrial productivity.

does not suggest that there are no firm-level variations in productivity. Rather, market concepts are most powerful for explaining industry-level productivity variation, which is the theoretical thrust of this chapter. Marginal productivity theory, especially when amended by attention to the quality of labor–management relations (i.e., corporate culture or managerial effectiveness), is probably most useful for explaining intraindustry productivity variation.

III. DATA, MEASURES, AND METHODS

A. Data

To test the expanded model of industrial productivity proposed above, data for all concepts were assembled from a variety of sources for three-digit 1970 census code manufacturing industries for circa 1970.

Like this analysis, Galle *et al.* (1985) only used data for manufacturing industries. There are two good reasons for limiting analysis to manufacturing industries. The first has to do with the economic measurement of value added. Traditionally, value added is more difficult to measure for industries that do not produce an observable physical product (e.g., schools or barbershops). The second reason is that less accurate data are available for some indicators (i.e., concentration) for nonmanufacturing industries. While these two factors do support limiting analysis to manufacturing, a strong theoretical argument can be made as to why the full range of industrial activity should be taken into account. First, the concepts of "structural power" and "potential disruption" both depend upon the place of an industry within a total national division of labor. Manufacturing industries are likely to be in more structurally powerful positions within the national economy than service industries. Similarly, the dual economy literature that points to concentration as a key determinant of market power is based on a full range of industries in the economy. In preliminary analysis I endeavored to use the full range of productivity in the U.S. economy. However, I found that data were unavailable for many indicators for nonmanufacturing industries. Data analysis for a subset of non-manufacturing industries for which indicators were available produced results somewhat comparable to those reported below for manufacturing, but coefficients tended to be unstable under different models and explanatory power low. Better data on concentration, interindustry sales, and value added for nonmanufacturing industries is needed for a more complete analysis of this problem.

B. Measures

Productivity will be measured as total value added divided by full-time equivalent employees. (This measure can be converted to hours simply by dividing it again by 40.)

Investment in physical capital, the quantity and quality of tools the labor force has at its disposal, will be measured as gross fixed assets divided by full-time equivalent employee. This is not the measure that Galle *et al.* (1985) used. In their paper physical investment is measured as current capital expenditure per worker. Although they note that gross fixed assets may be the more *theoretically* implied measure, they choose current capital expenditure because it was more strongly related to productivity in preliminary analysis. Empirical power rather than theoretical selection is not a compelling argument for operationalizing a concept, and the theoretical discussion developed in this chapter suggests why current expenditures have a stronger relationship with productivity. The level of current capital expenditures is, in part, a function of current receipts. Current capital expenditures, like productivity, are likely to be effected by the market concentration and structural power of an industry.

The median education and median age of the labor force will be the primary human capital measures of the quality of the labor force. The final "human capital" measures will be the percent of the labor force female and the percent black. These serve as crude controls for employment continuity, as well as proxies for any other productivity differentials that may exist between race or sex groups, such as the higher productivity of blacks suggested by Galle *et al.* (1985).

Market power will be measured with traditional concentration ratios. The measure is a 50-firm sales concentration ratio. This particular measure was chosen (rather than a 4-, 8-, or 20-firm concentration ratio) because it was the strongest predictor of productivity in exploratory models and no clear-cut theoretical criterion was evident for the selection of a concentration ratio level.

Both Perrone (1984) and Burt (1983) operationalized the structural power of an industry in terms of its position within an input-output matrix of industries. Perrone (1984) used two measures of structural power—"direct" and "total" out degrees in the matrix. An out degree in the matrix for Perrone was a sale to another industry of at least 500,000 lira per employee. A direct out degree was a direct sale to another industry of this amount or more, and an indirect out degree was scored if a direct out-degree industry had large sales to an industry or industries further downstream in the economy. While this measure is attractive in its ability to follow a hypothetical stream of transactions, it does not utilize information on the dollar value of transactions, and it is fairly cumbersome. This study will use two different measures of the structural power of an industry. The first I label "industrial centrality." It is the natural logarithm of all sales to other industries (but not to final consumers) divided by the total of all interindustry sales within the economy. Like Perrone's measures, this variable will tap the importance of an industry's sales to other production activity in the economy. The logarithmic transformation was utilized because preliminary analysis showed that it better captured the relationship with productivity, and the theoretical discussion does not suggest the exact form of the relationship. The second measure is the percent of total industry sales to other industries (rather than final consumers) and is labeled

Table 1. Correlation Matrix, Means and Standard Deviations for Variables Used in the Analysis of 76 (3-Digit SIC) Manufacturing Industries

	Productivity	Capital assets	Median education	Median age	Percent female	Percent black	Sales concentration	Industrial centrality	Inter-industry sales
Capital assets	0.693								
Median education	-0.011	0.157							
Median age	0.238	-0.163	-0.202						
Percent female	-0.032	-0.163	-0.202	0.022					
Percent black	0.235	0.034	-0.695	0.266	-0.105				
Sales concentration	0.282	0.308	0.506	-0.180	-0.133	-0.213			
Industrial centrality	0.316	0.232	0.102	0.196	-0.277	0.071	-0.003		
Interindustry sales	-0.138	-0.068	-0.040	0.161	-0.343	0.048	-0.266	0.527	
Mean	5,112	0.564	11.83	39.91	26.1	8.7	70.6	-5.8	0.635
SD	8,374	1.193	0.765	2.22	15.4	4.2	20.9	0.7	0.289

interindustry sales. Conceptually this variable measures the importance of interindustry sales to the productive activity of the industry. Following Burt (1983), it should be negatively related to productivity. This is because the extent that sales are to other industries rather than to final consumers should reflect (somewhat crudely) the extent of consumer concentration. The assumption here is that, in general, industrial consumers are more concentrated and so more powerful than final consumers (households). Table 1 presents the means and standard deviations and correlations between all variables used in the analysis.

C. Methods

I utilize ordinary least squares as the primary statistical tool for investigating interindustry productivity variation. The two blocks of variables (physical and human capital; market power and structural power) are entered separately, and then a full model that uses both blocks of variables will be explored.

IV. RESULTS

Table 2 provides the results of the regression analysis for manufacturing industries. Equation 1 is the basic physical and human capital model. The quality of tools (capital assets per employee) is strongly related to realized productivity. Percent black is found to have a statistically significant positive relationship with productivity. Education, age, and percent female all have (positive) nonsignificant relationships with productivity. The findings are essentially similar to those of Galle et al. (1985) except that I do not find education to be significantly related to productivity.

Equation 2 reports the regression of productivity upon market concentration, industrial centrality, and interindustry sales. Concentration is weakly positively related to realized productivity. Industrial centrality is strongly positively associated with realized productivity. All three relationships are in the predicted direction and significant.

Equation 3 reports the full productivity model. Productivity is most strongly determined by the quality of the physical tools (capital assets), and the structural power of the industry in the national economy (industrial centrality) and the degree of interindustry sales. In addition, percent black in the labor force is associated with *higher* productivity among manufacturing industries.

V. DISCUSSION

The productivity equations reported in Table 2 strongly support the proposal that productivity is a function of both internal organization of produc-

Table 2. Regression of Manufacturing Productivity
(Value Added/Full-Time Equivalent Employee)
upon Human Capital, Market Power, and
Structural Power Variables[a]

	1	2	3
Capital assets	0.66[e]		0.57[e]
Median education	0.17		0.00
Median age	0.13		0.12
Percentage female	0.14		0.11
Percentage black	0.31[d]		0.21[c]
Sales concentration		0.19[b]	0.13
Industrial centrality		0.51[e]	0.28[d]
Inter-industry sales		−0.35[d]	−0.28[c]
Multiple r	0.747	0.465	0.791
r^2	0.555	0.195	0.625

[a]Data are for three-digit census industry codes for circa 1970. $N = 76$.
 Coefficients are standardized betas.
[b]$p < 0.10$.
[c]$p < 0.05$.
[d]$p < 0.01$.
[e]$p < 0.0001$.

tion and external relationships to markets. The amount of capital investment per worker is the strongest predictor of productivity in the analysis. Human capital explanations of the variation in productivity across manufacturing industries were generally not supported. Neither median age nor median education of the work force were significantly associated with productivity in either model. The race composition of the labor froce is related to productivity, with percent black increasing productivity. Since blacks have lower employment continuity than white males, this finding is the opposite of what human capital theory would predict. While the results provide no support for neoclassical economic predictions of human capital–productivity linkages, the neoclassical notion that the quantity and quality of tools is connected to productivity is upheld.

The market power of manufacturing industries was found to be associated with their realized productivity. More concentrated industries were likely to have higher productivity net of other market structure variables. In the full model, however, we find that the effect of sales concentration is mediated by capital investment. This finding is congruent with discussions of oligopolistic markets (Averitt, 1968; O'Connor, 1973; Scherer, 1970) in which one of the benefits of oligopoly is that high receipts can be diverted to increased capital investment, increasing productivity, and limiting the ability of newcomers to enter the market. The structural position of an industry in the national economy was found to be related to realized productivity. The "structural power" (centrality) of an industry in terms of all interindustry activity in the economy was the second best predictor of variations in manufacturing productivity in the final model. The proportion of an industry's sales that are to other industries (not to final consumers) has a strong negative association with productivity, suggesting that the concentration of consumers is important to realized industry productivity.

The effects of human capital measures upon productivity in these data are negligible. In these data on manufacturing industries, I found no relationship between the age, sex, or education credentials of the work force and productivity. The absence of a human capital effect in manufacturing suggests that the theory is not particularly useful for explaining interindustry productivity variation. This does not mean, however, that human capital does not say something useful on the individual level about productivity. Human capital may be a useful theoretical tool for understanding individual-level productivity variation within comparable occupational positions. It may, for this reason, also be useful for explaining intraindustry, firm-level variations in productivity. However, here the differences in factor mix in the production process and any potential market power associated with firm reputation must be taken into account as well. It seems reasonable to posit (and the correlation matrix in Table 1 supports) that manufacturing industries, particularly industries with high levels of capital investment and market concentration and powerful structural positions within the economy, will be able to afford older and more educated work forces.

The last two labor force composition variables had an ambiguous status from the outset. Human capital theory has explained black–white and male–female individual earnings gaps as a function of differences in human capital and associated productivity. This argument leads to a prediction of negative effects of percent black and percent female upon industrial productivity. For manufacturing industries, just the opposite is the case. Higher concentrations of black labor are associated with *higher* productivity net of physical investment, market concentration, and structural position. This suggests that either blacks work harder with the same tools or are disproportionately recruited into manufacturing industries whose productivity is higher for some reason not specified in the model (e.g., managerial efficiency).

VI. CONCLUSION

This chapter has developed a theory of realized productivity. In addition to the neoclassical economic insights that human and physical capital determine productivity, I have argued that the relationship of the industry to markets and the national economy play a role in determining the realized productivity in an industry. Productivity is potentially interesting to social scientists as a measure of the store of value produced in a society. As such, it represents the amount of resources available for distribution, the size of the pie that stratification processes will later distribute. Given this understanding, productivity is best measured and explored as *value realized* from the sale of goods and services rather than as simple physical output. Value realized in consumer markets will be a function not only of physical production but also of the relative ability of the industry and its members to influence prices. Following the dual economy literature (e.g., O'Connor, 1973) I predicted that market concentration is a resource for price determination. In addition, industries in more structurally powerful positions (Perrone, 1984) within the national economy and those facing disorganized consumers (Burt, 1983) were predicted to have disproportionate ability to manipulate prices.

The data analysis supported the more complex understanding of productivity as a function of both the internal organization of production, particularly physical capital investment, and external market organization, particularly interindustry sales concentration and industrial centrality.

Future research should extend this analysis to other time points. Measures of international market activity and nonmanufacturing market structure would also strengthen this line of research. More fundamentally, the next step is to see how internal industrial organization and external market resources are related to the division of the value produced within industries. If productivity represents the size of the pie, then the next step is to see how it is sliced.

ACKNOWLEDGMENTS

An earlier version of this chapter was presented at the 1986 meetings of the American Sociological Society. The work has benefited from the comments of Jeff Leiter, Arne Kalleberg, Paula England, and George Farkas.

REFERENCES

Averitt, Robert. 1968. *The Dual Economy*. New York: W. W. Norton.

Baran, Paul, and Paul Sweezy. 1969. *Monopoly Capital*. New York: Monthly Review Press.

Beck, E. M., Patrick, M. Horan, and Charles M. Tolbert III. 1978. "Stratification in the Dual Economy: A Sectoral Model of Earnings Discrimination." *American Sociological Review* 43:704–720.

Becker, Gary S. 1964. *Human Capital: A Theoretical and Empirical Analysis with Special Reference to Education*. New York: Columbia University Press.

Becker, Gary S. 1971a. "Investment in Human Capital: Effects on Earnings." Pp. 159–177 in *Readings in Labor Market Analysis*, edited by John Burton. New York: Holt, Rinehart & Winston.

Becker, Gary S. 1971b. *The Economics of Discrimination*, 2nd ed. Chicago: University of Chicago Press.

Bibb, Robert, and William H. Form. 1977. "The Effects of Industrial, Occupational, and Sex Stratification on Wages in Blue-Collar Markets." *Social Forces* 55:974–996.

Blau, Peter, and Otis Dudley Duncan. 1967. *The American Occupational Structure*. New York: Wiley.

Bluestone, Barry. 1968. "Lower-Income Workers and Marginal Industries." Pp. 273–302 in *Pover-

ty in America, edited by Louis Ferman, Joyce L. Kornbluh and Alan Haber. Ann Arbor: University of Michigan Press.

Bluestone, Barry, William M. Murphy, and Mary Stevenson. 1973. *Low Wages and the Working Poor.* Ann Arbor: Institute of Labor and Industrial Relations, University of Michigan.

Burt, Ronald S. 1983. *Corporate Profits and Co-optation.* New York: Academic Press.

Burt, Ronald S., Christman, K. K., and Kilburn, H. C. 1980. "Testing a Structural Theory of Corporate Co-optation: Inter-organizational Directorate Ties as a Strategy for Avoiding Market Constraints on Profits." *American Sociological Review* 45:821–841.

Corcoran, Mary, and Gregory Duncan. 1979. "Work History, Labor Force Attachment, and Earning Differences between the Races and Sexes." *Journal of Human Resources* 14:3–20.

Denison, Edward F. 1974. *Accounting for U.S. Economic Growth 1929–1969.* Washington, D.C.: Brookings Institution.

Doeringer, Peter, and Michael Piore. 1971. *Internal Labor Markets and Manpower Analysis.* Lexington, MA: D. C. Heath.

Gailbraith, John K. 1967. *The New Industrial State.* Boston: Houghton Mifflin.

Galle, Omer R., Candace Hinson Wiswell, and Jeffrey A. Burr. 1985. "Racial Mix and Industrial Productivity." *American Sociological Review* 50:20–33.

Gallop, Frank, and Dale Jorgenson. 1980. "U.S. Productivity Growth by Industry 1947–1973." Pp. 17–136 in *New Developments in Productivity Measurement and Analysis,* edited by John W. Kendrick and Beatrice N. Vaccara. NBER Studies in Income and Wealth 44. Chicago: University of Chicago Press.

Gordon, David M. 1972. *Theories of Poverty and Underemployment.* Lexington, MA: D. C. Heath.

Hodson, Randy D. 1978. "Labor in the Monopoly, Competitive, and State Sectors of Production." *Politics and Society* 8:141–193.

Hodson, Randy. 1984. *Workers' Earnings and Corporate Economic Structure.* New York: Academic Press.

Kalleberg, Arne, Michael Wallace, and Robert Althauser. 1981. "Economic Segmentation, Worker Power, and Income Inequality." *American Journal of Sociology* 87:651–683.

Kaufman, Robert L. 1980. Racial Discrimination and Labor Market Segmentation. Unpublished doctoral dissertation, Department of Sociology, University of Wisconsin, Madison.

Kendrick, John. 1973. *Postwar Productivity Trends in the United States, 1948–1973.* Prepared for the National Bureau of Economic Research. New York: Columbia University Press.

Kunze, Kent. 1979. "Evaluation of Work Force Adjustment." Pp. 334–362 in *Measurement and Interpretation of Productivity,* edited by Panel to Review Productivity Statistics. Washington, D.C.: National Academy of Sciences.

Mincer, Jacob. 1974. *Schooling, Experience, and Earnings.* New York: Columbia University Press.

O'Connor, James. 1973. *The Fiscal Crisis of the State.* New York: St. Martin's Press.

Panel to Review Productivity Statistics (ed) 1979. *Measurement and Interpretation of Productivity.* Washington, D.C.: National Academy of Sciences.

Perrone, Luca. 1984. "Positional Power, Strikes and Wages." *American Sociological Review* 49:412–426.

Scherer, F. M. 1970. *Industrial Market Structure and Economic Performance.* Chicago: Rand McNally.

Tomaskovic-Devey, Donald. 1986. April. "Organizational Resources, the Social Organization of Production, and the Quality of Jobs." Paper presented at the Southern Sociological Society Meetings, New Orleans.

Treiman, Donald J., and Heidi Hartmann. 1981. *Women, Work, and Wages: Equal Pay for Jobs of Equal Value.* Washington, D.C.: National Academy Press.

Waldorf, William. 1973. "Quality of Labor in Manufacturing." *Review of Economic Statistics* 55:284–291.

Wright, Erik Olin, and Luca Perrone. 1977. "Marxist Class Categories and Income Inequality." *American Sociological Review* 42:32–55.

IV

FIRMS AND INTERNAL LABOR MARKETS

The chapters in this section focus on the firm as an employer, worker compensation, and mobility within and between firm internal labor markets. These topics have long held the interest of both sociologists and economists.

Williamson, a key figure in the development of the "new institutional economics," summarizes a number of its features. Focusing on transactions as the units of analysis, he presents "transaction cost economics," in which opportunistic individuals economize on bounded rationality (actions that are intendedly rational, but only limitedly so). Transaction costs are economized by assigning transactions (which differ in their attributes) to governance structures (which differ in their adaptive capacities and costs). Thus, variations in the characteristics of transactions (particularly their asset specificity—the ease with which an investment in a particular productive relationship can be successfully transferred to a different relationship) give rise to alternative incentive structures, governance structures, and trading regularities. Study of these permits new institutional economists to address issues such as the following: Which transactions will be organized within the firm's boundaries (via hierarchy), and which outside these boundaries (via the purchase of goods and services in markets)? How does on-the-job training affect implicit and explicit labor contracts? How are the characteristics of contracts and other social and economic institutions determined by the characteristics of transactions? Williamson suggests that the new institutional economics "occupies or shares territory once exclusively that of sociologists," so that "economics and sociology are no longer passing at a (comfortable) distance from one another." He claims that the time is therefore ripe for a productive joinder of the two. This joinder is most likely to occur through a shared interest in four consequences of a world characterized by both bounded rationality and opportunism. First, contracting is incomplete; at the time the contract is agreed to, it is impossible to foresee every contingency that may later arise. Thus, it is important to study those institutions that facilitate the actual execution of contracts. Examples include both informal and formal bargaining and arbitration, as well as the mobilization of law. Second, contracts involve promises regarding future behavior, yet economic agents are given to opportunism, so it is important to study institutional practices designed to minimize losses from this source. Examples include incentive schemes such as deductibles in insurance contracts, as well as the loss of reputation associated with various forms of "cheating" or "poor citizenship." Third, transactions are embedded in social structural contexts, as noted by Granovetter (see below). This is where Williamson sees sociologists making a contribution. Finally, transactions give rise to unintended consequences, whose antecedents and consequences for institutional structure would also repay investigation.

By contrast, Granovetter compares sociological and economic approaches to firms and labor markets in a wide-ranging review organized around two propositions. First, all individual behavior is embedded within networks of personal relations. Second, most behavior involves both economic and noneconomic motives. Consequently, neither the economist's focus on atomistic, instrumental behavior and efficient institutional arrangements, nor the sociologist's focus on group and personal loyalties is adequate by itself to fully explain employment and earnings behavior. Rather, the two views must be joined, and seen to operate simultaneously.

Much of Granovetter's discussion is designed to show what is still left out by the "new" institutional economics, which includes implicit contract theory as well as Williamson's transaction cost economics. In Granovetter's view, these theories fail to see how networks of personal contacts and hierarchy affect training, effort, cooperation, promotion, norms of fairness, compensation, and turnover. In this view, two key notions within the atomistic economic perspective—worker productivity and the "quality" of the worker/job match—are both difficult or impossible to measure at the individual level. This is because they are as much properties of group and network relations as of the individual's own characteristics and efforts. Thus, Granovetter believes that economists' emphasis upon individual characteristics is misplaced. In addition, he points out that economizing behavior occurs jointly with individual striving for sociability, approval, status, and power. Ultimately, the cumulation of these behaviors, jointly determined by social and economic motives, occurring within a social structural context of networks and hierarchy, leads to patterns that are typically identified as "institutions," "culture," or "atmosphere." Yet, in Granovetter's view, these are epiphenomenal outgrowths of the more fundamental patterns of network and hierarchy.

DiTomaso's approach to firms and their internal labor markets is more empirical. Focusing on three firms, one each in the core, periphery, and state sectors, she combines statistical and ethnographic data on the process of income determination. She argues that many taken-for-granted notions in the theoretical literature are considerably more complicated in real life. These include the distinction between professional and managerial workers versus others, firm unionization status, the job to which one has "rights" and the job one is assigned to work on any given day, and the determinants and consequences of gender and ethnic composition across occupations within the firm. DiTomaso highlights firm-specific idiosyncrasies in job access and wage determination, and the extent to which the implementation of internal labor market policies constitutes a constant source of tension among management, unions, and workers.

Yet the chapters by Williamson and Granovetter suggest theoretical perspectives that might provide useful guidance for future efforts such as DiTomaso's. In particular, the following questions might be addressed. First, to what extent, if at all, do personnel policies economize on firm specific training costs, and the transaction costs of hiring and promotion? Second, how do workers and their organizations (e.g., unions) respond to these policies? Third, what role is played in this labor process by networks of individuals, the group structure of organizations, and the interrelatedness of economic and social motives? Finally, is individual opportunism, by workers or management, important in these transactions? How is it curtailed and/or expressed within firm-specific institutional structures? Ethnographic and statistical studies explicitly addressing these and related questions would move us toward the truly interdisciplinary understanding of firms and labor markets advocated by both Williamson and Granovetter.

The Economics and Sociology of Organization
Promoting a Dialogue

Oliver E. Williamson

I. INTRODUCTION

The intellectual appeal of a single, unified theory of organization notwithstanding, we are at present operating in a preunified stage of development. Even if a comprehensive, integrated theory were in prospect, which it is not, our understanding of some complex organizational phenomena might be better served by working out of several well-focused perspectives. Exposing the powers and limits of each of the leading approaches and the tensions and complementarities between them can be, and often is, a productive enterprise.

What I characterize as the New Institutional Economics holds out the prospect that the study of economic organization will benefit from a richer dialogue between economists and sociologists. As discussed below, the New Institutional Economics adopts a much more microanalytic perspective than was characteristic of economics during the "applied price theory" era.[1] This microanalytic focus brings economists and sociologists into much closer contact. Albeit using different lenses, both are often looking at very similar and sometimes identical market, hierarchical, and hybrid phenomena.

A rich dialogue is usually attended by controversy. I fully expect that to be the case here. Needless disputes can be avoided, however, if each side has an appreciation for the distinctive contributions that the other has made and/or prospectively offers. As discussed below, the pervasive importance of

---

[1]The issues are developed more fully in Williamson (1985a:23–32).

Oliver E. Williamson • Yale University Law School, New Haven, Connecticut 06520.

economizing is where the New Institutional Economics has made greatest headway and has the most to offer. By contrast, the importance of process to economic organization is widely neglected and undervalued by economists. Greater appreciation for the past and prospective contributions of sociologists on matters of process is needed.

Lon Fuller, in his posthumously published paper, "The Forms and Limits of Adjudication," distinguishes between "essentials" and "tosh." He maintains that the essentials are to be discovered by adopting a "rational core" approach to human institutions (Fuller, 1978:359–362). To focus on tosh—which has reference to "superfluous rituals, rules of procedure without clear purpose, needless precautions preserved through habit," (1978:356) —is to "abandon any hope of fruitful analysis" (1978:360). Although that is a somewhat stronger position than I advance here, the importance of distinguishing between core and fringe is one to which I fully subscribe.

This chapter mainly emphasizes the economizing perspective. I begin, however, by laying out what I see to be the leading commonalities to which both economists and sociologists can relate if not subscribe (Section II). The economizing approach is then described and the rudiments of transaction cost economics are developed in Section III. Some recent sociological critiques of the transaction cost economics approach are examined in Section IV. Functionalist modes of explanation are discussed and an illustration of a "successful" application of functionalism in the social sciences is advanced in Section V. Concluding remarks follow.

II. SOME COMMONALITIES BETWEEN ECONOMICS AND SOCIOLOGY

A. Rationality Orientation

Paul Samuelson once remarked that "many economists would separate economics from sociology on the basis of rational or irrational behavior" (1947:90). A division of effort was thus contemplated whereby rationality was the province of economics, irrationality was relegated to sociology, and never the twain shall meet.

This was a bad bargain for sociology. As George Homans observed, "Of all our many 'approaches' to social behavior, the one that sees it as an economy is the most neglected, and yet it is the one we use every moment of our lives—except when we write sociology" (1958:606). To concede rationality reasoning to others is to blinker sociology needlessly.

Herbert Simon has recently counseled that all of the social sciences operate out of a rationality framework and that the rationality/nonrationality dichotomy is unhelpful (1978:2–6). The real differences are ones of degree. Economists more readily impute high-powered cognitive capacities to human agents than do other social scientists. Although this difference will doubt-lessly continue, economists today are much more amenable to the condition of bounded rationality—at least where this is defined as behavior that is *"intendedly* rational, but only *limitedly* so" (Simon, 1957:xxiv) and is not impli-cated with "satisficing," which is a contentious and separable issue—than was the case 10 and 15 years ago. If bounded rationality is our common ground, as I think it is, we should acknowledge this and work constructively out of this basic framework rather than endlessly dispute rationality excesses of both over- and underdeveloped kinds.

If mind is a scarce resource, which is what bounded rationality contem-plates, then the study of structures and procedures that serve to economize on bounded rationality are unavoidably part of the economics research agen-da. Bounded rationality is not, therefore, a threat but, instead, expands the scope of economics. Sociologists, moreover, who justifiably boggle at as-sumptions of hyperrationality can relate easily and productively to a bounded rationality framework.

To be sure, sociologists may place greater emphasis on the limits of rationality and some may reserve judgment on economizing. Both aspects are important, however, and need to be studied. Assumptions of hyperra-tionality and irrationality too often obfuscate or trivialize complex phe-nomena. Bounded rationality relocates the action in an arena where both economists and sociologists can participate.

B. Secondary Consequences

Intended rationality emphasizes purposiveness. The parties act with ref-erence to an intended set of consequences. Means are ssembled to accomplish ends. Responses to disturbances are expected to be adaptive.

Albeit instructive, a "machine model" of organization is also simplistic. ThIngs do not always go according to plan; efforts to be adaptive are not always successful. Some of these misfires occur because systems are more complex than imagined. Incumbents and other interested parties who are (1) strategically situated and (2) differentially affected may be able to tilt—accel-erate or delay; expand, defeat, or otherwise distort—new programs during implementation. Persistent failure to acknowledge these "unanticipated con-sequences"—which, however, predictably recur—and thereafter take them into account in the design calculus is the source of avoidable error.

Although sociologists have long been alert to this condition (Gouldner, 1954; March and Simon, 1958:36–47; Merton, 1936), the study of these matters needs more systematic development. Unintended consequences intrude in subtle ways that we have just begun to plumb. Organizations, like the law, have a life of their own. Greater attention to the spontaneous processes of organization to which sociologists insistently refer, including an awareness that history matters, is sorely needed if we are to deal with some of the key issues of organization in an informed way.

C. Unit of Analysis

The firm-as-production-function approach to economic organization held that (1) the natural boundary of the firm was largely determined by technology, (2) price and output were the relevant data, and (3) nonstandard forms of organization (contracting restraints, vertical integration) had monopoly purpose and intent. The New Institutional Economics in general, and transaction cost economics in particular, takes issue with each of these. Since most technologies can be supported by several forms of organization, technology can scarcely be determinative. Sequential attention—first to technology and only later to organization—is not warranted either. Rather, technology and organization are determined simultaneously. A parity between technology and organization thereby obtains.

Such an approach to economic organization requires that more microanalytic features and different purposes of organization be addressed. Transaction cost economics adopts the view advanced by John R. Commons in the 1930s that the transaction is the basic unit of analysis (Commons, 1934:6).[2] This much more microanalytic orientation brings economics into closer contact with observations and phenomena of long-standing interest to sociologists. The requisite degree of cooperation between parties to a transaction arises not from a presupposed harmony of interests but from active efforts to craft harmonizing safeguards and structures between parties whose interests are often opposed.

D. Organizational Form Matters

Identifying the microanalytic attributes of transactions is only the first half of the problem. The second half entails an examination of the costs and competencies of alternative governance structures. A comparative assessment of alternative market, hybrid, and internal forms of organization is required. Economists again find themselves addressing many phenomena identical to those of interest to sociologists. For example, differences *between* firm and market in incentive and due process respects are germane. Also, differences *within* internal organization require scrutiny. The decomposition rules of hierarchical organization are among the relevant internal features. Issues of corporate governance, including the purposes served by, and, relatedly, the appropriate composition of, the board of directors likewise come under study.

Although differences among as well as between economists, political

---

[2]I do not, however, mean to suggest that the New Institutional Economics and the older version associated with the work of Commons are tightly linked. The older version lives largely in the pages of the history of economic thought, in large measure because it did not develop a rival research agenda but spent its energies on methodological controversy (Coase, 1984). Some sociologists nevertheless express a preference for the earlier form. Whether that is because they believe that the older form can, with effort, be operationalized or whether it is because of a predilection for methodology is unclear. The history of science records that methodological critique is inconclusive. It takes a theory to beat a theory (Kuhn, 1970).

scientists, and sociologists on these matters are real, it is no longer the case that the different disciplines are everywhere addressing different issues. To the contrary, additional common ground—or contested terrain—results. The refutable implications of several distinct viewpoints can now be *compared* and the relevant data brought to bear.

E. Process Matters

The study of governance goes beyond structure and incentive and control instruments to include an examination of process. This is an area in which economists have been loath to enter. Some express the view that it can be avoided: "study of the firm as an organization . . . is not, strictly speaking, necessary: one can hope to divine the correct 'reduced form' for the behavior of the organization without considering the micro-forces within the organization. But study of the organization is likely to help in the design of reduced forms that stress the important variables" (Kreps and Spence, 1985:374–375).

I am persuaded that the self-conscious study of process has already played a vital role in the development of transaction cost economics (see the discussion of the Fundamental Transformation below) and that additional study of process is sorely needed if core issues are to be exposed. Sociologists are well positioned to guide and lead this inquiry. An understanding of the sources of "bureaucratic failures" and of the ways by which these may be mitigated is essential to, but currently is an underdeveloped part of, the study of economic organization. As a consequence of the large disparity between our current understanding of market and bureaucratic failures, the comparative study of organization suffers from a debilitating limp.

The foregoing developments provide the basis for a significant convergence between economists and sociologists. Old hang-ups over hyperrationality versus irrationality can be set aside in favor of a common interest in bounded rationality—with all of the rich organizational ramifications that such a view invites. Microanalytic interest in transactions and organization form brings economists and sociologists together on a common terrain. And the need to make more prominent allowance for unanticipated consequences and, more generally, for process-induced outcomes has become increasingly clear—although this is by no means the prevailing economic opinion. The upshot is that economists and sociologists are no longer passing at a (comfortable) distance from one another. A collision and/or productive joinder is in prospect.

III. RUDIMENTS OF TRANSACTION COST ECONOMICS

A. Economizing

Almost no one believes, much less would insist, that the only purpose of organization is economizing. But most economists, and many social scientists, would now agree that economizing is a leading if not central purpose. This was not always so. The economizing perspective advanced by Frank Knight in 1941 was slow to take hold. Thus, Knight argued that

> men in general, and within limits, wish to behave economically, to make their activities *and their organization* "efficient" rather than wasteful. This fact does deserve the utmost emphasis; and an adequate definition of the science of economics . . . might well make it explicit that the main relevance of the discussion is found in its relation to social policy, assumed to be directed toward the end indicated, of increasing economic efficiency, of reducing waste. (1941:252, emphasis added)

Although economists were long accustomed to thinking about efficiency from the standpoint of the division of labor, efficient factor proportions, gains from trade, and the like, this did not extend to the treatment of organization. To the contrary, the "applied price theory" approach to industrial organization, whereby the firm was described as a production function, regarded organizational variety with grave skepticism: "if an economist finds something—a business practice of one sort or other—that he does not understand, he looks for a monopoly explanation" (Coase, 1972:67). This orientation, which was characteristic of the study of industrial organization at both Harvard and Chicago (Coase, 1972:61–62), was responsible for the inhospitality tradition within antitrust.[3] Unfamiliar or nonstandard contracting and organizational practices were thus held to be presumptively antisocial.

The possibility that organizational variety was responsive to economizing considerations was accordingly given short shrift. The New Institutional Economics takes exception with this and maintains that, except where market power preconditions are satisfied, lasting organizational innovations normally serve economizing purposes. Transaction cost economics adopts and develops this perspective. Numerous refutable implications obtain. Much of antitrust economics as well as the studies of labor organization, regulation, corporate governance, and the corporate form have been reshaped as a consequence.

As compared with other approaches to the study of economic organization, transaction cost economics (1) is more microanalytic, (2) is more self-conscious about its behavioral assumptions, (3) introduces and develops the economic importance of asset specificity, (4) relies more on comparative institutional analysis, (5) regards the business firm as a governance structure rather than a production function, and (6) places greater weight on the *ex post* institutions of contract, with special emphasis on private ordering (as compared with court ordering). The underlying viewpoint that informs the comparative study of issues of economic organization is this: Transaction costs are economized by assigning transactions (which differ in their attributes) to

---

[3]The inhospitality tradition in antitrust works out of the aperture of monopoly. Donald Turner succinctly put it as follows: "I approach customer and territorial restrictions not hospitably in the common law tradition, but inhospitably in the tradition of antitrust" (address by Donald F. Turner before the New York State Bar Association, February 2, 1966, p. 1). For a discussion of the gradual undoing of this orientation and continuing antitrust dilemmas, see Williamson (1985a: Chapter 14).

governance structures (the adaptive capacities and associated costs of which differ) in a discriminating way.

B. Behavioral Assumptions

Behavioral assumptions are often regarded casually. This reflects a widely held opinion that the realism of the assumptions is unimportant and that the fruitfulness of a theory turns on its implications (Friedman, 1953).

This view has been variously disputed, but none more effectively than Nicholas Georgescu-Roegen's prescription for serious science: "Some claim that the purpose of science is prediction. . . . However, even though prediction is the touchstone of scientific knowledge—'in practice man must prove the truth,' as Marx said—the purpose of science in general is not prediction but knowledge for its own sake" (1971:37). Note the balance in these remarks. On the one hand, an important role is reserved for prediction—lest analysis become speculative and undisciplined. This is absolutely essential for sorting the wheat from the chaff. As between theories with substantially identical predictive content, however, those theories that employ more plausible behavioral assumptions are presumably preferred. Thus, "Parsimony recommends that we prefer the postulate that men are [boundedly rational] to the postulate that they are supremely rational when either . . . will do our work of inference as well as the other" (Simon, 1978:8). Or as Tjalling Koopmans put it, if mechanism B rather than A is believed to be generating the phenomena of interest, the intellectually respectable thing to do is to move toward, and eventually work out of, theory B constructions (1957:140). A single-minded quest for refutable implications is checked by acknowledging that the fundamental purpose is to achieve understanding. Anything that deepens our knowledge, which a careful statement of the behavioral assumptions does, is therefore valued.

The key behavioral assumptions on which transaction cost economics relies are bounded rationality and opportunism. The first of these holds that contractual man's cognitive competence is limited. The second makes allowance for self-interest seeking with guile. Calculated efforts to mislead, disguise, obfuscate, and confuse are thus admitted.

It is noteworthy that renewed interest in Machiavelli in the past century, in which *The Prince* is recognized as a contribution to political theory rather than a scurrilous handbook of power politics, has had an invigorating effect on political science. In contrast with Aristotle, who imbued his officeholders with virtue, Machiavelli set out to deal with "men as they are" (Gauss, 1952:14). Transaction cost economics subscribes to Knight's view that we need to deal with "human nature as we know it" (1965:270).

The assumptions of bounded rationality and opportunism have massive ramifications for economic organization. Consider the following:

1. *Incomplete contracting.* Although it is instructive and a great analytical convenience to assume that agents have the capacity to engage in comprehensive *ex ante* contracting (with or without private information), the condition of

bounded rationality precludes this. The only complex contracts that fall within the feasible set are those that are incomplete. Accordingly, the study of structures that facilitate gap filling, dispute settlement, adaptation, and the like are brought within the ambit of economic organization. The institutions of contract execution thus play a central role in the transaction cost economics scheme of things, whereas these same institutions are ignored (indeed, suppressed) by the fiction of comprehensive *ex ante* contracting.

2. *Contract as promise.* Another convenient concept of contract is to assume that economic agents will reliably fulfill their promises. Such stewardship behavior will not obtain, however, if economic agents are given to opportunism. *Ex ante* efforts to screen economic agents in terms of differential reliability and, even more, *ex post* safeguards to deter opportunism arise under these circumstances. Institutional practices that would be unneeded, and hence would be regarded as anomalous or antisocial in a pure promise regime, may actually be performing valued economizing purposes when the hazards of opportunism are admitted.

3. *Context.* Although the main predictive content of transaction cost economics turns on the attributes of transactions, this is not to say that context is unimportant. To the contrary, making allowance for the embeddedness of transactions (Granovetter, 1985), as well as the attributes of transactions themselves, can yield added predictive content.

4. *Secondary consequences.* The full ramifications of organizational innovations can often be discerned only when their secondary consequences are assessed. The bounded rationality/opportunism framework comes to terms easily with and helps to inform the study of unintended consequences. Regimes of hyperrationality and promise, by contrast, disallow these or regard unintended outcomes as aberrations. As previously noted,[4] such casual disregard can be and sometimes is responsible for serious organizational error.

C. Operationalizing Transaction Cost Economics

1. A Simple Contractual Schema[5]

As stated earlier, transaction costs are economized by assigning transactions to governance structures in a discriminating way. The transaction is thus made the basic unit of analysis. The basic attributes of transactions thereafter have to be identified. The costs and competencies of alternative governance structures likewise need to be determined. A discriminating (mainly, transaction cost economizing) match is thereupon attempted.

Of the several critical dimensions for describing transactions, the most important is the condition of asset specificity—which has reference to the ease with which durable investments can be redeployed to alternative uses and users without sacrifice of productive value. The simple contractual sche-

[4]See the discussion in the section on the rationality orientation, above.
[5]This is based on Williamson (1985a:32–35).

ma set out below works off of this distinction. Thus, assume that a good or service can be supplied by either of two alternative technologies. One is a general-purpose technology, the other a special-purpose technology. The special-purpose technology requires greater investment in transaction-specific durable assets and is more efficient for servicing steady-state demands.

Using k as a measure of transaction-specific assets, transactions that use the general purpose technology are ones for which $k = 0$. When transactions use the special-purpose technology, by contrast, a $k > 0$ condition exists. Assets here are specialized to the particular needs of the parties. Productive values would therefore be sacrificed if transactions of this kind were to be prematurely terminated. A bilateral monopoly condition thus applies to such transactions.

Whereas classical market contracting—"sharp in by clear agreement; sharp out by clear performance" (Macneil, 1974:738)—suffices for transactions of the $k = 0$ kind, unassisted market governance poses hazards whenever nontrivial transaction-specific assets are placed at risk. Parties have an incentive to devise safeguards to protect investments in transactions of the latter kind. Let s denote the magnitude of any such safeguards. An $s = 0$ condition is one in which no safeguards are provided; a decision to provide safeguards is reflected by an $s > 0$ result.

Figure 1 displays the three contracting outcomes corresponding to such a description. Associated with each node is a price. So as to facilitate comparisons between nodes, assume that suppliers (1) are risk-neutral, (2) are

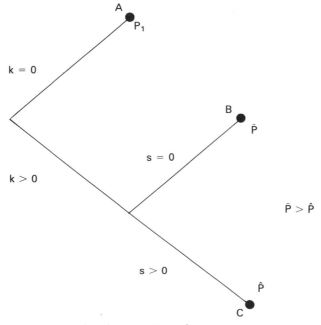

Figure 1. Simple contracting schema.

prepared to supply under either technology, and (3) will accept any safeguard condition whatsoever so long as an expected break-even result can be projected. Thus, node A is the general-purpose technology ($k = 0$) supply relation for which a break-even price of p_1 is projected. The node B contract is supported by transaction-specific assets ($k > 0$) for which no safeguard is offered ($s = 0$). The expected break-even price here is $\bar{p}$. The node C contract also employs the special-purpose technology. But since the buyer at this node provides the supplier with a safeguard ($s > 0$), the breakeven price, $\hat{p}$, at node C is less than $\bar{p}$.

The protective safeguards to which I refer normally take on one or more of three forms. The first is to realign incentives, which commonly involves some type of severance payment or penalty for premature termination. A second is to create and employ a specialized governance structure to which to refer and resolve disputes. The use of arbitration, rather than litigation in the courts, is thus characteristic of node C governance. A third is to introduce trading regularities that support and signal continuity intentions. Expanding a trading relation from unilateral to bilateral exchange—through the concerted use, for example, of reciprocity—thereby to effect an equilibration of trading hazards is an example of this third form of protective safeguard.

This simple contracting schema applies to a wide variety of contracting issues. It facilitates comparative institutional analysis by emphasizing that technology (k), contractual governance/safeguards (s), and price (p) are fully interactive and are determined simultaneously. It is furthermore gratifying that so many applications turn out to be variations on a theme. As Friedrich Hayek (1967:50) observed, "whenever the capacity of recognizing an abstract rule which the arrangement of these attributes follows has been acquired in one field, the same master mould will apply when the signs for those abstract attributes are evoked by altogether different elements."

By way of summary, the nodes A, B, and C in the contractual schema set out in Figure 1 have the following properties:

1. Transactions that are efficiently supported by general purpose assets ($k = 0$) are located at node A and do not need protective governance structures. Discrete market contracting suffices. The world of competition obtains.
2. Transactions that involve significant investments of a transaction-specific kind ($k > 0$) are ones for which the parties are effectively engaged in bilateral trade.
3. Transactions located at node B enjoy no safeguards ($s = 0$), on which account the projected break-even supply price is great ($\bar{p} > \hat{p}$). Such transactions are apt to be unstable contractually. They may revert to node A (in which event the special purpose technology would be replaced by the general-purpose ($k = 0$) technology) or be relocated to node C (by introducing contractual safeguards that would encourage the continued use of the $k > 0$ technology).
4. Transactions located at node C incorporate safeguards ($s > 0$) and thus are protected against expropriation hazards.

5. Inasmuch as price and governance are linked, parties to a contract should not expect to have their cake (low price) and eat it too (no safeguard). More generally, it is important to study *contracting in its entirety*. Both the *ex ante* terms and the manner in which contracts are thereafter executed vary with the investment characteristics and the associated governance structures within which transactions are embedded.

2. The Company Town Example[6]

The company town is mainly regarded as a painful reminder of labor abuses associated with an earlier era. Surely there is nothing favorable, much less redeeming, that can be said about such a condition.

Still, company towns were the exception rather than the rule. The question, moreover, needs to be asked: Why would anyone accept employment under patently unfavorable terms? More generally, what are the relevant contractual alternatives for which a comparative assessment is needed? Inasmuch as the study of extreme instances often helps to illuminate the essentials of a situation (Behavioral Sciences Subpanel, 1962:5), an examination of the problems of organization faced by the company town may be instructive.

The issues are addressed in two stages, analysis and commentary. The first illustrates the advantages and the second the limitations of studying economic organization from the standpoint of "contracting in its entirety."

In order to analyze the issues, assume the following: (1) A remote mineral source has been located, the mining of which is deemed to be economical; (2) the mineral can be mined only upon making significant investments in durable physical assets that are thereafter nonredeployable; (3) requisite labor skills are not firm-specific to any significant degree, but there are setup costs associated with labor relocation; (4) the weather in the region is severe, which necessitates the provision of durable housing for protection from the elements; (5) the community of miners is too small to support more than one general store; and (6) the nearest city is 40 miles away.

I wish to focus on two issues: Should the workers or the mining firm own the homes in the community? And how should the general store be owned and operated? So as to display the relevant features more clearly, two different mobility scenarios will be considered.

What I will refer to as the immobile society corresponds to the pre-automobile era. The firm advertises for workers and describes the terms of employment. Given the remote location, workers will be concerned not merely with wages but also with housing and with the economic infrastructure.

Were the firm to decide to construct housing itself, it could then (1) sell the homes to the workers, (2) rent the homes to workers on short-term leases, (3) write long-term leases with severe penalties for early termination by the lessee, or (4) write long-term leases that bind the firm but permit easy termi-

---

[6]This is based on Williamson (1985a:35–38).

nation by the lessee. Alternatively, the firm could (5) require workers to construct their own housing.

Given the thin market, workers who constructed their own homes would, in effect, be making firm-specific investments. Lacking contractual safeguards—buy-back clauses (whereby the company guarantees a market in the event of layoff or termination), long-term employment guarantees, lump sum severance awards, death benefits, and the like—workers will agree to make such investments only if offered a sign-on bonus and/or a wage premium. Expressed in terms of the contractual schema in Figure 1, that last corresponds to a node B rather than a node C result (which is to say, a $\overline{w} > \hat{w}$ outcome).

Node B outcomes, however, are notoriously inefficient. The marginal costs of the firm will be driven up by a $\overline{w}$ wage bargain, whence the firm will make layoffs according to an inefficient criterion. Home designs chosen by the workers will likewise be compromised in consideration of the hazards. The advantages of concentrating all the specific investments on the mining firm are thus apt to be apparent to both parties at the outset (or will become obvious during negotiations). Accordingly, home ownership by the mining firm coupled with efficient lease terms ought to be observed. Option 4—long-term leases that bind the lessor but provide easy release for the lessee—has obvious attractions.

Consider the general store. The leading possibilities here are these: (1) The store is owned by the mining firm and (a) operated as a monopoly, (b) placed under a fair rate of return constraint, or (c) placed under a market basket (index number) constraint; (2) a multiyear franchise is awarded to the highest bidder, the receipts from which bidding competition are (a) paid to the company treasury, (b) divided among the initial group of workers, or (c) placed in a money market fund and paid out to customers over the life of the franchise in proportion to purchases; and (3) the store is owned and operated by the workers as a cooperative. Although none of these is unproblematic, options 2c and 3 have much to recommend them. Whatever the determination, the more general point is this: The wage bargain to which the workers agree will be conditional on, rather than independent of, the way in which the general store is owned and operated if, as assumed, contract realizations reflect all of the salient features—of which the ownership and governance of the general store are plainly germane.

Suppose now that mobility is introduced. The appearance of the automobile, mobile homes, home freezers, mail order houses, and the like greatly relieve the contracting difficulties of the premobility era. The need for site-specific investments in homes is alleviated by the invention of suitable assets on wheels, which is what the mobile home option represents. Exclusive reliance on the general store is relieved by the possibility of shopping at a distance, which cheap transportation to the nearby city and purchase from mail order houses permit. Changes in markets and technology thus have sweeping contracting ramifications. In effect, a viable node A alternative has been introduced into what had previously been a contractually complicated node B/node C choice set.

To be sure, remote mining communities may present still other issues for which careful comparative institutional assessments will be needed. Plainly, however, contractual strains of the earlier era are greatly alleviated by the mobility that assets on wheels and competition permit.

If contracting in its entirety reliably obtains, then an efficient configuration of wages, home ownership, company store operations, and the like will appear, whatever the mobility condition of the population. What then explains the widespread discontent with the organization of company towns in the premobility era?

There are two leading possibilities. One is that students of company towns have not performed the relevant comparative institutional tests. Rather than describe and evaluate the actual set of contractual choices from which company town organization is constrained to choose, company towns are compared instead with noncompany towns. Unsurprisingly, company towns fare poorly in the comparison. Inasmuch, however, as such a comparison is operationally irrelevant, it is wholly unhelpful to an understanding of the organizational problems with which the company town is faced.

The second possibility is that, especially in the context of labor market organization, contracting in its entirety is rarely realized. Company towns would be a good deal less objectionable if they were actually organized along efficient contracting principles. But what company store was ever organized as a cooperative? A chronic problem with labor market organization is that workers and their families are irrepressible optimists. They are taken in by vague assurances of good faith, by legally unenforceable promises, and by their own hopes for the good life. Tough-minded bargaining in its entirety never occurs or, if it occurs, comes too late. An objective assessment of employment hazards that should have preceded any employment agreement thus comes only after disappointment. "Demands" for redress in those circumstances are apt to be regarded as a bluff—based, as they are, on weakness. Collective organization may help, but it entails a struggle. Ensuing settlements may stanch the losses rather than effect a transfusion.

I submit that both factors contribute to the low opinion with which company towns are held. The transaction cost economics assumption that the parties to a contract are hardheaded and that the ramifications of alternative contracts are intuited if not fully thought through thus comes at a cost. Omissions and distortions sometimes result. Such costs are less severe, I believe, where commercial contracting practices (including vertical integration and supporting internal governance structures) are under review than when labor market organization is being studied. As an interim measure, my emphasis on previously neglected transaction cost features is meant to redress an earlier imbalance. I fully concur, however, that complex contracting will be better understood if examined from several well-focused perspectives.

3. The Fundamental Transformation

What has been called the Fundamental Transformation is an illustration of how the study of process can be vital to an understanding of economic organization. Economists have long been inured to the view that the number of qualified suppliers influences the quality of bids—large numbers favoring a competitive outcome, small numbers yielding a more problematic or, in the limit, monopolistic outcome. Indeed, this was thought to be settled beyond dispute. The number of noncollusive bidders being decisive, the study of process was simply irrelevant.

Transaction cost economics views these matters anew. It starts from the premise that all long-term contracts are unavoidably incomplete. It further maintains that a condition of asset idiosyncrasy is a much more widespread condition than had previously been acknowledged. And it insists that the contracting process needs to be studied in its entirety.

Contrary to the prevailing view that large numbers of qualified bidders at the outset assured an efficient and competitive contracting outcome, transaction cost economics asks whether a large-numbers condition continues during the supply period and at contract renewal intervals. Transactions that are supported by nontrivial investments in transaction-specific assets (the $k > 0$ condition referred to above) are not ones for which parity at the outset implies parity thereafter. To the contrary, a condition of bilateral dependency between buyer and initial winning bidder *evolves*. In the degree to which continuity is valued and/or an expropriation hazard to transaction-specific assets is posed, a large-numbers supply condition at the outset is transformed into one of small numbers bargaining thereafter. This transformation is called the Fundamental Transformation.

Given the gaps in long-term incomplete contracts (by reason of bounded rationality) and the unenforceability of general clauses (because of the proclivity of human agents to make false and misleading (self-disbelieved) statements), the following hazards must be confronted: Joined as they are in a condition of bilateral monopoly, both buyer and seller are strategically situated to bargain over the disposition of any incremental gain whenever a proposal to adapt is made by the other party. Although both have a long-term interest in effecting adaptations of a joint profit-maximizing kind, each also has an interest in appropriating as much of the gain as he or she can on each occasion to adapt. Efficient adaptations that would otherwise be made thus result in costly haggling or even go unmentioned, lest the gains be dissipated by costly subgoal pursuit. Governance structures that attentuate opportunism and otherwise infuse confidence are evidently needed.

The Fundamental Transformation scarcely exhausts the issues of process that are germane to an informed assessment to economic organization. To the contrary, it is merely illustrative. A careful examination of the intertemporal propensities of bureaucracy, to include an assessment of how these propensities vary with internal organization, is sorely needed. An extensive literature on "market failure" needs to be joined by an assessment of "bureaucratic failure" if a balanced treatment of economic organization is to be reached. Sociologists and organization theory specialists obviously have much to contribute if the studies of bureaucratic and market failures are to be placed on a parity.

D. Variations on a Theme

The company town example sketched above is merely a finger exercise. As it turns out, however, the simple contracting schema has broad applicability. A wide range of seemingly disparate phenomena are variations on a theme.

Thus, the very same transaction cost economics apparatus helps to inform the study of intermediate product market transactions (both nonstandard contracting practices, such as reciprocity, and vertical integration), labor market organization, project financing, regulation, corporate governance, and even aspects of family organization. This is gratifying, since "A fundamental hypothesis of science is that appearances are deceptive and that there is a way of looking at or interpreting or organizing the evidence that will reveal superficially disconnected and diverse phenomena to be manifestations of a more fundamental and relatively simple structure" (Friedman, 1953:33).

The primitive state and other limitations of transaction cost economics notwithstanding, the cutting edge by which theories are judged is their refutable implications. Transaction cost economics invites comparison with alternative theories on this criterion.

IV. RECENT CRITIQUES OF TRANSACTION COST ECONOMICS

Although transaction cost economics traces its origins to the 1930s,[7] it is only in the past 15 years that concerted efforts have been made to operationalize this approach. Earlier criticisms of transaction cost economics dealt with its tautological character (Alchian and Demsetz, 1972:783; Fisher, 1977: 322, fn. 5). These concerns have been relieved, though not entirely dissipated, by the aforementioned strategy of assigning transactions (which differ in their attributes) to governance structures in a discriminating way. In a crude and preliminary way, moreover, the data that bear on the predictions are corroborative.[8]

This focus on refutable implications and the data that bear thereon marks a significant shift in the dialogue. Rival hypotheses must offer competing (same or different) implications if they wish to be heard on these matters. The study of economic organization is coming of age. The conceptual schema and analytic apparatus out of which transaction cost economics operates are nonetheless legitimate objects of concern. This is where most of the recent sociological objections focus.

I begin with a brief self-critique of the transaction cost economics framework. Standards of peer group organization are then considered and claims that transaction cost economics commits excesses of functionalism are ad-

[7]For a discussion of the antecedents, see Williamson (1985a:2–7).
[8]See Anderson and Schmittlein (1984), Bjuggren (1985), Joskow (1985, 1986), Masten (1984), Masten and Crocker (1985), Mulhern (1986), Palay (1984, 1985), Williamson (1985a: Chap. 5).

dressed. A new mode of criticism—the "lighthearted vignette"—to which transaction cost economics has recently been subjected is then assessed.

A. Self-Critique

Transaction cost economizing is an instructive but narrow way of conceiving of the problem of economic organization. This approach needs to be located in the larger framework of which it is a part. Consider the following[9]:

1. Holding the nature of the good or service to be delivered constant, economizing takes place with reference to the sum of production and transaction costs, whence trade-offs between the two must be recognized.
2. More generally, the design of the good or service to be delivered is a decision variable that influences demand as well as costs of both kinds, whence design is appropriately made a part of the calculus.
3. The social context in which transactions are embedded—the customs, mores, habits, and so on—have a bearing, and therefore need to be taken into account, when moving from one culture to another.
4. The argument relies in a general, background way on the efficacy of competition to perform a sort between more and less efficient modes and to shift resources in favor of the former. This seems plausible, especially if the relevant outcomes are those that appear over intervals of five and ten years rather than in the very near term. This intuition would nevertheless benefit from a more fully developed theory of the selection process. Transaction cost arguments are thus open to some of the same objections that evolutionary economists have made of orthodoxy (Nelson and Winter, 1982:356–370), though in other respects there are strong complementarities between transaction cost economics and the evolutionary economics view (Nelson and Winter, 1982: 34–38).
5. Whenever private and social benefits and costs differ, the social cost calculus should govern if prescriptive treatments are attempted.

B. Peer Groups

Raymond Russell's recent treatment of "Employee Ownership and Internal Governance" (1985a) usefully contributes to our understanding of employee owned enterprise. My favorable opinion of this work and of Russell's general approach are stated elsewhere (Williamson, 1985a:238, fn. 26, 1985b). It bears repeating that both Russell and I agree that his empirical findings concerning the organization of employee-owned firms are consonant with transaction cost economics reasoning. Russell and I nevertheless differ on how to describe the peer group standard to which actual employee ownership

---

[9]The list is from Williamson (1985a:22–23).

organizations should be compared. Specifically, Russell contends that I have invented a peer group standard that bears little resemblance to the literature on peer group organization. Lest others conclude that I am guilty as charged, I take occasion here to dispute this claim.

The original charge reads as follows (Russell, 1985a:218):

> As [Louis] Putterman . . . has already noted, Williamson has loaded up [the Peer Group] model with so many economic disabilities that it cannot help but look inferior to any realistic organizational form. Among these disabilities, . . . [are] the absence of hierarchy or any form of strategic leadership . . . [and] the absence of "metering" or any form of performance measurement. . . . If Williamson had consulted the sociology literature on actual "peer groups," he would have been hard pressed to find a single one that did not have leaders, and in which members did not regularly monitor each other's behavior and punish members whose behavior did not conform to the standards of the group.

The charge is thereafter repeated as follows: Williamson's Peer Group "bears no relation to any actual peer groups or actual firms, and even as a 'vision' it exists only in Williamson's own mind" (Russell, 1985b:247).

I agree that all forms of organization, peer groups included, need to come to terms with both bounded rationality and opportunism. Very small groups aside, all viable forms of organization employ hierarchy—as a concession to bounded rationality. Moreover, all viable forms of organization employ a combination of screening, social conditioning, monitoring, and reward/penalty instruments to check opportunism. I count it as a significant gain that there is increasing agreement—perhaps even approaching unanimity—on this.

A curious schizophrenia, however, characterizes much of the peer group literature. Utopian visions of work organization are repeated by successive generations of scholars without reference to either of these troublesome behavioral features. Rather than concede that the pure peer group form is unattainable because of the relentless pound of bounded rationality and opportunism, the fiction that the utopian ideal would succeed gloriously but for the opposed interests of the establishment is introduced and promulgated instead.

This being the case, any comparative assessment of alternative forms of work organization in which idealized forms favored by the New Left are included should presumably start with a statement of the pure peer group ideal. To begin otherwise would be contrary to the letter and spirit of New Left reform—which regards compromise forms as the problem, not the solution.

Unfortunately, however, careful and complete statements of the pure peer group mode are rarely provided. Assar Lindbeck nevertheless observes that the decentralized, producer cooperatives favored by the New Left contemplate a "nonhierarchical decision-making structure" and traces this view of organization "to such pre-Marxist socialists as Francois M. C. Fourier, Pierre Joseph Proudhon and Robert Owen" (Lindbeck 1971:5). Although Ernest Mandel recognizes that even peer groups require administration, he holds that communitarian economic organization will successively evolve into "self-management of *free communes of producers and consumers,* in which every-body will take it in turn to carry out administrative work, in which the difference between 'directors' and 'directed' will be abolished, and a federation of which will eventually cover the whole world" (Mandel, 1968:677).

To be sure, these are the aspirations of political philosophers. But sociologists who have examined producer cooperatives also describe the cooperative ideal in very similar terms. Thus, Joyce Rothschild-Witt (1979:512) characterizes, without endorsing, the collectivist-democratic ideal as:

> . . . premised on the belief that social order can be achieved without recourse to authority relations (Guerin, 1970). Thus it presupposes the capacity of individuals for self-disciplined, cooperative behavior. Indeed, collectivist organizations routinely emphasize these aspects of human beings. Like the anarchists, their aim is . . . the abolition of the pyramid in toto: organization without hierarchy.

And Howard Aldrich and Robert Stern (1983:373) indicate that the "ideal form of producers' cooperatives includes such characteristics as one person—one vote, limits to the amount of stock held by single individuals, rotation or election of managers, limited specialization, minimal levels of hierarchy, and extensive member involvement in decisions."

Plainly, the ideal peer group form that I described and to which Putterman and Russell take exception is akin to, if not identical with, that described by the sociologists. If, however, there is now general agreement that the pure peer group form is hopelessly naive, I am fully prepared hereafter only to examine viable peer groups—by which I (and presumably others) mean those that expressly come to terms with "human nature as we know it."

C. Functionalism

Mark Granovetter's recent paper, "Economic Action and Social Structures: A Theory of Embeddedness," attributes functionalist excesses to transaction cost economics and to the New Institutional Economics of which it is a part: "The general story told by members of this school is that social institutions and arrangements previously thought to be the *adventitious* result of legal, historical, social or political forces are better viewed as the efficient solution to certain economic problems. The tone is strikingly similar to the structural-functional sociology of the 1940s to the 1960s, and much of the argumentation fails the elementary tests of a sound functional explanation laid down by Robert Merton in 1947" (Granovetter, 1985: 481–482, emphasis added). Granovetter (1986) takes particularly strong exception with the readiness with which economists invoke economic natural selection arguments.

Whether an adventitious theory of economic organization is superior to an efficiency theory is better settled, I submit, by pressing each to show its hand. What are the implications of each, and what do the data support?

Perhaps, indeed, the issue is less efficiency versus adventitiousness than a productive joinder of each. Few economists would insist on an unrelieved efficiency theory of economic organization. Weak-form efficiency and selection is all that can usually be claimed. Simon thus distinguishes between weak- and strong-form selection as follows: "in a relative sense, the *fitter* survive, but there is no reason to suppose that they are *fittest* in any absolute sense" (1983:69; emphasis in original).

To be sure, a more well-developed theory of weak-form selection—when it works well and poorly—is greatly needed. The important work of Richard Nelson and Sidney Winter (1982) notwithstanding, much remains to be done to assess the efficacy of the selection process. That does not, however, entitle sociologists to dismiss economizing arguments because "the selection pressures that *guarantee* efficient organization are nowhere clearly described" (Granovetter, 1985:503; emphasis added).

Indeed, Granovetter advances an unreasonably demanding and asymmetric standard. Why not insist that efficiency skeptics describe the circumstances under which efficiency is assuredly *defeated*? If an unambiguous case *for or against* efficiency can rarely be made on selection grounds, then plausible efficiency arguments must be assessed differently. Abstract selection logic thus gives way to an examination of refutable implications.

Note in this connection that "adventitious" explanations of economic organization to which no evolutionary litmus test is applied no longer win by default. Not only are alternative efficiency explanations assessed in terms of their predictive content,[10] but adventitious explanations are held to the same standard.

There is a certain irony, moreover, in Granovetter's claim that transaction cost economics is guilty of functionalist excesses when in fact transaction cost economics provides one of the very few cases in the social sciences in which full functionalism, as defined by Jon Elster (1983), goes through. The issues are developed in a later section.

D. Analyzing Vignettes

Charles Perrow's critique of transaction cost economics is unique. He does not offer a rival theory to explain the same vertical integration phenomena to which transaction cost economics has been applied and with which interpretations he takes exception. He does not offer a contrary assessment of the main empirical studies of vertical integration/contracting to which transaction cost economics has been applied. He does not demonstrate that the modeling apparatus on which transaction cost economics relies is defective. And he does not offer new evidence that contradicts earlier findings.

Instead, he employs a new genre, which he characterizes as a "lighthearted . . . vignette" (1986:245). The vignette is entertaining, but it lacks the discipline that is ordinarily associated with scientific discourse. There are simply too many degrees of freedom. The conditions of asset specificity out of which the vignette works are ambiguous. Perrow neither supplies his own trade-off framework nor makes use of those of others.[11] Considerations of contracting in their entirety are not even acknowledged, much less ad-

[10]I have elsewhere expressed my deep skepticism of efficiency theories that turn entirely on differential risk aversion (Williamson, 1985a:388–389).

[11]He makes no use, for example, of Williamson (1981; 1985:90–96) or Riordan and Williamson (1985).

dressed. Perrow thus blithely asserts that buyers can shift adjustment costs onto suppliers with impunity. The proposition that contractual hazards are reflected in prices is never addressed, much less disputed—possibly because vignette analysis invites myopia.

The vignette completed, Perrow concludes with "two cheers for markets, and only one for hierarchies" (1986:246.[12] Although I am more inclined to regard alternative forms of organization as instruments, I am pleased that Perrow does not repeat a position that he took in 1975—when he asserted that "bureaucracy is a form of organization superior to all others we know or can hope to afford in the near or middle future" (Perrow, 1975:6).

V. FUNCTIONALIST EXPLANATION

Functionalist explanations of four kinds can be distinguished. The hopelessly naive version is Panglossian. At the other extreme is full functionalism, which is associated with Elster. Located in between are functionalist explanations that follow Malinowski and Merton.

The Panglossian view is that all is for the best in this best of all possible worlds. Almost no one subscribes to this view, but Granovetter claims that some economists come close (1985:503; 1986).[13] I submit, however, that Panglossian functionalism is better disregarded and attention focused on the three more carefully stated kinds. These are examined next, after which an illustration of full functionalism is offered.

A. Types of Functionalism

1. Malinowski

According to Elster, Malinowski's Principle states, "All social phenomena have beneficial consequences (intended or unintended, recognized or unrecognized) that explain them" (1983:57). This invites *ex post* rationalization, in that events that at first appear to be a contradiction to a preferred hypothesis are simply reinterpreted. As Elster notes, "This principle can be harnessed to conservative as well as to radical ideologies: the former will explain social facts in terms of their contribution to social cohesion, the latter according to their contribution to oppression and class rule" (1983:57). Elster illustrates the latter with the following quotation from Marx (Elster, 1983:59):

[12]Perrow nevertheless maintains, "Markets tend to be concentrated, rigged, protected, and inefficient" (1986:246). Not all markets are equally defective, however. Many are unconcentrated, difficult to rig, highly contested, and relatively efficient. Since we plainly need to make choices among alternatives, *all* of which are defective, Olympian statements that cast a pox on all alternatives do not advance the dialogue. When do markets fail *comparatively* is the issue.
[13]Although Granovetter includes me among the offenders, Dennis Mueller specifically exempts *The Economic Institutions of Capitalism* from Panglossian excesses (Mueller, 1986).

> The circumstance that a man without fortune but possessing energy, solidity, stability and business acumen may become a capitalist in this manner . . . is greatly admired by apologists for the capitalist system. Although this circumstance continually brings an unwelcome number of new soldiers of fortune into the field and into competition with the already existing individual capitalists, it also reinforces the supremacy of capital itself, expands its base and enables it to recruit ever new forces for itself out of the substratum of society. In a similar way, the circumstance that the Catholic Church, in the Middle Ages, formed its hierarchy out of the best brains in the land, regardless of their estate, birth or fortune, was one of the principal means of consolidating ecclesiastical rule and suppressing the laity.

The natural or first-order interpretation of elitist systems, of which capitalism and the Catholic Church are candidates, is that merit selection will be denied in favor of the establishment. Incumbents and their heirs will thus systematically suppress qualified intruders. Upon examination, however, the data do not perfectly line up: Some qualified intruders regularly make "unwelcome" headway. So a more subtle or second-order interpretation is needed. The new prediction is that the security of the establishment is favored by admitting "the best brains in the land, regardless of their estate, birth or fortune." If the data were still recalcitrant, a still more subtle third-order explanation would be advanced. Malinowski's Principle is thus too elastic, in that any outcome can eventually be rationalized.

2. Merton's Principle

Merton's Principle states, "Whenever social phenomena have consequences that are beneficial, unintended and unrecognized, they can also be explained by these consequences" (Elster, 1983:57). This is a deeper form of functional explanation, in that functional explanation is reserved for phenomena that yield unintended and unrecognized consequences. Elster nevertheless insists that even this more cautious form of functionalist explanation is invalid because it lacks reproductive feedback. This brings us to full functionalism.

3. Elster

Elster maintains that a "valid functional explanation in sociology" takes the following form (1983:57):

> An institution or a behavioural pattern X is explained by its function Y for group Z if and only if:
> (1) Y is an effect of X;
> (2) Y is beneficial for Z;
> (3) Y is unintended by the actors producing X;
> (4) Y—or at least the causal relation between X and Y
> —is unrecognized by the actors in Z;
> (5) Y maintains X by a causal feedback loop passing through Z.

Elster argues that full functional explanations are rarely satisfied in the social sciences. Rather, functionalism is mainly reserved for biology. This is because in biology "the theory of natural selection creates a presumption that whatever benefits reproductive capacity can also be explained by these benefits. In the social sciences there is no such theory of comparable generality, and so the actual mechanism must be specified for each particular case" (Elster, 1983:20). This being rarely possible, Elster urges that social scientists eschew full functional explanation in favor of "intentional explanation [, which] differs from functional in that the former can be directed to the distant future, whereas the latter is typically myopic and opportunistic" (1983:20).

Efforts to apply functional explanation in the social sciences should recognize that "condition (4) is fulfilled only if the rules are spread by takeover, not if they are spread by imitation" (Elster, 1983:58). Also, "many purported cases of functional explanation fail because the feedback loop of criterion (5) is postulated rather than demonstrated" (Elster, 1983:58). Unlike biologists, social scientists must show in each instance how the feedback operates (Elster, 1983:61).

B. A Full Functionalist Example

I am persuaded by Elster that social scientists can and should use intentional explanation to good advantage. Intentional behavior is goal-oriented, whence intentional explanation "involves showing that the actor did what he did for a reason." This excludes flukes (Elster, 1983:70). By contrast with natural selection, which can only choose from among actual alternatives, men can create unactualized future possibilities (Elster, 1983:71). For example, the contracting schema set out in Figure 1 contemplates that contracting agents can describe alternative modes of contracting in which technologies and governance structures differ and expressly price these differences out. More generally, the study of contracting in its entirety is part of an intentional explanation scheme.

Anything, however, that deepens our understanding of complex phenomena has merit. Full functionalism, in those few cases where it can be shown to apply, is one of the possibilities. Interestingly, one of these exceptions comes out of the transaction cost literature.

I have reference to the appearance and diffusion of the multidivisional (M-form) organizational innovation. As described elsewhere (Chandler, 1962; Williamson, 1975: Chaps. 8–9), the M-form innovation was developed in the 1920s as a response to the organizational problems that beset the large, functionally organized (U-form) corporation. Although there is reason to believe that the innovators anticipated many of the benefits that accrued to this organizational reform (Brown, 1924), there were also unanticipated and unexpected consequences.

The M-form innovation began as an effort to cope. Chandler's statement of the defects of the large U-form enterprise is pertinent (Chandler, 1962:382–383):

> The inherent weakness in the centralized, functionally departmentalized operating company . . . became critical only when the administrative load on the senior exec-

utives increased to such an extent that they were unable to handle their entrepreneurial responsibilities efficiently. This situation arose when the operations of the enterprise became too complex and the problems of coordination, appraisal, and policy formulation too intricate for a small number of top officers to handle both long-run, entrepreneurial, and short-run operational administrative activities.

Bounds on rationality were evidently reached as the U-form structure labored under a communication overload. Moving to a decentralized structure relieved some of these strains.

But there was more to it than this. Not only did the M-form structure serve to economize on bounded rationality, but it further served (in comparison with the U-form structure that it supplanted) to attenuate subgoal pursuit (reduce opportunism). This is because, as Chandler (1962:382) puts it, the M-form structure "clearly removed the executives responsible for the destiny of the entire enterprise from the more routine operational activities, and so gave them the time, information, and even psychological commitment for long-term planning and appraisal."

The upshot is that the M-form innovation (X), which had mainly bounded rationality origins, also had unanticipated effects on corporate purpose (Y) by attenuating subgoal pursuit. Benefits of two kinds were thereby realized in the process.

There were still further unexpected consequences in store, moreover. Once the M-form organization had been perfected and extended from specialized lines of commerce (automobiles, chemicals) to manage diversified activities, it became clear that this structure could be used to support takeover of firms in which managerial discretion excesses were occuring (Z). A transfer of resources to higher-valued purposes arguably obtains (Williamson, 1985a: 319–322).

The spread of multidivisionalization through takeover thus yields the *reproductive link* that Elster (1983:58) notes is normally missing in most functional arguments in social science. The requisites of full functionalism are evidently satisfied.

Indeed, there is an additional process of spreading the M-form that ought also to be mentioned: mitosis. The large and diversified M-form structure may discover that the benefits associated with new activities or acquisitions do not continue indefinitely. Acquired components or diversified parts may there-

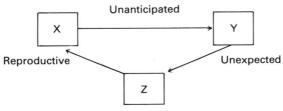

Figure 2. Full functionalism. X—M-form innovation, Y—attenuated subgoal pursuit, Z—takeover.

fore be divested. To the extent that these are spun off or otherwise divested as discrete multidivisional units themselves, propagation through cell division may be said to exist. This quasi-biological process would also presumably qualify as a reproductive link and thereby contribute to successful functional explanation. Figure 2 summarizes the argument.

VI. CONCLUSIONS

It is arguable whether economists and sociologists ever divided the domain along the rational/irrational lines described by Samuelson (1947). The earlier approaches to economic organization employed by each were nevertheless consonant with this general oreintation. Thus, hyperrationality was featured in the economic approach whereby the firm was described as a production function to which a profit maximization objective was ascribed. The relevant data were price and output. Sociologists, by contrast, viewed the firm as a bureaucracy within which a struggle between opposing interests were waged. Attention was focused on the dysfunctional consequences that attend efforts to exercise control and on the adventitious results of legal, historical, social, or political forces. There being little overlap in the phenomena of interest, and there being data that corroborated each view, sociologists and economists could happily coexist without the prospect of being challenged by the other.

The New Institutional Economics threatens to upset this *modus vivendi*. It supplants the firm as production function approach by a much more microanalytic orientation, which brings it into active contact with issues that were once relegated to sociology. It maintains that the details of organization have economic content to which an appropriately microanalytic economizing approach can be systematically applied.

Once the transaction has been made the basic unit of analysis, questions such as the following are posed: Which transactions are organized within the firm and which outside (the efficient boundaries issue)? How do the employment hazards posed by human asset specificity influence the organization of labor? How do the contracts for the goods and services that are procured from outside sources vary as a function of the attributes of the transactions? What are the lessons for economic organization—peer groups included—of the twin assumptions of bounded rationality and opportunism? What purposes are served by the board of directors, and how does the composition of the board vary with the internal structure of the firm and the lines of business in which the firm is engaged? How does contracting in its entirety help to inform the study of the fairness and efficacy of contracts of all kinds (e.g., company towns, franchising, regulation, career marriages, executive compensation, consumer durables)? And the list goes on.

The upshot is that the New Institutional Economics occupies or shares territory that was once thought to be the exclusive domain of sociologists. The "problem" is that it introduces efficiency principles to predict that a whole series of organizational regularities will be observed. Theories of organization in which adventitiousness is featured must now come to terms with rival theories of organization that employ an economizing framework.

Sociologists can respond, with cause, that there is more to the study of economic organization than efficiency. The real challenge, however, is to demonstrate that the sociological viewpoint adds predictive content and in other respects deepens our understanding of complex organization. Put differently, it would be unfortunate if sociologists were mainly to get caught up in methodological critique and did not develop the refutable implications that their viewpoint distinctively affords. Granovetter (1985) is surely correct in his insistence that embeddedness matters. This orientation is greatly in need of systematic development, however.

Sociologists who accept the challenge to advance a predictive theory of organization will presumably want to become familiar with the powers of efficiency reasoning—if only for the purpose of more accurately assessing its limits. The shoe will be on the other foot as sociologists begin to generate predictive statements that are not contradicted by the data and that are different from, if not alien to, an economic approach to these matters. The time for a two-footed treatment of economic organization is now.

REFERENCES

Alchian, Armen, and Harold Demsetz. 1972. "Production, Information Costs, and Economic Organization." *American Economic Review* 62:777–795.

Aldrich, Howard, and Robert Stern. 1983. "Resource Mobilization and the Creation of U.S. Producer Cooperatives, 1835–1935." *Economic and Social Democracy* 4:371–406.

Anderson, Evin, and David Schmittlein. 1984. "Integration of the Sales Force: An Empirical Examination." *Rand Journal of Economics* 15:385–395.

Behavioral Sciences Subpanel, President's Science Advisory Committee. 1962. *Strengthening the Behavioral Sciences*. Washington, D.C.: U.S. Government Printing Office.

Bjuggren, Pev-Olof. 1985. *A Transaction Cost Approach to Vertical Integration*. Lund, Sweden: Lund University Press.

Brown, Donaldson. 1924. "Pricing Policy in Relation to Financial Control." *Management and Administration* 1:195–258.

Chandler, Alfred, Jr. 1962. *Strategy and Structure*. Cambridge, MA: M.I.T. Press. (Subsequently published 1966. New York: Doubleday.)

Coase, Ronald. 1972. "Industrial Organization: A Proposal for Research." Pp. 59–73 in *Policy Issues and Research Opportunities in Industrial Organization*, edited by V. R. Fuchs. New York: National Bureau of Economic Research.

Coase, Ronald. 1984. "The New Institutional Economics." *Journal of Institutional and Theoretical Economics* 140:229–231.

Commons, John R. 1934. *Institutional Economics*. Madison: University of Wisconsin Press.

Elster, Jon. 1983. *Explaining Technical Change*. Cambridge: Cambridge University Press.

Fisher, Stanley. 1977. "Long-Term Contracting, Sticky Prices, and Monetary Policy: Comment." *Journal of Monetary Economics* 3:317–324.

Friedman, Milton. 1953. *Essays in Positive Economics*. Chicago: University of Chicago Press.

Fuller, Lon. 1978. "The Forms and Limits of Adjudication." *Harvard Law Review* 92:353–409.

Gauss, Christian. 1952. "Introduction" to N. Machiavelli, *The Prince*. New York: New American Library.

Georgescu-Roegen, Nicholas. 1971. *The Entropy Law and Economic Process.* Cambridge, MA: Harvard University Press.

Gouldner, Alvin. 1954. *Industrial Bureaucracy.* Glencoe, IL: Free Press.

Granovetter, Mark. 1985. "Economic Action and Social Structure: The Problem of Embeddedness." *American Journal of Sociology* 91:481–510.

Granovetter, Mark. 1986. "Labor Mobility, Internal Markets, and Job Matching." In *Research in Social Stratification and Mobility,* edited by R. Robinson. Greenwich, CT: JAI.

Hayek, Friedrich. 1967. *Studies in Philosophy, Politics, and Economics.* London: Routledge & Kegan Paul.

Homans, George. 1958. "Social Behavior as Exchange." *American Journal of Sociology* 62:597–606.

Joskow, Paul. 1985. "Vertical Integration and Long-Term Contracts." *Journal of Law, Economics and Organization* 1:33–80.

Joskow, Paul. 1986. "Contract Duration and Durable Transaction Specific Investments: The Case of Coal." Unpublished manuscript.

Knight, Frank. 1941. "Review of Melville J. Herskovits' 'Economic Anthropology.'" *Journal of Political Economy* 49:247–258.

Knight, Frank. 1965. *Risk, Uncertainty and Profit.* New York: Harper & Row.

Koopmans, Tjalling. 1957. *Three Essays on the State of Economic Science.* New York: McGraw-Hill.

Kreps, David, and Michael Spence. 1985. "Modelling the Role of History in Industrial Organization and Competition." Pp. 340–378 in *Issues in Contemporary Microeconomics and Welfare,* edited by G. Feiwel. London: Macmillan.

Kuhn, Thomas. 1970. *The Structure of Scientific Revolutions,* 2nd ed. Chicago: University of Chicago Press.

Lindbeck, Assar. 1971. *Political Economy of the New Left: An Outsider's View.* New York: Harper & Row.

Macneil, Ian. 1974. "The Many Futures of Contracts." *Southern California Law Review* 72:854–906.

Mandel, Ernest. 1968. *Marxist Economic Theory,* rev. ed., vol. 2, translated by B. Pearce. New York: Monthly Review Press.

March, James, and Herbert Simon. 1958. *Organizations.* New York: John Wiley & Sons.

Masten, Scott. 1984. "The Organization of Production: Evidence from the Aerospace Industry." *Journal of Law and Economics* 27:403–418.

Masten, Scott, and Keith Crocker. 1985. "Efficient Adaptation in Long-Term Contracts." *American Economic Review* 75:1083–1093.

Merton, Robert. 1936. "The Unanticipated Consequences of Purposive Social Action." *American Sociological Review* 1:894–904.

Mueller, Dennis. 1986. "Review of 'The Economic Institutions of Capitalism.'" *Antitrust Bulletin* 31:827–834.

Mulhern, J. H. 1986. "Complexity in Long-Term Contracts: An Analysis of Natural Gas Contractual Provision." *Journal of Law, Economics and Organization* 2:105–118.

Nelson, Richard, and Sidney Winter. 1982. *An Evolutionary Theory of Economic Change.* Cambridge, MA: Harvard University Press.

Palay, Thomas. 1984. "Comparative Institutional Economics: The Governance of Rail Freight Contracting." *Journal of Legal Studies* 13:265–288.

Palay, Thomas. 1985. "Avoiding Regulatory Constraints: Contracting Safeguards and the Role of Informal Agreements." *Journal of Law, Economics and Organization* 1:155–176.

Perrow, Charles. 1975. *Complex Organizations.* New York: Random House.

Perrow, Charles. 1986. *Complex Organizations,* 3rd ed. New York: Random House.

Riordan, Michael, and Oliver Williamson. 1985. "Asset Specificity and Economic Organization." *International Journal of Industrial Organization* 3:365–378.

Rothschild-Witt, Joyce. 1979. "The Collectivist Organization: An Alternative to Rational-Bureaucratic Models." *American Sociological Review* 44:509–527.

Russell, Raymond. 1985a. "Employee Ownership and Internal Governance." *Journal of Economic Behavior and Organization* 6:217–241.

Russell, Raymond. 1985b. "Reply to Williamson." *Journal of Economic Behavior and Organization* 6:247.

Samuelson, Paul. 1947. *Foundations of Economic Analysis*. Cambridge, MA: Harvard University Press.

Simon, Herbert. 1957. *Models of Man*. New York: Wiley.

Simon, Herbert. 1978. "Rationality as Process and as Product of Thought." *American Economic Review* 68:1–16.

Simon, Herbert. 1983. *Reason in Human Affairs*. Stanford: Stanford University Press.

Williamson, Oliver. 1975. *Markets and Hierarchies*. New York: Free Press.

Williamson, Oliver. 1981. "The Economics of Organization: The Transaction Cost Approach." *American Journal of Sociology* 87:548–577.

Williamson, Oliver. 1985a. *The Economic Institutions of Capitalism*. New York: Free Press.

Williamson, Oliver. 1985b. "Employee Ownership and Internal Governance: A Perspective." *Journal of Economic Behavior and Organization* 6:243–245.

9

The Sociological and Economic Approaches to Labor Market Analysis
A Social Structural View

Mark Granovetter

I. INTRODUCTION: THE SOCIOLOGICAL AND ECONOMIC APPROACHES TO LABOR MARKETS

This chapter reviews recent economic and sociological work on labor markets, concentrating on studies whose comparison is particularly revealing of differences in strategies and underlying assumptions between the disciplines. The sociological studies reviewed are especially those stressing the embeddedness (Granovetter, 1985) of labor market behavior in networks of social interaction and demographic constraints. Most of these studies share with microeconomics the stance of "methodological individualism" (see Blaug, 1980:49–52) that attempts to ground all explanations in the motives and behaviors of individuals, but they differ in emphasizing social structural constraints and in avoiding the functionalist arguments now common in neoclassical work.

From a sociological viewpoint, it is an exaggerated version of methodological individualism that often appears in economics, in which individual actors are analyzed as if atomized from the influence of their relations with others, of these others' decisions and behaviors, and from the past history of

Mark Granovetter • Department of Sociology, State University of New York at Stony Brook, Stony Brook, New York 11794-4356.

these relations.[1] This atomized view of economic action has a long history in classical and neoclassical economics. Aside from leading to incorrect understanding of how labor market institutions actually function, it also makes it difficult to give an adequate account, even within a strictly methodologically individualist framework, of how individual actions can aggregate up to the level of institutions, since that aggregation takes place through networks of relationships. Because of the unavailability, in this atomized view, of a persuasive causal account of how institutions arise, there is a powerful temptation to trot out "culture" as a *deus ex machina*, or to make the classic functionalist assumption that those institutions arise that are best suited to the circumstances at hand. When functionalist assumptions are defended—and usually they are not—it is asserted that inefficient arrangements will have failed the test of the marketplace, and surviving ones are thus the result of some sort of "natural selection."[2] Though the mechanism of this selection is usually vague, the most common account is that suboptimal arrangements are short-lived because they present the opportunity for beneficial trade or profit to those who develop more efficient ones. But this arbitrage-type argument, when developed in detail, depends crucially on stylized assumptions about information, productivity, and motivation that can be accurate only in the absence of social structure—i.e., in the presence of atomized actors.

A second major difference between economic and sociological work on labor markets is the general failure in the economic literature to consider the intertwining of economic and noneconomic motives. When we seek economic goals in our interactions with others, these are usually combined with striving for sociability, approval, status, and power as well. Though such motives have largely been absent from economic thinking since Adam Smith (see Hirschman, 1977), it does not follow that their pursuit is nonrational. Though there may be more sociologists than economists who *study* nonrational behavior, the study of rational action has nevertheless often been central in sociological work (Blau, 1964; Heath, 1976; Homans, 1974; Tilly, 1978; Weber, 1968). While it is an interesting intellectual exercise to construct models that assume *only* economic motives, to see how far such a position can be pushed before its limits of explanation are reached—and to ferret out self-interest in altruistic guise—much neoclassical work goes beyond this, insisting on principle that no other motives "significantly" affect the economic sphere. This insistence is sometimes defended by the imprecise and unfalsifiable assertion that noneconomic motives are "randomly distributed" among units of interest and may thus be assumed to "cancel out" in their overall effects.

In the following account, I shall try to show in some detail how these disciplinary differences affect the interpretation and explanation of concrete economic action and institutions.

---

[1]For an extended argument on atomization in economic discourse see Granovetter, 1985.

[2]For critical views of this neo-Darwinian argument see Blaug (1980:114–120) and Elster (1979:133–137).

II. SHIFTING ECONOMIC APPRAISALS OF LABOR MOBILITY

The classical economic appraisal of labor mobility was favorable. Mobility reallocates labor from locations of lower to those of higher demand; hence, Adam Smith's denunciation of legal institutions restricting free movement (1776/1976, Book I:Chap. 10). But when early 20th-century institutional economists confronted the extent of turnover costs, the evaluation changed and the word *turnover* came into vogue. While *mobility* and *turnover* have slightly different denotations, one having the individual and the other the firm as unit of analysis, the connotations diverge more widely. *Turnover* almost invites the suffix applied to it by Sumner Slichter in his 1920 article, "The Scope and Nature of the Labor Turnover Problem"; Paul Brissenden and Emil Frankel (1922:46) went so far as to assert that 54 to 86% of job changes in firms they surveyed had been "unnecessary."

The pendulum shifted back with the landmark SSRC volume *Labor Mobility and Economic Opportunity* (Bakke, 1954). The title could hardly have been *Turnover and Economic Opportunity*, and much of it sings the praises of mobility. The "free movement of labor," commented Bakke, "is in large part responsible for the flexibility with which millions of people and an amazing variety of jobs have been matched, for the vast potential of enterprise, initiative, incentive, invention and for the self-development and acquisition of skills which contributed greatly to our economic development" (1954:3). In 1954 mobility seemed relevant even to the Cold War: "Had the Marxists given appropriate attention to the human initiative, inventiveness and adaptive skill unleashed by the freedom of labor movement, they would have been less confident of the internal decay of a 'business civilization'" (Bakke *et al.*, 1954:3).

The 1970s saw still another shift, back to a negative view of labor mobility. This can be better understood by noting that an attitude to mobility entails a corresponding view of long job tenures and well-developed internal labor markets. Early institutionalists stressed the value of long-time employees to the firm, and the advantages of promoting from within. Slichter commented: "How much would the employment man not give to know as much concerning the skill, willingness to work, reliability and loyalty of applicants . . . as he already knows of the men on the force from his own acquaintance with them. . . . By promoting men who have made good on simple operations to more difficult ones and by hiring outsiders for the simple jobs the risk of a misfit is largely eliminated . . . where misfits are costly, and transferred to the simple jobs where they are less costly" (1919:290). By contrast, the post-World War II approval of mobility entailed a denunciation of long tenures in internal labor markets. Using medieval language, Clark Kerr described such markets as "manorial" (1954), and Arthur Ross summed up the prevailing fear in his article "Do We Have a New Industrial Feudalism?" (1958).

Mobility was deplored early in the century because it was perceived as exceptionally high, and applauded nostalgically in the 1950s when it seemed too low to ensure flexible responses to changes in economic needs (Doeringer and Piore, 1971; Hall, 1982; Ross, 1958). Both responses were critical of existing labor market conditions. The recent shift to approval of immobility in internal markets did not, however, result from a belief that mobility had become excessive; on the contrary, it resulted from a new trend in economics—broadly encapsulated by the term *new institutional economics*—that reclaims much of labor economics and other subjects from the "old" institutionalists by sophisticated demonstrations that what had appeared to be inefficiencies of historical, legal, or sociological origin could instead be interpreted as efficient solutions to economic problems more complex than initially recognized. In this new yet determinedly neoclassical spirit, internal labor markets, property rights, some unemployment, corporate hierarchy, and various legal arrangements have been rehabilitated as economically efficient.

Such a view makes criticism of observed trends unlikely. It is riddled with Panglossian pitfalls of the sort that Robert Merton warned against in his account of the difficulties in assuming that every social practice fills a well-defined function in an integrated whole (1947). Similar difficulties arise in biology, where Gould and Lewontin have recently complained about the tendency to explain behavioral traits as optimal by telling "adaptive stories" about what environmental exigency they can be viewed as meeting. The comment that evolutionists often "consider their work done when they concoct a plausible story. But plausible stories can always be told. The key to historical research lies in devising criteria to identify proper explanations among the substantial set of plausible pathways to any modern result" (1979:587–588).

Adaptive stories about long tenures and internal labor markets followed assertions that these were more prevalent than previously suspected (Hall, 1980, 1982; Main, 1982; Sekscenski, 1980). Rather than responding to this finding by further pursuit of the "industrial feudalism" concerns of the 1950s, economists have discovered the virtues in existing arrangements. Doeringer and Piore's 1971 book argued, much like the early 20th-century institutionalists, that given the costs of turnover, long tenures were economically rational. Growing attention to internal markets sparked an interest in "implicit labor contracts," to explain how rational individuals could produce institutional structures that seemed at first glance inconsistent with neoclassical assumptions (Azariadis, 1975; Baily, 1974).

With minor variations, the adaptive story line about long tenures goes as follows: Young workers "job-shop" (Johnson, 1978; Pencavel, 1972; Reynolds, 1951), trying out jobs to learn about the market and their own skills. By their mid-30s they settle into jobs that nicely match their tastes and abilities. The better the match, the longer the tenure will be. Most workers "do wind up in lifetime work . . . multiple tries eventually succeed" (Hall, 1982:720–721). Length of tenure is taken as a proxy for quality of a match (e.g., Bartel and Borjas, 1981:66; Jovanovic, 1979b:1257). High mobility is seen as suitable only in the job-shopping stage. Mincer and Jovanovic suggest that workers highly mobile prior to current job have little investment in firm-specific human capital, and one reason for this is "inefficiency in job-matching" (1981:35). When mobility persists beyond the job-shopping stage, it is pathological and ought to be designated "persistent turnover denoting little investment in specific capital" (Mincer and Jovanovic, 1981:38).

I will assess the "stories," old and new, about labor mobility by juxtaposing sociological and economic accounts, and stressing the embeddedness of mobility in social structural constraints. I consider various factors that determine mobility, beginning with those closest to the individual worker and proceeding to broad features of market organization. I neglect the current macroeconomic situation—e.g., the rate of unemployment—though this is widely acknowledged to affect the rate of mobility (see Ross, 1958).

III. MODELS OF "INDIVIDUAL PROPENSITY" IN LABOR MARKETS

It is a frequent empirical observation that individuals who have already experienced an event (such as mobility or unemployment) are more likely than others to do so again. This observation could be due to those individuals' having high but stable probabilities for the event ("heterogeneity") or to each recurrence's making the next more likely ("state-dependence") (see Heckman, 1978). Which is the case matters a great deal. If current unemployment makes that state more likely in the future, then policies that reduce it reduce future unemployment as well, and the benefits are amplified by a hidden multiplier effect, not present if only heterogeneity explained differential chances of unemployment.

Though the concept of "heterogeneity" has no intrinsic theoretical content, it has been treated in the economic literature as indexing personal "propensities" exogeneous to the economic frame of reference. Stayers are, in effect, "sticks in the mud" and movers have "ants in their pants." Corcoran and Hill (1980), for example, attribute heterogeneity in the "propensity to work" to differences in "personal preferences, motivations and talents" and counsel that to reduce unemployment we must "identify and alter those skills, attitudes and habits which influence work stability" (1980:41, 54). They go on to attribute persistence in observed unemployment to "unmeasured personal differences in the propensity for unemployment" (1980:54). The word *propensity* unfortunately strongly connotes voluntary behavior with little sense of constraints; one might as well say that big-game hunters have a high propensity to be eaten by lions. Sociologists discussing heterogeneity have been more eclectic, suggesting that it may index not only personal differences but also those in characteristics of jobs and local labor markets and of the attachments between employers and employees (DiPrete, 1981:290; March and March, 1977:399–403; Tuma, 1976:357–358).

Not only are "heterogeneity" and "state-dependence" without intrinsic theoretical content, but which of these applies may depend crucially on model specification. Flinn and Heckman note that heterogeneity may include unobserved state-dependent components. If being unemployed has no effect on the probability of future unemployment, yet people vary in their chance of unemployment, we have pure heterogeneity. If it affects everyone's probability of future unemployment to exactly the same extent, we have pure state-dependence. But the economic losses caused by unemployment, that affect future behavior, may vary across workers in ways not fully measured: Flinn and Heckman call this interaction effect "state-dependent heterogeneity" (1982a:112).

What accounts for this variation in losses? The "unmeasured personal differences" approach to heterogeneity would suggest that individual characteristics are the reason. But variations in local labor markets might also create this outcome. Unemployment stemming from a plant's closing in a company town inflicts worse losses than temporary layoffs in a large city. But the crude specification of states in a stochastic model as "employed" and "unemployed" aggregates these situations. With more distinctions among states, individuals might no longer appear heterogeneous in how these states affected them, and data that had been taken to show heterogeneity would be reinterpreted as indicating state-dependence.

The category "employed" also conceals enormous differences among individuals' jobs. If these differences lead to different chances of mobility, this variation will appear to indicate unmeasured heterogeneity of individuals. Defining the states in a stochastic model is thus not a theoretically neutral procedure. When states are crudely specified, the dice are loaded for a finding of heterogeneity. This predisposition may result from the unspoken assumption, typical in economics, but also to some extent in sociological work on "status attainment," that personal differences underlie variation in individual outcomes. If one thinks, by contrast, that jobs and careers are embedded in social and bureaucratic structures that strongly affect the chances of mobility or unemployment, it is appropriate to define the state space in more detail. Such a specification would be more likely to produce findings of state-dependence.

The distinction between heterogeneity and state-dependence as influences on transition probabilities is thus arbitrary; more important, the attention focused on choosing between these deflects theoretical interest from the actual process of transition. Knowing what variables are nonspuriously correlated with these probabilities hardly gives a sufficient account of how transitions are accomplished, though it may be a valuable starting point for such an account and can cast doubt on explanations statistically inconsistent with the findings. As with many methodological innovations the danger lies in mistaking a starting point for the end of the theoretical road.

These considerations enter a discussion of labor mobility on account of the frequent observation that length of tenure and separation probability have a strong inverse relation. The question is whether this is the causally spurious result of heterogeneity, since, as Rosen points out, "those with greater propensities to move will always exhibit greater separation rates and lower tenure than those with the opposite propensities" (Rosen, 1981:3). Unless carefully formulated, the attribution of mobility "propensity" to heterogeneity may undercut the claim that job tenure is a good proxy for the quality of a match, since this attribution implies that long tenures result instead from a low propensity to move. Mincer and Jovanovic (1981) attempt to surmount this dilemma by interpreting heterogeneity as closely related to quality of job matches. They measure heterogeneity by the extent of mobility prior to current job, and relate the resulting estimate of "propensity to move" to current separation probability. This is justified by interpreting prior mobility as reflecting the level of specific human capital investment, which is, in turn, determined in part of the quality of previous job matches. They conclude that heterogeneity "biasses the steepness of the tenure-turnover profile upward by 50% on average," with the effect growing with age since prior mobility is a better predictor of separation for older workers (Mincer and Jovanovic, 1981:35).

In Flinn and Heckman's terminology, "state-dependent heterogeneity" is asserted here. Differences in jobs lead individuals to different levels of specific human capital investment that affect future separation probabilities. With more detail on what the differences are in jobs or matches that shape these investments, a statistical finding of state-dependence might thus emerge. But either is consistent with the human capital argument offered, showing again that the statistical distinction between heterogeneity and state-dependence is of little direct theoretical import.

I suggest here a sociological interpretation of mobility history. The meaning of individuals' history of mobility is inadequately captured by human capital arguments. As one moves through a sequence of jobs, one acquires not only human capital but also, and more difficult to interpret as an investment phenomenon (though see Boorman, 1975), a series of co-workers who necessarily become aware of one's abilities and personality. This awareness occurs without cost, as a by-product of the interactions necessary for work; this costless feature is difficult to reconcile with most economic models in which investment assumes direct or opportunity costs. Because of the often-documented fact that employers acquire a great deal of information about prospective employees from individuals known to both (Granovetter, 1974, 1983), one's market situation changes significantly with the number of individuals who know one's characteristics and with the number of firms in which they are located.

The former has to do with the number of jobs one has held, the latter with the number held by one's contacts—since their immobility would concentrate them in a small number of firms that, ceteris paribus, would have fewer vacancies than a larger number. When economic action is embedded in social structure in this way, the usual distinction between heterogeneity and state-dependence is inadequate; both implicitly assume atomized actors. This can be seen in terms of the urn models used to represent these processes (e.g., Heckman, 1981:94–96)—where each individual has an urn containing red and black balls (corresponding to two states such as mobility and immobility). In each period one randomly draws a ball from the urn and is assigned to the corresponding state. In pure heterogeneity, each individual has an urn with a different proportion of red and black balls. The contents of the urn "are unaffected by actual outcomes and in fact are constant" (Heckman, 1981:95). State dependence means that the contents of the urn change as a consequence of outcomes. For example, "if a person draws a red ball, . . . additional new red balls are added to his urn" (Heckman, 1981:95). But in neither case are the contents of one's urn affected by what other individuals draw from their urns. As in most economic models, independent individuals are assumed, not directly affected by the behavior of others. My theoretical account requires precisely, however, that the composition of each person's urn change depending on what color balls are drawn by others: One's mobility depends on that of others. Nor would it suffice to model the interdependence by simple aggregation rules, such as modifying one's urn according to the average outcome of others. Urn composition is changed only by the draws of those others with whom one has direct connections; thus, the overall structure of this network of connections is implicated in total system functioning.[3]

Correspondingly, the mobility of the random sample of professional, technical, and managerial job-changers I studied was heavily mediated by personal contacts acquired at various stages of the career, and before. Their "mobility appears to be self-generating; the more different work and social settings one moves through, the larger the reservoir of personal contacts . . . who may mediate further mobility. It is because ties from past jobs and from before work are as likely to be used as more recent ones that we have a cumulative effect, as if individuals "stockpile" their contacts. If only strong or recent ties mediated mobility, this could not be true, but since relatively weak ones may be crucial, working on a job for two or three years may be sufficient to build a tie that will later be useful (though this is generally unanticipated). Too short a time may not be enough, since one's contact must have a definite impression of one's abilities and personality; staying too long in one's jobs, on the other hand, may foreclose future mobility by truncating the pool of personal contacts one might otherwise have built up" (Granovetter, 1974:85).

I found, correspondingly, that those whose average job tenure over the career was intermediate were much more likely to have found the current job through contacts than those with short or long tenures. Moreover, the modal categories for proportion of jobs in career found through contacts, in my sample, were none and all, suggesting strong individual differences in the extent to which contacts have been "stockpiled" (Granovetter 1974:90). This outcome may result from a stochastic process in which early events are crucial: Initial mobility generates contacts, who facilitate further mobility, and so on. Branching processes, a reasonable analogue for this "snowball" sequence of events, yield bimodal results under relatively simple assumptions (see, e.g., Feller, 1957:274–276).

Many job separations may thus be voluntary and may reflect perception

---

[3]Stochastic processes with a network component are more complex than those involving independent units, and resulting mathematical arguments would have to be correspondingly recast (see Boorman, 1975; Erdos and Renyi, 1960; Kleinrock, 1964).

of better opportunities, rather than otherwise unexplained personal "propensities" to move. This suggestion is supported by cases in my sample where long tenures reduced mobility. I was struck by the dilemma of individuals whose long tenures were interrupted by conglomerate acquisition of their firm and attendant "housecleaning." Despite what appeared excellent qualifications, they were enormously disadvantaged in the job market because they knew almost no one in other firms and were consequently not taken seriously by employers accustomed to recruiting via personalized information. These individuals were typically in firms where others also had long tenures; thus, those who knew them well had themselves never moved to other firms where they might be in a position to help. This points up that tenure length is a characteristic of firms, not only of individuals, and thus results in part from organizational characteristics (see Granovetter, 1974:88–90; Pfeffer, 1983). My argument is inconsistent both with assertions that long tenures represent a "good match" and a high "propensity" to "stay put." Instead, long tenures may indicate a deficiency of opportunity attributable in part to the details of previous mobility history; short tenures may, conversely, result from ample opportunity rather than poor matches or "ants in the pants."

What does other empirical evidence show? Mincer and Jovanovic (1981:38ff) found that prior mobility does not influence current wages for younger men but reduces them for older. But they did not distinguish between voluntary and involuntary mobility. Sorensen (1974:55–60) showed, with longitudinal data, better gains in income and occupational prestige, for voluntary than for involuntary moves. Bartel and Borjas's (1981) analysis of the NLS indicated that older men have negative and younger men positive returns to quits. At first glance this supports the story of job-shopping and increasingly better matches but they then disaggregate quits into those caused by "pushes" (job dissatisfaction) and "pulls" (better opportunities). When older men quit to pursue a better opportunity, their wage growth is positive, and greater than that of younger men who do so. The overall lower return to quits for older men results from the higher proportion of "dissatisfaction" quits they report; these do not create wage growth because most workers in this category "gave reasons relating to nonwage aspects of the job. Thus there is no obvious reason to expect any kind of wage increase for this group" (Bartel and Borjas, 1981:69). These findings are consistent with my sociological argument, and they show the need to disaggregate mobility events rather than assuming that all mobility at a given career stage is similar. Some studies consider explicitly the relation between contact networks and economic returns. In my own data, voluntary mobility among older men is overwhelmingly in response to better opportunities offered through contacts. I cannot assess wage growth, but it is clear in cross section that those who found their current jobs through contacts reported substantially higher wages than those using other methods (Granovetter, 1974:14–16). Corcoran, Datcher, and Duncan (1980:33–36) use PSID data and show positive wage returns to the use of contacts only for some groups and in certain specifications. But the levels of aggregation used in their analysis of men and women under 45, from all occupational groups, were too high to sort out the impact of contacts: Only distinctions of race and sex were made. Since information found via contact networks carries the main burden of allocating workers among jobs, we cannot expect that higher wages will invariably result; the variety of circumstances where contacts are used is simply too great. Important distinctions beyond race, sex, and age are as follows. (1) Voluntary versus involuntary mobility. When mobility is involuntary, individuals are much more likely to take the first job that comes along, and may then use personal contacts less well placed than those they might access from a position of greater security (Granovetter, 1974:44). This suggests the importance of (2) the kinds of resources available to individuals through their contacts. There is mounting evidence, hardly surprising, but important in any general account, that resources available from one's contact network will not exceed those characteristic of it. Thus, Mostacci-Calzavara (1982:153), in her Toronto sample, found that blue-collar, same-ethnic-group ties often led to jobs even in ethnic groups with low incomes, but the lower the income in one's group, the less advantage in income from using one's same-group contact network over other means of finding jobs. Also important is (3) the characteristics of the relationship that mediates mobility. Mostacci-Calzavara (1982) and Ericksen and Yancey (1980:24–25) found that jobs located through weak ties have higher incomes than those resulting from strong ties. This is explained by my 1973 argument that since one's acquaintances are less likely to know one another than are one's close friends, information received from them is less likely to be redundant (see also Granovetter, 1981, 1983). Lin, Ensel, and Vaughn (1981) showed that the use of weak ties in finding jobs has a strong association with occupational standing achieved, but only insofar as these ties connected respondents to others well placed in the occupational structure, a connection achieved with much greater probability through weak than strong ties. This combination of factors (2) and (3) may explain why the income advantage associated with weak ties in the Ericksen and Yancey study is found only for those with a high school diploma or greater, and increases in size with education. Finally, some implications of my general argument are consistent with results from studies of unemployment. Some unemployment is made up of those out of work for long periods (Akerlof and Main, 1980; Clark and Summers, 1979; Disney, 1979; Feldstein, 1973; Stern, 1979). For such workers, my argument suggests reasons different from the usually cited personal disabilities. The bimodality in size distribution of labor-market contacts and the self-sustaining character of job mobility imply that certain workers will have great difficulty finding work once unemployed: those with small numbers of contacts to "signal" their productivity (cf. Spence, 1974). Their continuing failure in the labor market dampens their prospects not only by hurting their reputations (cf. Ghez, 1981) but also by continuing to prevent acquisition of contacts.

The process may begin early in the career. Economists Meyer and Wise (1982) found that the number of hours worked in high school is strongly related to weeks worked after high school—even four years after graduation. Effects on wages are weaker but positive. They comment that the strength and duration of this effect suggests that it results less from what is learned at the early jobs than from "personal characteristics not gained through work but leading to work in high school as well as greater labor force participation following graduation" (Meyer and Wise, 1982:306). These personal characteristics are identified as "ill-defined attributes associated with working hard and 'doing well,'" such as the "work ethic" and a high "propensity to work" (Meyer and Wise, 1982:327).

Though not so cast explicitly, this is yet another heterogeneity-state-dependence formulation that interprets the former as a matter of personal characteristics. To fall back on the "work ethic" is not exactly a neoclassical argument, but it is consistent with an atomized view of behavior. A more sociological interpretation would be that those who work in high school are indeed "heterogeneous," but that their difference consists of being those whose families and friends have offered significant help in finding jobs. This would help explain why, net of parents' income and education, nonwhites work much less in high school than whites (Meyer and Wise, 1982:309): Nonwhites are less connected to the structure of jobs and have less influence on hiring even when they are connected. This interpretation is consistent with Clark and Summers's (1982:204) argument that "for many teenagers, job search is a passive process in which the main activity is waiting for a job to be presented." In their data, while "only about a third of the unemployed find a job within a month, almost two-thirds of [teenage] labor-force entrants are successful within a month. This strongly suggests that many people only enter the labor force when a job is presented" (Clark and Summers, 1982:204–205). They also conclude that racial differences in youth unemployment rates are not due to blacks' being laid off or quitting but rather to their difficulty in initially entering the labor force (Clark and Summers, 1982:218). Thus, long-term unemployment may be traceable for some to a weak early start, making it difficult for contacts to snowball over time as they do in successful careers. Each period of failure feeds on the previous one. Not only unemployment but underemployment may have this effect since poor matching of one's abilities to jobs will make it difficult for one's actual skills to become widely known even to those in one's own workplace.

The empirical studies reviewed here present substantial evidence consistent with my sociological arguments on labor mobility, but since most were not directly addressed to arguments of this kind, this is not a conclusive demonstration. More studies are needed that directly consider the social embeddedness of labor mobility as a determinant of labor market outcomes.

IV. IMPLICIT CONTRACTS, EFFICIENCY WAGES, AND EMPLOYEE BEHAVIOR

Many of the perplexing puzzles of recent labor economics involve the existence of employee "loyalty" to firms. Of special interest is the impact of such loyalty on employee work effort, and on decisions to remain in or leave a firm. Two branches of the economic literature on these questions are those on "implicit contracts" and on "efficiency wages."

By "implicit contracts" is meant nonbinding commitments from employers to offer such advantages as continuity of wages, employment, and working conditions, and from employees to forgo such temptations as shirking and quitting for better opportunities (Akerlof and Miyazaki, 1980; Azariadis, 1975; Baily, 1974). Such "contracts" are said to stem mistrust: Long-term relationships require employees and employers to believe that the other will not act against one's interest at every opportunity to do so. Arthur Okun (1980:84), who refers to implicit contracts as the "invisible handshake," comments that if "neither explicit nor implicit contracts could be developed that curbed the role of distrust, firms would be obliged to pursue the strategy of hiring casual workers." Much of this literature finds that apparently inefficient practices such as wage stickiness, seniority, and worker attachment to firms result from implicit contracts that are (by various criteria) optimal.

Efficiency wage arguments (see the useful summary in Yellen, 1984) have a less Panglossian tone. They address the much neglected aspect of labor supply that concerns individual work effort. All the models assume that workers' productivity depends in part on their wage—a major departure from the orthodox assumption that the productivity of labor is simply given by the technical conditions summarized by a production function. Some efficiency-wage models nevertheless stay on firm neoclassical ground, by assuming that the relation between wage and productivity is a matter of how incentives are arranged: Higher than market-clearing wages for some results in involuntary unemployment for others, and these conditions raise the cost of being fired, thus discouraging the low productivity that is called "shirking" in this literature. But some efficiency-wage arguments depart from purely economic motivations, arguing that higher wages may encourage worker loyalty to the firm, and thereby affect production by their impact on group output norms (Akerlof, 1982, 1984).

Here I focus on the social context in which employers and employees actually *develop* expectations about one another's behavior. Arguments about implicit contracts and efficiency wages depict workers' behavior in too atomized a way to capture the most important forces in the labor situation that affect loyalty and effort. My criticism has two main aspects. First, both literatures treat the relations between employers and employees as occurring between individuals whose information about one another is limited to formal education signals or generalized employer reputation. Second, both take the relations between employer and employee, and that among members of a work group, out of their context in a larger work organization, and thus neglect the way relations *among* groups and cascades of effects from group to group affect individual behavior and social relations, and vice versa.

There is substantial empirical evidence that employers and employees do not face one another as strangers, thus needing to rely on institutional arrangements to determine incentives. Rather, they often know a great deal about one another before ever entering the employment relationship. In my study of newly hired professional, technical, and managerial workers, nearly one in five reported having found out about the current job directly from the employer, whom he already knew. Another one in three heard from someone who worked in the same firm or from a business friend of the employer (Granovetter, 1974:46). Though these data do not reveal how many of those contacts who worked in the firm actually knew the employer, responses from a more intensively studied subsample indicate that about three out of four did (Granovetter, 1974:57). It thus appears that 80 to 90% of the cases where contacts are used involve the employer or the employer's own contacts. If learning of a job through contacts mainly meant that information came from friends of friends of friends of employers—long diffusion chains—this information would not differ much in quality from what could be found through want ads or the employment service. In fact, however, diffusion chains were overwhelmingly short, indicating focused and reliable information connecting employers and employees before hiring occurs.

From evidence in other studies (Corcoran et al., 1980; Langlois, 1977; Shack-Marquez and Berg, 1982) it appears that, depending on the exact question asked, from one-sixth to one-half of those entering new employment contracts have prior information about, and/or relations with, the other party that are bound to affect expectations and trust. In small firms the actual employer is highly likely to be part of this prior information, and since workers are substantially more likely to enter small firms than large through personal contacts (Granovetter, 1974:128—where "small" means less than 100), we may surmise that many "new" employer–employee relations in small firms are actually continuations of earlier dealings. Such small firms are more important in economic life than suggested by the image of typical employees as working in large manufacturing firms. Various estimates put the proportion of private sector U.S. employees in establishments of 100 workers or fewer at between 49 and 60%, and 26 to 38% are in those of 20 or fewer (Granovetter, 1984:327). Of particular interest for the present argument, there is evidence that the smallest firms, of 20 or fewer, generate from one-half to two-thirds of all new jobs (Greene, 1982).

In larger firms, employees' prior information may be less likely to be *directly* about those with authority to alter implicit or explicit agreements, but it still has implications for expectations of employer behavior, for worker effort, and for likely job tenure; this is because those entering a workplace through personal contacts have a ready entree to the informal relations that not only create a comfortable social niche but also smooth the way for learning "the ropes"—the subtle and idiosyncratic features of jobs whose understanding may spell the difference between success and failure.

Furthermore, the fact that employees have begun their jobs with personal information about the firm, the employer, or other employees should reduce the chance of separation by making unlikely gross mismatches due to ignorance. It should also enhance the level of trust, not only because of previous knowledge but also because of social relationships that have become overlaid on initially economic ones. Difficulties and grievances may be a source of separation where no mechanism exists for resolving them, as has been shown in the effect of unions in reducing quit rates (Freeman, 1980). Reservoirs of trust and interpersonal knowledge may serve a similar function, especially in small nonunion firms. Empirical evidence is generally supportive of these arguments (e.g., Bluedorn, 1982:89; Granovetter, 1974:15; Price, 1977:70–73; Shack-Marquez and Berg, 1982:20–21; Shapero, Howell, and Tombaugh, 1965:50).

It is also misleading to suppose that expectations, wage and separation decisions, and level of worker loyalty and effort evolve entirely as the result of pairwise relations—between employees and employers—or even from the norms of a work group, taken in isolation from other work groups. Particularly in organizations characterized by long tenures, and this is especially where implicit contract and efficiency wage arguments are directed, it is inappropriate to view employees as engaged in separate agreements that do not impinge on one another. Such a conception is more appropriate to spot markets. Solow (1980:9) notes that "the stability of the labor pool makes it possible for social conventions to assume some importance. There is a difference between a long-term relationship and a one-night stand, and acceptable behavior in one context may be unacceptable in another." When many employees have long tenures, the conditions are met for a stable network of relationships, shared understandings, and political coalitions to be constructed (see Homans, 1950, 1974, for relevant social psychological discussions). Lincoln (1982) notes that in Max Weber's conception of bureaucracy, formal organizations are "designed to function independently of the collective actions which can be mobilized through interpersonal networks. Bureaucracy prescribes fixed relationships among positions through which incumbents flow, without, in theory, affecting organizational operations." He goes on to summarize sociological studies, however, showing that "when turnover is low, relations take on additional contents of an expressive and personal sort which may ultimately transform the network and change the directions of the organization" (Lincoln, 1982:26).

Such internal organizational "atmospheres" (Williamson, 1975), "cultures," or "esprits de corps" may themselves make an important further contribution to individual attachments and relate closely to expenditure of effort. Though concepts like these have become popular in the economic literature, there is rarely an attempt to show how such cultural phenomena originate; rather, they are treated as givens, with some impact in situations where more purely economic variables have failed to explain all behavior. My claim is that these "atmospheres" are the accumulated outcome of social relations whose structure and history must be analyzed to understand what has occurred. William Foote Whyte (1955:Chap. 11), for example, tells the story of industrial relations at the Chicago Inland Container plant that resulted in a substantial rise in productivity from 1946 to 1948. What was crucial was the development of good relations between low- to mid-level management and union officials; these relations then acted as bridges to higher management to lever changes in how time rates were set. Once this happened, the "atmosphere" in the plant changed and production rose "phenomenally." Yet there had been only minor changes in the incentive rates—the object of wage-efficiency theories. While the level of abstract analysis offered by Whyte of the process by which this occurred is not adequate to lead to a general argument about the conditions under which this takes place, it is clear from the account that a neglect of social relations and their accumulated results would leave us with no understanding whatever of the crucial changes that occurred.

It is similarly problematic to call on the "norms" of a work group to explain its productivity in the absence of some account of whence those norms derive. Akerlof (1982, 1984), in his arguments about "partial gift exchange" and efficiency wages, attempts to ground these norms in employer wage policy, suggesting that "in most jobs, keeping busy makes the time go faster. . . . Payment of a fair wage legitimizes for the worker the use of this busyness for the advantage of the firm" (Akerlof, 1984:82). This statement is apt as far as it goes, but it leaves up for grabs the crucial issue of how groups decide what is a fair wage, and assumes that industrial work groups are merely passive recipients of whatever wage employers offer. In fact, highly paid work groups and categories may have this high wage as the result of concerted political activity, especially in unionized settings. It is clear that some work groups are characteristically much more involved in such concerted action than others (Sayles, 1958), and the groups that are successful in this action are often highly productive. One might then look in cross section at their high wages and argue that these wages have led to loyalty. But Sayles suggests instead that groups that have successfully pursued their own economic interests develop, for this reason, a sense of efficacy, cohesion, and esprit de corps that shows up in higher productivity (Sayles, 1958:112–113).

The question of which groups in large industrial firms are active in forwarding their own economic interests is one that can be successfully answered only by considering the place of a group in the firm's overall social structure. In Sayles's comprehensive study of 300 work groups in 22 plants (1958), there were two identifying characteristics of such groups. One was that they consisted of members whose work was similar to one another's, as opposed to complementary and interdependent, but who worked together; the other was that their relative status in the firm was ambiguous. In explaining why highly interdependent groups have difficulty mounting collective action, Sayles (1958:76) points out that the intensity of interaction in such groups can reduce its ability to combine with other groups with similar economic interests. "Each crew or short assembly line . . . can become really a world to itself. The close ties of the members to this work unit make loyalty to some larger interest group difficult to sustain." In the terms of an argument I have made, the strong ties within highly interdependent groups close the group off, making difficult the formation of weak ties to other groups of the sort that have the potential to channel activity from one part of the social structure to another (Granovetter, 1973, 1983).

Furthermore, active groups tended to be in the middle range of the plant hierachies, in jobs neither "obviously and inevitably undesirable" nor "manifestly the most superior available" (Sayles, 1958:49), so there was some room to seek a change in relative status. They were also often jobs not well defined by the local labor market. Being in the middle of the hierarchy, they were not hiring-in jobs like many jobs at the bottom or the top, but steps on an internal promotional ladder. "As a result, what are fair and equitable wage rates, in terms of the 'going rate' in the community, tend to be substantially more ambiguous for the middle range of occupations" (Sayles 1958:49).[4]

As a general matter, the question of how workers make the wage comparisons that determine whether they think they are fairly paid has received little research attention (see Gartrell, 1982, for one important exception). Yet as far back as the 1940s, labor economist John Dunlop and his students had noticed that certain jobs are "key jobs" in that if their wages change, this sets off a chain reaction of other changes in associated jobs, which, all together, make up a "job cluster"; and among firms, certain ones are key firms in this sense and there are correspondingly sets of firms that make up a "wage contour" (Dunlop, 1957). Doeringer and Piore (1971:89) later noted that jobs "which involve wide contacts with other workers acquire a strategic position in the internal wage structure which makes it impossible to change their wages without adjustments throughout the system." There is here an implicit social structural argument that workers are more likely to compare their wages to those of workers they frequently interact with. Sayles's general argument that these patterns of interaction are mainly determined by what he calls "technology"—including the way the firm arranges the flow of work within and between groups—remains to be investigated fully. Gartrell's (1982) empirical study indicates that there are a substantial number of wage comparisons made between workers in *different* internal labor markets, and that these comparisons are generally not, in the nature of the case, based on work interactions but rather follow the contours of existing social networks. He suggests that by "ignoring social networks outside of internal labor markets and the wage information which is conveyed through them, the institutional literature underestimates the extent of interdependence between wage-determining units" (Gartrell, 1982:29–30).

V. INTERNAL LABOR MARKETS AND PROMOTION

One of the major factors that affects worker performance and the likelihood of mobility between firms is the chances of promotion within internal labor markets. Labor economists have treated promotion as an important aspect of implicit contracts, which matches revealed productivity to wages. Jovanovic asserts that individual "contracting creates a structure of rewards that provides proper signals for the attainment of optimal matches. . . . a widely prevalent example is a system of promotion . . . based on the quality

---

[4]Compare the similar difficulty of determining transfer prices for intermediate goods with no external market (Eccles, 1985).

of workers' performance" (Jovanovic, 1979a:974; see also Malcolmson, 1984). Williamson, Wachter, and Harris (1975:275–276) believe that though wages and marginal productivity may not correspond closely at "ports of entry," "productivity differentials will be recognized over time and a more perfect correspondence can be expected for higher level assignments in the internal labor market job hierarchy."

A different—though equally functionalist—interpretation is the Marxist argument that fine distinctions among jobs and multiplication of levels serve mainly to create artificial barriers among workers, via competition for promotion, thus avoiding a united working class (Gordon, Edwards, and Reich, 1982). Edwards's related account of "bureaucratic control" has in common with the neoclassical version that it assumes promotions to result principally from workers' performing according to bureaucratically stated criteria.

All of these accounts neglect the embeddedness of promotion judgments and actions in social structure. I will first argue that even if productivity were easily measurable it would not be the sole or even main explanation of promotion chances. I then discuss some of the difficulties in measuring productivity. Among the bases for promotion unrelated to productivity are seniority and ethnicity. Abraham and Medoff (1983:8) surveyed 392 firms and estimate that about 60% of private sector, nonagricultural employees are in settings where senior employees are favored for promotion even over junior ones thought more productive. In one-third of firms employing mainly unionized hourly employees, respondents asserted that junior employees are *never* promoted ahead of senior ones, regardless of the size of productivity differential (Abraham and Medoff, 1983:9).

Evidence on ethnic and personal bases for promotion is mostly anecdotal. Dalton's (1959:184) data on a midwestern chemical plant show, for example, that "ethnics composing probably less than 38% of the community filled 85% of . . . advisory and directive forces." Informants described the situation less politely: "Nearly all the big boys are in the Yacht Club, and damn near all of 'em are Masons. . . . Hell, these guys all play poker together. Their wives run around together. . . . Seniority, knowledge or ability don't count. You've got to be a suckass and a joiner" (Dalton, 1959:154). But even here Dalton stresses the importance of minimal qualifications and the desire of superiors to recruit and promote individuals politically useful to them in the complex coalitions that have so much impact on what gets done in the plant.

Promotion by seniority may have similar roots: More senior employees will have had a longer time to develop pivotal roles in networks of political influence and coalition within workplaces, and to have performed important services over the years for those in a position to promote. Supervisors who promote do not merely winnow talent but also act politically to place strategically those loyal to their personal aims and procedures. This may help explain why even in nonunion settings, more than half the firms responding to Abraham and Medoff's survey indicated promotion preference for more senior employees. Such an account sees the preference for promotion by seniority as the result of actors with strategic motives pursuing their aims—some economic, some noneconomic—in established networks of social relations, rather than merely as an exercise of union power on behalf of older employees, or as part of some elaborate structure of incentives in an unobservable implicit contract.

Rosenbaum has extensively studied promotions in a large investor-owned company having "offices in many cities and towns in one region of the United States" (Rosenbaum, 1979a,b, 1981, 1984). Conceding that promotions do serve the need to recruit to higher levels and thus will be decided on productivity criteria in part, he also points out the importance of promotions in the social comparisons workers make. Since "promotions are . . . one of the most important rewards in an organization, . . . they must be allocated in a way that gives hope and motivation to the maximum number of employees." Promotion chances, that is, "are likely to be an effective way of controlling employees, offering the possibility of material rewards and symbolic status to a far larger number of people than can possibly receive the actual promotions" (Rosenbaum, 1979a:27).

A pure productivity criterion might limit promotion to younger employees with more years to contribute, who are likely to be recognized as deserving soon if at all. But an age cutoff would depress the motivation of older employees; Medoff and Abraham (1980:732) note that within a grade level, those with most experience are behind their cohort in relative advancement and thus are likely to doubt they are on the "fast track," with consequent reduction in effort. Rosenbaum (1979a:28) thus suggests that sharp age discontinuities in the distribution of those promoted are avoided so "no age group suddenly perceives itself disproportionately deprived relative to its immediately younger cohort." His analysis of promotions from 1962 to 1972, based on personnel data, substantiates this argument. He finds, further, that periods of high growth increase promotion chances only for older employees, whose chances decline correspondingly in downturns. This further suggests the discretionary and motivational component of such promotions. The importance of social comparisons thus makes promotion policy a way to affect productive effort even among those not promoted—a more complex process than envisioned in wage-efficiency arguments.

Another determinant of promotion independent of productivity is demographic: the sheer availability of advancement opportunities. White (1970) points out that opportunity occurs in chains: A retirement or the creation of a new job creates a vacancy that pulls someone in. This new incumbent creates a vacancy in his previous job, which pulls in another person, and so on. The chain of vacancies ends when an individual enters without having previously held a job (e.g., a student) or when the job in which the vacancy appears is left unfilled. Rates of retirement or labor force entry have to do with general population demographics (see also Sorensen and Tuma, 1981), whereas rates of creation and abolition of jobs depend on the business cycle. These four rates, determining the lengths of "vacancy chains," closely determine the number of promotion opportunities. Stewman and Konda (1983) have shown that formal models in demography can be adapted to help explain promotion rates; this effort indicates complex interactions between the structure of organizational hierarchies and the sizes of various cohorts moving through them.

Now consider some problems in measuring productivity. March and March (1978) develop a model of "performance sampling," where skill exists unambiguously, but those in charge of promotion cannot observe it continuously but only take occasional samples, either because they are not in constant contact or because situations that indicate competence only arise from time to time. This argument is statistically related to the literature on quality control and implies that even in a skill-homogeneous population, career success would result in part from sampling variation. This suggests one reason why tenure is related inversely to chances of separation: Early in the job, samples of performance will be small, so the proportion of successes inferred to be characteristic will err substantially on the high or low side, leading to promotion or dismissal. Those with longer tenures will have larger samples of performance with less variance, and thus will not be promoted or dismissed for these statistical reasons alone (March and March, 1978:450–451).[5] Some "stars" will thus be thrown up by the promotion system without regard to actual ability. Stewman and Konda (1983:672) obtain a similar result from purely demographic considerations of cohort size.

In his empirical study, Rosenbaum correspondingly found great importance in early promotion histories. As in high school curriculum tracking, early winners are "seen as 'high-potential' people who can do no wrong, and who are given additional opportunities and challenges while those who do not win the early competition are given little or no chance to prove themselves again." By the "third year of employment, an employee's eventual career chances have been fundamentally affected" (Rosenbaum, 1981:236, 238). In Rosenbaum's account, productivity seems less a fixed trait of individuals than an outcome of social expectations and interactions endogenous to promotion history. *The parallel to interfirm mobility, where I also argued early mobility to be self-sustaining, is important.*

Where productivity is ambiguous, those in charge of promotion must rely on various signals. Rosenbaum (1981:112) finds that the quality of college attended has substantial net effects, and that having attended a local college has greater impact than could be expected from its quality level alone. I suggest that this entails the role of key personal contacts acquired in local colleges who have connections to this corporation; the role of such contacts in conferring initial and continuing advantages in promotion deserves further investigation. The importance of contacts between educational institutions and corporate settings for early career advantage has been extensively documented for Japan (Taira and Wada, 1987). Pfeffer (1977:556) argues that certain situations make productivity evaluation especially hard: staff rather than line positions, small rather than large organizations, and industries where

---

[5]But note that this explanation assumes individuals' true ability to lie in the moderate range, suitable for retention, but not promotion or dismissal.

"personal contact is likely to be more important" in one's work, such as financial services as opposed to manufacturing. He finds that in such situations, socioeconomic origins affect salary more, for a sample of business school graduates at a "large, prestigious state university."

Ample evidence shows that productivity is rarely measured well except in certain well-defined and individualized jobs such as typing (e.g., Medoff and Abraham, 1981). The difficulties of measurement are not merely technical. Rather, the productivity of individual workers is inextricably intermeshed in a network of relations with other workers. Slichter pointed out in 1919 that inadequate instruction "in how to do the work frequently causes men to appear to be incompetent, when, if properly taught, they could do the new job easily" (Slichter, 1919:207). But why should training be inadequate? Economists have suggested some institutional reasons. Freeman and Medoff (1980:77) assert that under unionism, rewards depend less on performance and more on seniority, so competition among individuals is mitigated and workers will give one another more informal assistance. Thurow (1975:81) suggests that competition for jobs is typically limited to the entry level and employment security provided beyond that level, so workers will not be afraid to provide on-the-job training to those less experienced.

These arguments are apt but recognize insufficiently the embeddedness of helping relationships in a network of informal exchanges closely tied to status distinctions, friendships, and sponsor–protégé relations. Since the Western Electric studies first demonstrated the intimate relation between productivity and group structure (Homans, 1950; Roethlisberger and Dickson, 1939; Sonnenfeld, 1980), this connection has been pursued vigorously by industrial sociologists (Sayles, 1958; Whyte, 1955). Some of the processes are subtle and might easily escape attention. Dalton describes the case of a black worker in a chemical plant who had the seniority to operate some delicate and complex equipment, and the necessary experience with similar but less intricate machines. His promotion was resisted by the group of all white workers he would have joined, who did not want such a "precedent" set. He filed a successful grievance with the union and was promoted, but was told that "he would be 'entirely' on his own and would 'assume all responsibility for the job'. [This] meant that he would not receive the usual preliminary guidance given to others taking these jobs. The processes in this department were dangerous in that both the product and chemicals used . . . were either corrosive, lethal to inhale or highly inflammable and explosive" (Dalton, 1959:128–129). The worker withdrew from the promotion.

The white workers had violated no explicit rule but had made clear that the social position of the black worker was such that he would not receive the usual assistance necessary to perform the job properly. His "productivity" in the job was thus shown to be not the individual attribute of human capital formulations but rather the result of a structure of social relations oriented to noneconomic as well as economic aims. This example should not be pigeonholed into the category of "discrimination"; it is only a variant of group processes that affect the productivity of all workers where informal on-the-job training is significant.

To sum up this section: Even if productivity were easily gauged, promotions often result from motives or causes not clearly related to it, but easily understandable when relevant social structures and motives are analyzed. When one adds to this consideration the evidence of problems in measuring productivity, and that such measurement is ambiguous in part because of the strong effects of the social context of production, it seems naive to suppose that promotion systems are nothing more than efficient talent sieves and that firms can thus be in a position to promise implicitly or explicitly that employees' productive efforts will always be appropriately rewarded.

VI. INTERNAL LABOR MARKETS, INTERFIRM MOBILITY, AND THE OPTIMALITY OF LABOR ALLOCATION

The prevalence of large internal labor markets with extensive promotion ladders and implicit or explicit promises of long tenures must discourage interfirm mobility. This implies that internal markets have a self-perpetuating character quite independent of their efficiency characteristics, which casts doubt on adaptive stories that trumpet the optimality of these employment arrangements. The dynamics of this self-perpetuation have to do in part simply with the relative proportions of positions inside and outside such internal labor markets. Doeringer and Piore (1971:38) comment that "the relative security of an open market is a function of its size and of the diversity of industries within it. If any employer withdraws jobs from a competitive market and allocates them internally, the job security of workers in other establishments is thereby reduced and the value of an internal market to them is correspondingly enhanced." The structure of contact networks generated in systems with large internal markets also contributes to their perpetuation. This is so because interfirm mobility generates contacts who make possible further mobility; thus, in systems with little such movement one knows mainly others in one's own firm and is thus less able to move to other firms since one's ability cannot be certified there with the confidence that comes through personalized information.

These arguments, rather than widely alleged "cultural" differences, may help explain why, comparing the individual mobility experiences of Yokohama versus Detroit workers, Cole found that, in every cohort, the proportion never changing employer in Yokohama is two or three times greater than in Detroit, and that those who do change employers in Yokohama do so significantly less often than those in Detroit (Cole, 1979:64, 68). The self-perpetuation of internal markets seems especially likely in a large urban location like Yokohama, where the large firms that contain such markets are much more important than in other parts of Japan.

But if internal markets perpetuate themselves and workers move within and among firms for reasons having more to do with social structure than with how well they are matched to jobs, it becomes hard to credit the equation of long tenure to good job matches current in neoclassical labor economics. Moreover, the very notion of the "quality" of a job match is poorly developed. For this concept to have clear denotation requires well-developed theory and evidence on the comparative advantage of workers in the set of available jobs, similar to the concept of comparative advantage in the theory of international trade.

The few discussions of this kind in the economics literature are extremely stylized (Rosen, 1978; Roy, 1953; Sattinger, 1980; Willis and Rosen, 1979), and the empirical prospects of assessing quality of matches in comparative advantage terms are dim. In the section on promotion I suggested the difficulty of measuring productivity on account of its embeddedness in a structure of social relations. Comparative advantage calculations require us to know not only one's productivity in the current job but also that in all other jobs one might have filled but did not. The theoretical literature in labor economics takes such calculations to involve the imputing of one or more dimensions of "ability" to workers and various levels of requirements for these dimensions to jobs. But this is precisely to ignore the empirical reality that productivity does not result from the characteristics of individuals and jobs alone. Individuals in jobs are not atmoized from individuals in other jobs, but all together they make up a system that must be treated as such. Nor is it reasonable to take the set of jobs available as given independently of the population of workers. Many job accessions represent the filling of entirely new positions rather than of previously held vacancies. This was true of more than one in three for my sample of professional, technical, and managerial workers (Granovetter, 1974:15); many of these new jobs had in fact been tailored to the needs, preferences, and abilities of the workers recruited. Correspondingly, jobs found through personal contacts were much more likely than those found through other means to have been newly created (44% vs. 24%) and made up 70% of all newly created jobs in the sample (1974:15). Difficulties of this kind may explain why the theoretical literature on comparative advantage of workers in jobs has not yet been systematically linked with assertions about match quality in the empirical literature on labor mobility.

Some skepticism is thus warranted as to whether the praise of labor mobility in classical and postwar economics could have been utterly and completely misplaced. It seems too good to be true that after a period of job shopping ending around age 35, most workers will have found an optimal match. This is even less credible when workers are in a system of lifetime employment, so that the firm where one begins must be asserted to be just the one where his or her talents can be best utilized in the entire economy. Further, considerations of both equity and efficiency should lead us to ask whether any match advantages that do accrue to that part of the labor force in long tenures might be at the expense of others not able to take advantage of such arrangements. Firms that normally subcontract part of their operations may be able to guarantee employment to regular workers in a downturn only because of the possibility of dropping the subcontracts (Okun, 1980:107). Strong firms with well-developed internal labor markets can thus transfer the risk of cyclical fluctuations to weaker "peripheral" firms that depend on their subcontracts and must engage in large layoffs when demand falls off (Doeringer and Piore, 1971:173; Gordon *et al.*, 1982:191, 200–201).

Japanese "permanent employment" conceals large numbers of temporary subcontract workers, whose numbers are underreported and who receive poor benefits and little job security. Many such workers are actually relatively long-term employees classified as temporary precisely to save the firm the expense of benefits and job security (Somers and Tsuda, 1966; Taira, 1970:161–162). In the 1974–1975 recession large firms dismissed temporary workers, and as many as 600,000 women may have left the labor force. "In short," remarks Cole, "employment security is much better for white-collar workers than blue-collar workers, for young workers than older workers . . . for employees in large firms than small firms . . . for male workers than female workers. . . . This overall system, with its ascriptive age and sex discrimination and dualistic labor market practices, hardly represents a model for the solution of the problems facing the United States" (Cole, 1979:263).

At the level of the firm, the efficiency of internal labor markets has been challenged. The 1950s emphasis on inflexibility of systems with low mobility is echoed for the Japanese case by Cole, who argues that internal labor markets were inefficient in recent periods of rapid technological change: "The education and training costs associated with having to upgrade established employees (who did not have the requisite skills) relative to recruitment on the external market may have been substantial" (Cole, 1979:120) but could be borne because of the expanding economy and the dominant position of these firms in their product markets.

Whether turnover adversely affects efficiency of firms is the subject of a complex literature. Price summarizes sociological studies indicating that the level of turnover is positively related to formalization and bureaucratization in firms, because without long-term relations a web of informal understandings is less likely to develop (Price, 1977:96–102). Increased turnover is associated also with increases in the ratio of administrative to productive employees, in part because of the increase in supervision, recruitment, and training activity, and in part because new administrators attempt to bring in additional staff loyal to themselves (Price, 1977:93–96). But the impact of formalization and increased proportions of administrators on productivity cannot be determined on abstract grounds alone; it is rather embedded in the particular history of the firm. In Gouldner's (1954), classic study of a gypsum mining and processing plant, managerial turnover resulted in bureaucratization that replaced in inefficient set of informal arrangements. One cannot conclude in general, however, that informal coalitions are less efficient than clear-cut formal procedures; if anything, the former are more often reported as having been adopted to escape the rigidities of the latter (Blau, 1963; Dalton, 1959).

In organizations where turnover is variable among units, those with lower turnover become more powerful because their continuity of personnel gives them advantages in understanding and manipulating the system (Bluedorn, 1982:108–109). In this connection one thinks of the French Third and Fourth Republics, where it was widely asserted that the civil bureaucracy was the real center of power since it stayed in place while governments came and went at revolving-door speed. Such unplanned devocation of power on persisting units may be efficient and adaptive in stable periods but they produce rigid resistance to change when it is needed. Pfeffer (1983) suggests that firms with long-term employment may become ingrown and that industries composed of such firms may suffer by losing the coordination that results from extensive interfirm mobility. By contrast, the frequent movement of personnel among firms may generate an industry-wide perspective since managers in each firm will know managers in most others from having once worked with them (Granovetter, 1974: Chap. 8; Pfeffer, 1983).

All in all, the impact of labor mobility and turnover at the level of firms, industries, and the economy as a whole cannot be easily assessed, and it presents far more complex questions than have yet been appreciated in the more microscopically oriented economic literature. One must agree with economist Robert Hall's comment that economists "have only just begun to examine the issues in the efficient movement of workers among firms" (Hall, 1980:108). Despite their potential to do so, sociologists have contributed even less to assessment of this question. I believe this is in large part because the general discrediting of structural-functional theory in macrosociology has discouraged them from asking questions about efficiency. Healthy suspicion of Panglossian pitfalls and hidden value judgments has created an intellectual climate in which scholars do not even think of asking whether systems are functioning well; but this can be asked with reference to clearly stated criteria of efficient functioning and need not be oriented to showing that all is for the best.

VII. CONCLUSIONS

I have tried to show that the characteristically atomistic explanatory approaches of neoclassical economic theory to problems of labor markets give inadequate accounts both of individual economic action and of how this action cumulates into larger patterns, some of which come to be called "institutions." The failure to consider the embeddedness of individual behavior in networks of social and economic relations, and the mixture of economic and noneconomic motives, leads to the use of "adaptive stories" and appeal to "cultures" or "atmospheres" where institutional developments cannot be otherwise derived. Yet the use of such stories and appeals is broadly inconsistent with the usual methodological individualist stance of most economists; closer attention to social structure would provide a more satisfactory account of how economic patterns arise.

For analytical purposes let me separate the two main issues I have raised: the embeddedness of economic action in networks of relations, and the intertwining of economic with noneconomic motives. Suppose that actors had only the economic motives and goals attributed to them in most economic analyses and, in addition, could be conceived as perfectly rational, given the information at hand. Then at least some of the spirit of neoclassical analysis could carry over to a treatment that took seriously the embeddedness of these actors in a network of relations. If, for example, as I have argued, the number of contacts one has in other firms who know one's characteristics both depends on one's past mobility and influences one's chance of future moves, it would be natural to construct models for "investment" in contacts and perhaps to assess optimal stopping rules for number of job changes. Such models would yield predictions of turnover and would also make the structure of networks partially endogenous to the economic process. Boorman's interesting model of investment in contacts for the purpose of acquiring job information (1975) has been amplified by Delany (1980) in a dynamic setting (see my further comments, Granovetter, 1981:25–26).

But while formal models may well be useful in elucidating such problems, I am skeptical as to what extent the usual neoclassical apparatus will be suitable. In particular, it is problematic whether utility functions—originally developed to represent an isolated individual's ordinal preferences over a universe of goods—can easily capture network effects. While Becker (1976) and others have used interdependent utility functions, where the utility of some other becomes an argument of your own function, this usage is usually confined to pairs of individuals, and the structure of a broader network of relations can probably not easily be incorporated, at least not in the current state of technical development.

The example of investment in contacts also points up the extent to which noneconomic motives are mixed with economic ones. One's interaction with others is generally not confined to "economic investment activity": As with other aspects of economic life, striving for sociability, approval, status, and power also enter in. Indeed, a perception by others that one's interest in them is mainly a matter of "investment" will make this investment less likely to pay off; we are all on the lookout for those who only want to use us. Whether noneconomic motives can easily be incorporated into the typical formal models of neoclassical economics is again problematic, though there are some interesting attempts in this direction (Iannaccone, 1986; Kuran, 1986).

Whatever turns out to be the best methodology, better models of the labor market will result from a merger of the economists' sophistication about instrumental behavior and concerns with efficiency, and the sociologists' expertise on social structure and relations and the complex mixture of motives present in all actual situations. By laying economic and sociological models side by side for detailed comparison, I hope here to have clarified the advantages of, and obstacles to, such a merger, and thus to have brought it closer to fruition.

Acknowledgments

I am indebted to Robert Averitt, Paula England, George Farkas, Randy Hodson, Kevin Lang, and Oliver Williamson for their helpful comments.

REFERENCES

Abraham, Katharine, and James Medoff. 1983. "Length of Service and the Operation of Internal Labor Markets." Sloan School of Management Working Paper, 1394–83. Massachusetts Institute of Technology.

Akerlof, George. 1982. "Labor Contracts as Partial Gift Exchange." *Quarterly Journal of Economics* 97:543–569.

Akerlof, George. 1984. "Gift Exchange and Efficiency-Wage Theory: Four Views." *American Economic Review* 74:79–83.

Akerlof, George, and Brian Main. 1980. "Unemployment Spells and Unemployment Experience." *American Economic Review* 70:885–893.

Akerlof, George, and H. Miyazaki. 1980. "The Implicit Contract Theory of Unemployment Meets the Wage Bill Argument." *Review of Economic Studies* 47:321–338.

Azariadis, C. 1975. "Implicit Contracts and Underemployment Equilibria." *Journal of Political Economy* 83:1183–1202.

Baily, Martin. 1974. "Wages and Unemployment Under Uncertain Demand." *Review of Economic Studies* 41:37–50.

Bakke, E. W., editor. 1954. *Labor Mobility and Economic Opportunity.* Cambridge, MA: MIT Press.

Bartel, Ann, and George Borjas. 1981. "Wage Growth and Job Turnover: An Empirical Analysis." Pp. 65–90 in *Studies in Labor Markets*, edited by S. Rosen. Chicago: University of Chicago Press.

Becker, Gary. 1976. *The Economic Approach to Human Behavior.* Chicago: University of Chicago Press.

Blaug, Mark. 1980. *The Methodology of Economics.* New York: Cambridge University Press.

Blau, Peter. 1963. *The Dynamics of Bureaucracy.* Chicago: University of Chicago Press.

Blau, Peter. 1964. *Exchange and Power in Social Life.* New York: Wiley.

Bluedorn, Allen. 1982. "The Theories of Turnover: Causes, Effects and Meaning." Pp. 75–128 in *Research in the Sociology of Organizations*, Vol. 1, edited by S. Bacharach. Greenwich, CT: JAI Press.

Boorman, Scott. 1975. "A Combinatorial Optimization Model for the Transmission of Job Information Through Contact Networks." *Bell Journal of Economics* 6:216–249.

Brissenden, Paul, and Emil Frankel. 1922. *Labor Turnover in Industry: A Statistical Analysis.* New York: Macmillan.

Clark, Kim, and Lawrence Summers. 1979. "Labor Market Dynamics and Unemployment." *Brookings Papers on Economic Activity* 1:13–60.

Clark, Kim, and Lawrence Summers. 1982. "The Dynamics of Youth Unemployment." Pp. 199–234 in *The Youth Labor Market*, edited by R. Freeman and D. Wise. Chicago: University of Chicago Press.

Cole, Robert. 1979. *Work, Mobility and Participation: A Comparative Study of American and Japanese Industry.* Berkeley: University of California Press.

Corcoran, Mary, Linda Datcher, and Greg Duncan. 1980. "Information and Influence Networks in Labor Markets." Pp. 1–37 in *Five Thousand American Families: Patterns of Economic Progress*, Vol. 8, edited by Greg Duncan and James Morgan. Ann Arbor: Institute for Social Research.

Corcoran, Mary and Martha Hill. 1980. "Persistence in Unemployment among Adult Men." In *Five Thousand American Families: Patterns of Economic Progress*, Vol. 8, edited by Greg Duncan and James Morgan. Ann Arbor: Institute for Social Research.

Dalton, Melville. 1959. *Men Who Manage.* New York: Wiley.

Delany, John. 1980. Aspects of Donative Resource Allocation and the Efficiency of Social Networks: Simulation Models of Job Vacancy Information Transfers Through Personal Contacts. Unpublished doctoral dissertation, Yale University, Department of Sociology.

DiPrete, Thomas. 1981. "Unemployment over the Life Cycle." *American Journal of Sociology* 87:286–307.

Disney, R. 1979. "Recurrent Spells and the Concentration of Unemployment in Great Britain." *Economic Journal* 89:109–119.

Doeringer, Peter, and Michael Piore. 1971. *Internal Labor Markets and Manpower Analysis.* Lexington, MA: D. C. Heath.

Dunlop, John T. 1957. "The Task of Contemporary Wage Theory." Pp. 117–139 in *New Concepts in Wage Determination,* edited by G. Taylor and F. Pierson. New York: McGraw-Hill.

Eccles, Robert. 1985. *The Transfer Pricing Problem.* Lexington, MA: D. C. Heath.

Elster, Jon. 1979. *Ulysses and the Sirens.* New York: Cambridge University Press.

Erdos, P., and A. Renyi. 1960. "On the Evolution of Random Graphs." *Publications of the Mathematical Institute of the Hungarian Academy of Sciences* 5A:17–61.

Ericksen, Eugene, and William Yancey. 1980. "The Locus of Strong Ties." Mimeo, Department of Sociology, Temple University, Philadelphia.

Feldstein, Martin. 1973. "The Economics of the New Unemployment." *Public Interest* 33:3–42.

Feller, William. 1957. *An Introduction to Probability Theory and Its Applications,* Vol. 1. New York: Wiley.

Flinn, Christopher, and James Heckman. 1982a. "New Methods for Analyzing Individual Event Histories." Pp. 99–140 in *Sociological Methodology,* edited by S. Leinhardt. San Francisco: Jossey-Bass.

Freeman, Richard. 1980. "The Exit-Voice Tradeoff in the Labor Market: Unionism, Job Tenure, Quits and Separations." *Quarterly Journal of Economics* 94:643–676.

Freeman, Richard, and James Medoff. 1980. "The Two Faces of Unionism." *Public Interest* 39:69–93.

Gartrell, C. David. 1982. "On the Visibility of Wage Referents." *Canadian Journal of Sociology* 7:117–143.

Ghez, Gilbert. 1981. "Comment on Bartel and Borjas." Pp. 84–89 in *Studies in Labor Markets,* edited by S. Rosen. Chicago: University of Chicago Press.

Gordon, David, Richard Edwards, and Michael Reich. 1982. *Segmented Work, Divided Workers.* New York: Cambridge University Press.

Gould, Steven, and Richard Lewontin. 1979. "The Spandrels of San Marco and the Panglossian Paradigm: A Critique of the Adaptationist Programme." *Proceedings of the Royal Society of London* B205:581–598.

Gouldner, Alvin. 1954. *Patterns of Industrial Bureaucracy.* Glencoe, IL: Free Press.

Granovetter, Mark. 1973. "The Strength of Weak Ties." *American Journal of Sociology* 78:1360–1380.

Granovetter, Mark. 1974. *Getting a Job: A Study of Contacts and Careers.* Cambridge, MA: Harvard University Press.

Granovetter, Mark. 1981. "Toward a Sociological Theory of Income Differences." In *Sociological Perspectives on Labor Markets,* edited by I. Berg. New York: Academic Press.

Granovetter, Mark. 1983. "The Strength of Weak Ties: A Network Theory Revisited." *Sociological Theory* 1:201–233.

Granovetter, Mark. 1984. "Small Is Bountiful: Labor Markets and Establishment Size." *American Sociological Review* 49:323–334.

Granovetter, Mark. 1985. "Economic Action and Social Structure: The Problem of Embeddedness." *American Journal of Sociology* 91:481–510.

Greene, Richard. 1982. "Tracking Job Growth in Private Industry." *Monthly Labor Review* 105 (9):3–9.

Hall, Robert. 1980. "Employment Fluctuations and Wage Rigidity." *Brookings Papers on Economic Activity* 1:91–123.

Hall, Robert. 1982. "The Importance of Lifetime Jobs in the U.S. Economy." *American Economic Review* 72:716–724.

Heath, Anthony. 1976. *Rational Choice and Social Exchange*. New York: Cambridge University Press.
Heckman, James. 1978. "Simple Statistical Models for Discrete Panel Data Developed and Applied to Test the Hypothesis of True State Dependence against the Hypothesis of Spurious State Dependence." *Annales de l'INSEE* 30–31:227–269.
Heckman, James. 1981. "Heterogeneity and State Dependence." Pp. 91–139 in *Studies in Labor Markets*, edited by S. Rosen. Chicago: University of Chicago Press.
Hirschman, Albert. 1977. *The Passions and the Interests*. Princeton: Princeton University Press.
Homans, George. 1950. *The Human Group*. New York: Harcourt Brace World.
Homans, George. 1974. *Social Behavior*. New York: Harcourt Brace Jovanovich.
Iannaccone, Laurence. 1988. "A Formal Model of Church and Sect." *American Journal of Sociology*.
Johnson, William. 1978. "A Theory of Job Shopping." *Quarterly Journal of Economics* 93:261–277.
Jovanovic, Boyan. 1979a. "Job Matching and the Theory of Turnover." *Journal of Political Economy* 87:972–990.
Jovanovic, Boyan. 1979b. "Firm-Specific Capital and Turnover." *Journal of Political Economy* 87:1246–1260.
Kerr, Clark. 1954. "The Balkanization of Labor Markets." Pp. 92–110 in *Labor Mobility and Economic Opportunity*, edited by E. W. Bakke, P. Hauser, G. Palmer, C. Myers, D. Yoder, and C. Kerr. Cambridge, MA: M.I.T. Press.
Kleinrock, L. 1964. *Communication Nets: Stochastic Message Flow and Delay*. New York: McGraw-Hill.
Kuran, Timur. 1986. "Preference Falsification, Policy Rigidity and Social Conservatism." Mimeo, Department of Economics, University of Southern California.
Langlois, Simon. 1977. "Les Reseaux Personnels et la Diffusion des Informations sur les Emplois." *Recherches Sociographiques* 2:213–245.
Lin, Nan, M. Ensel, and J. Vaughn. 1981. "Social Resources and Strength of Ties: Structural Factors in Occupational Status Attainment." *American Sociological Review* 46:393–405.
Lincoln, James. 1982. "Intra- (and Inter-) Organizational Networks." Pp. 1–38 in *Research in the Sociology of Organizations*, Vol. 1, edited by S. Bacharach. Greenwich, CT: JAI Press.
Main, Brian. 1982. "The Length of a Job in Great Britain." *Economica* 49 195:325–333.
Malcolmson, James M. 1984. "Work Incentives, Hierarchy and Internal Labor Markets." *Journal of Political Economy* 92:486–507.
March, James C., and James G. March. 1977. "Almost Random Careers: The Wisconsin School Superintendency, 1940–1972." *Administrative Science Quarterly* 22:377–408.
March, James C., and James G. March. 1978. "Performance Sampling in Social Matches." *Administrative Science Quarterly* 23:434–453.
Medoff, James, and Katharine Abraham. 1980. "Experience, Performance and Earnings". *Quarterly Journal of Economics* 95:703–736.
Medoff, James, and Katharine Abraham. 1981. "Are Those Paid More Really More Productive? The Case of Experience." *Journal of Human Resources* 16:186–216.
Merton, Robert. 1947. *Social Theory and Social Structure*. New York: Free Press.
Meyer, Robert, and David Wise. 1982. "High School Preparation and Early Labor Force Experience." Pp. 277–348 in *The Youth Labor Market Problem*, edited by R. Freeman and D. Wise. Chicago: University of Chicago Press.
Mincer, Jacob, and Boyan Jovanovic. 1981. "Labor Mobility and Wages." Pp. 21–63 in *Studies in Labor Markets*, edited by S. Rosen. Chicago: University of Chicago Press.
Mostacci-Calzavara, Liviana. 1982. *Social Networks and Access to Job Opportunities*. Doctoral disseration, Department of Sociology, University of Toronto.
Okun, Arthur. 1980. *Prices and Quantities*. Washington D.C.: Brookings Institution.
Pencavel, John. 1972. "Wages, Specific Training and Labor Turnover in U.S. Manufacturing Industries." *International Economic Review* 13:53–65.
Pfeffer, Jeffrey. 1977. "Toward an Examination of Stratification in Organizations." *Administrative Science Quarterly* 22:553–567.
Pfeffer, Jeffrey. 1983. "Organizational Demography." Pp. 299–357 in *Research in Organizational Behavior*, Vol. 5, edited by L. L. Cummings and B. Shaw, Greenwich, CT: JAI Press.
Price, James. 1977. *The Study of Turnover*. Ames: University of Iowa Press.

Reynolds, Lloyd. 1951. *The Structure of Labor Markets*. New York: Harper.

Roethlisberger, Fritz, and William Dickson. 1939. *Management and the Worker*. Cambridge, MA: Harvard University Press.

Rosen, Sherwin. 1978. "Substitution and the Division of Labour." *Economica* 45 179:235–250.

Rosen, Sherwin. 1981. "Introduction". In *Studies in Labor Markets*, edited by S. Rosen. Chicago: University of Chicago Press.

Rosenbaum, James. 1979a. "Organizational Career Mobility: Promotion Chances in a Corporation during Periods of Growth and Contraction." *American Journal of Sociology* 85:21–48.

Rosenbaum, James. 1979b. "Tournament Mobility: Career Patterns in a Corporation." *Administrative Science Quarterly* 24:220–241.

Rosenbaum, James. 1981. "Careers in a Corporate Hierarchy." In *Research in Social Stratification and Mobility*, Vol. 1, edited by D. Treiman and R. Robinson. Greenwich, CT: JAI Press.

Rosenbaum, James. 1984. *Career Mobility in a Corporate Hierarchy*. New York: Academic Press.

Ross, Arthur. 1958. "Do We Have a New Industrial Feudalism?" *American Economic Review* 48:903–920.

Roy, A. D. 1953. "Some Thoughts on the Distribution of Earnings." Oxford Economic Papers.

Sattinger, Michael. 1980. *Capital and the Distribution of Labor Earnings*. New York: North-Holland.

Sayles, Leonard. 1958. *The Behavior of Industrial Work Groups*. New York: Wiley.

Sekscenski, E. 1980. "Job Tenure Declines as Work Force Changes." Special Labor Force Report No. 235. Washington, D.C.: Bureau of Labor Statistics.

Shack-Marquez, Janice, and Ivar Berg. 1982. "Inside Information and the Employer-Employee Matching Process." Fels Discusssion Paper 159, School of Public and Urban Policy, University of Pennsylvania.

Shapero, A., R. Howell, and J. Tombaugh. 1965. *The Structure and Dynamics of the Defense R and D Industry: The Los Angeles and Boston Complexes*. Menlo Park, CA: Stanford Research Institute.

Slichter, Sumner. 1919. *The Turnover of Factory Labor*. New York: Appleton.

Slichter, Sumner. 1920. "The Scope and Nature of the Labor Turnover Problem." *Quarterly Journal of Economics* 34:329–345.

Smith, Adam. 1976. *The Wealth of Nations*. Chicago: University of Chicago Press. (Originally published 1776)

Solow, Robert. 1980. "On Theories of Unemployment." *American Economic Review* 70:1–11.

Somers, G., and M. Tsuda. 1966. "Job Vacancies and Structural Change in Japanese Labor Markets." In *The Measurement and Interpretation of Job Vacancies*, edited by R. Ferber. New York: Columbia University Press.

Sonnenfeld, Jeffrey. 1980. "Hawthorne Hoopla in Perspective: Contextual Illumination and Critical Illusions." Working Paper No. HBS 81-60. Boston, MA: Harvard Business School.

Sorensen, Aage. 1974. "A Model for Occupational Careers." *American Journal of Sociology* 80:44–57.

Sorensen, Aage, and Nancy Tuma. 1981. "Labor Market Structures and Job Mobility." In *Research in Social Stratification and Mobility*, Vol. 1, edited by D. Treiman and R. Robinson. Greenwich, CT: JAI Press.

Spence, Michael. 1974. *Market Signaling*. Cambridge, MA: Harvard University Press.

Stern, Jon. 1979. "Who Bears the Burden of Unemployment?" In *Slow Growth in Britain*, edited by W. Beckerman. Oxford: Oxford University Press.

Stewman, Shelby, and Suresh Konda. 1983. "Careers and Organizational Labor Markets: Demographic Models of Organizational Behavior." *American Journal of Sociology* 88:637–685.

Taira, Koji. 1970. *Economic Development and the Labor Market in Japan*. New York: Columbia University Press.

Taira, Koji, and Teiichi Wada. 1987. "The Japanese Business–Government Relations: A Todai-Yakkai-Zaikai Complex?" Pp. 264–297 in *The Structural Analysis of Business*, edited by M. Schwartz and M. Mizruchi. New York: Cambridge University Press.

Thurow, Lester. 1975. *Generating Inequality*. New York: Basic Books.

Tilly, Charles. 1978. *From Mobilization to Revolution*. Reading, MA: Addison-Wesley.

Tuma, Nancy. 1976. "Rewards, Resources and the Rate of Mobility: A Non-Stationary Multivariate Stochastic Model." *American Sociological Review* 41:338–360.

Weber, Max. 1968. *Economy and Society*. Translated and edited by G. Roth and C. Wittich. Totowa, NJ: Bedminster Press. (Originally published 1921)

White, Harrison. 1970. *Chains of Opportunity: System Models of Mobility in Organizations*. Cambridge, MA: Harvard University Press.

Whyte, William F. 1955. *Money and Motivation*. New York: Harper.

Williamson, Oliver. 1975. *Markets and Hierarchies*. New York: Free Press.

Williamson, Oliver, M. Wachter, and J. Harris. 1975. "Understanding the Employment Relation: The Analysis of Idiosyncratic Exchange." *Bell Journal of Economics* 6:250–278.

Willis, Robert, and Sherwin Rosen. 1979. "Education and Self-Selection." *Journal of Political Economy* 87:S7–S36.

Yellen, Janet. 1984. "Efficiency-Wage Models of Unemployment." *American Economic Review* 74:200–210.

10

Income Determination in Three Internal Labor Markets

Nancy DiTomaso

I. INTRODUCTION

Early research by economists on dual, segmented, and internal labor market theories (Andrisani, 1973; Averitt, 1968; Bluestone, 1973; Cain, 1976; Doeringer and Piore, 1971; Edwards, Reich, and Gordon, 1975; Freedman, 1976; Gordon, 1972; Harrison, 1972; Reich, Gordon, and Edwards, 1973; Rosenberg, 1975; Thurow, 1975; Wachter, 1974) told us that the labor market was differentiated but not the specifics of the differentiation. The lack of precision in conceptualization became evident as empirical analyses proliferated. For example, while the early research hypothesized that there were dual sectors to the economy (Averitt, 1968) and subsequent analyses used 3 sectors (e.g., Hodson, 1978), later research identified as many as 16 distinct sectors (Kaufman, Hodson, and Fligstein, 1981). In fact, the notion of different sectors has given way to a focus on multivariate models of the effects of firm or organization-level characteristics, such as size or capital intensity (Baron and Bielby, 1980, 1982, 1984; Hodson, 1986; Kalleberg, Wallace, and Althauser, 1981; Lincoln and Kalleberg, 1987).

Neither dual-sector nor multivariate models sufficiently explained the reward processes within firms for different types of workers, even though wage or income determination has been a primary emphasis of this literature (Beck, Horan, and Tolbert, 1978, 1980b; Bibb and Form, 1977; Bridges and Berk, 1974, 1978; Hodson, 1978; Horan and Tolbert, 1980; Stolzenberg, 1975; Talbert and Bose, 1977; Zucker and Rosenstein, 1981). Recent work on internal labor markets has concentrated on occupational linkages and mobility. But it has also not sufficiently addressed how the income determination pro-

Nancy DiTomaso • Rutgers Graduate School of Management, Newark, New Jersey 07102.

cess within firms relates to the structure of internal labor markets (Baron, Davis-Blake, and Bielby, 1986; Berg, 1981; Halaby, 1979; Rosenbaum, 1975; Smith, 1983; Stewman and Konda, 1983, 1986).

In the research reported here, findings regarding the income determination process within three firms are discussed. Some of the results of previous work are confirmed, while raising questions about the context in which the findings might apply. The results of other previous work are called into question. The research here addresses three basic questions: (1) What factors determine income? (2) How does the income determination process differ across different types of firms? (3) How do the differences across firms affect workers of different race/ethnicity and sex characteristics? Answers to these questions must be received with caution because the number of firms and the size of the sample are small. But because so few studies provide insight at the level of the firm, the findings should help us understand some of the issues about what future research is needed.

II. DATA

Interviews were conducted with 360 workers in three firms in the Chicago consolidated labor market in 1980. The three firms were chosen to fit the definitions of three labor market sectors as they existed in the literature at the time (primarily, Beck *et al.*, 1978; Bluestone, 1973; Edwards *et al.*, 1975; Hodson, 1978) with the exception that all three firms are large. The sectors represented are core, periphery, and state. The firms include, respectively, (a) a heavy *manufacturing* firm, in a capital-intensive industry, with high productivity, historically inelastic and oligopolistic markets, large assets, a strong union, and primarily male employees; (b) a *nonmanufacturing* firm, in a labor-intensive industry, with low productivity, competitive markets, large assets, but no union, and primarily female employees; (c) a *public* agency, in a labor-intensive but relatively professional industry, with low productivity, a captive market of poor clients in an industry that in the private sector is competitive, insufficient assets, several comparatively weak unions, and primarily minority and female employees. In each firm, a stratified, random sample of 120 *nonprofessional and nonmanagerial* employees were interviewed, on company time, in face-to-face interviews.

Each firm sample consisted of 20 each black males, black females, white males, white females, Latino (or Hispanic) males, and Latina (or Hispanic) females. The definition of nonprofessional and nonmanagerial was unique to each firm to account for differences in occupational structure and history. Interviews were conducted in English or Spanish, depending on the preference of the respondent. The questionnaires were translated by six bilingual persons, including five native Spanish speakers, from different Hispanic ethnicities (Chicano, Mexican-American, Puerto Rican-American, Costa Rican, and Peruvian). The interview team included blacks, whites, and Hispanics, and as much as possible, the ethnicity and sex of the interviewer were matched with those of the respondent.

Although the three firms in this study may not be representative of all firms in the economy, the construction of the sample and the design of the study are themselves instructive of some of the problems with existing labor force literature. Because we wanted to include Hispanics as well as blacks and whites in the study, we found early on that we were restricted to very large firms to obtain even a sample size of 20 for either Hispanic males or females, even though the Chicago metropolitan area has a large Hispanic population. Evidently, most Hispanics either work in smaller firms that are highly segregated or are spread widely across work organizations in the area. We strongly suspect that the former is more true than the latter. Overall, the racial, ethnic, and sexual composition of each of these three firms was very skewed, but not in the ways that would be suggested by the labor force literature. The manufacturing firm, with the concentration of "good jobs," was only 60% white, while the nonmanufacturing firm, with the concentration of "bad jobs," was 90% white. The public agency was less than 40% white. Thus, there was not a direct relationship between the income level and security of jobs across firms with the racial and ethnic composition of the firms. In addition, the definition of who is a minority was problematic in the selection of subsamples in each firm. For example, firm's managers initially included Iranians, Filipinos, and others within the Hispanic group. It appears that they included anyone who "looked" Hispanic to them.

A second factor that was evident when the study was first designed was that there was not a neat pattern to the occupational composition or the organizational structure across these firms. I want to discuss just a few issues that suggest how complex and variable these employment organizations are in contrast to our often simple and elegant theories about them.

First, the study was designed to include only nonprofessional and nonmanagerial employees, and we assumed that this distinction would be clear. It was necessary, however, within each firm to develop an operational definition of who should fall into the sampling frame. An easy demarcation would have been exempt (from overtime pay as defined by legislation) and nonexempt status, but these groups did not always coincide with the distinction between professional and managerial employees versus others. Many professional employees, for example, are paid overtime in some firms up to a given salary level. Also, there is a large group of semiprofessional or technical occupations that do not neatly fit the census categories frequently used by sociologists. Many of these jobs require some college education, if not a degree; they are distinct from clerical staff; and yet they are not really professional in the usual sense of that term. In the nonmanufacturing company, where we first completed the interviews, we decided to include these people within our sampling frame. The same definition did not, however, fit the public agency. There, it was decided that the only workable demarcation was by who was in a bargaining unit.

A second item of ambiguity was the notion of unionization. Sociologists often talk about firms as being either unionized or not unionized, but this is not sufficient. In the manufacturing firm, where most of the production employees belong to a once-powerful national industrial union, it is clear that the firm should be categorized as "unionized." However, a small proportion of black employees, within production, are not part of the union for historical reasons, and the office staff in the corporate headquarters, as well as in various parts of the plant, are not unionized, although many clerical employees among the production workers are part of the union. In the public agency, there are at least five unions that each represent different groups of employees. Some of these are craft unions, but others, for example, representing the clerical staff, are not. Because job rights exist only within each of the five bargaining units and not between them, it is more difficult to specify what an internal labor market means within this agency. Further, not all of the jobs within the agency are unionized. Many firms have multiple establishments and separate departments or divisions, some of which are entirely unionized, some of which deal with unions for only some employees (e.g., maintenance workers), and some of which have no unionized workers.

Another issue, often assumed in the sociological literature to be straightforward, we found not to be. This is the identification of one's job. We were interested, among other things, in knowing the current job held by the respondent, as well as the jobs they previously held and expected to hold in the future. We found that this was not a simple question, aside from the expected complexity of understanding the meaning of job titles and tasks in different organizations. In the manufacturing firm, for example, where there exist clearly defined promotion ladders for some production jobs, there is an important distinction made between the job to which one has "rights" and the job to which one may be assigned to work. We found that they were frequently not the same thing. In this company with good jobs and "stable" work, we found that as many as 5% of the employees were absent on any given day, necessitating both overhiring by the firm and reassigning people to different jobs on any given day. Production employees in that company who are part of the bargaining unit hold rights to only one job but may work different jobs frequently and may work in another job for an extended period of time. While doing so, these employees would be paid either the rate of their frequently held job or their permanently assigned job rate, whichever was higher, making the linkage between pay and task also difficult to determine clearly if one were not aware of these distinctions.

Finally, for reasons that will be discussed below, the meaning of different occupations also differed by firm. Since this point will be clearer following the data analysis, I now turn to the empirical analysis.

III. VARIABLES AND METHOD

The income determination model used here includes variables to test aspects of the claims of internal, dual, and segmented labor market theories. The full model includes six types of variables: characteristics endogenous to the worker but exogenous to our model (race/ethnicity and sex), human capital investment, amount of time worked, occupation, and hourly wage rate. The dependent variable is annual personal income *at this firm* for each respondent for the year prior to the interview in dollars.[1] The dependent variable does not include income from other sources or family income. Questions on other related variables were asked for the same time period.

Dummy variables, coded 1 and 0, were constructed for six race/ethnic and sex categories (black female, white female, Latina female, black male, white male, and Latino male), firm (manufacturing, nonmanufacturing, and public), and occupation (technical or semiprofessional, craft, operative, clerical, laborer, and service). In all equations, the omitted categories are white male, nonmanufacturing, and service.

The firm variables are indicators of "sector" to the extent that these three firms represent the sectors as defined in the literature. Given previous definitions of three sectors (e.g., Hodson, 1978), the manufacturing firm corresponds most closely to the descriptions of the core sector, the nonmanufacturing firm (although large and predominantly white) to the competitive (or periphery) sector, and the public agency to the state sector. This study broadens the focus of income determination studies, many of which have restricted their samples to manufacturing. As will be seen subsequently, this study confirms that existing theories of the labor force, including both human capital theory and its alternatives, best fit the manufacturing sector but are not as easily applied to others.

The occupational variables used here are indicators of "segment" to the extent that the occupations can be matched to the characteristics defined in the literature. If Edwards's (1979) categories are used to classify occupations, then technical and craft would be classified as "independent primary," operative and laborer as "subordinate primary," and clerical and service as "secondary." However, one of the findings from the study is that the characteristics of occupation differ depending on the firm in which it is located, so these definitions should be received with caution. The very fact that in only three firms, all of which are large, it is not possible to match the Edwards definitions to jobs in terms of their conditions and rewards should give pause to those who have adapted these definitions to secondary data analysis without any on-site contact with organizations and workers. Although more will be said about this following the data analysis, let me illustrate the point briefly here.

The technical or semiprofessional category that we included within our sampling frame is quite variable across the three firms. In the manufacturing firm, jobs in this category are clearly semiprofessional, held mostly by men,

[1]In separate analyses, the same equations were analyzed with log dollars as the dependent variable, but the semilog form did not substantially improve the fit (difference of 0.02 in explained variance for the total sample), and the extent of improvement differed by firm. Thus, for ease of interpretation and to account for the poor fit of the semilog model in the public agency data, the dollar form of the equation was used. We assume that the reason the semilog form does not provide a better fit for these data is that each firm does represent a distinct sector or segment of the labor market and income is, therefore, less likely to be overwhelmingly skewed within each firm. Because the sample includes only three firms, with one representing good jobs, one bad jobs, and one in between, and for each including only nonprofessional and nonmanagerial employees, the income distribution of the three together is also less likely to be skewed than would be true of the distribution in a national data set.

and relatively well paid. Similar jobs in the nonmanufacturing firm, however, are more like clerical jobs in both tasks and rewards. In neither firm are such jobs likely to lead to promotions to higher-level positions without further training by the incumbent. But such promotions are more likely in the non-manufacturing firm, despite the absence of *formal* job ladders linking one job to another. For various reasons, the same complexities in meaning exist for each of the six job categories across the three firms, yet the categories are meaningful because the bundle of job tasks within each category make the jobs more like each other than like jobs in one of the other categories.

Human capital investment is defined in this study similar to Mincer's use of it (1958, 1974), although our data permit a more complete specification of experience. Work experience is measured in terms of both tenure (number of years with current employer) and total work experience (number of years employed for 3 months or more since respondent was 16). The correlation between tenure and work experience is 0.753. The choice of the work experience measure was intended to eliminate part-time work while the respondent was still a full-time student. (See Griffin, 1978, for a discussion of in-school versus postschooling experience.) A variable for the square of experience was also included to account for the deterioration of human capital over time (Mincer, 1974). Our measure of work experience is taken from a direct question to the respondent, in contrast to the calculated measure used by Mincer and others of age minus years of schooling minus 5. Because our measure was self-reported, it may include some measurement error, but it should provide a far superior measure, especially for our female respondents, than the commonly used estimate, which does not account for time out of the labor force.

Education was measured on an 8-point scale (1 = none, 2 = grades 1–7, 3 = grade 8, 4 = grades 9–11, 5 = grade 12, 6 = grades 13–15, 7 = grade 16, and 8 = grade 17 or more). Because of the relatively low educational level of Hispanic respondents in these types of occupations, it was felt that this would be a less intimidating question than a question regarding years of schooling.

Amount of time worked was measured by both weeks (in the year prior to the interview) and hours worked (on average, in the year prior to the interview). Both were self-reported. While weeks and hours are defined as labor supply within a human capital framework, some have argued that the same variables can be indicators of labor demand, which reflect characteristics of the employing organizations within a segmented labor market framework (Beck, Horan, and Tolbert, 1980a). For our respondents, the distinction is not directly relevant, at least for the weeks worked variable, because these are all full-time, year-round workers. Weeks worked, therefore, partly accounts for workers who began their employment with the company during the year for which the question was asked or indicates long illnesses or periods of layoff. Hours worked does vary owing to differences in the amount of overtime worked, but most of the respondents worked a normal 40-hour week.

Finally, we include hourly wage rate as a predictor of annual personal income in the firm. Income is often defined as the wage rate times weeks times hours, on the assumption that income is perfectly defined by the cost of labor and its supply. A less than perfect correspondence between income and

Table 1. Means and Standard Deviations, Total Sample and by Company.

Independent variables[a]	Total sample		Manufacturing		Nonmanufacturing		Public agency	
	Mean	SD	Mean	SD	Mean	SD	Mean	SD
INCM	14,811.275	7,263.486	21,441.441	7,206.494	10,115.208	3,311.029	12,628.357	4,575.164
TEN	7.955	8.185	8.318	9.382	6.499	7.109	9.306	7.684
EXP	16.757	13.185	16.137	11.668	12.894	11.824	22.233	14.180
EXPSQ	449.703	614.143	395.110	501.426	304.647	482.371	692.856	790.893
EDUC[b]	5.201	1.170	5.118	1.204	5.156	1.046	5.357	1.269
WEEKS	49.027	8.119	48.138	9.025	49.985	6.385	48.915	8.818
HOURS	40.824	4.391	41.855	3.714	39.735	5.499	40.922	3.182
WAGE	683.986	231.225	906.485	117.740	516.021	109.083	623.440	233.865
BF	0.207	—	0.160	—	0.070	—	0.432	—
WF	0.238	—	0.263	—	0.382	—	0.032	—
LF	0.046	—	0.085	—	0.031	—	0.017	—
BM	0.161	—	0.095	—	0.094	—	0.323	—
LM	0.054	—	0.092	—	0.034	—	0.032	—
MFG	0.350	—	—	—	—	—	—	—
PUBLIC	0.292	—	—	—	0.073	—	—	—
TECH	0.049	—	0.013	—	—	—	0.061	—
CRAFT	0.099	—	0.215	—	—	—	0.082	—
OPER	0.091	—	0.122	—	0.036	—	0.120	—
CLER	0.442	—	0.189	—	0.724	—	0.398	—
LABOR	0.158	—	0.352	—	0.080	—	0.021	—
N	273		96		98		80	

[a]The variables are as follows: INCM = annual personal income at this company, TEN = tenure, EXP = experience, EXPSQ = experience squared, EDUC = education, WEEKS = weeks worked last year, HOURS = average hours worked last year, WAGE = hourly wage rate in cents per hour, BF = black female, WF = white female, LF = latina female, BM = black male, LM = latino male, MFG = manufacturing company, PUBLIC = public agency, TECH = semiprofessional or technical occupations, CRAFT = craft occupations, OPER = operative occupations, CLER = clerical occupations, LABOR = laborer occupations. In all equations, dummy variables are coded 1 and 0, and the left-out categories in all equations are white male, nonmanufacturing company, and service occupations.
[b]Education is coded on an 8-point scale, 1 = none, 2 = some grade school, 3 = completed grade school, 4 = some high school, 5 = completed high school, 6 = some college, 7 = completed college, 8 = graduate or professional school.

Table 2. Correlations ($N = 273$)

	INCM	TEN	EXP	EXPSQ	EDUC	WEEKS	HOURS	WAGE	BF	WF	LF	BM	LM	MFG	PUBLIC	TECH	CRAFT	OPER	CLER	LABOR
INCM	1.000																			
TEN	0.187	1.000																		
EXP	0.216	0.753	1.000																	
EXPSQ	0.151	0.731	0.960	1.000																
EDUC	0.095	−0.335	−0.218	−0.262	1.000															
WEEKS	0.224	0.178	0.201	0.171	−0.016	1.000														
HOURS	0.373	0.081	0.078	0.029	0.074	0.018	1.000													
WAGE	0.801	0.207	0.237	0.189	0.039	0.051	0.205	1.000												
BF	−0.104	0.039	0.089	0.044	0.063	0.013	0.060	−0.100	1.000											
WF	−0.136	0.115	0.041	0.031	−0.089	−0.007	−0.123	−0.022	−0.286	1.000										
LF	0.018	−0.112	−0.147	−0.124	−0.011	0.004	−0.028	0.049	−0.112	−0.122	1.000									
BM	−0.014	−0.085	−0.006	−0.022	0.107	−0.066	0.084	−0.110	−0.224	−0.245	−0.096	1.000								
LM	0.067	0.051	−0.002	0.002	−0.217	−0.085	0.006	0.054	−0.122	−0.133	−0.052	−0.104	1.000							
MFG	0.671	0.033	−0.035	−0.065	−0.052	−0.080	0.173	0.707	0.043	−0.086	0.136	−0.132	0.125	1.000						
PUBLIC	−0.193	0.106	0.271	0.255	0.086	−0.009	0.014	−0.169	0.356	−0.311	−0.087	0.283	−0.062	−0.471	1.000					
TECH	−0.036	0.003	−0.065	−0.076	0.144	0.082	0.170	−0.068	−0.004	0.070	−0.050	0.021	0.014	−0.120	0.037	1.000				
CRAFT	0.530	0.117	0.223	0.197	0.138	0.057	0.147	0.533	−0.093	−0.140	−0.039	−0.085	0.031	0.284	−0.037	−0.075	1.000			
OPER	0.119	0.100	0.124	0.133	−0.198	0.044	0.087	0.092	−0.078	−0.130	−0.058	0.147	0.052	0.080	0.066	−0.072	−0.105	1.000		
CLER	−0.415	−0.112	−0.151	−0.170	0.136	0.115	−0.264	−0.399	0.083	0.245	−0.018	−0.043	−0.051	−0.373	−0.056	−0.201	−0.295	−0.281	1.000	
LABOR	0.200	−0.114	−0.160	−0.139	−0.127	−0.069	0.064	0.223	−0.137	−0.057	0.127	−0.012	−0.013	0.391	−0.242	−0.098	−0.144	−0.137	−0.385	1.000

measures for wage rate and weeks and hours worked is assumed to be an indication of measurement error. But in the process of collecting these data, we discovered that there is more to annual income than this: The manufacturing firm in our sample paid employees in different types of jobs an "incentive pay" that was based on departmental production and was over and above hourly pay. The incentive pay could make up as much as 10 to 20% of the employee's annual income, and access to it differed by type of job. Also, since the respondents are all nonmanagerial and nonprofessional employees, they all received overtime pay for work beyond 40 hours a week. (A correction for overtime was not included in the equation because our question asked average number of hours per week over the year, and the amount of overtime pay would vary depending on when it was worked and whether other time was taken off during the week.) In addition, sick leave policies vary, many do not get paid for days absent, and some get docked for being late.

Thus, annual personal income may vary because of these factors, independent of hourly wage rate or the average weeks or hours worked. Indeed, the type of job one holds and the type of firm in which one works can determine how each of these affects annual income. Wage rate is also associated with a specific job, but in the manufacturing firm, as noted, a given employee may work different jobs, with different wage rates from one day to the other. Further, inequality—a major concern of this study—has more to do with income over a year's time than it does with the wage rate for an hour worked, and we wanted the dependent variable to reflect the overall economic advantages and disadvantages that a given occupation has in a given firm. Of course, given the choice of annual income as a dependent variable, hourly wage rate is also a control variable. As will be seen subsequently, the effects of wage rate on annual personal income vary across the firms for many of the reasons noted here.

The means and standard deviations for the total sample and by firm are given in Tables 1 and 2.

In the following analyses, we use OLS regressions for each firm to compare the differences between the firms in the determinants of annual personal income. In all equations a listwise deletion of missing data was used, which significantly reduces the sample size because of missing data on either annual income or hourly wage rate. In most analyses, the results with pairwise deletion do not differ significantly from those with listwise deletion, but the education variable was affected, so the more conservative approach of listwise deletion was chosen. The data are also weighted by the proportion of each race/ethnic and sex group within each firm because the distribution varied so widely across firms.

IV. RESULTS

Table 3 shows the results of our analysis of personal annual income for each firm, both with and without wage rate in the equation as an independent

Table 3. Regression of Personal Annual Income at This Company, by Company, with and without Wage Rate as an Independent Variable: Unstandardized Coefficients, (Standard Error), ⟨Standardized Coefficients⟩

Independent variables	Manufacturing		Nonmanufacturing		Public agency		Total sample
	1	2	3	4	5	6	7
BF	-3,513.14[b]	-3,569.77[b]	1,048.52	1,356.20[b]	720.98	894.17	-1,208.47[a]
	(1,477.96)	(1,685.72)	(1,114.54)	(659.39)	(1,430.73)	(890.78)	(727.52)
	⟨-0.18463⟩	⟨-0.18249⟩	⟨0.07717⟩	⟨0.10524⟩	⟨0.06655⟩	⟨0.09742⟩	⟨-0.06757⟩
WF	-1,499.26	-937.70	-661.97	-43.22	1,057.57	1,451.55	-1,791.34[c]
	(1,377.48)	(1,599.22)	(728.97)	(459.72)	(2,179.93)	(1,437.44)	(657.49)
	⟨-0.09560⟩	⟨-0.05761⟩	⟨-0.09616⟩	⟨-0.00638⟩	⟨0.04051⟩	⟨0.05600⟩	⟨-0.10526⟩
LF	-989.31	-1,340.86	-65.75	526.13	1,258.68	1,007.08	-1,414.46
	(1,703.82)	(1,946.56)	(1,521.18)	(896.10)	(3,157.36)	(1,764.17)	(1,079.65)
	⟨-0.04096⟩	⟨-0.05203⟩	⟨-0.00330⟩	⟨0.02769⟩	⟨0.02948⟩	⟨0.02889⟩	⟨-0.04075⟩
BM	-632.96	-191.10	498.44	776.07	3,244.46[b]	2,857.70[c]	642.31
	(1,524.61)	(1,790.48)	(966.25)	(571.62)	(1,415.62)	(934.90)	(726.69)
	⟨-0.02810⟩	⟨-0.00781⟩	⟨0.04219⟩	⟨0.06872⟩	⟨0.28301⟩	⟨0.29385⟩	⟨0.03256⟩
LM	425.10	1,196.33	-66.84	-23.65	3,006.64	1,879.36	424.08
	(1,588.65)	(1,984.05)	(1,436.47)	(875.76)	(2,679.50)	(1,447.76)	(1,039.36)
	⟨0.01983⟩	⟨0.04820⟩	⟨-0.00361⟩	⟨-0.00130⟩	⟨0.08929⟩	⟨0.07261⟩	⟨0.01317⟩
EDUC	1,289.85[c]	1,352.88[c]	925.72[c]	89.34	773.12[b]	398.80[a]	542.80[b]
	(445.43)	(501.18)	(276.01)	(178.30)	(386.55)	(220.32)	(213.90)
	⟨0.22452⟩	⟨0.22605⟩	⟨0.29943⟩	⟨0.02823⟩	⟨0.18513⟩	⟨0.11057⟩	⟨0.08745⟩
EXP	633.51[c]	644.44[c]	6.71	-32.47	101.02	-62.98	132.60[b]
	(158.46)	(179.58)	(112.41)	(69.19)	(114.20)	(64.32)	(64.63)
	⟨1.07764⟩	⟨1.04341⟩	⟨0.02296⟩	⟨-0.11597⟩	⟨0.25278⟩	⟨-0.19518⟩	⟨0.23771⟩
EXPSQ	-12.33[c]	-13.34[c]	-.68	.46	-1.49	.81	-2.52[a]
	(3.78)	(4.28)	(2.59)	(1.59)	(1.92)	(1.08)	(1.30)
	⟨-0.90523⟩	⟨-0.92854⟩	⟨-0.09530⟩	⟨0.06719⟩	⟨-0.20678⟩	⟨0.13998⟩	⟨-0.21334⟩
TEN	-2.37	19.78	242.90[c]	21.46	27.63	64.82	32.97
	(79.71)	(89.20)	(56.44)	(39.55)	(94.76)	(52.87)	(40.96)
	⟨-0.00329⟩	⟨0.02575⟩	⟨0.50377⟩	⟨0.04607⟩	⟨0.03953⟩	⟨0.10887⟩	⟨0.03715⟩

WEEKS	326.06[c] (52.75) ⟨0.40394⟩	343.45[c] (57.54) ⟨0.43012⟩	106.23[b] (44.10) ⟨0.19564⟩	36.14 (26.55) ⟨0.06970⟩	87.86 (50.69) ⟨0.13205⟩	91.34[c] (26.82) ⟨0.17604⟩	189.76[b] (27.60) ⟨0.21212⟩
HOURS	341.53[c] (126.30) ⟨0.17695⟩	319.26[b] (143.02) ⟨0.16453⟩	223.63[c] (52.27) ⟨0.36093⟩	192.42[c] (31.76) ⟨0.31958⟩	-57.94 (62.84) ⟨-0.07624⟩	240.69[c] (83.84) ⟨0.16738⟩	278.40[c] (51.08) ⟨0.16830⟩
TECH	8,711.87[c] (2,725.36) ⟨0.22714⟩	9,466.51[b] (4,679.67) ⟨0.15170⟩	-2,253.32[a] (1,255.15) ⟨-0.21345⟩	-2,197.76[b] (857.36) ⟨-0.15885⟩	1,350.59 (1,684.01) ⟨0.06028⟩	-2,215.78[a] (1,142.61) ⟨-0.11685⟩	-1,045.99 (1,158.42) ⟨-0.03104⟩
CRAFT	5,784.96[c] (1,818.64) ⟨0.34000⟩	5,858.68[c] (2,117.36) ⟨0.33586⟩	—	—	13,234.21[c] (1,707.34) ⟨0.69698⟩	3,287.43[b] (1,621.15) ⟨0.19859⟩	2,712.61[b] (1,047.42) ⟨0.11189⟩
OPER	5,639.99[c] (1,894.66) ⟨0.27333⟩	5,010.04[b] (2,153.09) ⟨0.22892⟩	-287.59 (1,674.01) ⟨-0.01555⟩	-150.34 (984.92) ⟨-0.00852⟩	1,470.86 (1,366.09) ⟨0.09030⟩	-1,541.57[a] (818.87) ⟨-0.11030⟩	242.32 (916.43) ⟨0.00961⟩
CLER	2,364.01 (1,623.39) ⟨0.14615⟩	2,609.68 (1,872.78) ⟨0.14250⟩	-3,301.04[c] (1,049.53) ⟨-0.45402⟩	-2,308.36[c] (632.07) ⟨-0.31330⟩	-2,000.22[b] (966.01) ⟨-0.17880⟩	-1,654.85[c] (556.59) ⟨-0.17818⟩	-973.84 (682.04) ⟨-0.06670⟩
LABOR	4,250.25[c] (1,561.33) ⟨0.29201⟩	4,284.96[b] (1,755.80) ⟨0.28548⟩	-3,100.41[b] (1,292.41) ⟨-0.24350⟩	-1,932.70[b] (766.75) ⟨-0.15885⟩	3,866.35 (3,231.83) ⟨0.09263⟩	786.54 (1,775.61) ⟨0.02454⟩	-179.23 (836.06) ⟨-0.00901⟩
WAGE	—	3.38 (4.63) ⟨0.05515⟩	—	21.97[c] (1.85) ⟨0.72371⟩	—	14.31[c] (1.71) ⟨0.73161⟩	13.43[c] (1.62) ⟨0.42755⟩
MFG	—	—	—	—	—	—	4,408.40[c] (835.66) ⟨0.28988⟩
PUBLIC	—	—	—	—	—	—	-427.15 (688.28) ⟨-0.02867⟩
Constant	-23,576.07	-26,891.30	-7,273.77	-9,171.11	3,566.09	-13,251.12	-19,790.05
Adjusted R^2	0.61909	0.62356	0.45146	0.80611	0.57818	0.84572	0.78055
N	114	96	105	98	97	80	273

[a] $p < 0.10$.
[b] $p < 0.05$.
[c] $p < 0.01$.

variable. In each of the sets of two equations (Models 1 through 6 in Table 3), most of the differences have to do with the variables for human capital and the amount of time worked. In the equations in which hourly wage rate is excluded, education has approximately the same effect across the three very different firms (in none of the pairs is the t value statistically significant). Yet when wage rate is included in the equation, the effect of education varies dramatically across the three firms. It is strongly significant in the manufacturing firm, moderately significant in the public agency, and not at all significant in the nonmanufacturing firm. The differences between the education coefficients for the manufacturing firm and the nonmanufacturing firm is significant at the 0.05 level. In contrast to the results for education, the firms differ even without hourly wage rate in the equation on tenure, experience, and weeks and hours worked, and the effects of these variables change in some equations when wage rate is added.

That the coefficients vary across firms and that they change depending on whether hourly wage rate is in the equation or not does not reflect problems with the stability of the estimates, but rather indicates that there are clear differences across these three firms in the way income is determined. More will be said about the differences below. For now, suffice it to say that the direction of the changes all make sense given an understanding of the structure and characteristics of the firm in the labor market. The differences in coefficients between firms suggest that the previous research has not been sufficiently sensitive to the variations across firms. Indeed, many past analyses restricted the sample to male employees of prime working age in manufacturing jobs. Since Mincer (1974) is among these, it is not surprising that the results for our manufacturing firm are most consistent with Mincer's findings. However, the fact that the results for the other two firms vary on important dimensions underscores the necessity for studies at this level of analysis.

Across the three firms there are also differences in the effects of race/ethnicity and sex, but most of the coefficients are not statistically significant. One exception is that in the manufacturing firm, the coefficient for black females is negative and significant. In this firm, black females were disproportionately likely to have some college education, but it did not translate into high-paying jobs for them as it did for white males. Further, in the nonmanufacturing firm, the coefficient for black females is positive and significant (only in the equation with hourly wage rate included). Finally, in the public agency, the coefficient for black males is positive and significant. Since these effects are net of occupation, the results do not suggest that there is income equality across race/ethnicity and sex in this sample. White men dominate highly paid craft jobs, and women are concentrated in low-paid clerical jobs in all firms. The sex composition and income advantage or disadvantage of the other occupational categories is mixed and depends on the firm.

There are differences between the firms in the effects of occupation on income, whether or not hourly wage rate are controlled. Strongly positive and significant effects of being in a technical occupation in the manufacturing firm contrasts sharply with the negative and significant effects in both the nonmanufacturing firm and the public agency. In the manufacturing firm, the technical jobs are primarily held by men and are semiprofessional, if not managerial, jobs. In the other two firms, technical jobs are more likely to be similar to clerical positions, even if semiprofessional, and the incumbents are primarily female.

Firms also differ markedly in the effects of being in a service occupation. It is similar to being in a clerical job in the manufacturing firm, but it pays more than all but craft jobs in the other two firms. An example of a service job in the manufacturing firm is cleaner; in the other two firms, an example of a service job is security guard. Also, in the manufacturing firm, the clerical and service jobs are more likely to be held by women and/or by older workers, while in the other two firms, the service jobs are more likely to be held by male and younger workers. Consistent across the equations is the income advantage of being in a craft job and the disadvantage of being in a clerical job.

In Model 7 of Table 3, the equation is analyzed for the total sample.[2] Here we can see the effects on income of human capital and of amount of time worked, net of hourly wage. Education, experience (but not tenure), and weeks and hours worked all have significant positive effects. They contribute to an increase in annual personal income, net of the other variables in the equation. Mincer (1974) found the same variables to be significant predictors of hourly wage. Sex and race/ethnicity do not have significant effects on income after hourly earnings are controlled. Among the occupational variables, craft continues to be positive and significant, even net of firm, while the coefficients for the other occupations vary and are not statistically significant. Hourly wage rate is significant, net of firm and the other variables in the equation. Among the three firms, being in the manufacturing firm pays significantly more than the nonmanufacturing firm, even net of wage rate, occupation, human capital, the amount of time worked, and race/ethnicity and sex.

Given the importance of hourly wage rate in explaining the variability in annual personal income in this sample, analyses were also done using hourly wage rate as the dependent variable (results shown in Table 4). In this step we can see some of the reasons for the findings in the other equations. Here we find that being black (either female or male) means receiving a lower hourly wage rate, compared with white males. These effects are significant in the total sample, although none of the effects are significant in the firm-level equations. This implies that the distribution of blacks across the firms works to the disadvantage of blacks, even if they are not paid less in any given firm, given their occupation and human capital characteristics.

Table 4 also shows that education and experience both have significant effects on hourly wage rate, but these effects vary by firm. Only experience

---

[2]Because one of the major questions of the research is the reason for the differences among the firms, I intended to include interaction terms in Equation 7 of Table 3. Although interaction is clearly evident in Equations 1 through 6, it was not possible to include interaction terms in Equation 7 because of the multicollinearity in the matrix. This is especially due to high correlations among the interactions for firm times the other variables.

Table 4.   Wage Rate in Cents per Hour Regressed on Selected Variables,
by Total Sample and by Company: Unstandardized Coefficients,
(Standard Error), ⟨Standardized Coefficients⟩

Independent variables	Total sample	Manufacturing	Nonmanufacturing	Public agency
BF	−66.301[b]	−42.127	−0.946	−1.649
	(25.592)	(40.477)	(36.050)	(53.816)
	⟨−0.11861⟩	⟨−0.13016⟩	⟨−0.00235⟩	⟨−0.00370⟩
WF	−7.857	−23.236	4.196	15.141
	(23.695)	(37.760)	(25.742)	(86.126)
	⟨−0.01468⟩	⟨−0.08818⟩	⟨0.01872⟩	⟨0.01279⟩
LF	−21.616	−14.866	−24.008	2.666
	(38.707)	(47.250)	(46.989)	(110.162)
	⟨−0.01980⟩	⟨−0.03481⟩	⟨−0.04164⟩	⟨0.00161⟩
BM	−51.547[b]	−4.230	0.510	−18.098
	(25.921)	(42.503)	(32.773)	(56.561)
	⟨−0.08203⟩	⟨−0.01073⟩	⟨0.00133⟩	⟨−0.03764⟩
LM	−45.126	−48.399	−9.231	58.681
	(36.884)	(46.225)	(48.903)	(88.874)
	⟨−0.04506⟩	⟨−0.12168⟩	⟨−0.01544⟩	⟨0.04980⟩
EDUC	13.600[a]	−1.154	23.805[c]	22.441
	(7.606)	(12.066)	(8.967)	(14.383)
	⟨0.06920⟩	⟨−0.01166⟩	⟨0.23692⟩	⟨0.12449⟩
EXP	5.385[b]	10.142[b]	1.070	5.496
	(2.270)	(4.188)	(3.795)	(3.955)
	⟨0.30322⟩	⟨1.00039⟩	⟨0.11285⟩	⟨0.34615⟩
EXPSQ	−0.068	−0.222[b]	−0.047	−0.043
	(0.047)	(0.101)	(0.088)	(0.069)
	⟨0.02384⟩	⟨−0.93780⟩	⟨−0.20050⟩	⟨−0.14597⟩
TEN	1.778	0.409	9.541[c]	−3.368
	(1.508)	(2.160)	(1.994)	(3.333)
	⟨0.06185⟩	⟨0.03164⟩	⟨0.59743⟩	⟨−0.11323⟩
WEEKS	1.224	1.055	2.704[b]	−1.102
	(0.909)	(1.360)	(1.080)	(1.728)
	⟨0.04662⟩	⟨0.07983⟩	⟨0.21871⟩	⟨−0.04198⟩
HOURS	0.737	1.050	1.443	3.665
	(1.858)	(3.369)	(1.820)	(5.256)
	⟨0.01379⟩	⟨0.03349⟩	⟨0.06939⟩	⟨0.05270⟩
TECH	60.478	199.258[b]	−51.844	61.846
	(42.131)	(111.108)	(50.322)	(73.072)
	⟨0.05448⟩	⟨0.19250⟩	⟨−0.11762⟩	⟨0.06304⟩
CRAFT	251.951[c]	138.271[c]	—	689.271[c]
	(34.983)	(48.399)		(72.457)
	⟨0.31967⟩	⟨0.48536⟩		⟨0.80602⟩
OPER	72.688[b]	87.943[a]	−29.452	117.855[b]
	(32.900)	(51.157)	(58.235)	(51.251)
	⟨0.08907⟩	⟨0.24269⟩	⟨−0.04789⟩	⟨0.17031⟩
CLER	28.357	73.523	−67.671[a]	3.016
	(23.871)	(44.724)	(36.265)	(34.318)
	⟨0.06144⟩	⟨0.24279⟩	⟨−0.26791⟩	⟨0.00655⟩
LABOR	76.698[b]	58.930	−68.687	279.720[b]
	(30.092)	(41.732)	(44.916)	(113.749)
	⟨0.12007⟩	⟨0.24192⟩	⟨−0.16235⟩	⟨0.16827⟩

Table 4. *(Continued)*

Independent variables	Total sample	Manufacturing	Nonmanufacturing	Public agency
MFG	324.431[c]	—	—	—
	(24.096)			
	⟨0.66543⟩			
PUBLIC	93.439[c]	—	—	—
	(24.045)			
	⟨0.18743⟩			
Constant	273.392	678.317	196.860	264.519
Adjusted R^2	0.68963	0.17565	0.37027	0.69016
Mean	670.585	904.360	508.230	611.155
SD	229.773	117.801	109.709	222.892
N	298	98	109	91

[a]$p < 0.10.$
[b]$p < 0.05.$
[c]$p < 0.01.$

predicts hourly wage rate in the manufacturing firm, while education and tenure are significant predictors in the nonmanufacturing firm. Neither has a significant effect on hourly wage rate in the public agency. These effects, of course, are net of occupation in these equations. From these analyses it seems that claims about the effects of human capital need to be specified in terms of either the hourly wage rate or the annual income and be related to specific types of firms or industries. Too often generalizations have been made about inequality, specifically about discrimination, using only one or the other indicator and without acknowledging important differences in the level of application.

If we further compare the results in Table 4 with Models 2, 4, and 6 in Table 3, we see that the process of income determination varies across the firms. In the manufacturing firm, both education and experience have direct effects on annual income net of hourly wage rate, but only experience has an indirect effect through the wage rate. In the nonmanufacturing firm, the effects of human capital are only through the wage rate; there are no additional direct effects of either education, experience, or tenure. In the public agency, education has a moderate direct effect on annual income, but no indirect effects through the wage rate.

The firm variables (in the Total Sample equation of Table 4) are both significant predictors of the wage rate, with the nonmanufacturing firm paying only 67% and the public agency paying 76% of the manufacturing firm wage rate. It is in reference to the wage rate that these firms appear to fit the definitions of economic sectors, with the manufacturing firm paying most, the nonmanufacturing firm paying least, and the public agency in between. But in terms of annual personal income (Model 7 of Table 3), controlling for hourly wage rate, the manufacturing firm is differentiated from the other two, but they are not differentiated from each other. The difference in this respect between hourly wage rate and annual personal income has to do with the fact that incentive pay is available only in the manufacturing firm, which makes the firm even more distinct from the others than it would be if we compared only hourly wage rate. It also relates to the fact that the nonmanufacturing firm requires more overtime than the public agency, making annual income for employees at that firm higher than it would be if we considered only their hourly wage rates. These differences, however, are not accidental or incidental; they are part of what makes these firms and the kinds of jobs within them unique and distinct from the others. Again, we are cautioned in future analyses of inequality to specify the type of reward measure (whether wage or income), as well as the firms or industries to which we want to generalize.

Finally, we want to consider what accounts for the differences in reward patterns among these three firms. The three firms vary on a number of important dimensions that have been discussed in the literature on dual and segmented labor markets: size, proportion male, proportion black and Hispanic, and whether unionized or not. We cannot statistically separate the effects of these dimensions because they are too highly intercorrelated in this sample to include them in the regression analyses. We can, however, suggest a possible relation between them and the regression analyses by comparing the distribution of the firms on these dimensions with the magnitude of the coefficients on the firm variables in the equations predicting annual income and hourly wage rate. Table 5 gives the values of the dimensions for the three firms.

The *size* of the firm has the same distribution as the coefficients on the firm variables in the equation predicting hourly wage rate (Total Sample equation of Table 4); none of the other dimensions in Table 5 do. That is, size is ordered from largest to smallest: manufacturing (24,200), public (5,300), and nonmanufacturing (3,500). The coefficients on the firm variables in the equation for hourly wage rate are ordered the same way: manufacturing (324.431), public (93.439), and nonmanufacturing (omitted category), with both manufacturing and public significantly larger than nonmanufacturing. *Proportion male* has the same distribution (manufacturing largest and no difference between nonmanufacturing and public) as the coefficients on the firm variables in the equation predicting annual personal income (model 7 of Table 3; manufacturing is significantly different from the nonmanufacturing firm, but the public agency is not significantly different in this equation). None of the other dimensions in Table 5 have this ordering.

While both size and proportion male do seem to underlie the strong firm effects in these equations, it does not appear that either unionization or per-

Table 5. Selected Characteristics by Firm

	Manufacturing	Nonmanufacturing	Public
Size	24,200	3,500	5,300
Percent male	95	30	28
Union	1	0	1
Percent black and hispanic	39	17	61

cent minority are possible explanations. That is not to say that unionization does not have an effect, but only to note that there are major differences among unions. Both the manufacturing firm and the public agency are unionized, but the unions in the two firms are of a very different sort. In the manufacturing firm, the union has been very strong and dominant; in the public agency, the unions have been relatively weak. The labor force literature often refers to unionization as a piece and does not always make distinctions, especially in empirical work, between strong and weak unions. Distinctions are also rarely made in the literature on dual and segmented labor markets between the job situations for women and minorities. They are often lumped together as a category and both assumed to be concentrated in the "periphery" or "competitive" sectors. In this sample there is a different distribution. Although we cannot generalize from these three firms to the whole labor force, these firms are typical of other firms in their respective industries. The manufacturing firm has a large proportion of minority employees (40%) and this is true of many heavy manufacturing firms. The nonmanufacturing firm is predominantly female, with only a small minority (especially of black and Hispanic) population. It, too, is typical of its industrial category, which is finance, insurance, and real estate. (We promised the firm not to reveal the exact industry.) Finally, the public agency is predominantly minority (especially black) and female, which is true of many public agencies, especially in large cities.

Both firm size and proportion male (of either occupation, industry, or firm), which are the dimensions that seem to provide an interpretation to the firm effects in this study, have been found to be important determinants of earnings in past studies (Bibb and Form, 1977; Bridges, 1982; Bridges and Berk, 1974, 1978; Cassell, Director, and Doctors, 1975; England, 1984; Halaby, 1979; Snyder, Hayward, and Hudis, 1978; Stolzenberg, 1978). But there is one further aspect to these firms that may provide a possible explanation for the relation of both size and proportion male to both hourly wage rate and annual income. That is the occupational composition across the three firms *in relation to the "maleness" or "femaleness" of the job* (see Table 6 for the value of each variable for each race/ethnic and sex group). The point here is the effect of composition differences, not mean differences. That the coefficients for sex and race/ethnicity are not always significant in the regression analyses shows only that there are no mean differences between groups when relevant variables are controlled. But it is still possible, and I argue that it is very likely, that there are composition effects of sex, race/ethnicity, and occupation. The following provides some explanation of what I mean.

In the manufacturing firm, females in male jobs are paid well, but so are females in female jobs. Even so, females make less than males in the manufacturing firm, but this is primarily accounted for by their differences in human capital, net of their occupational assignments. The manufacturing firm also has mostly "male" jobs, with only a few "female" jobs, and the distribution of employees reflects this difference in occupational composition. In the nonmanufacturing firm, females in female jobs are paid poorly, but so are males in female jobs. The few males in male jobs in this firm (primarily service jobs)

Table 6.   Selected Characteristics by Race/Ethnicity and Sex[a]

Variable	BF	WF	LF	BM	WM	LM
Tenure	7.117	9.350	4.483	7.417	8.733	7.517
	(60)	(60)	(60)	(60)	(60)	(60)
Experience	16.783	20.100	10.750	15.339	19.133	15.350
	(60)	(60)	(60)	(59)	(60)	(60)
Education	5.267	5.000	4.983	5.250	5.433	4.500
	(60)	(60)	(59)	(60)	(60)	(60)
Hours	41.678	39.917	40.350	42.450	41.117	40.390
	(59)	(60)	(60)	(60)	(60)	(59)
Weeks	48.933	48.034	46.717	48.561	50.267	46.052
	(60)	(58)	(60)	(57)	(60)	(58)
Hourly wage	635.509	660.160	599.642	658.519	780.245	615.920
	(53)	(50)	(53)	(52)	(53)	(50)
Income	14,270.635	13,303.444	12,825.200	16,969.929	17,964.965	15,020.408
	(52)	(54)	(50)	(56)	(57)	(49)
Technical	1.7%	6.7%	0	3.3%	8.3%	6.7%
	(1)	(4)	(0)	(2)	(5)	(4)
Craft	5.0%	1.7%	1.7%	8.3%	25.0%	10.0%
	(3)	(1)	(1)	(5)	(15)	(6)
Operative	1.7%	5.0%	6.7%	16.7%	13.3%	6.7%
	(1)	(3)	(4)	(10)	(8)	(4)
Clerical	63.3%	53.3%	61.7%	31.7%	20.0%	55.0%
	(38)	(32)	(37)	(19)	(12)	(33)
Laborer	6.7%	10.0%	15.0%	23.3%	18.3%	8.3%
	(4)	(6)	(9)	(14)	(11)	(5)
Service	21.7%	23.3%	15.0%	16.7%	15.0%	13.3%
	(13)	(14)	(9)	(10)	(9)	(8)

[a]Tenure, experience, education, hours, weeks, hourly wage, and income means; the occupational variables are in percents. Numbers in parentheses represent the N of valid cases in the cell.

do better, but not nearly as well as if they were in male jobs in one of the other firms. In the nonmanufacturing firm, there are primarily "female" jobs, with only a few "male" jobs. Consequently, it is hard for the company to recruit and keep males in their hire. In the public agency, in contrast to the other two firms, there is more segregation by occupation, with females primarily in female jobs (clerical, service, and technical in this agency) and males primarily in male jobs (craft, operative, and laborer). The occupational composition in this agency is also more evenly balanced with both "male" and "female" jobs than in the other two firms. (This explains the occupational effects on hourly wage rate in the agency.) Even with this distinction, however, the only well-paid jobs in the public agency are the craft jobs, and, as is true for the manufacturing firm, these positions are held overwhelmingly by white men, while the operative and laborer jobs are disproportionately held by minority men.

Thus, both the sex and occupational composition of each of these firms are important determinants of how well the employees within each firm fare. The studies that have used, for example, proportion male in occupation or industry have not always been sufficiently attuned to how the location of a job in a particular firm makes the meaning of the job different and makes the meaning of the compositional differences variable. The relations between and among firm, occupation, and wage are related to the historically developed sex and occupational composition of each. The following provides some background for each firm to show how each has been subject to different pressures in the development of their labor forces. It is imperative that the labor force literature recognize the variations within the labor market that have created the kinds of differences represented, for example, by these three firms.

The manufacturing firm is part of heavy industry and is in a historically oligopolistic market where wage concessions to employees could be passed along in higher prices to consumers. The jobs are both dirty and dangerous and require a well-skilled labor force to prevent in-plant disasters. One former executive from this firm reported (in private conversation) that the norm for the industry is that employees have to have an IQ of at least 115 even to be able to walk around in the plant. In this environment it has been possible for the firm to be very selective in their recruitment and hiring, but the free decisions of the firm have been circumscribed in two ways.

First, the unionization of the industry, which was gained only after a long and bloody struggle over many years, has contributed to the strong defense of seniority as the primary criterion for promotion decisions within the firm. At the same time, management has tried over the years to break the power of the skilled trades within the industry. Seniority is important in an industry where the hard physical nature of many jobs makes them more difficult for older workers to do, and where the complex and dangerous nature of the work requires intelligence and years of experience and training. For all these reasons, a complex system of job ladders and an internal labor market system have developed within this industry. The implementation of the internal labor market is a constant source of tension among management, the union, and the workers. As such, the occupation to which one gains access and the experience within it are important determinants of both the wage rate and annual income. But given the added incentive pay and the structure of overtime, occupation is especially important for explaining annual income. Who holds what occupation has some relationship to race/ethnicity and sex, although there are few direct effects of race/ethnicity and sex on rewards within the company after occupation is controlled.

Although foreign competition in the industry has forced dramatic changes over the last decade that were just beginning to be evident at the time this study was completed, many working-class people still see these jobs as highly desirable. At the time the interviews were done, the company had a backlog of applications of up to two years for jobs at this firm. Because of the high pay and protection of seniority in this industry, it was a specific target of equal employment opportunity policies when they were legislated in the mid-1960s. This is a second factor that has affected the company's ability to make decisions about hiring and promotion.

About 20% of the employees are Hispanic, and many of them were recruited by the company in Mexico during the labor shortages of World War

II. About 20% of the employees are black, and many of them were hired only after affirmative action legislation required the company to do so. There are differences in the types of jobs held in this firm by Hispanic versus black versus white males, with white males overrepresented in the highly paid craft jobs, black males overrepresented in the most dangerous, dirty, and relatively lower-paid jobs in the firm, and Hispanic males overrepresented in the other, noncraft, but less dangerous and dirty jobs. Access to different types of jobs, with the attendant wage and incentive possibilities and the relative physical comfort of doing the job, is a highly charged issue in this firm.

In addition, less than 10% of the employees in the manufacturing firm are female. Many females worked in the industry during World War II, but as was true for other heavy industries, many also left when males returned from the war at its end. Only recently has there been an increase again in the hiring of females, which is also in response to pressure brought on the firm from equal opportunity legislation. Females in the firm are overwhelming likely to be found in either clerical or service jobs, both of which are lower paid. In interviews with the women in the firm, it was clear that they felt entitled to access to the physically easier jobs if they preferred, but yet they did not want to be barred from the higher-paying, more physically demanding jobs if they felt they were able. In fact, some felt that the company should make the higher-paying jobs easier to do so that it would be more possible for them to manage them, and many of them felt ambivalent at best toward seniority rights.

All of the women we interviewed in the manufacturing firm were quite aware that they had few options outside this firm and this industry to make as much money as they did. Although concerned about their ability to do the jobs, these women were determined to keep them. Women in this firm were more likely to hold "female" jobs even though in a "male" environment, and for the most part, they claimed that they would rather have the "female" jobs than the "male" jobs. Although they desired access to higher pay, few, in their conversations with us, expressed interest in doing the more physically demanding but higher-paying jobs. In fact, because so many of the women in this firm—disproportionate to the other two—were single mothers, many expressed their hope to one day get married and leave the company. Because the firm overall paid so well, these women made substantially more than if they had held similar types of jobs in either of the other two firms.

The nonmanufacturing firm is opposite in almost every characteristic from the manufacturing firm. There are few physically demanding jobs in the largely "paperwork" firm. The few "physical jobs," such as maintenance, transportation, and security, were almost all held by males. Although relatively well paid compared to others in this firm, they nevertheless were much less well paid than if they had been doing similar jobs in the manufacturing firm. Thus, these males in "male" jobs were still not paid "male" wages in this largely female firm. This was even more true for males holding "female" jobs in this firm. As noted above, the semiprofessional or technical jobs in this firm were more like clerical positions than they were like management.

Consequently, the firm had high turnover and a bimodal age distribution, with very young and very old employees. The personnel policies of the firm were very paternalistic, which was frequently mentioned in the interviews we conducted with these employees. To accommodate the high turnover problems without increasing wages, the firm developed a unique policy of hiring older workers and also of rewarding employees more for tenure than for experience. The women in this firm were disproportionately likely to be married and living with their husbands. This is probably because women with sole responsibility for breadwinning could not "afford" to work here.

Finding qualified workers to do the "male" jobs at this firm at largely "female" wages was the primary personnel problem for the company. But management, in this nonunionized firm, was free to assign both wage rate and jobs to accommodate their problems of recruitment and retention. Service jobs in the firm, which are the "male" jobs most difficult for them to staff, therefore paid more than others, while clerical jobs, which were easier to fill, paid the least. Net of occupation, the company primarily rewarded education and tenure in the assignment of wage rate. Given that the company had so few well-trained workers, those with better skills stood out. Because of the relative lack of complexity to the internal job structure in the firm, annual income for the employees in this firm is primarily a function of the wage rate and the hours worked.

Like many public agencies, the one in this sample was disproportionately black, and this was true for management as well as nonmanagement jobs. Even so, the most highly paid craft jobs at this firm were held almost exclusively by white men, in part because access to the craft is not a decision of the firm but of the union through which they get their training. As noted above, the jobs within this firm were more sex-segregated than were those in the other two firms, with males primarily in "male" jobs and females primarily in "female" jobs. The wage rate for the jobs within the firm follows the sex distribution, with the male jobs paying most (craft, operative, and laborer) and the female jobs paying least (clerical, service, and technical or semiprofessional).

With no incentive pay and a relatively less complex internal labor market structure compared with the manufacturing firm, annual income in the public agency is primarily a function of wage rate and occupation. The major exception is that black males, net of wage rate and occupation, earn significantly more, and there is a modest direct effect of education. Both are probably also affected by the sex and occupational composition within the agency, although the exact reasons are not clear.

V. SUMMARY AND DISCUSSION

Past empirical research has been indeterminant regarding the relative importance of human capital investment and firm or occupational characteristics for determining income and for explaining differences by race, ethnicity, or sex. Part of the differences between studies in their findings can be attributed to differences in sample selection, concept definition, and statistical procedures. By analyzing data at the level of the firm, this chapter has helped to decompose some of the complexity of labor market structure and rewards. However, precisely because the data are firm-level, we need to be cautious in claiming generalizability.

The truncation of the sample especially to nonmanagerial and nonprofessional employees means that the findings I have presented do not describe the labor force as a whole. However, they do apply to the strata about which dual and segmented labor market theories have been developed.[3] None of the workers in the sample is likely to be promoted to a managerial or professional job within these or other companies, *unless* he or she obtains further training or education. Furthermore, the experience that workers have in these jobs would not necessarily work to their advantage in obtaining higher-level employment. Thus, jobs have distinct linkages. People are likely to move within a limited range in most cases, but how these moves are made and how they are rewarded depend on the occupation itself, on its requirements and associated conditions of work, and on the firm within which it is located.

In this sense, Thurow (1975) is correct in pointing to job versus wage competition, but he does not give sufficient attention to the location of jobs within a firm context, which makes some jobs, in some kinds of firms, relatively more open to some categories of workers than others. And if the firm does not have a structured internal labor market, then the job itself may be less important than the wage rate assigned to the worker. For example, a craft union, where control is at the level of the occupation even though employees may be distributed across many firms, may function quite differently from industrial unions, which leave hiring decisions to the individual employer but negotiate the job rules, wages, and working conditions. And both may be quite distinct from a nonunionized firm, where all such decisions are at the discretion of the employer, who, nevertheless, has to make those decisions in

---

[3]The dual and segmented labor market theories originated in the aftermath of the War on Poverty programs and as part of the analysis of the failure of the programs to bring about equality in the labor market. The primary emphasis was on the employment problems of blacks, especially males, and their exclusion from craft jobs in heavy industry. Thus, the dual and segmented labor market theories were applied to explain discrimination not in managerial and professional employment but rather within blue-collar manufacturing jobs. It is also in this context that theories of internal labor markets were developed, and so it is not surprising that much of the earlier work on labor markets restricted the samples to males of prime age in manufacturing jobs. Because dual and segmented labor market theories were originally proposed as critical of mainstream economics, they have been thought of as supporting liberal policies. They have, even so, served a conservative purpose by coinciding with the efforts of companies such as the one in our sample to try to circumscribe craft unions to hire and train black men in craft jobs, albeit in shortened training programs that were not under union control. Their motivation had more to do with the shortage of skilled workers during the Vietnam War than with civil rights or labor market theories. The solution to their hiring problem simultaneously provided them with an avenue of response to pressures from the civil rights movement and with a means to take training out of the hands of unions.

competition for qualified employees with other employers, including some who are unionized. In the case of craft unions, job incumbents have been able to gain advantage in both hourly wage rate and working conditions, which translate into high annual incomes. For those in other types of jobs, the determinants of annual income are primarily determined by the firm, especially whether or not it is unionized, by the strength of the union, and by the circumstances in the labor market, especially whether jobs are scarce or plentiful.

Thus, as Bluestone (1970) argued earlier, an occupation may have a very different meaning depending on which firm it is in and on the occupational incumbent. In other words, the interaction between the type of firm and the type of occupation, as well as their independent effects, is important for understanding the structure and rewards of the labor market as they affect the lives of workers of different race/ethnicity and sex. For example, secretaries within the manufacturing firm fare much better than secretaries within the nonmanufacturing firm or the public agency, while craft workers fare well no matter which firm employs them. Yet workers who may do the same job, but without the occupational title of craft, do not do as well in a firm like the nonmanufacturing company in our sample. Further, the same occupational distribution in two similar firms may affect workers quite differently if one has a well-structured internal labor market and the other does not. In a company with a structured internal labor market, workers in the same job are likely to be paid similarly, but in a company without a structured internal labor market, it is possible to pay workers in the same job differently, depending on judgments about their actual or potential performance.

One conclusion that we could draw from these findings is that the world is much more complex than we have allowed (owing to limitations of our data and our samples). But this is not the only lesson from this study. More important, we can suggest that the labor market is a political as well as a structural entity and that the unevenness of outcomes is related to the unevenness of the political struggles that have shaped the definitions of occupations and the pattern of wage rates within particular firms or industries. There is a structure to the labor market that, when put into practice (Giddens, 1979), reproduces the structure of inequality that we generally observe. But we often overconceptualize both the structure and the inequality, because we fail to see the accommodations that both employers and workers make to economic conditions, to political and/or legal pressures, constraints, and opportunities, and to social norms and conventions. Heavy industry was once a mecca for good jobs sought by working-class people; now the privileges and rewards are under siege, while the physical demands and risks remain. Changes are also very much under way in organizations like the public agency and the nonmanufacturing firm in this study. The outcomes for the workers and the jobs they hold are still being sorted out. Our theories will have to change as well if we are to understand what is going on around us. Even more, they need to be continually sensitive to the variability of both structure and process and their interrelation.

ACKNOWLEDGMENTS

I would like to thank Marisa Alicea, Nancy Hartline, Audrey Henderson, Charles Kyle, Patricia Passuth, Alicia Ordonez Sequeira, and David Torres for their assistance, along with others, in the data collection, and Martin Selzer for assistance in data analysis. I would also like to thank E. M. Beck, Paula England, Neil Fligstein, Randy Hodson, Arne Kalleberg, Charles Ragin, and D. Randall Smith for helpful comments on previous drafts of this work. This research was supported in part by grants from the U.S. Department of Labor, Grant No. 21-17-78-66, and from The Rockefeller Foundation, Grant No. GA-EO, C EO 8208, from Northwestern University's Center for Urban Affairs and Policy Research, from Rutgers University Research Committee, and from Rutgers Graduate School of Management Research Resources Committee.

REFERENCES

Andrisani, Paul James. 1973. An Empirical Analysis of the Dual Labor Market Theory. Doctoral dissertation, Ohio State University.

Averitt, Robert T. 1968. *The Dual Economy: The Dynamics of American Industry Structure.* New York: Horton.

Baron, James N., and William T. Bielby. 1980. "Bringing Firms Back In: Stratification, Segmentation, and the Organization of Work." *American Sociological Review* 45:737–765.

Baron, James N., and William T. Bielby. 1982. "Workers and Machines: Dimensions and Determinants of Technical Relations in the Workplace." *American Sociological Review* 47:175–188.

Baron, James N., and William T. Bielby. 1984. "The Organization of Work in a Segmented Economy." *American Sociological Review* 49:454–473.

Baron, James N., Alison Davis-Blake, and William T. Bielby. 1986. "The Structure of Opportunity: How Promotion Ladders Vary within and among Organizations." *Administrative Science Quarterly* 31:48–273.

Beck, E. M., Patrick M. Horan, and Charles M. Tolbert III. 1978. "Stratification in a Dual Economy: A Sectoral Model of Earning Determination." *American Sociological Review* 45:704–720.

Beck, E. M., Patrick M. Horan, and Charles M. Tolbert III. 1980a. "Social Stratification in Industrial Society: Further Evidence for a Structural Alternative." *American Sociological Review* 45:712–719.

Beck, E. M., Patrick M. Horan, and Charles M. Tolbert III. 1980b. "Industrial Segmentation and Labor Market Discrimination." *Social Problems* 28:113–130.

Berg, Ivar, ed. 1981. *Sociological Perspectives on Labor Markets.* New York: Academic Press.

Bibb, Robert, and William H. Form. 1977. "The Effects of Industrial, Occupational, and Sex Stratification on Wages in Blue-Collar Markets." *Social Forces* 55:974–996.

Bluestone, Barry. 1970. "The Tripartite Economy: Labor Markets and the Working Poor." *Poverty and Human Resources* 5:15–35.

Bluestone, Barry. 1973. *Low Wages and the Working Poor.* Ann Arbor: Institute of Labor and Industrial Relations.

Bridges, William P. 1982. "The Sexual Segregation of Occupations: Theories of Labor Stratification in Industry." *American Journal of Sociology* 88:270–295.

Bridges, William P., and Richard A. Berk. 1974. "Determinants of White Collar Income: An Evaluation of Equal Pay for Equal Work." *Social Science Research* 3:211–233.

Bridges, William P., and Richard A. Berk. 1978. "Sex, Earnings, and the Nature of Work: A Job-level Analysis of Male-Female Income Differences." *Social Science Quarterly* 58:553–565.

Cain, Glen G. 1976. "The Challenge of Segmented Labor Market Theories to Orthodox Theory: A Survey." *Journal of Economic Literature* 14:1215–1257.

Cassell, Frank H., Steven M. Director, and Samuel I. Doctors. 1975. "Discrimination within Internal Labor Markets." *Industrial Relations* 14:337–344.

Doeringer, Peter B., and Michael J. Piore. 1971. *Internal Labor Markets and Manpower Analysis.* Lexington, MA: Lexington Books.

Edwards, Richard C. 1979. *Contested Terrain.* New York: Basic Books.

Edwards, Richard C., Michael Reich, and David M. Gordon, eds. 1975. *Labor Market Segmentation.* Lexington, MA: Lexington Books.

England, Paula. 1984. "Wage Appreciation and Depreciation: A Test of Neoclassical Economic Explanations of Occupational Sex Segregation." *Social Forces* 62:726–749.

Freedman, Marcia. 1976. *Labor Markets: Segments and Shelters.* New York: Allanheld, Osmun Land Mark Studies, Universe Books.

Giddens, Anthony. 1979. *Central Problems in Social Theory: Action, Structure, and Contradiction in Social Analysis.* Berkeley: University of California Press.

Gordon, David M. 1972. *Theories of Poverty and Underemployment.* Lexington, MA: D. C. Heath.

Griffin, Larry J. 1978. "On Estimating the Economic Value of Schooling and Experience: Some Issues in Conceptualization and Measurement." *Sociological Methods and Research* 6:309–335.

Halaby, Charles N. 1979. "Job-Specific Sex Differences in Organizational Reward Attainment: Wage Discrimination versus Rank Segregation." *Social Forces* 58:108–127.

Harrison, Bennett. 1972. *Education, Training, and the Urban Ghetto.* Baltimore: Johns Hopkins Press.

Hodson, Randy. 1978. "Labor in the Monopoly, Competitive, and State Sectors of Production." *Politics and Society* 8:429–480.

Hodson, Randy. 1986. "Industrial Structure as a Worker Resource." *Social Science Journal* 23:277–292.

Horan, Patrick, and Charles M. Tolbert III. 1980. "The Market Homogeneity Assumption: On the Theoretical Foundations of Empirical Knowledge." *Social Science Quarterly* 61:278–292.

Kalleberg, Arne L., Michael Wallace, and Robert P. Althauser. 1981. "Economic Segmentation, Worker Power, and Income Inequality." *American Journal of Sociology* 87(3):651–683.

Kaufman, Robert L., Randy Hodson, and Neil D. Fligstein. 1981. "Defrocking Dualism: A New Approach to Defining Industrial Sectors." *Social Science Research* 10:1–31.

Lincoln, James R., and Arne L. Kalleberg. 1987. *Culture, Control Systems, and Commitment.* Under review.

Mincer, Jacob. 1958. "Investment in Human Capital and Personal Income Distribution." *Journal of Political Economy* 66:281–302.

Mincer, Jacob. 1974. *Schooling, Experience, and Earnings.* New York: Columbia University Press.

Reich, Michael, David M. Gordon, and Richard C. Edwards. 1973. "A Theory of Labor Market Segmentation." *American Economic Review* 63:359–365.

Rosenbaum, James E. 1975. "Organizational Career Mobility: Promotion Chances in a Corporation during Periods of Growth and Contraction." *American Journal of Sociology* 85:21–48.

Rosenberg, Sam. 1975. The Dual Labor Market: Its Existence and Consequences. Doctoral dissertation, Brandeis University.

Smith, D. Randall. 1983. "Mobility in Professional Occupational-Internal Labor Markets: Stratification, Segmentation, and Vacancy Chains." *American Sociological Review* 48:289–305.

Snyder, David, Mark D. Hayward, and Paula M. Hudis. 1978. "The Location of Change in the Sexual Structure of Occupations, 1950–1970: Insights from Labor Market Segmentation Theory." *American Journal of Sociology* 84:706–717.

Stewman, Shelby, and Suresh L. Konda. 1983. "Careers and Organizational Labor Markets: Demographic Models of Organizational Behavior." *American Journal of Sociology* 88:637–685.

Stewman, Shelby, and Suresh L. Konda. 1986. "Demographic Models of Internal Labor Markets." *Administrative Science Quarterly* 31:212–247.

Stolzenberg, Ross M. 1975. "Occupations, Labor Markets, and the Process of Wage Attainment." *American Sociological Review* 40:645–665.

Stolzenberg, Ross M. 1978. "Bringing the Boss Back In: Employer Size, Employee Schooling, and Socioeconomic Achievement." *American Sociological Review* 43:812–828.

Talbert, Joan, and Christine Bose. 1977. "Wage Attainment Processes: The Retail Clerk Case." *American Journal of Sociology* 83:403–423.

Thurow, Lester G. 1975. *Generating Inequality*. New York: Basic Books.

Tolbert, Charles M., III. 1982. "Industrial Segmentation of Men's Career Mobility." *American Sociological Review* 47:457–477.

Wachter, Michael L. 1974. "Primary and Secondary Labor Markets: A Critique of the Dual Approach." *Brookings Papers on Economic Activity* 3:637–693.

Zucker, Lynne G., and Carolyn Rosenstein. 1981. "Taxonomies of Institutional Structure: Dual Economy Reconsidered." *American Sociological Review* 46:869–884.

V
THE FUTURE OF WORK

Profound changes are reshaping American workplaces, resulting from developments in the international economy as well as from (related) technological change. Whether these trends render previous analyses of employment and earnings obsolete, and whether the changes threaten the well-being of American workers, are both subjects of debate. The three chapters in this section provide an early view of the consequences for workers of the growth of the service and high-technology sectors.

Hodson reports on in-depth interviews with workers and managers in high-tech firms in "Good Jobs and Bad Management: How New Problems Evoke Old Solutions in High-Tech Settings." He reviews past literature, highlighting debates about whether "high-tech" employment will increase or decrease job skill levels, inequality in the distribution of skill and pay, hierarchical authority relations in the workplace, job safety, and job satisfaction.

Hodson conducted interviews with 48 managers, engineers, and other workers in 22 large and small companies, representing electronics, telecommunications, aerospace, and biotech companies in a medium-size southwest city. The result is a rich "snapshot" of working life in high-tech firms.

Hodson reports that many of the production workers have some post-high school education, but few find this helpful on the job. Rather, their on-the-job training is viewed by both themselves and their supervisors as significantly more important. Hodson describes this pattern as neither deskilling nor upgrading but as "skill disruption."

The women and minorities Hodson interviewed complained of discrimination and blocked mobility. Indeed, the perception of blocked upward mobility is widespread, extending even to Anglos and males, and resulting in a serious problem of turnover, particularly within larger firms. Yet employers are failing to use internal labor markets, efficiency wages, or implicit contracts to deal with this problem. If this observation is accurate, some of our theories of internal labor markets need revision.

Hodson notes a discrepancy between managers' verbalized adherence to ideologies of participation and their actual practice of allowing only very superficial participation while measuring productivity with traditional time-and-motion studies. Both engineers and production workers complain bitterly about the incompetence of management, claiming that managers are insufficiently concerned with production itself. Workers in nonunionized plants complain about favoritism and arbitrary discipline.

Hodson concludes that "there appears to be an intensive, if fairly quiet, crisis of organizational structure and managerial competence and style" in high-tech firms. He believes that the roots of this crisis reside in rapid technological change, insufficient worker participation, and unmediated managerial power. However, workers liked certain aspects of their jobs in high-tech settings, such as the informal workplace atmosphere and the ability to learn skills on the job.

Hodson portrays managers as choosing strategies that are beneficial neither to workers nor to the firms' bottom line. An economist might ask why competition between high-tech firms isn't leading those making such errors to go bankrupt or at least lose market share to firms doing more to enhance productivity and profits. But the real challenge is to consider the possibility that employers are behaving in a way inconsistent with their own interests, and to investigate what systematic factors lead such behavior to persist despite competitive forces that work to eliminate inefficient behavior. Or, if employers are acting rationally, what is it about high-tech firms that makes it less profitable for them to use implicit contracts, internal labor markets, and efficiency wages to motivate and retain workers, than it is for large employers in the traditional manufacturing sector? It is with regard to such questions that hypotheses from sociology and economics can be empirically tested and we can seek an integrative view that neither precludes nor is limited to the operation of market forces.

In "Dueling Sectors: The Role of Service Industries in the Earnings Process of the Dual Economy," Leann Tigges argues that the rise of the service sector renders older views of economic segmentation at least partially obsolete. She begins with the development of a "new segmentation" view that takes into account changes in both the "how" of production (i.e., core and peripheral sectors) and the "what" of production (i.e., transformative and service sectors).

Tigges provides an empirical analysis of industrial determinants of earnings in both 1960 and 1980. Individuals were categorized into either core or periphery according to the industry in which they were employed, using the scheme proposed by Tolbert and his colleagues. They are also categorized into the cross-cutting categories of transformative or service industries. Tigges finds that the earnings advantage of core employment declined between 1960 and 1980, particularly for core industries within the service sector. This suggests that the "new structuralist" emphasis on the dimensions of industrial segmentation that determine core or peripheral status are decreasingly useful for predicting earnings. Contrary to the prediction of optimistic "postindustrial" theories, the increment in earnings for professional or managerial employment did not increase across the 20 years, returns to education did not increase, and education was not more highly rewarded in the service sector. However, the failure of professional and managerial occupations to increase their earnings advantage over other workers between 1960 and 1980 also casts doubt on pessimistic views that see occupational bifurcation and an elimination of middle-level jobs.

The final chapter in the section is "The Impact of Technology on Work Organization and Work Outcomes: A Conceptual Framework and Research Agenda," by Form, Kaufman, Parcel, and Wallace. These authors analyze the effects of technological change in production processes upon work organization and outcomes. Dependent variables include skill demands, authority relations, autonomy, job satisfaction, and alienation.

Form et al. begin by reviewing the sociological and economic literature on technological change. A pessimistic view argues that work is being deskilled and degraded by strategies of technological rationalization. An optimistic view argues that technology is upgrading the skill levels of work, leading to the professionalization of many jobs. In contrast to either of these two views, the authors propose a "contingency model" that specifies how upgrading or downgrading is contingent upon a complex array of organizational and societal factors.

Their contingency view predicts that, at the worker level, the effects of technological innovation depend upon the type of the innovation, the position of the firm in the segmented economy (e.g., its size, capital intensity, oligopoly, and unionization), and the firm's organizational structure. At the departmental level, their contingency approach predicts that effects of technological change will vary with the size of the department and its role within the organization (e.g., staff or line). At the establishment level, the contingency approach predicts that the effects of technological change will depend upon whether or not the establishment is a subsidiary of a larger firm and the characteristics of the product market in which the establishment operates.

Form et al. propose that empirical work in this area be based upon a three-stage hierarchical design that begins with a household probability sample. Respondents would be asked about their work situation, including the name of their establishment, department, and supervisor. These data are then employed in subsequent stages of the design to gather departmental and establishment-level measures as contextual variables that help define the contingencies of effects of technological change on outcomes for work and workers.

Taken together, the chapters in this section point out that, even within disciplines, there has been insufficient attention to the implications of theories about services and "high-tech" production for theories about industrial and labor market segmentation, and vice versa. For example, Hodson finds that production jobs in high-tech industries use firm-specific more than general human capital, yet there is little development of internal labor markets, implicit contracts, or explicit union contracts. The "new institutional economics" would expect to find that an emphasis upon firm-specific training is accompanied by these features. Tigges finds the advantage of employment in core industries declining between 1960 and 1980 precisely in service industries, suggesting a need to revise dual economy theories to take into account the rise of these industries. In view of these observations, the theoretical indeterminacy of the contingency approach proposed by Form et al. may be necessary to capture the complexity and flux of the current situation, at least until the "new segmentation" theory that Tigges calls for is further developed.

Development of this theory might best proceed by attending to those issues that capitalize on the respective strengths of the economic and sociological perspectives. Such questions include these: Why do certain characteristics of industries, such as the technology of production and the product type (e.g., services) affect workers' outcomes as they do? Is the key to answering such questions to search for why personnel policies that maximize profits differ between sectors? This would be the economists' approach. Or are there systematic deviations from market-driven predictions? If so, the challenge is to describe and specify the causes of these. For example, are there features of certain product markets that make information acquisition and rational calculation particu-

larly difficult or unlikely? Do employer and worker networks create perceptions and loyalties that in turn alter calculations of self-interest? Serious study of trends in work require a sensitivity to both market processes and such systematic deviations from them. It also requires a perspective encompassing both sociological and economic concerns.

11

Good Jobs and Bad Management
How New Problems Evoke Old Solutions in High-Tech Settings

Randy Hodson

I. INTRODUCTION

It is generally agreed that new technologies are having a profound effect on the character of work in modern society. The nature of these changes, however, is as yet little understood. Which areas are being most effected? Which areas are less effected? Which consequences are desirable and which are undesirable? This article will address these issues by investigating some of the consequences of "high-tech" production systems for the skill content of jobs, for labor market segmentation, for organizational structure, and finally, for the satisfactions and frustrations that workers derive from their employment.[1]

The analysis presented in this chapter is based on in-depth interviews with workers, engineers, supervisors, and managers in a variety of high-tech settings. This technique allows us to investigate the detailed issues and nuances that have been identified as most relevant in the existing literature on technology and work and to evaluate these changes in the immediate present.

---

[1]Conceptually, "high-tech" industries can be defined as having continuous flow technology (as opposed to unit or batch technology), as employing flexible production techniques, as having a low division of labor, and as producing customized products for differentiated (as opposed to mass) markets (Warner, 1986). In more concrete terms, researchers typically operationalize "high-tech" in terms of industries that utilize greater-than-average numbers of engineers and scientists and expend greater-than-average amounts on research and development. This operational definition includes electronics, machinery, ordnance, chemicals, instrumentation, pharmaceuticals, aerospace, genetic engineering, and communication equipment. All of the firms surveyed for this project operate primarily in these industries.

Randy Hodson • Department of Sociology, Indiana University, Bloomington, Indiana 47401.

This technique offers several benefits unavailable with secondary data analysis. In order to be useful for addressing issues of general interest, social surveys frequently have to be so broad that they are limited in their ability to intensively investigate any single issue. In addition, secondary data quickly become dated, particularly when the phenomena we are studying are changing rapidly. In-depth interviews avoid both of these problems. In addition, in-depth interviews produce information and insights that would be unavailable in more structured contexts. Resulting serendipitous findings are one of the chief benefits of this technique. The major limitation of our small-sample, in-depth interview method is that it cannot tell us very reliably about the *distribution* of consequences, only about their *nature*. In addition, because of the small and potentially nonrepresentative samples utilized, generalizations based on in-depth interviews must remain highly tentative.

Four major themes will emerge in the following analysis. First, high-tech production systems cause a major disruption of skill requirements entailing both extensive deskilling and the demand for new skills. Second, multiple tendencies toward strong segmentation of labor markets result in a substantial reduction of middle-level jobs. The most important of these segmentation tendencies result from organizational and market factors rather than from changing skill requirements. Third, increasing utilization of high-tech production systems has resulted in an extensive organizational crisis involving both organizational structure and the commitment and competence of employees at all levels. Finally, in spite of skill disruption and organizational crisis, workers generally like working with advanced technology because they experience increased levels of "craftlike" ability to do quality work.

II. WHAT THE EXISTING LITERATURE TELLS US

Before reporting on my own observations, it will be useful to review briefly what the existing literature has to say about the issues of high technology and skills, labor market segmentation, organizational structure, and job satisfaction.

A. Skill Upgrading as a Central Theme

Among the most frequently referenced empirical works dealing with advanced technology and skill requirements is Blauner's (1964) classic study of continuous process automation in the chemical industry. Blauner finds that continuous process automation requires a greater proportion of skilled maintenance workers than mass production and that operators in automated settings have greater responsibility for the care and proper functioning of expensive capital equipment. At the broader societal level, Bell (1973) has made similar arguments about the rise of a new intellectual class and the general upgrading of work in "postindustrial" society.

More recently, Adler (1984) argues that "technology has a major positive effect on skill requirements and working conditions." He cites a 1979 Communication Workers of America poll in which 78% of the respondents indicated that technological change had increased the skill requirements of their jobs. Adler adds that automated machines require increasing levels of worker responsibility and that it is easy to underestimate the depth of knowledge required by the technicians who operate automated equipment.

Several studies have emphasized the *new skills* that workers have to learn in order to operate technologically advanced production systems. Cross (1983) investigated 36 continuous-process companies that were "technical leaders in their industries" and found an increasing use of electronics in the control and monitoring of production. In interviews with over 100 workers in these 36 firms, Cross discovered that as a result of the introduction of new technology, workers had to learn important new skills, including the ability to use and maintain a particular type of technology and the ability to diagnose systems problems. Cross argues that these new skill requirements arise from the use of more complex and expensive equipment, from greater integration of different production processes, and from greater demands for product quality. Riche (1982) notes that, even in conventional areas like materials handling, mechanization (or even the utilization of machines with faster speeds) is often a major impetus requiring workers to develop new skills. He adds that unskilled workers in industrial manufacturing settings frequently become monitors of very expensive equipment as manual tasks are increasingly mechanized.

B. Deskilling as a Central Theme

In contrast to Adler (1984) and others, who identify a consistent upgrading pattern in skill requirements, there are many who believe that deskilling is the dominant consequence of the adoption of new technology. For example, Bright (1966), while noting that increasing automation implies increasing levels of responsibility for some workers, concludes that overall, automation creates a tendency toward declining skill requirements. Bright argues that as mechanization progresses, initial changes that demand increased skills give way under automation to a progressive loss of skill, resulting in an inverted "U-shaped" skill curve. Moreover, Bright suggests that the growing demand for trained technicians to operate automated equipment may be just a form of "credential inflation," rather than true skill upgrading. This "deskilling" thesis has been given popular expression by the work of Braverman (1974), who argues that skill degradation is an inherent and pervasive characteristic of capitalist economies because capitalists are constantly driven to reduce labor costs in order to increase profits and maintain their competitive position.

Through the use of case studies, Boddy and Buchanan (1981) describe in detailed terms how new technologies are creating a growing proportion of deskilled occupations. They present two case studies, the first of which involves the transformation of copy typists into video typists. According to Boddy and Buchanan, deskilling occurs because, with automated equipment, there is less need to type text correctly the first time. With the new equipment, corrections are made more easily or are even made automatically. The printer positions the paper and the computer takes over other functions formerly executed by copy typists. Boddy and Buchanan do, however, cite some new skills required of video typists. These include the need to concentrate more and the need to become familiar with codes for formatting and editing text on the automated system.[2]

The other case documented by Boddy and Buchanan (1981) involves the introduction of automated mixing equipment at a biscuit factory. The major effect cited in this study is the transformation of the "doughman" into a mixer-operator. Formerly, the position of doughman was held by a master baker. But when the computer replaced the need for human intervention in the mixing process, the doughman suffered a radical loss of craft skills. The new automated equipment left the doughman with the residual responsibility of pressing a button to start the mixing cycle. Further, the doughman was left with less discretion over other aspects of his work as the overall control of the operation was moved higher into the organizational hierarchy. Boddy and Buchanan found no aspects of the automatic technology that demanded that the mixer-operators acquire new skills or knowledge in order to perform effectively.[3]

The *training* needs of workers are also being affected by the changing skill requirements of new technologies. Riche (1982) sums up much of the literature on this point when he writes that there is now "less demand for manual dexterity, physical strength, and for traditional craftsmanship." Instead, he sees "employers stressing formal knowledge, precision, and perceptual aptitudes." Riche argues that, in general, the new occupations can be filled by retraining existing workers. Hunt and Hunt (1983) also argue that the new technologies will require much more technical background than manufacturing jobs in the past. However, they anticipate that retraining workers displaced by robots for the new jobs created by robotics may not always be realistic. For example, they feel that it would be difficult to retrain an assembly welder to maintain and repair the welding robot that will be doing his job in the future. On the other hand, they conclude that it would be feasible to retrain skilled plant maintenance workers to also maintain industrial robots.

C. Labor Market Segmentation

An important issue, and one that has drawn increasing attention, concerns the consequences of advanced technology for the overall *shape* of the occupational distribution. Francis, Snell, Willman, and Winch (1981) find that new technologies tend to create dual occupational structures, one highly

---

[2]For further research on the deskilling consequences of automated office systems, see Cornfield (1984) and Murphee (1981).

[3]See also the Wallace and Kalleberg (1982) study of mechanization, automation, and deskilling in the printing industry.

skilled, the other composed of unskilled workers. The AFL-CIO has also issued a report (1983) voicing concern over the possibility that the growing use of advanced technology will increase the schism between professional workers and production workers. Baran and Teegarden (1984), in their study of automation in the insurance industry, find that technological restructuring has raised average skill requirements as a result of reducing the number of less-skilled positions. But they also see the work force in insurance firms becoming polarized through a breakdown in conventional mobility ladders. They specifically note the growing gap between clerical workers on the one hand, and professionals and managers on the other.

Burris (1984) suggests that such labor market splits are being intensified by the increasing use of educational credentials as an employment screen between two nonconnecting career lines. And Ingham (1967) notes how such limits on mobility opportunities can lessen motivation for all employees. Baran and Teegarden (1984) point out that the changing occupational structure affects mainly women. Minority women, concentrated in the lowest-level clerical jobs, will face displacement, while better-educated white women will confront deskilling and blocked mobility opportunities.

Further cautions against the idea of an egalitarian occupational structure emerging as a consequence of new technology are offered by Rumberger and Levin (1983). They note that most of the new jobs in high-technology settings will be in occupations with less-than-average earnings. Further, they point out that in 1980, only one-quarter of the jobs in high-tech industries could be truly classified as high-tech occupations. Perhaps even more compelling, Rumberger and Levin note that the vast majority of new jobs generated by our "high-technology" economy in the next 15 years will be in such low-skill occupations as janitorial services, nurse's aides, and waitressing.

Data gathered by Eisenscher (1984) also support the idea that the new technologies are producing a more bottom-heavy occupational distribution. For example, among workers in Santa Clara county, California, there is a lower proportion of professional and technical workers in the electronics industry than in manufacturing as a whole. In the electronics industry, professional and technical occupations account for only 28% of all jobs, while among all manufacturing workers, these two occupations account for 34% of total employment. Further, there are fewer craft workers in the high-tech sector (10%) than in manufacturing as a whole (12%). In contrast, there is a higher proportion of operatives in the high-tech sector (32%) than in manufacturing as a whole (25%).

Rumberger and Levin (1983) argue that this distribution is unlikely to improve with advancing technology because the profit imperative demands that highly paid labor be automated before poorly paid labor. As an example, they note that one of the most dramatically successful areas of automation in computer manufacture is in computer-assisted design. This technological breakthrough has displaced large numbers of reasonably well paid draftsmen. Meanwhile, the development of automatic equipment for inserting microchips into printed circuit boards has advanced much more slowly, partly because this work is being done by poorly paid minority and female workers and by workers in third world nations.[4]

D. New Technology and Workplace Organization

A common theme that emerges in the literature on technology and work is that the organization of the workplace is being fundamentally altered by the introduction of advanced technologies. One version of this theme argues that the new technologies are creating a personalized, even family-like management style. A number of researchers argue that alienation is reduced under these circumstances. For example, Zisman (1978) argues that workers in automated environments are less alienated than workers in earlier mechanized environments. He attributes this to job enlargement and to less need for functional specialization. Shepard (1971) agrees, arguing that "automated technology reduces the level of alienation among office employees as well as factory workers."

An important element in the thesis that technological change leads to improved working conditions is the argument that advanced technology disperses information and authority. This thesis has gained popular recognition in such forms as Naisbitt's (1984) slogan that "computers destroy hierarchy" and in Cleveland's (1985) thesis concerning the "twilight of hierarchy." This thesis, ultimately based on technological determinism, is further supported by current management schemes that attempt to increase productivity through the involvement of "*all* employees" (Peters and Waterman, 1982).

In direct contrast to those who believe that advanced technology erodes organizational inequalities, other researchers have observed a connection between technology and the centralization of authority. Mowshowitz (1976) sounds a common theme in this tradition when he writes that the natural tendency of automation is to centralize the functions of control and decision making and to concentrate these functions in the upper levels of management. Organizational analysts have noted a persistent connection between mechanization, technology, and administrative intensity (Freeman, 1973) and between mechanization, technology, and organizational centralization (Blau, Falbe, McKinley, and Tracy, 1976).

A variety of other organizational changes besides increasing hierarchy also suggest the possibility of deteriorating working conditions under high-technology systems. One commonly cited problem is the stress caused by working on accelerated project schedules. Perhaps more important is the problem of incompetent management in high-technology industries (Juravich, 1985). This problem arises for two reasons. First, even when managers are promoted from within the professional staff, rapid product changes typical of high-tech industries quickly make their knowledge obsolete. Without continu-

---

[4]For further analysis of segmentation along race and gender lines in high-tech settings, see Applebaum (1983), Kraft (1977, 1984), and Rogers and Larsen (1984).

ing hands-on involvement in design and production, even engineering managers rapidly begin to lose touch with the technology, with its problems, possibilities, and limitations. Second, learned managerial orientations toward short-run profit considerations frequently come into conflict with maximizing the technical efficiency of the production process. This may occur through overreliance on cost-cutting techniques or through demands for getting the product out on too tight a schedule (Burawoy, 1979). These problems appear exaggerated in high-tech industries because of the highly competitive nature of these industries. Whatever its cause, working under chronically incompetent management is devastating to worker morale and long-run productivity.

E. New Technology and Job Satisfaction

In light of the mixed reviews high technology receives for its effects on skill levels and on organizational structure, evidence for a variety of divergent effects of high technology on job satisfaction can also be expected. Basing their analysis on large-sample survey data, Form and McMillen (1983) find that both men and women experience technological change favorably in terms of self-reported job satisfaction. Also using large-sample survey data, Hodson (1984) finds that worker satisfaction rises with the increasing use of expensive capital equipment. Similarly, Riche (1982) observes that isolation and constant monitoring can create new stresses but that the new technologies are eliminating much tedious and dangerous work. Reviewing the literature on job satisfaction and computer technology as a whole, Danziger (1985) argues that workers tend to experience technological change as mildly benign.

In contrast, other observers see advanced technology as having less favorable consequences for job quality. For example, examining the work of machinists, Shaiken (1984) argues that new numeric-control systems create heightened alienation and stress. Specifically, he sees increased alienation stemming from workers' loss of input into the design of the production process. He traces additional stress to the experience of growing isolation at the workplace, as proportionately more machines and fewer workers are involved in production.[5] Shaiken is not completely negative in his evaluation of numeric control, however, noting that it also means less noise, more accuracy, and greater cleanliness. In particular, Shaiken notes that numeric control and computer-assisted numeric control in the machine tool industry have created a situation in which workers are less frequently confronted with chronically "cranky" machines that are difficult or impossible to operate within prescribed standards.

Because so much high-technology work takes place within very large companies, there may be additional negative effects on workers' job satisfaction that arise from the size of these monolithic companies and from their

[5]On the basis of his overview of computer-assisted production systems, Danziger (1985) arrives at a similar conclusion about the growing isolation of workers in high-tech settings.

highly bureaucratic procedures. For example, Hodson and Sullivan (1985) find a strong negative relationship between job commitment and corporate "sphere of influence," with workers being much less committed in large, nationally recognized corporations than in smaller, locally based companies.

F. New Technology and Worker Health and Safety

The major health and safety issue that confronts production workers in high-tech settings is contamination from industrial chemicals. A 1980 survey by the California Department of Industrial Relations found an occupational illness rate of 1.3 per 100 electronics industry workers compared with a rate of 0.4 per 100 general manufacturing workers (Ladou, 1984). Electronics workers also suffer from a systemic poisoning rate *twice* that of other manufacturing workers. Electronics workers are routinely exposed to highly toxic and carcinogenic arsenic and arsine gas. In addition to these hazards, production workers in electronics are exposed to hundreds of other chemicals, some 5,000 of which are used by the industry as a whole. Many of the problems associated with exposure to hazardous chemicals take years to develop, but more immediate ailments such as skin irritations and blisters have been well documented. There is also evidence that some workers develop severe eyestrain from wiring tiny electronic chips under microscopes and from the repetitive nature of other very detailed work in this industry. Production workers also face a serious risk of electrical shock. At a recent Semiconductor Safety Association meeting, five deaths were reported from this source alone.

Despite the potential severity of health and safety concerns in the electronics industry, Eisenscher (1984), in his digest on the Silicon Valley, reports that semiconductor companies spend less than 1% of their revenues on health and safety programs, compared with 2.5 to 3% spent by firms in other industries. This low level of spending may well contribute to the underrecognized, and very likely underreported, character of safety and health problems in the electronics industry.

G. What Have We Learned to Date?

An important theme in the debate between deskilling and skill upgrading concerns the role of formal education. The bulk of the evidence indicates that requirements for formal education are increasing but that, simultaneously, this education is becoming less general and more specific in nature. We do not believe that this seeming contradiction results solely from the increasing use of educational requirements as a screening mechanism, resulting in "credential inflation." Rather, we believe that the resolution of this seeming contradiction rests on taking seriously the idea that advanced education can be both formal *and* narrow at the same time. Indeed, this tension is at the root of much of the current debate in colleges and universities between a broad "liberal arts" education and more narrowly defined "professional" training. The reality of this and other developments should warn us that no simple measure of "skill" is adequate for understanding the consequences of high technology for job requirements (see also Spenner, 1983).

With respect to the consequences of advanced technology for occupational structure, many divergent conclusions have been advanced. However, most studies favor the notion that a more divergent or "dual" occupational structure emerges following the introduction of new technologies. In fields such as computer and scientific instrument manufacturing, large numbers of lower-level production workers are required along with smaller numbers of skilled technicians and highly trained engineers.

The findings on the consequences of advanced technologies for working conditions are also controversial. But there appears to be substantial agreement that, particularly at the lower levels, advanced technologies are producing new sources of alienation and stress for workers. Increasingly, whether the context is industrial manufacturing or the automated office, control and discretion are being removed from workers and built into automated equipment or into more comprehensive computer-assisted management information systems. Under these conditions, it becomes apparent that the types of participative management schemes currently in vogue are in essence stopgap measures. Selected elements of participation, carefully monitored by management, are being given back to the workers, after new management-selected technologies have destroyed more traditional forms of participation. The resulting loss of control over the production process denies workers an essential ingredient for a satisfying job.

Finally, it is apparent that there are a host of underrecognized safety and health problems confronting workers in the wake of new technologies. The hundreds of dangerous chemicals, solvents, and resins that workers are exposed to in the production of electronic components belies the claim made by some analysts that new high-technology forms of production are cleaner and safer than previous industrial systems.

III. RESEARCH METHODS

Employers included in our survey were selected from the Chamber of Commerce's list of high-tech companies operating in the southwestern city being studied. Twenty-two companies were selected, representing electronics, telecommunications, aerospace, and biotech industries. The sample was stratified by company size, with an equal number of large, nationally recognized companies and small, locally based companies being selected. In addition, the two largest unions operating in the high-tech field in the city were also contacted.

Access was arranged to interview workers through both of the unions. Additional workers, as well as engineers, supervisors, and managers who were employed in 12 of the 22 companies contacted, were also interviewed. Access was arranged from the top down in seven companies and through alternative contacts in five others. Three companies refused access. Access to seven others was still pending when the survey stage of the project was completed. Access and refusal did not follow any clear pattern related to either the industry or the size of the company. However, the rationale offered for refusals did. Large companies declining to participate had explicit policies against participating in outside-sponsored surveys. Small companies declining to participate said that they did not have the free time or available personnel to participate.

A total of 48 respondents were interviewed in the spring and summer of 1985. These respondents included 19 managers, personnel directors, and supervisors who were interviewed for an average of 75 minutes each, 23 workers who were interviewed for an average of 28 minutes each, and 6 degreed engineers who were interviewed for an average of 90 minutes each. In addition, the author was taken on extended tours at most of the facilities where interviewing took place and, in one case, was given access to supplemental company records. In general, we interviewed managers as well as workers at each company, as well as engineers at some companies. At one company we were able to interview only engineers, at two companies we were able to interview only managers, and at one company we were able to interview only workers (the contact for this latter company had been secured through its union).

During the course of the interviews it was discovered that many of the smaller companies contacted were in fact owned by larger, nationally recognized corporations. Thus, of the 14 companies in our sample (12 accessed directly plus the 2 accessed through their unions), 10 were listed in Moody's *Industrial Manual* (1984). Additional data were secured from this source for these 10 companies. These companies were mostly directly owned branch plants, but 2 were subsidiary companies and 1 was a corporate headquarters. Local employment for these companies ranged from 450 to 7,000, with an average employment of 2,200. *Company-wide* employment ranged from 8,300 to 370,000, with an average employment of 42,000. Annual company-wide sales ranged from $424 million to $40 billion. By way of contrast, the 4 locally based companies in which we interviewed had employment sizes of approximately 12, 70, 80, and 150.

Thus, it can be seen that the high-tech companies in our study are not primarily new entrepreneurial enterprises. Rather, they were parts of large, diversified national and international conglomerate empires. The ten companies in our sample that were listed in Moody's had an average of 13 domestic and 29 international subsidiaries each. Their profit on net worth for 1984 (the last completed calendar year) ranged from 4.9 to 31.8% (the latter figure being for a major defense contractor) and averaged 17.1%. Profit per worker averaged $10,600. Sales per worker and assets per worker both averaged just under $100,000. In sum, the majority of the companies in which we interviewed were parts of huge multinational corporations. The contrast in size between the truly locally owned companies and these industrial giants is quite dramatic, and we will see that this contrast has a major influence on working conditions.

IV. FINDINGS: THE NATURE OF WORK IN HIGH-TECH SETTINGS

A. The Skill Content of Jobs

Managers and supervisors reported that the workers in their sections did a variety of tasks, with assembly work being the most frequently mentioned category. Workers' reports were in congruence but lent further specification to the meaning of "assembly work" in high-tech settings: Equal numbers of workers reported being engaged in assembly production work, troubleshooting components while in the assembly stage, bringing complex assembled devices up to running order before shipping, and repair of assembled components that had been damaged or improperly assembled. This diverse set of activities suggests that "assembly work" in high-tech settings may be a more varied and highly skilled set of job tasks than the term generally implies.

The engineers interviewed were split evenly between software engineering and hardware engineering. They worked in a wide range of engineering specialties, including chemical, mechanical, and electrical engineering. Engineers reported spending an average of 44% of their time working with information, 38% working with people, and 18% working with things. Their detailed descriptions of their activities suggest that they were almost exclusively engaged in activities directly relating to development and production. Accordingly, although half reported that they supervised other workers occasionally, none reported having input into hiring, firing, or the setting of pay.

When engineers were asked if their work in high tech was different or unique from work in other settings, the majority said that it was not. When asked further about any differences between work in high-tech settings and other settings, many engineers reasserted the lack of difference, but others responded by noting the pervasiveness of the "project orientation" and the powerful roles of customers and of the government as customer and rule-maker. Managers were generally also quite firm in their view of an overall lack of difference between work in high-tech and other settings, but some noted the importance of rule orientations, the complex nature of the production process, and the importance of quality.

Workers were asked to rate their jobs on a variety of dimensions. They characterized their jobs as being very high on the dimensions of skill, learning new things, and repetition, suggesting an unusual combination of characteristics that is perhaps distinctive of assembly work in high-tech settings. They characterized their jobs as being somewhat high on the dimensions of hard work and having to work very fast. They almost never characterized their jobs as requiring hard physical labor. More mixed responses were recorded on the dimensions of freedom, decision making, creativity, variety, and manual dexterity. When managers were asked to what extent work in their sections required greater precision, reliability, and responsibility than work outside high-tech settings, a majority agreed that this was true, with the strongest confirmation recorded for responsibility rather than for precision or reliability. But, again, these responses were not overwhelmingly strong or unanimous.

Engineers characterized their jobs as requiring extremely high degrees of responsibility and autonomy and spoke frequently of the high demands on their intelligence and creativity. Precision and reliability were seen as secondary to taking responsibility for maximizing one's own substantive contribution.

Both the workers and the engineers interviewed were, in general, quite well educated. A slight majority of workers had some post-high school education and only two had not finished high school. Two workers also had college degrees, but neither was working in a field even vaguely related to his or her college training. The most common source of post-high school training for workers was community college or trade school, with many having completed two-year programs. However, large numbers also reported extensive formal training in areas directly relating to their current employment either in the military or in company training programs. A slight majority of workers also had at least one vocational training course while in high school. However, these were not primarily in areas directly related to their current work. The largest number had taken some sort of shop class, with electronics being the second most likely vocational class, and clerical training ranking third.[6] Two-thirds of the engineers reported having a four-year degree in an engineering or computer science field, while the remaining third reported either master's or doctoral level training in engineering.

First-line supervisors, many of whom had risen through the ranks, frequently had lower levels of formal education than the workers they supervised. The majority held only a high school degree, with equal numbers not completing high school and having some formal post-high school training. This difference suggests a rapid shift in the sources of training for workers in high-tech settings. The earliest workers gained their training almost exclusively on the job, while a majority of contemporary workers receive fairly extensive formal training.

When workers were asked what level of formal training was required to do their jobs properly, 71% said that a high school degree or less was all that was necessary. This suggests that the rather extensive post-high school training of these workers was experienced by many as unnecessary for their current jobs. However, when workers were asked how long it would take someone with their same general level of training to learn to do their job properly, the modal response was *one to two years.* In sum, workers see a need for extensive on-the-job training in order to do their work properly. The specific skills workers reported acquiring on the job mainly concerned the correct operation of complex machinery and instrumentation devices. Significant numbers of workers also reported having to learn basic chemistry, engineer-

[6]For the *labor force as a whole,* the largest number of technicians, craftsmen, and operators receive their training on the job (59%). The next largest group (31%) receive their training through a formal school. In addition, company schools provide training for 22%, and 6% receive training in the military (Bureau of Labor Statistics, 1985).

ing, electronics, and drafting skills on the job. Only one worker reported that she did not have to acquire any new skills to perform her job properly.

Managers and supervisors also strongly confirmed the importance of on-the-job training. When asked if the skills required in their sections were primarily learned on the job or through formal programs, 63% said on-the-job training was the primary source of skill acquisition. However, in spite of managers' agreement that on-the-job training was the most significant source of training for workers, they estimated the required training time as *one to six weeks*, an estimate that is several orders of magnitude lower than workers' estimates. This is probably due to differences between managers and workers in the meanings given to *skill* and *competence*. Workers tend to see their training on several different but related tasks as "required" for the competent performance of their current job. Managers tend to view competence only in terms of "getting the work out" on the current job.

The agreed-upon importance of on-the-job training results in managers' looking primarily at *attitude* rather than *formal training* when hiring new workers. Criteria relating to "desire" and "fitting in" outnumbered criteria relating to skill by five to one. The specific characteristics identified as desirable were persistence, initiative, and good health. The characteristics identified as negative were a lackadaisical attitude and a poor work history. Several managers even noted that they preferred workers with no prior training at related jobs because they felt that such training only taught "bad work practices." The major exception to this attitude concerned soldering skills, where formal training, especially military electronics training, was highly desired.

Engineers also reported training requirements for their jobs that were somewhat less than they themselves possessed. None thought their jobs required graduate work in engineering, although several did note a need for additional skills, such as the ability to communicate. Engineers also reported that on-the-job training was more important than formal training for their jobs. The length of time needed to gain job competence was generally described as "one project cycle," with elapsed time ranging from six to nine months.

Overall, workers seemed very proud of the new skills learned on their high-tech jobs. This pride rested both on a sense of craftsmanship and on the possession of unique skills that could not be learned elsewhere. One worker described an older technique for locating a bad circuit by taking the circuits out individually and smelling each one. He then described with pride his ability to locate and replace bad circuits utilizing a sophisticated electronic testing device and how this allowed him to do his work much more quickly and reliably.

When asked if they had any skills from previous jobs that they would like to be using on their current jobs but could not use, workers reported a scattering of machinists' skills, equipment-related skills, and interpersonal skills. But, in general, the satisfaction derived from their new skills seemed to outweigh any sense of loss over not being able to utilize previous skills. Engineers also described with enthusiasm and pride the new skills developed on their jobs. Developing original techniques and processes was seen as central to their work and provided a genuine sense of satisfaction and pride.

In summary, on-the-job training appears to provide the major source of skill acquisition for workers in high-tech settings. Many of the workers interviewed had extensive formal education, but their on-the-job experiences were seen by both themselves and their supervisors as much more important. As the literature on training for high-tech jobs suggests, one reason for this may be that formal training programs prepare workers in a set of skills that are different from the ones they are called upon to use on the job. The discrepancy between the skills taught in formal educational settings and those actually needed on the job may be particularly acute in high-tech settings because of rapid changes in production technologies. These conclusions support Spenner's (1983:35) thesis that skill changes over time are uneven and offsetting. The specific skills needed in high-tech settings are highly volatile. New skills come into being with new production technologies and diminish in importance just as rapidly. Rather than describing this process as either one of skill upgrading or deskilling, it seems more appropriate to describe it as one of chronic *"skill disruption."*

B. Labor Market Segmentation

Generally one expects wages in an industry to be grouped around some middle level, with smaller numbers of people receiving especially high or especially low wages. In contrast to this expectation, the high-tech workers we surveyed reported a relatively flat distribution of wages, with an equal number making less than $15,000 per year, between $15,000 and $25,000 per year, and greater than $25,000 per year. What this distribution suggests is a flattening of the middle-level positions, which make reasonable (though hardly "middle-class") earnings, and an expansion of more poorly and more highly paid positions. In other words, there was evidence that high-tech industries are increasing the inequality of earnings.[7]

This inequality is also evidenced by the fact that well over half the workers reported family savings of less than a month's income, making these workers extremely vulnerable to the most damaging effects of layoffs and unemployment. Almost 15% of the workers interviewed reported a period of unemployment within the past 12 months. This occurred even within a geographic area with a tight labor market where the unemployment rate averaged 3 to 5% during the previous year. About one-third of the workers also reported that they currently held other jobs for pay in addition to their main job.

---

[7]This relatively flat distribution could be a result of idiosyncratic characteristics of our sample. However, this seems unlikely in that managers tended to prefer that we interview more senior, better-paid, and presumably more loyal employees. A more representative sample of workers might have produced an even larger number of low earners, suggesting a more bottom-heavy earnings distribution.

1. Mobility Opportunities

Workers reported, on average, one to two job moves with their current employers. However, the overwhelming majority of these were *lateral moves* rather than *promotions*. Managers also reported a great deal of lateral mobility among workers, both between companies in pursuit of "10 to 15 cent per hour wage differentials" and "just for the change" and within their own companies from one job to the next. A few managers noted that upward mobility was possible for workers into the position of lead worker, supervisor, or inspector, but most managers said that there was "little or no" upward mobility for workers. A pervasive image emerges from these reports of very constrained intrafirm mobility opportunities for workers in high-tech settings.

This reality was also evidenced by managers' denials of the existence of formal job structures for workers that delineated specific upward mobility routes. Mobility was viewed as much more loosely structured than this, leaving ample room for expectations of mobility without formal structures and commitments in this regard. These reports contrast sharply with the image of internal labor markets prevalent in the literature on complex organizations: Loosely structured internal labor markets are more frequently associated with small, marginal operations than with huge multinational corporations that supposedly rely on complex, bureaucratically structured internal labor markets.

The absence of within-firm mobility opportunities violates the "implicit contract" that economists have argued stabilizes employment relations in modern complex production systems (England and Farkas, 1986:Chap. 6). In order to maximize efficiency, employers and employees develop "implicit contracts" that limit shirking, quitting, and other counterproductive activities in exchange for benefits forthcoming at some time in the future (such as promotions). Without trust on both sides such implicit contracts cannot exist, and work relations are reduced to "spot contracts" in which a given amount of labor time is exchanged for a given wage. Our observations in the high-tech enterprises we visited suggest that such implicit contracts are largely absent in these firms.

The opportunity structure for high-tech engineers is also limited, though for different reasons. Because of their highly specialized skills, engineers have relatively few options for mobility. Outside of the position of "project engineer," there are few opportunities for either lateral or vertical mobility for engineers. Half the engineers interviewed reported *no* previous job with their current employer besides the one they held now. And engineers spoke with some discontent about the seemingly endless cycle of projects and how this rapidly loses interest after the first half dozen projects are completed. Once again, the absence of formal job ladders was glaringly apparent.

Because of this lack of structured internal labor markets, managers were forced to spend a great deal of time hiring and training new workers. Training demands were further increased by the importance of on-the-job training noted above. This situation seemed to exist for every level of personnel and caused managers to express repeated concern over recruitment and training.

Recruitment, training, and opportunity problems were also reflected in tenure figures and turnover rates. Managers reported the average tenure of workers as two to three years, with a greater number reporting average tenure below rather than above this figure. Less than 15% of the work force had spent five years or more with the company, and the average annual turnover rate was 27%. Workers also reported that they did not expect to remain at their current jobs. When asked "what they expected to be doing five years from now," the largest number of workers replied that they would be working in some other job, with the remainder split between the "same job" and moving up within their current company. This high level of lateral mobility obviously creates a situation in which it is more difficult for the existing work force at a company to become an important carrier of production skills.

Engineers reported even less tenure than workers, with an average employment length of *one and a half years* with their current employer! A majority also reported either that this was their first job or that their last job was in some way connected with their college training, either as a formal apprenticeship or as work to support themselves while in college. It appears that recent employment expansion in the high-tech field has created job opportunities for a large number of engineers with little or no experience.

In sharp contrast, the average length of tenure for first-line supervisors was 10.8 years, highlighting the upward mobility that supervisors have experienced within their organizations in the past. This finding suggests that high-tech organizations have been successful in the past in retaining at least some workers. However, these organizations are currently experiencing a crisis in turnover and tenure rates among production workers.

Turnover problems were experienced much more keenly in large organizations than in small ones. The smaller high-tech firms reported fewer problems with employee retention in spite of more limited internal labor markets due to their smaller size. This small size appears to contribute to employee retention because the lower division of labor in these firms results in employees' experiencing changes and advances in production techniques as "upward mobility" in their job content rather than just as "lateral moves" within a stagnant internal labor market. As a result, workers in small companies expressed much greater commitment to their organizations than did workers in large corporations.

2. Social Divisions

Managers reported that their work forces contained about 40% minority workers and about 44% female workers, and that the average worker was 30 years old. The representation of minority workers in these firms is similar to the representation of minority workers in other production jobs in the local labor market. The representation of women in these firms is about double that in other production jobs in the local labor market. Managers also noted that many of the female workers were single parents. A significant minority of companies employed handicapped workers, and several had explicit policies promoting this.

The social characteristics of engineers are startlingly different from those of production workers. All of the engineers we interviewed were Anglo. The representation of women among engineers, at 15 to 20%, was much lower than among production workers, where it ranged from 40 to 45%. And, perhaps surprisingly because of the four to five years of college education required to become an engineer, the median age of the engineers, at 27, was substantially lower than that of production workers. In terms of self-description, engineers typified themselves as "hardworking, competitive, homogeneous 'nerds' and 'yuppies.'"

The existence of a substantial amount of race and sex discrimination was hinted at during our conversations with workers, engineers, and managers. About 50% of the Hispanics we interviewed complained about racial discrimination, both in promotions and in terms of subtle interpersonal harassment. Similarly, nearly 50% of the women complained about sexual discrimination. The women complained almost exclusively about blocked promotion opportunities, rather than about interpersonal harassment, and they complained about it much less stoically than did the Hispanics.[8] Many of the women were furious about blocked opportunities and suppressed their anger only with visible effort.

3. Ancillary Workers

In recent years, large corporations have increasingly utilized various sorts of ancillary workers as an alternative to expanding their core work force. We were interested in investigating the nature and consequences of this phenomenon in high-tech settings as an additional potential basis of segmentation. In particular, we sought information about several types of ancillary workers: part-time workers, temporary workers, subcontracting, and offshore production.

On the basis of our interviews with workers, engineers, and managers, we found little indication that part-time workers were used extensively. Given the importance of a high level of skill in many high-tech jobs, and the importance of on-the-job training in learning these skills, this is perhaps to be expected. Part-time work simply does not appear to be a viable employment option in the high-tech settings we studied.

Temporary workers, however, were used in a wide range of positions. Temporaries were used most frequently as clerical workers and as receptionists, but they were also used for janitorial work and for production work under a variety of situations. Temporaries were used in production work to

---

[8]Women who had faced sexual harassment seemed to accept this as an inevitable part of "work life" and felt that there was little they could do to change this that would not make the situation worse.

help handle emergency situations such as accidents, moves, or regularly scheduled activities requiring additional labor. They were also used to fill in for absent workers as an alternative to hiring additional workers to adjust for predictable absence rates in large companies. Finally, they were used as a captive labor pool from which to select workers for permanent positions after a period of on-the-job evaluation. We found only one incident in which temporary workers were used to displace permanent employees on a regular basis. At one company, as many as half of the production workers on some assembly lines were temporary workers. These workers were hired for three-month stints on a staggered basis so that the disruption involved in their turnover could be lessened.

Perhaps more significant as a potential basis of segmentation, and certainly more pervasive, is the use of subcontracting. Subcontracting is used for a seemingly endless variety of purposes. Traditional uses include cafeteria work and plant security. More innovative uses include drafting, publishing, marketing, shipping, design, component testing, assembly, meeting production deadlines that exceed current company capacity, and any special task for which the company does not have in-house facilities. One engineer, commenting about his own company (a nationally recognized giant in electronic instruments), said, "In a few years, R&D may be ended completely and we'll just be evaluating vendors' products and putting our name on them."

Offshore facilities also appeared to be extensively utilized by the high-tech companies we studied. Unfortunately, this was one of the most sensitive topics we broached, and respondents were often quite guarded in their comments. The typical response was that they "assumed such facilities were used," but they denied any knowledge of which components were manufactured offshore or what proportion of the company's activity this involved. Not only were respondents guarded in their responses, but it seemed as if there was a widespread and concerted effort *not* to know too much about this topic.

In summary, a variety of dimensions of segmentation were evidenced in the high-tech workplaces we studied, including economic segmentation, limited mobility opportunities, race and gender segmentation, and extensive use of ancillary workers and production facilities. The combined influence of these various dimensions of segmentation exerts a strong downward pressure on wages and conditions for middle-income, blue-collar workers. The source of this pressure does not seem to lie in a decline in workers' skills in high-tech settings. Rather, the source of this pressure appears to lie primarily in organizational and market factors that are used expressly to engineer such downward pressure on wages. These factors include the availability of cheap female, minority, and third world labor and the lack of any organizational or trade union ability on the part of workers to defend themselves against these pressures.

The organization of work for high-tech engineers is similar to what has come to be thought of as the Japanese model, based on teamwork and diffuse commitments (Ouchi, 1981). Williamson (1981) labels such task organizations "relational teams" and argues that they tend to emerge in situations where the skills needed are specific to the task at hand but there is no easy way to measure individual contributions to productivity. Such a characterization fits well with the nature of the work tasks and problems described by the engineers we interviewed. The task organization for production workers, on the other hand, was organized as what Williamson (1981) would describe as an "internal spot market" in which a given quantity of labor is exchanged for a given wage. Such task organizations tend to emerge where the skills needed are nonspecific and individual contributions to productivity are relatively easy to measure. Such labor markets generate relatively weak attachments between workers and employers, a situation that very accurately characterizes the relations we observed between high-tech workers and employers. However, in addition to limiting their attachment and commitment to their employers in accord with their treatment, workers also attempted to *redefine* the nature of their tasks in order to argue for more favorable treatment. Workers felt that their skills were highly specific in nature and took a long time to acquire. On the basis of these *job specific skills*, they felt entitled to better treatment, greater opportunities for promotion, and in general greater attachment and concern on the part of their employers.

C. High-Tech Effects on Organizational Structure and Management Styles

Managers were asked about the most important strategies used in their companies to address ongoing problems. Responses to this question identified marketing and quality control as key strategies, with cost control also being mentioned as an important consideration. Daily production management was not seen as a high priority. This ranking of company strategies is somewhat incongruent when seen in light of the pressing problems of labor force recruitment, training, and retention noted above. Little consideration was given to fostering teamwork and cooperation. Work group sizes ranged from 15 to 300 and were in general quite large.

Over 90% of the managers interviewed typified their operations as being strongly organized around stated rules and procedures. Interestingly, few workers thought of their jobs in this way. Rather, they tended to see their jobs as organized by the direct supervision of their immediate boss. Engineers likewise saw only a small role for explicitly stated procedures in their work. The work of engineers was basically to create new procedures and techniques, and explicitly stated procedures were of little use in this effort.

1. Quality Control

When asked about the importance of quality control in their operations, every manager and supervisor with whom we spoke stressed this as a key focus of concern. The chief method of quality control for production work was review by external quality control departments. Peer review, establishing "feelings of ownership," incentives, training films, and feedback were also mentioned as quality control techniques, but only about half as frequently as external quality control departments. Managers frequently stated that they were moving toward "building quality in" rather than "checking it after the fact." But there appears to be a major discrepancy between this proposed direction of change and the actual practices in effect.

Engineers, on the other hand, said quality control was pursued in their departments first and foremost by peer review, second by external quality control departments, and third by customer interaction. Both managers and engineers offered frequent examples of the failure of external quality control departments. They even suggested that such departments sometimes did more damage than good because they generated interdepartmental conflict and allowed workers, and even engineers, to "externalize" their quality control problems rather than dealing with them directly.

2. Productivity

Productivity was generally measured with quite conventional techniques and did not seem to be a major focus of concern. The most frequent technique for measuring productivity noted by managers was time-and-motion studies. These were done by industrial engineers who then devised time estimates for projects. The next most frequent technique, a rather indirect one, was to evaluate the bottom line of sales and revenues. Other techniques mentioned were cost containment, annual review by immediate supervisors or project leaders, and machine pacing. In general, many more individual- than group-based measures were utilized, and the bulwark of these was the time estimate developed by the industrial engineer.

This treatment of productivity suggests that labor was seen as an interchangeable component of production rather than as a uniquely human entity in need of being motivated to do quality work. This vision of work and workers accords well with the older neoclassical economic view of productivity but relatively poorly with more recent views. A widely recognized example of these more modern views is provided by the Japanese system. Wage systems in the industrial core of the Japanese economy encourage low worker turnover and high labor productivity. "In Japan if the wage of the average twenty to twenty-four-year-old is set at 100, those from thirty to thirty-four will make 153, and those forty to forty-four years old 194. Wages essentially double over the first twenty years of seniority. In such a system to move is to face a large cut in income" (Thurow, 1983:177). Thurow (1983:171) further estimates that a 50% reduction in turnover raises productivity by almost 30% over five years. If American high-tech firms are to compete with Japanese firms in world markets, they may be forced to join workers in embracing such an "efficiency wage" theory of productivity.

As with the discussions above of internal labor markets and quality control, there again appears to be a considerable gap between verbalized adherence to currently popular management ideologies and actual practices. In the case of productivity, this gap is measured by the degree of reliance on traditional measures of individual output in situations where verbalized ideologies proclaim a focus on group productivity.

3. Commitment

The issue of worker commitment, unlike that of measuring productivity, did appear to be a principal focus of concern for managers. Pride and dedication, on the one hand, and turnover and absenteeism, on the other, were identified as central problems by the majority of the managers and supervisors we interviewed. The principal techniques for instilling commitment were raises and promotions, direct praise, good supervisory relations, and "parties" or other ancillary morale-building tactics. Various forms of participative management were also sometimes mentioned as a technique for instilling pride and creating a "feeling of ownership" in the work.

Engineers mentioned two major strategies used to build commitment. The most important of these was the granting of autonomy to pursue their work as they thought best. The second was monetary incentives, including "embarrassingly high" salaries and stock options. Of these two strategies, the first was described with more enthusiasm and considerably less cynicism. The majority of engineers we interviewed seemed genuinely committed to their work. The major motivation they voiced for this was that their high degree of autonomy enabled them to experience the projects to which they were assigned as "their own work."

What is most striking about the strategies used to develop worker commitment is that, even on this issue, which managers identify as highly significant to their organizations, there is a large gap between actual practices and verbalized ideologies. In spite of being verbally committed to worker participation, the main strategies of commitment that were utilized with production workers were monetary and career incentives and good supervisory relations. These strategies are important and time-honored, but they may not be sufficient in light of the great need in high-tech settings for commitment and responsibility.

4. Involvement in Decision Making

When managers were asked who makes the key decisions concerning production, a variety of responses were evoked, including project engineers, division heads, plant managers, industrial engineers, inspectors, and research and development specialists. What was conspicuously absent was any mention of worker involvement in decision making.

Managers were also directly asked what areas of autonomy and discretion were allowed workers in their sections. Their responses indicated that workers had important areas of autonomy in getting equipment to work properly and in troubleshooting to determine what in a component being assembled was not working properly. When asked further about informal work practices among workers, managers acknowledged that many informal work practices represent positive contributions to getting the work out on time and to getting it done properly. In particular, they noted that workers help each other solve difficult assembly problems and that more experienced workers often show newer recruits how to work more efficiently. They also said that workers offer many useful suggestions to supervisors about production techniques that are later incorporated into standard operating procedures.

The above discussion suggests that workers have an important informal role in determining work practices in high-tech settings. However, that informal role does not readily become institutionalized into a recognized, formal form of participation. The principal techniques for integrating workers into production decisions that were reported by managers were feedback, creating a "feeling of ownership," training in quality control, and periodic parties and festivities. None of these define a clear role for workers as full partners in production.

Engineers, on the other hand, both according to their own reports and according to the reports of supervisors, have a high degree of both formal and informal participation in production decisions. When asked who makes important decisions about production in their areas, engineers frequently stumbled, and, although they would sometimes name particular positions such as project engineer, more frequently their answer contained the idea that "a lot of people" participate in decision making. This participation includes both a ready acceptance of individual creative contributions to projects and frequent group meetings. Every engineer we interviewed spoke favorably of periodic project meetings in which ongoing problems are discussed and solutions are brainstormed. This high level of interaction and participation represents a central component in engineers' sense of commitment to their work.

In sum, for engineers, the work group represents a very real and vital system for facilitating involvement, participation, and commitment. For workers, formal and informal means of participation are much more limited and many of the forms of participation are of a superficial character.

Forms of participation emergent from the production technology, such as worker self-help and instruction, are not actively encouraged by management but are rather tolerated as essential though vaguely undesirable. Informal forms of participation existing in small companies also appear to be obliterated in larger companies by the increasing spatial isolation of workers from each other, by sophisticated "management information systems," and by extensive management hierarchies that develop elaborate planning strategies. Workers in large companies are asked to "participate" in superficial and facile ways that are a thin substitute for more genuine forms of participation, such as those existing for engineers and, to a certain extent, even for workers in smaller companies. Thus, such participation schemes can be seen as giving back to workers, in watered-down and partial form, aspects of participation in production that technology and organizational structure have recently taken away from them, but only those aspects that have been selected by management as being compatible with their goals. An alternative interpretation would be that management has not yet had time to implement genuine participation schemes. However, given that we observed little effort to retain and legitimate worker involvement, this more generous interpretation must be viewed with some skepticism.

The lack of participation for production workers coupled with strong forms of participation for engineers suggests the "contingency" theory of management popular during the 1970s (Morse and Lorsch, 1970). This theory argues that management styles should *vary* according to the characteristics of the group being supervised. Under this theory, professional workers are seen as desiring and needing a high degree of autonomy and involvement, and production workers are seen as preferring to not get involved in the decision-making process. While current management theories proclaim the importance of involvement for *all* employees, the actual programs we observed in place were much more reminiscent of the earlier contingency theory of management in which different styles are used with different groups of workers.

5. Managerial Incompetence

One of the most interesting findings of our study emerged when we asked workers an open-ended question about what they liked least about their jobs. Their overwhelming response was bad management. They spoke of incompetent management as well as arbitrary and abusive managerial styles. When workers complained about management incompetence they offered two different explanations for this problem. One explanation stressed lack of management understanding of the intricacies of high-tech production. Workers felt that continuing direct, hands-on involvement was required to understand the nature of production problems, solutions to these problems, time allotments needed to do quality work, and so on. A second line of explanation focused on the promotion of individuals into supervisory positions on the basis of favoritism rather than competence. Again and again, this point was stressed. One worker commented that it had gotten so bad that good workers were being driven out because they could not stand to work under such incompetent supervisors.[9]

In addition to complaining about management incompetence, workers also complained about arbitrary and abusive management styles. Here again, favoritism was a pervasive theme, not only in terms of promotion decisions but also in terms of the supervision of day-to-day operations. Workers also complained about strict and rigid enforcement of rules, excessive pressure, excessive red tape that bogged down production, absence of two-way communication with management, and excessive delays due to unplanned and

[9]This sort of problem has also been reported at IBM, a company known for its paternalistic relations with workers. "There are two sides to IBM's paternalism, . . . On the one hand, people say the company will take care of them. But then you also see resentment over favoritism in promotions, raises and hiring" (*In These Times*, 1985:7). See Juravich (1985) for a more extended discussion of managerial incompetence.

uncoordinated retooling and product shifts. Even supervisors complained about unrealistic management time frames for project completion and said that this was one of their most significant problems.

Engineers were also asked what they liked least about their jobs, and, perhaps surprisingly, given their much greater degree of autonomy, they also complained most bitterly about bad management. Engineers stressed the issue of distance from the actual production process as the root cause of managerial incompetence rather than past promotions into managerial positions based on favoritism. Engineers also complained about problems that arose directly from the group organization of their work. We heard many complaints about competition with co-workers and the negative atmosphere generated by office politics.

To some extent these problems result from the speed of technological change. That is, managers and supervisors do not understand the current parameters of the production process they are supervising because it has changed substantially within the last few years, or even within the last few months. They do not have sufficient direct, hands-on experience with the new production technologies to understand their capabilities and problems.

There was also a feeling that management was insufficiently concerned with production issues and overly concerned with rules, bureaucratically measurable outcomes, and marketing. There was resentment that these considerations took priority over production issues. Rather than workers' being actively involved in "participative management" and committed to their work in high-tech settings, we saw very little genuine participative structure and saw instead a pervasive discontent with managers for their frequent incompetence and for their arbitrary and (from the workers' standpoint) counterproductive practices.

This situation was moderated somewhat in the unionized workplaces. Here workers still complained about management incompetence and favoritism, but they did not complain with the same mixture of fear and anger. Although distrustful of management practices, they did not feel as individually vulnerable to these practices. The union grievance structure provided them with protection against the worst abuses, and this dissipated much of their resentment. This contrast between union and nonunion plants suggests that the issue of arbitrary management styles is partially a result of the unbridled nature of management power in high-tech settings where unions are extremely weak. The existence of even a few more union shops could have a decisive impact on limiting such demoralizing and counterproductive management styles in high-tech industries.

In sum, there appears to be an intensive, if fairly quiet, crisis of organizational structure and managerial competence and style in the high-tech settings we studied. The causes of this crisis appear to reside in too-rapid technological change, insufficient genuine participation for workers, and unmediated management power. The consequences of this crisis are a tremendous discrepancy between stated agendas and actual practices in areas ranging from internal labor markets to quality control, to measuring productivity, to participative management. This crisis is all the more significant because it is occurring in core industrial sectors that are highly significant to the overall health of the economy. Although our research design does not allow us to evaluate the existence of similar problems in other industries, the strong discrepancy we observed between stated and actual management practices observed in high-tech settings suggests this as an important area of investigation in coming to terms with the continuing malaise of American industry.

D. Job Satisfaction

As well as asking workers what they *disliked* about their jobs, we also asked them what they *liked* about their jobs. When workers were asked to evaluate their jobs on a scale ranging from 1 to 7, with 7 representing an ideal job, the modal responses were 4 and 5. This level of response is typical of the mildly favorable answers workers in most situations give when they are asked a general question about their level of job satisfaction. Once again, the responses were strongly differentiated by the size of the employing organization, with workers in the smaller companies frequently giving their jobs the very highest ratings and workers in larger companies registering more cautious responses.

When workers were asked what they liked *best* about their jobs, their primary response was autonomy. Thus, autonomy to do one's job as one sees fit was seen as providing a source of pleasure and satisfaction, as well as a source of discontent when it was absent. The second most frequent category of responses was challenging or satisfying work, frequent learning, and variety. Pay and benefits was the third most frequent response. Promotion opportunities were mentioned next most frequently. Only two workers indicated that what they liked best about their jobs was the equipment they used. Thus, organizational and management considerations appear to represent much more salient issues for workers than do the direct consequences of technology itself.

When engineers where asked what they liked *best* about their jobs, they named autonomy and challenge. Engineers also mentioned that they liked to do work requiring thought and intelligence. Engineers also made frequent mention of the pleasures derived from friendships that had originated at the workplace. Repeated mention was made not only of lunching together and going to "happy hour" together after work but also of activities suggesting more substantial friendships. These friendships typically revolved around recreational activities such as boating and golfing. As one might expect, given their involvement in a cohesive group structure at work, engineers appeared interested in developing lingering and diffuse friendships with their colleagues outside of the work setting.

When workers were asked to indicate the specific problems they were having at their workplaces, they often appeared reluctant to discuss this, even in situations where they were being interviewed outside the work setting. Many declined to name specific problems. The largest number of those who responded named a physical problem, such as the workplace's being too hot or too cold, high levels of tension and pressure, noise, restrictive clothing, dangerous equipment, or having to use VDTs with resulting eye- and back strain.

One concern that workers did mention repeatedly was workplace safety. Safety problems seemed to be a source of genuine concern for workers.[10] A majority of the workers we interviewed mentioned at least one area of concern regarding safety and health. The most common hazards mentioned were chemicals and gases, but many workers were also concerned about the danger of electric shock. A wide variety of other concerns were mentioned as well, depending on the nature of the worker's job task. These included equipment hazards, welding and soldering hazards, falling, and back problems from heavy lifting. Managers also mentioned the importance of health issues, noting especially the dangers of acids, cuts, and the inability of non-English-speaking workers to read warning labels and instructions.

When managers were asked what problems workers reported to them, they named two major categories: boredom and too rapid a work pace. Managers complained that workers frequently responded to these problems by withdrawing from work through inattention, tardiness, absenteeism, and quitting. Managers also said that workers frequently complained about being underutilized and having inadequate opportunity to learn new tasks and to move upward. In addition, managers indicated that some workers reported problems of isolation at the workplace and problems of family stress due to shift work and to the extensive demands for overtime associated with production pushes.

Engineers spoke quite freely of their problems at the workplace. The most recurrent themes reported by engineers centered around the strongly competitive and achievement-oriented situations in which they worked. In particular, they complained about the pace of work, about the fact that their life-styles and home lives suffered in relation to work, and about feelings of boredom and underutilization when there were lulls between projects.

When engineers were asked about the ways in which the high-tech setting specifically influenced their satisfactions with work, they noted its damaging effects due to long hours. But they also noted positive consequences. They derived substantial satisfaction and pride from the high-tech focus on quality and also from the strong commitment to customer satisfaction. This latter aspect was especially salient for engineers working on expensive customized instrumentation devices to be used in workplace automation and related applications.

---

[10]One workplace we visited smelled pervasively of ammonia and other, unidentified chemicals, even in the front offices. Fiberglass dust clouded one whole section, and another section had miniature canyons etched in the concrete floor by the drainage of caustic chemicals running toward open drains.

V. CONCLUSIONS: THE COSTS AND BENEFITS OF HIGH-TECH PRODUCTION SYSTEMS

A. Organizational Costs and Benefits

Late in the interview, we asked workers how much of the time they understood what they were supposed to do and how they were supposed to do it. We were somewhat shocked by their answers. The majority said they understood what they were supposed to do only between 50 and 90% of the time. An even stronger majority said that at least 95% of their work was reviewed and inspected by someone else. These responses suggest that not only do managers not understand what is going on with production but, all too frequently, workers do not understand either. As a result, a tremendous amount of time and energy is expended inspecting work already completed. It appears that the high-tech companies we studied are experiencing a major organizational crisis in this regard.

Managers tended to see these problems as personnel problems rather than as organizational problems. Managers indicated that while they had little problem in recruiting qualified personnel for managerial and professional positions, they had substantial problems recruiting skilled trade, clerical, and assembly workers. Skilled craftsmen (e.g., machinists and electricians) were unwilling to stick with a job in a high-tech industry because of the low pay scale. Skilled and experience clerical workers were hard to find because the level of pay did not provide sufficient encouragement to stick with the job any longer than absolutely necessary. Similarly, production workers had little commitment to their work and would frequently leave one line of work for an unrelated job, just for the change of pace.

In the workplaces we visited, there was little indication that wage structures were used as a mechanism to increase efficiency and productivity through encouraging employees to work to their fullest potential. Rather, wages for production workers tended to be set at the lowest possible level sufficient for procuring the desired number of bodies. Similarly, there was little evidence of the development of trust between workers and employers of the sort necessary for the establishment of long-term implicit contracts in which employees give their best efforts in anticipation of future rewards. Because of the absence of such trust, production workers rejected commitment to their organizations and often held back from working at their greatest efficiency.

In response to these concerns, managers identified their key needs as (1) better compensation schemes, (2) better technical background and more experience among the available labor force, and (3) a more cooperative and facilitative group orientation. Unfortunately, given the downward pressures on the wages of middle-income workers, more adequate compensation schemes are unlikely to be forthcoming. And, given the fact that attitudes are considered more important than skills in recruitment decisions, it is unlikely that high-tech companies will be able to recruit, or to keep, skilled and experienced workers. Although the current cohort of first-line supervisors have been with their companies for an average of over a decade, this situation seems unlikely to be replicated with future cohorts, owing to more limited promotion opportunities in the industry as it matures. Instead, lateral mobility between different jobs within and between companies will in all likelihood continue to be the most common form of mobility for high-tech workers.

Engineers reported problems of conflictual interdepartmental relations, inadequate routes of communication with middle and top management, and also a concern with compensation schemes for supporting personnel because of rapid turnover in these positions. In the view of engineers, the primary solution to these problems lies in the reduction of bureaucratic procedures. In many ways, this proposal is similar to the complaint voiced by workers of too close supervision. The goal of both proposals is to remove the obstacles that limit and constrain participation in the production process. The difference between engineers and workers in this regard is that the participation of engineers is limited by too many bureaucratic rules, while the participation of workers is limited by too close and too arbitrary supervision.

In sum, there is substantial evidence that high-tech companies are experiencing quite serious, even if hidden, organizational crises. These crises involve management incompetence of a structural and systemic nature rather than on an individual basis. They involve arbitrary decision making and favoritism. They involve an excess of bureaucratic planning and red tape and too great a focus on marketing and financial issues unrelated to production. And, finally, they involve a personnel strategy that expects skill, commitment, and involvement from workers but does not provide adequate compensation or participation, and that selects workers for their docility rather than their training.

High-tech production systems generate a new set of problems for organizations. But in the majority of the settings we studied, outdated solutions are being applied to these new problems. Problems of retaining qualified labor are addressed by strategies based on positive supervisory relations rather than by strategies based on the creation of internal labor markets offering genuine upward mobility within the company. A labor market situation characterized by increasingly large barriers to upward mobility seems to be emerging. Workers are trapped in the heavily segmented lower tiers of the labor market with relatively limited opportunities for mobility out of their particular niche. Problems of quality control are addressed primarily by external quality control departments in spite of the widely acknowledged failure of such strategies. Productivity continues to be measured largely on an individual basis rather than on a group basis. And the problem of maximizing worker commitment and involvement is addressed either by traditional incentive structures or by limited and superficial participative schemes rather than by the genuine integration of workers into the decision-making process at every level.

Because of our sample design, we were unable to determine the extent of these problems outside high-tech settings. However, given that adherence to new management ideologies seems at least as high, if not higher, in the high-tech sector than in other sectors, we should probably not expect that the situation is much better in other industries, and it could be much worse. In either case, the tensions we have identified between stated and actual agendas certainly warrant serious investigation in current research on organizational structure and productivity.

B. Costs and Benefits for Employees

For workers, one benefit of working in a high-tech setting appears to be the informal workplace atmosphere. This aspect of the high-tech workplace was present at every cite we visited, but two were particularly remarkable in this regard. The first was a small branch plant of a multinational corporation specializing in automated scientific instruments. Everyone wore blue jeans and completely informal clothes, work schedules were readily adapted to meet individual needs, and interactional patterns more closely resembled those of a primary group than a formal organization. The second cite was a circuit board assembly operation. Here acceptable attire included cutoffs for both men and women, muscle shirts for men, and no bras for women. Group solidarity was strongly in evidence among the workers in the various sections at this plant as they helped each other through the various stages of production. The informal atmosphere seemed to be an important facilitating element in this solidarity and group effort.

More significantly, high-tech production systems offer important potential resources for the development of heightened worker power. Many of the jobs in high-tech production settings require high levels of skill. And much of this skill has to be learned on the job, making workers more difficult to replace. In addition, informal shop-floor knowledge and practices play an important role in facilitating production. The significance of these potential sources of power is further increased by the fact that workers operate expensive and complex production equipment and by the fact that quality control is so important in high-tech settings. In light of our observations at the high-tech settings we studied and our interviews with workers, engineers, and managers, it does not appear that workers' skills have been eliminated by "building them into the automated machinery." Unfortunately, workers had not yet devised methods for translating these *potential* sources of power into improved wages and conditions.

The ability of workers to translate these new sources of power into better working conditions is limited by a number of factors. First, the antiunion environment of the industry, the times, and the region makes collective action to improve working conditions very difficult. Second, the increasing use of ancillary workers and production facilities, including those located in the Third World, lessens the ability of workers to demand improved conditions. The continuing crisis of lagging competitiveness in the industrial core of American industry further aggravates these problems (Piore and Sabel, 1984).

For engineers, the most important benefit of working in high tech is the autonomy it allows them. The major day-to-day problem they experience is the imposition of unrealistic project deadlines on their work. The other negative aspect of working in a high-tech setting that was repeatedly reported by engineers was the narrow division of labor and excessive specialization in the way their skills were utilized. Several engineers complained that the only people who have an opportunity to use the full range of their skills are project engineers. The regular engineering staff, no matter how skilled they are at what they do, or perhaps *because* they are so skilled and specialized at what they do, do not typically have an opportunity to exercise and develop a broader range of engineering skills.

An additional reservation engineers have that specifically concerns high tech is a certain degree of concern about technological displacement. Many of the engineers we interviewed were working on various aspects of automated production systems. One group of engineers we interviewed was engaged in the development of computer systems for the computer-assisted design of microchips, systems that would directly replace engineers in their own field. In such situations, it is perhaps inevitable that engineers will feel a certain amount of anxiety about their futures. The engineers we interviewed were aware that computer-assisted design was only in its infancy and that its potential displacement effects were as yet to be felt. But many were uneasy about this.

Widespread problems were also reported by female workers concerning promotion opportunities. Lower-level production positions and poorly paid clerical positions are heavily female-dominated in high-tech companies, while professional and managerial hierarchies are staffed almost entirely by Anglo males. Female workers are quite realistically concerned about blocked mobility opportunities. Virtually every female worker and supervisor we interviewed complained about some aspect of this problem.

Finally, there are large costs to workers due to arbitrary and unmediated management power. This arbitrary authority influences every aspect of production, from promotions and work assignments to shift selections and discipline for tardiness. One of the most compelling examples of this we observed was the implementation of a new program to screen employees for drug use. Employees were terrified that evidence of prescription drug use would be used to identify workers or job applicants with chronic health problems and eliminate them from the labor pool. Management concern with health-related absences and past management abuses in this area had made it an especially sensitive issue.

In summary, workers tend to like the new skills required to work in high-tech settings. But they resent their low wages and they are not very impressed by the sorts of partial and superficial involvement offered by currently popular "participative management" schemes. Their resentment is heightened by the glaringly apparent need for more substantial forms of involvement to mediate genuine worker concerns and problems. These problems appear to result less from inherent characteristics of high-tech production systems than from specific organizational choices and policies. In particular, the use of market-clearing wages for recruiting labor rather than efficiency wage structures for encouraging worker productivity, and the lack of trust and long-term implicit contracts between workers and employers appear to be underlying causes of many of the problems observed. This interpretation again suggests that many of the problems noted in this chapter may not be restricted to high-tech industries but may, rather, be endemic to American industry as a whole. It is hoped that the observations made in this chapter will stimulate research efforts to further our understanding of these issues and of the intersection of sociological and economic considerations in promoting the vitality of our economy and the well-being of workers.

ACKNOWLEDGMENTS

I would like to thank Paula England, George Farkas, Mark Granovetter, Shelley Coverman, Dan Cornfield, Bob Kaufman, Mary Zey-Ferrell, Toby Parcel, Rob Robinson, Jackie Hagan, and Susan Hodson for invaluable critical comments on earlier versions of this chapter. I would also like to thank Bob Parker for help with the interviewing process. Any remaining errors of omission or interpretation are, inevitably, my own.

REFERENCES

Adler, Paul. 1984. "Tools for Resistance: Workers Can Make Automation Their Ally." *Dollars and Sense* 100:7–8.
AFL-CIO. 1983. *The Future of Work.* Washington, D.C.: AFL-CIO.
Applebaum, Eileen R. 1983. "Winners and Losers in the High-Tech Workplace." *Challenge* 26:52–55.
Baran, Barbara, and Suzanne Teegarden. 1984. Women's Labor in the Office of the Future. Unpublished manuscript, Department of City and Regional Planning, University of California.
Bell, Daniel. 1973. *The Coming of Post-Industrial Society.* New York: Basic Books.
Blau, Peter M., Cecilia McHugh Falbe, William McKinley, and Phelps K. Tracy. 1976. "Technology and Organization in Manufacturing." *Administrative Science Quarterly* 21:20–40.
Blauner, Robert. 1964. *Alienation and Freedom.* Chicago: University of Chicago Press.
Boddy, David, and David Buchanan. 1981. "Information Technology and the Experience of Work." Pp. 78–102 in *Information Technology: Impact on the Way of Life,* edited by European Economic Community Conference on the Information Society. Dublin, Ireland: Tycooly International.
Braverman, Harry. 1974. *Labor and Monopoly Capital.* New York: Monthly Review.
Bright, James R. 1966. "The Relationship of Increasing Automation and Skill Requirements." Pp. 203–221 in *The Employment Impact of Technological Change,* vol. 2, *Technology and the American Economy,* edited by National Commission on Technology, Automation and Economic Progress. Washington, D.C.: U.S. Government Printing Office.
Burawoy, Michael. 1979. *Manufacturing Consent.* Chicago: University of Chicago Press.
Bureau of Labor Statistics. 1985. *How Workers Get Their Training.* U.S. Department of Labor Bulletin 2226. Washington, D.C.: U.S. Government Printing Office.
Burris, Beverly H. 1984. Technocracy and Work Organization. Paper presented at the Southwestern Social Science Meetings: Houston, March.

Cleveland, Harlan. 1985. "The Twilight of Hierarchy." Pp. 1–27 in *Information Technologies and Social Transformation*, edited by Harlan Cleveland, National Academy of Engineering. Washington, D.C.: National Academy Press.

Cornfield, Daniel B. 1984. Office Automation, Clerical Workers and Labor Relations in the Insurance Industry. Paper presented at the Southern Sociological Society Meetings: Knoxville, Tennessee, April 11–14.

Cross, M. 1983. "Skill Requirements for Process Industries." *Employment Gazette* 91:184–187.

Danziger, James N. 1985. "Social Science and the Social Impacts of Computer Technology." *Social Science Quarterly* 66:3–21.

Eisenscher, Michael. 1984. *Silicon Valley: A Digest of Electronics Data*. San Jose, CA.

England, Paula, and George Farkas. 1986. *Households, Employment, and Gender: A Social, Economic, and Demographic View*. New York: Aldine.

Form, William, and David Byron McMillen. 1983. "Women, Men, and Machines." *Work and Occupations* 10:147–178.

Francis, Arthur, Mandy Snell, Paul Willman, and Graham Winch. 1981. "The Impact of Information Technology at Work: The Case of CAD/CAM and MIS in Engineering Plants." Pp. 182–193 in *Information Technology: Impact on the Way of Life*. Dublin, Ireland: Tycooly International.

Freeman, John Henry. 1973. "Environment, Technology, and Administrative Intensity of Manufacturing Organizations." *American Sociological Review* 38:750–763.

Hodson, Randy. 1984. "Corporate Structure and Job Satisfaction: A Focus on Employer Characteristics." *Sociology and Social Research* 69:22–49.

Hodson, Randy, and Teresa A. Sullivan. 1985. "Totem or Tyrant? Monopoly, Regional and Local Sector Effects on Worker Commitment." *Social Forces* 63:716–731.

Hunt, H. Allan, and Timothy L. Hunt. 1983. *Human Resource Implications of Robotics*. W. E. Upjohn Institute for Employment Research. Ann Arbor, MI: University of Michigan.

Ingham, Geoffrey K. 1967. "Organizational Size, Orientation to Work and Industrial Behavior." *Sociology* 1:239–258.

In These Times. 1985. "Starting from Scratch." *In These Times* November 20–26:7.

Juravich, Tom. 1985. *Chaos on the Shop Floor: A Worker's View of Quality, Productivity, and Management*. Philadelphia: Temple University Press.

Kraft, Philip. 1977. *Programmers and Managers: The Routinization of Computer Programmers in the U.S.* New York: Springer-Verlag.

Kraft, Philip. 1984. A Review of Empirical Studies of the Consequences of Technological Change on Work and Workers in the U.S. Paper prepared for the National Research Council, Committee on Women's Employment and Related Social Issues. Washington, D.C.

Ladou, Joseph. 1984. "The Not-So-Clean Business of Making Chips." *Technology Review* 7:23–36.

Moody's Investors Service. 1984. *Industrial Manual*. New York: Moody's Investors Service.

Morse, John, and Jay W. Lorsch. 1970. "Beyond Theory Y." *Harvard Business Review* 48:61–68.

Mowshowitz, Abbe. 1976. *The Conquest of Will: Information Processing in Human Affairs*. Reading, MA: Addison-Wesley.

Murphee, Mary. 1981. Rationalization and Satisfaction in Clerical Work: A Case Study of Wall Street Legal Secretaries. Doctoral dissertation, Department of Sociology, Columbia University.

Naisbitt, John. 1984. *Megatrends*. New York: Warner.

Ouchi, William G. 1981. *Theory Z*. New York: Avon.

Peters, Thomas J., and Robert H. Waterman, Jr. 1982. *In Search of Excellence: Lessons from America's Best-Run Companies*. New York: Warner.

Piore, Michael J., and Charles S. Sabel. 1984. *The Second Industrial Divide*. New York: Basic Books.

Riche, Richard W. 1982. "Impact of New Electronic Technology." *Monthly Labor Review* 105:37–39.

Rogers, Everett M., and Judith K. Larsen. 1984. *Silicon Valley Fever*. New York: Basic Books.

Rumberger, Russell W., and Harry M. Levin. 1983. "The Educational Implications of High Technology." Project Report No. 83–A4. Institute for Research on Educational Finance and Governance, Stanford University.

Shaiken, Harley. 1984. *Work Transformed: Automation and Labor in the Computer Age.* New York: Holt, Rinehart & Winston.

Shepard, Jon M. 1971. *Automation and Alienation: A Study of Office and Factory Workers.* Cambridge, MA: M.I.T. Press.

Spenner, Kenneth I. 1983. "Deciphering Prometheus: Temporal Change in the Skill Level of Work." *American Sociological Review* 48:824–837.

Thurow, Lester. 1983. *Dangerous Currents: The State of Economics.* New York: Random House.

Wallace, Michael, and Arne L. Kalleberg. 1982. "Industrial Transformation and the Decline of Craft: The Decomposition of Skill in the Printing Industry, 1931–1978." *American Sociological Review* 47:307–324.

Warner, Malcolm. 1986. "Microelectronics, Technological Change and Industrialized Economies: An Overview." *Industrial Relations Journal* 16:9–18.

Williamson, Oliver E. 1981. "The Economics of Organizations: The Transaction Approach." *American Journal of Sociology* 87:548–577.

Zisman, Michael. 1978. "Office Automation: Revolution or Evolution?" *Sloan Management Review* 19:1–16.

12

Dueling Sectors

The Role of Service Industries in the Earnings Process of the Dual Economy

Leann Tigges

I. INTRODUCTION: POSTINDUSTRIALISM AND ECONOMIC DUALISM

The literature on the transformation of the U.S. economy has two primary components, one dealing with the historical shift in what is produced and the other concerning changes in how production is organized. The first, centering on the industrial shifts from agriculture to manufacturing to services, is located primarily in the traditions of neoclassical economics and functionalist sociology (Bell, 1976; Fuchs, 1968). Although currently focusing on the growth of the service (postindustrial) society, these works have their base in classical modernization theory, sharing assumptions of evenness in development, stratification based on achievement, and convergence both within and between societies.

In contrast to this optimistic view of social change stands the literature on the changing organization of production. The foci here are considerably more varied. They include views of segmentation defined by classes (Wright, 1978), labor markets (Kalleberg and Sørensen, 1979), firms (Baron and Bielby, 1980), and industries (Hodson, 1978; Tolbert, Horan, and Beck, 1980). Generally, these views share a common base in the critical study of monopoly capitalism (Baran and Sweezy, 1966; Braverman, 1974; O'Connor, 1973) and assumptions of unevenness in development and divergence in outcomes.

Perhaps because of the very different theoretical assumptions involved, few social scientists have studied changes occurring in both the "what" and the "how" of production. (Notable exceptions include Browning and Sin-

Leann Tigges • Department of Sociology, University of Georgia, Athens, Georgia 30602.

gelmann, 1978; Stanback and Noyelle, 1982; Wright and Singelmann, 1982.) The failure to consider changes in both aspects of production has led to inaccurate assessments of the past and misguided prognoses about the future. Economic transformation in the post-World War II economy has entailed change in both what is produced and how that production is organized. In terms of the what of production, Stanback and Noyelle (1982) trace major shifts in employment to the increasing role of government, nonprofit, and producer services, and the declining importance of agriculture and manufacturing. They argue that the organization of production has become more hierarchical in service and nonservice industries alike, partly because of increased market size and the rise of the large corporation. One result is a greater polarization of skilled and unskilled workers, and a growing dichotomy, based on pay and mobility, of good and bad jobs—even in oligopolistic firms. The theory of segmentation is being redefined by these researchers; they see the conventional interpretation of core and periphery sectors as increasingly out of step with empirical reality. Similarly, Gordon, Edwards, and Reich (1982) argue that the parallelism between labor market outcomes and economic sectors began to break down in the 1970s. A new segmentation is emerging.

In order to investigate the validity of this charge, I analyze how changes in the organization of production and in what is produced have affected the power of workers to obtain high earnings. Specifically, I compare the income determination process of 1960 and 1980 in sectors defined by the cross-classification of core/periphery and transformative/service distinctions. I examine three hypotheses derived from the "new segmentation" theory, and consider what the regression analyses tell us about the validity of the conventional interpretations of economic transformation.

II. INCOME DETERMINATION AND ECONOMIC TRANSFORMATION

A. Industry Shifts: Technology Drives Capitalism

In the functionalist tradition, social scientists focus on shifts in production from agriculture to manufacturing to services. These shifts in the industrial base of societies are largely technological in nature but are believed to have positive consequences for the nature of work and for social structure. For example, the process of shifting from an economy based on agriculture to one based on manufacturing requires development of inanimate sources of energy that allow high productivity and specialization. As machines relieve workers of the heavy physical demands of labor, and workers become more specialized, skills also increase. Achievement of skill becomes an important basis of economic reward, undermining the traditional, ascriptive reward system (Davis and Moore, 1945).

The postindustrial thesis extends modernization theory to advanced capitalist societies (Bell, 1976). The primary economic activity of postindustrial society is in the provision of services because technological advances such as mechanization and automation allow food and goods to be produced by a relatively small proportion of the working population. The United States became a "service society" around 1960 when proportionately more workers were employed in service industries than in transformative or extractive sectors (Singelmann, 1978). Political and social consequences of the coming of postindustrial society revolve around the importance of theoretical knowledge. Technical expertise becomes increasingly important in the workplace. In this view, alienation is reduced by automation because workers have more control over the entire production process (Blauner, 1964). Decision makers in every field come to rely on technical experts for the information necessary to guide the organization (Bell, 1976).

Bell (1976) describes the implications of a service economy for postindustrial society's stratification system. The power base shifts from property and political position to scientific knowledge and technical skill. The character of the stratification system is determined by the division between scientific and technical classes and those who "stand outside." "The rise of the new elites based on skill derives from the simple fact that knowledge and planning . . . have become the basic requisites for all organized action in modern society" (Bell, 1976:362). Technical skill, which Bell equates with human capital, becomes an overriding condition of competence for place and position. Eventually theoretical knowledge will eliminate property as part of the society's power base.

Studies of earnings determination with this theoretical orientation focus on characteristics of individuals as workers; occupational position and educational attainment are increasingly important in a postindustrial society. Service industries provide the best setting for meritocratic stratification principles to guide earnings determination.

B. Organizational Shifts: Capitalism Drives Technology

Social scientists with a more critical view of social change in advanced capitalism argue that production has changed primarily in its organization (Baran and Sweezy, 1966; O'Connor, 1973). Capitalism's development has resulted in a segmented economic structure. Economic segmentation in monopoly capitalism is based on the degree of concentration of market power, and on the centralization of capital. Centralization of capital refers to the redistribution of capital into fewer hands, reflected by the number of firms within an industry and society. Concentration refers to the proportion of sales controlled by a small number of companies in a particular industry. Changing patterns of control, technological developments, and capital mobility are all intimately related to changes in concentration and centralization: "A firm that can both dictate price, free of market pressure, and restrict output by barring the entry of new firms is in a position to earn monopoly profits, to control the pace of technological progress, to more closely determine the rate of capital expansion, and to more easily ignore product quality or safety" (Bluestone and Harrison, 1982:119–120).

Although U.S. industries certainly exist along a continuum of these dimensions, it has become common to differentiate between core and peripheral sectors. The core is the sector of advantage for both capital and labor. Greater economic assets and monopoly-pricing power allow these industries to attract more highly skilled workers and to provide benefits to keep them. In manufacturing, core firms are likely to use large-batch or continuous-flow production techniques. These procedures keep labor costs a relatively small proportion of total costs (Averitt, 1968). Accordingly, there exists a stratification of workers by sector, and between sectors, workers' characteristics receive different rates of return. New structuralists include individual characteristics, such as education and experience, in their analyses of the earnings determination process. But they argue that the sector in which one is employed affects the economic returns to these individual characteristics (Beck, Horan, and Tolbert, 1978; Hodson, 1978).

In contrast to postindustrial theorists' emphasis on differences between industries in *what* is produced, the emphasis of new structuralists is on the differences between industries in *how* production is organized. Early work in the new structuralist tradition emphasized the importance of increased concentration and centralization of corporate power in monopoly capitalism, but few new structualists examined changes in workers' earnings in economic sectors over time. Hodson (1978) expected increased income inequality between core and periphery workers, a by-product of the increased economic resources of monopoly sector employers. His hypothesis was not supported. Between 1947 and 1976, monopoly and competitive sector wage differentials were relatively stable. More recently, Hodson (1983) noted that new forms of workplace organization (increases in firm size and national-level concentration, growth of conglomerates, and rise of multinational corporations) have broad implications for social stratification. These implications were not specified.

C. Monopoly Capitalism Shifts Gears

In a recent critique of the dual economy position, Stanback and Noyelle (1982) charge that, even in core manufacturing, a polarization between skilled and unskilled workers is being created by the rising importance of the service functions of the corporation. Production and administrative functions are separated spatially, resulting in "office-based employment structures." Although more pessimistic about the outcomes of this transformation for the stratification of workers, Stanback and Noyelle share with postindustrial theorists an emphasis on the occupational categories of professionals, technical workers, and managers. They argue that in transformative and service industries earnings are based less on capital segmentation and more on occupational position.

New structuralists have failed to theorize about the implications of the growth of services for workers' earnings within economic sectors. Indeed, Averitt's (1968) key work within this tradition is an analysis confined to manufacturing industries. Although those who struggled to derive an empirical model of economic segmentation have included all industry types, from agriculture and mining to personal services (Hodson, 1978; Tolbert *et al.*, 1980), they have not made explicit the relevance for services of the criteria used.

Granovetter (1984:331) points out one problem resulting from this neglect: "While average weekly wages of employees in manufacturing rise almost monotonically with establishment size—as suggested by dual-economy arguments—there is almost no correlation between these wages and establishment size in services." He goes on to argue that it is unclear that "the kinds of arguments adduced to explain the peripheral status of small manufacturing firms can readily be generalized beyond manufacturing." The declining proportion of private-sector workers involved in manufacturing industries, now one in four, affirms the importance of addressing the nature of services in the dual economy.

The literature on advanced capitalism has not left us totally without direction in our thinking about the interaction of the "how" and "what" of production. To make sense of this information, I consider characteristics of industries as resources available to workers and employers (Hodson and Kaufman, 1982). I explore three areas: (1) the organization of work, (2) geographic mobility, and (3) economies of scale. I highlight the importance of the type of industrial activity for earnings.

1. The Organization of Work

One major advantage of large manufacturing enterprises over those confined to small-batch production is the ability to organize production according to Frederick Winslow Taylor's principles of scientific management. Time-motion studies are used to set work pace standards. Work is divided in such a way that knowledge of the logic of production, as well as its technical aspects, is controlled by management. These combined forces result in a labor force with little skill; workers are largely interchangeable and adapt to a wide range of simple tasks.

In service industries, advances in technology are also accompanied by the increasing Taylorization of work done by highly trained professionals and technicians (Braverman, 1974). Recent actions of TRW, Inc., a major computer software firm, illustrate the successful application of Taylor's principles. TRW developed a plan that, in its first year, increased its software programmers' productivity 39%. The plan involved isolation of the technicians in specially designed separate offices, each with its own computer terminal, allowing the programmer to immediately test his or her designs. Work was individualized and yet monitored through the technical apparatus of the worker. A consultant for TRW stated that "improving white-collar efficiency depends less on structural changes, such as improving the efficiency of machines or layout, than on analyzing how people use their time" (Brooks, 1983:33). The cost of the investment, estimated at about $10,000 per worker, would probably be prohibitive to firms without oligopolistic or conglomerate resources available to them.

Deskilling does not necessarily lower workers' earnings. In core manufacturing firms unions were able to negotiate for a share of the gains from increased productivity. But service industries have low levels of unionization. Service sector workers in nearly all occupations may find their earnings, even their jobs, threatened by changes in the social and mechanical organization of work. When technological change affects occupations, the demand for high-skilled workers is reduced and opportunities in labor-intensive occupations that have not yet been or cannot be subjected to high technology increase (Braverman, 1974). These low-technology jobs have traditionally been found in the competitive sector of the economy, especially in service industries.

The largest numbers of new jobs are expected to be created in the very areas where technology is not available to mechanize or where availability of a low-cost labor force has made it unprofitable to do so. For example, the Bureau of Labor Statistics (Carey, 1981) estimates that between 1978 and 1990, janitorial and hospital aide work will provide at least 1.265 million new jobs, while the fast-growing occupations of computer systems analysts and computer operators and programmers will add only 349,000 new jobs. The "education-intensive" white-collar jobs are not expanding at the rate of the labor force available to do those jobs (Young and Hayghe, 1984). Although lower-level white-collar jobs, often referred to as pink-collar jobs because of the predominance of women in these positions, will probably grow at a rate slightly above the national average through 1990 (Carey, 1981), automation and capital flight may slow the growth of clerical positions more than previously thought (Reskin and Hartmann, 1986:33). Already, low value-added jobs such as keypunching have been moved overseas to places like Barbados, where workers are paid 30% of the U.S. rate (*Business Week*, 1986:81).

The growth of service industries also suggests that skill requirements will be more sharply divided among available jobs. Expansion of the education-intensive segment of the service industry seems to have slowed considerably in the 1970s and will probably continue to do so in the 1980s as opportunities for public sector employment decline. Movement from the lower to the upper occupational level in services is extremely restricted. Stanback and Noyelle (1982) note that upward mobility in services depends on a change of industry, not only of jobs—a difficult task in a tight job market.

2. Geographic Mobility

Some analysts of the service sector have suggested that services, by their nature, are immobile. They are unlikely to leave local markets because they cannot be stockpiled or shipped, or they are bound by geographical licensing (Sullivan, 1981). Although personal, social, and consumer services may fit these restrictions, other services, especially producer services, tend to be as footloose as nonservice industries. The permissive technologies of telecommunications, rapid transportation, and information management systems are freeing service industries from their ties to localities. It is increasingly possible to ship information and stockpile services, and the restrictions on geographical licensing within the United States are subject to change, with the prevailing political winds currently blowing toward corporate freedom.[1]

U.S. service companies are facing barriers to overseas expansion that manufacturing firms do not face. According to *Business Week* (1986:81), in special business services, such as engineering, consulting, and brokerage, the U.S. share of global trade had fallen to 8% by 1983, nearly half of what it had been ten years earlier. The federal government is having little success lowering the protectionist barriers of our trading partners to U.S. service companies.

The transformation to a service-based economy probably will not reduce the power of capital to determine its location. As white-collar labor is deskilled, service industries will not be bound to a particular region by the availability of a highly educated work force. Furthermore, it must be remembered that many service industries are closely related to manufacturing industries in function and location. The close ties between manufacturing and those services that aid in production and distribution mean that loss of jobs in the former sector has reverberations in the service sector as well. The deindustrialization of the United States is a broad-ranging experience likely to be felt by workers in all industries.

3. Economies of Scale

Service industries can also take advantage of economies of scale, despite the limits localities place on market size. If the firm operates on a multiunit basis, as many producer and consumer services do, the firm size will not be restricted by the size of local markets; only the size of the establishment will be so limited. Service firms also utilize transportation and communication advancements to expand the size of the market. Sears, Roebuck, and Company rose to dominance in the retail industry through its mail-order business that opened a national market in an industry characterized as small-scale and local. Sears has used its dominance in retailing to enter into other service industries, including real estate, insurance, and stock brokerage and investments. Thus, economies of scale are brought in by the parent firm, making it

---

[1]The banking industry represents a good example of the changes permissive technologies are bringing to service industries. Geographical restrictions have been transcended, despite the illegality of interstate banking, except for the few companies that already owned banks in several states before the law went into effect. Despite legal restrictions, banks do tend to own each other, and banking operations extend across state boundaries through a system that allows customers of member banks to use any bank in the system. Automated teller machines and bank cards have facilitated the "shipping" of banking services across the nation, and the programming of these machines to provide a range of services has allowed many routine banking operations to be "stockpiled" until the demand exists. In addition, the closing of many small-town banks has forced customers to go to the provider rather than the other way around.

possible to deliver a broad range of services on a national scale by utilizing existing resources.

This review of some of the changes in technology and organization of core service industries suggests that, overall, the transformations in the economy have increased the resources of capital but not those of labor. The lack of countervailing resources available to service workers, many of whom are women, suggests that they will be negatively affected by many of these changes.

D. New Segmentation and Earnings

Segmentation is a *process* of contradiction and change in the organization of production (Wilkinson, 1981). In their search for the parameters of segmentation, new structuralists have lost sight of the ongoing nature of segmentation, presenting a static view of the organization of production. Recent efforts to focus new structuralist research on class resources (Hodson, 1983; Hodson and Kaufman, 1982; Spaeth, 1985) have also failed to capture the process of segmentation. This failure is partially the result of a narrow focus on how production is organized within product markets or organizational contexts. Class resources are also affected by developments outside of the workplace, such as the internationalization of production and consumption (Bluestone and Harrison, 1982) and labor legislation (Burawoy, 1983).

In part, these developments are manifested in the shift toward services within the United States. As I have argued above, the service economy does not represent the fulfillment of the postindustrial dream. Stanback and Noyelle (1982) provide evidence that service employment has brought greater earnings inequality and lower job mobility. Service work, like transformative work, is subject to technological change; it can be deskilled, monitored, and paced. Social and material technologies that deskill workers also contribute to the mobility of capital and enable firms to take advantage of economies of scale, even in small-size establishments. The character of service work, as well as the rewards associated with it, probably vary with the economic resources of the firm.

Historically, services have been organized differently from transformative industries. Firm and establishment size have been smaller in service industries (Granovetter, 1984); service industries have been relatively free of union influence; and they operated in smaller, more competitive, product markets. These institutional differences have been subsumed into the industrial typologies of new structuralists. The assumption has been that these differences also reflect the structural differences in the labor markets of the sectors (Hodson and Kaufman, 1982). However, within the core and periphery, labor markets vary by the type of industrial activity. Some workers, especially women, are not able to choose employment in transformative industries; sex segregation in occupations pushes women into service industries where most "women's jobs" are (Reskin and Hartmann, 1986; also see the appendix of this chapter). Tolbert *et al.* (1980) note the overrepresentation of women in the periphery but do not directly associate it with the predominance of service industries in the periphery.

My argument is that even within core and periphery sectors, the type of industry represents a class resource of a dimension not tapped by commonly used indicators of the organization of production. The direction and character of change since 1960 have made industrial-type distinctions more important for workers' earnings. As Stanback and Noyelle (1982) argue, the rise of services represents a "new segmentation," with new consequences for workers.

Consideration of the changes in *what* is produced and *how* production is organized leads to hypotheses about the earnings process quite different from those of postindustrialists and new structuralists. Not only are different outcomes expected but different factors are considered. "New segmentation theory," as represented primarily in the work of economists Stanback and Noyelle (1982), Gordon *et al.* (1982), and Bluestone and Harrison (1982), suggests a reduction in the benefits of core employment, even in transformative industries. New structuralists have not hypothesized about the effect of changes in core industries on workers' earnings, and postindustrialists have not been concerned with organizational differences among services. Thus, an empirical study of industrial change and workers' earnings guided by a new segmentation theory is not really a test of competing theories. Rather, it is an exploration of advanced capitalism that can shed light on important dimensions of change, some of which have been neglected by postindustrial and new structuralist theorists. The following hypotheses emerge from the new segmentation perspective.

First, benefits of core sector employment for workers' earnings have declined. This decline is the result of increased employment in service industries in the core, and of the general decline in workers' power in core industries due to deindustrialization, deskilling, and declining levels of unionization.

Second, it has become more important for one's earnings to have a professional, technical, or managerial occupation than it was in the past. The greater inequality associated with service work means that fewer jobs have middle-level pay. According to Stanback and Noyelle (1982), this bifurcation of occupation is found in transformative as well as service industries of the core. They attribute this to the increased separation of production and administrative functions (manifested in the spatial separation of production and administrative establishments within a firm). Thus, the increased division of jobs based on pay will be found in transformative and service sectors of the core.

Third, lower job mobility means that age has less influence on men's earnings in core sectors. In core transformative industries, this is partially the result of the spatial separation of production and administrative functions within the firm. In services, upward mobility depends heavily on opportunities to advance through change of industries (Stanback and Noyelle,

1982). Changing employers is more difficult for workers than changing jobs within the organization because workers have more difficulty obtaining job information and often bear greater opportunity costs.

Finally, although the results of these analyses cannot be used to *disprove* postindustrial or new structuralist theories, the direction of change in the effects of certain variables can be used to support the reasoning behind the theories. Postindustrial theorists expect education and professional and technical occupations to increase in importance because knowledge plays a central role in the stratification system. The meritocratic basis of reward reduces the influence of ascriptive characteristics, race and sex. New structuralists tend to reject the meritocratic vision of postindustrialism and to emphasize the organizational context in which rewards are distributed. Although new structuralism has not been developed as a theory of social change, the early work of Hodson (1978) leads one to expect continued benefits from core sector employment.

III. DATA AND DECISIONS REGARDING ANALYSIS

In order to assess the changes in the structure of employment and its outcomes for workers, we need to look at a period of time characterized by the relevant changes in the economy. For this purpose, I have chosen 1960 as the baseline since this is when the service sector began to grow at the expense of the transformative sector (Singelmann, 1978). Thus, 1960 is seen as the beginning of the "new" economy. The 1980 economy represents a more fully developed service economy.

The study populations are drawn from machine-readable data files of the 1960 Public Use Samples and 1980 Public-Use Microdata Sample (A) of the U.S. Censuses of Population (one-in-a-thousand size). They comprise civilians aged 14 and older in 1960 and 16 and older in 1980 who had been gainfully employed in the year preceding the census (the experienced civilian labor force) and who were in nonextractive industries during the reference week of the census year or during the last employment period.[2]

The multivariate regression analyses use demographic variables of education (highest grade attended), sex, race (white/nonwhite), and age group membership (< 25, 25–34, 35–44, 45–54, 55–64, ≥ 65) as independent variables.[3] Consistent with the Stanback and Noyelle (1982) and the Gordon *et al.*

---

[2]Extractive industries of agriculture, fishing, forestry, and mining have been excluded since the processes of production and major occupational categories in extractive industries are qualitatively different from those in other industries.

[3]The use of dummy variables for age groups rather than a continuous variable for age, though unconventional in labor market research, has several advantages. First, it facilitates the comparisons of women's experiences in the labor force over time. For them, age is not a good proxy for experience (especially in 1960); however, comparisons of returns received by women of different ages are interesting. Second, if age has meanings other than those implied by human capital theory, for example, as a correlate of worker power (Tigges, 1987), then comparing age groups allows assessment of these nonlinear dimensions.

(1982) assertions that an occupational dualism is developing between high-level white-collar workers and all others, an occupational dummy variable that distinguishes professionals, technical workers, and managers from all other workers is included. The "what" of production is indicated by industrial sectors of transformative and service production. Based on the categorization by Browning and Singelmann (1978), the transformative sector comprises the construction industry, manufacturing, and utilities. The service sector includes transportation, communications, wholesale and retail trade, producer services, social services, and personal services.

I rely on the Tolbert et al. (1980) schema of core and periphery industries to classify dual economy sectors in 1960 and 1980.[4] There is a problem using this classification scheme derived since 1960 but not as recently as 1980 for analysis of data from these two times. This problem should not be prohibitive since the data sources for the Tolbert et al. variables cut across a wide swath of the 1960–1980 period, ranging from 1966 (four-firm adjusted concentration ratio) to 1976 (earnings data). Assuming decreasing industrial concentration (Shepherd, 1982), applying the Tolbert et al. categories to 1960 and 1980 census data might result in a slight underestimation of the core in 1960 and a slight overestimation in 1980. Using static classification schemes to study historical change is not ideal, but it does serve the purpose of exploring changes in economic structure.

An important part of this analysis is the cross-classification of industries by dual economy and industrial activity dimensions into the following categories: (1) core transformative industries, (2) core service industries, (3) periphery transformative industries, and (4) periphery service industries. Part of the analysis regresses annual earnings on these categories for men and women at each time.[5] In order for us to see changes in the patterns of earnings determination within economic sectors, earnings are also regressed separately for each sector.

To compare the influence of economic sector and the other independent variables on earnings over time, a measure of real earnings must be used. Constant dollars are computed by dividing 1979 earnings by the inflation factor since 1959, which is 2.5 (U.S. Department of Labor, 1980:185), and then aggregating the results into categories corresponding to those used in the 1960 census. (This aggregation results in the loss of the differentiation of

[4]With industry as the basic unit of analysis, Tolbert et al. (1980) use three types of empirical indicators of market structure: (1) measures of market concentration and economic scale, (2) measures of oligopolistic behavior in the industrial product market (especially profit), and (3) measures of the relative size of the bureaucratic work force and the extent of internal labor market development.

[5]Earnings are given for the year preceding the census. Industry and occupation, however, are current for the census year. The analysis of earnings associated with occupation and industry, therefore, is based upon the assumption of continuity of employment between the census year and the one preceding it. This assumption is necessary in 1960 since no information on industry or occupation for the earnings year is available. Although labor market information of this type is available in the 1980 census, the information pertaining to the census year is used in order to make the assumptions between the two data sets as similar as possible.

incomes between \$62,500 and \$75,000, since these now fall into the single 1960 category for incomes of \$25,000 and higher.) The categories are then equated to the dollar midpoints and the natural logarithm computed to minimize the effect of extremely high earnings.

IV. FINDINGS

The descriptive data presented in the appendix show the changes in the distribution of the nonextractive labor force between 1960 and 1980. The labor force as a whole is less white and less male in 1980. It is also younger, more highly educated, and more concentrated in the professional, technical, and managerial occupations. Service industries in the periphery grew the most and transformative industries in the core lost the most in terms of work force shares. The major differences in worker characteristics among the economic sectors appear in the high concentration of males in the core transformative sector, of professionals and managers in both service sectors, and of young workers in periphery service industries.

In order to assess the changes in the net influence of employment sector on annual earnings, three regression models are tested (Table 1). In Model 1, earnings are regressed on sex, race, education, professional/managerial occupation, age group, and core economic sector. The last variable is replaced by type of industrial activity in Model 2, and by the cross-classification of industrial activity and dual economy dimensions in Model 3. Using new segmentation theory as my guide, I hypothesized that the benefits of core sector employment, net of other worker characteristics, have diminished. Model 1 supports this hypothesis. New structuralists have failed to predict this result, expecting instead either stability or increasing advantage for the core.

Although the effect of type of industrial activity did not change (Table 1, Model 2), changes in the effects of industrial activity within dual economy sectors (Model 3) may help explain the decreased importance of core sector employment for workers' earnings. In 1980, workers in core service industries received significantly lower returns than their counterparts in core transformative industries. In contrast, there was no difference between the two core sectors in 1960. While the industry differences within the core increased, the differences between service employment in the core and the periphery were reduced. Given the growth of service employment, these changes are important.

Analysis of Model 3 by sex (Table 2) shows similar trends in the effects of economic sectors for men and for women. The major difference between men and women lies in the influence of periphery service employment. This sector was more detrimental to women's earnings than to men's in both years, though the penalty was less for women in 1980 than it had been in 1960. Within the core, employment in service industries was associated with lower earnings than was employment in transformative industries for both sexes in 1980, and for women in 1960. The differences between men and women in the

Table 1. Regression of Log Earnings Models, 1960 and 1980[a,b]

Variables	Model 1		Model 2		Model 3	
	1960	1980	1960	1980	1960	1980
Female	−0.799	−0.602	−0.858	−0.634	−0.788	−0.586
Contrast t					20.200[d]	
Nonwhite	−0.287	−0.095	−0.323	−0.104	−0.272	−0.096
Contrast t					11.131[d]	
Education	0.060	0.051	0.070	0.058	0.064	0.055
Contrast t					6.364[d]	
Professional/managerial	0.347	0.355	0.317	0.347	0.364	0.369
Contrast t	0.555		2.080[d]		0.347	
Age group[c]						
25–34	0.926	0.808	0.959	0.843	0.916	0.798
Contrast t					7.867[d]	
35–44	1.121	0.996	1.159	1.032	1.112	0.985
Contrast t					8.130[d]	
45–54	1.192	1.085	1.225	1.125	1.187	1.077
Contrast t					6.707[d]	
55–64	1.161	1.039	1.203	1.072	1.163	1.033
Contrast t					6.989[d]	
65+	0.641	0.226	0.670	0.242	0.652	0.233
Contrast t					15.149[d]	
Sector						
Core sector	0.503	0.472	—	—	—	—
Contrast t	3.100[d]					
Service industry	—	—	−0.348	−0.346	—	—
Contrast t			0.175			
Periphery service[e]	—	—	—	—	−0.400	−0.341
Contrast t					2.602[d]	
Core transformative[e]	—	—	—	—	0.170	0.200
Contrast t					1.323	
Core service[e]	—	—	—	—	0.153	0.134
Contrast t					0.811	
Core transformative/core service						
Contrast t					0.687	3.111[d]
Intercept	5.743	6.099	6.621	6.938	6.540	6.823
Adjusted R^2	0.399	0.343	0.378	0.323	0.405	0.347

[a]*Source:* Tigges (1987), adapted from Table 6.2.
[b]Private sector workers in nonextractive industries with annual earnings greater than $0 (1959 constant dollars). In 1960, $N = 58,054$; in 1980, $N = 99,338$. Coefficients are unstandardized (metric) betas and are all significant at the 0.05 level. The contrast t is the t statistic of the differences in the metric coefficients of 1960 and 1980. The t statistic is given only for Model 3, except where its values are significantly different for the other models.
[c]The excluded age group for 1960 is 14–24; for 1980, 16–24.
[d]Significant at the 0.05 level.
[e]Relative to the periphery transformative sector.

penalties associated with periphery service industry may be a reflection of the lack of full-time employment opportunities in this sector (Stanback and Noyelle, 1982) and of women's greater representation among part-time workers, including those involuntarily employed part time (U.S. Department of Labor, 1980:54–56). Indeed, analyses of year-round full-time workers' earn-

Table 2. Net Effects of Economic Sector for Men's and Women's Earnings, 1960 and 1980[a,b]

	Men		Women		Sex contrast	
Variables	1960	1980	1960	1980	1960	1980
Professional/managerial	0.304	0.275	0.473	0.463	6.298[c]	11.463[c]
Contrast t		1.857[c]		0.366		
Sector[d]						
Periphery service	−0.229	−0.258	−0.619	−0.417	11.249[c]	5.470[c]
Contrast t		1.079		5.549[c]		
Core transformative	0.190	0.208	0.198	0.188	0.215	0.649
Contrast t		0.688		0.246		
Core service	0.174	0.141	0.084	0.105	2.332[c]	1.176
Contrast t		1.196		0.511		
Core transformative/core service						
Contrast t	0.580	2.560[c]	2.480[c]	2.395[c]		
Intercept	6.382	6.709	5.891	6.360		
Adjusted R^2	0.387	0.368	0.222	0.201		
N	35,507	52,885	22,547	46,453		

[a]*Source:* Tigges (1987), adapted from Table 6.3
[b]Private sector workers in nonextractive industries with annual earnings greater than $0 (1959 constant dollars). Other variables included in the analysis are race, education, and age group. Coefficients are unstandardized (metric) betas and are all significant at the 0.05 level. The contrast t is the t statistic of the differences in the metric coefficients of 1960 and 1980. The sex constrast column contains t statistics for sex differences in the effects of the variables.
[c]Significant at the 0.05 level.
[d]Relative to the periphery transformative sector.

ings show no sex difference in the effect of periphery service employment in 1980, though there was one in 1960 (Tigges, 1987).

In my second hypothesis, I stated that occupational bifurcation would be apparent in increased influence of professional, technical, and managerial occupations on earnings, even in core transformative industries. This hypothesis receives little support. The net effect of professional/managerial occupation increased only in Model 2 (Table 1), where industrial activity represented the sectoral dimension. When the industrial organization dimension was present in the regression model (Models 1 and 3 of Table 1, and Table 2), occupation did not have a greater effect. In fact, it had less influence on men's earnings in 1980 than it had in 1960. The within-sector analyses of men's earnings (Table 3) show this reduced effect in core transformative and core service industries. There is evidence of increased earnings inequality by occupation only for men in periphery service industries (Table 3) and for women in core service industries (Table 4).

These findings show why there was no change in the effect of occupation when sex and economic sector variables were also in the regression models— the changes that did occur differed by sex within the same sector, and by sector for men and for women. Given the increased employment of women (on whose earnings occupation has a greater influence than on men's) and the growth of employment in periphery service industries (where occupation's effect is greater than in core sectors), overall occupational bifurcation would seem to be increasing. However, the evidence presented here suggests that this is not because professional/managerial occupations are inherently more important in the economy, as suggested by postindustrial theory. Neither can it be attributed to changes in how work is organized within transformative industries, as new segmentation theory suggests.

Stanback and Noyelle's (1982) argument about the consequences of the spatial separation of production and administrative functions in core transformative industries is not supported by the changes in the net effects of the occupation variable, especially for men. However, according to their reasoning, another result of the increased service functions of core transformative industries should be lower job mobility (hypothesis 3). Using returns to age groups of men as a rough indicator of mobility, we see that in core transformative industries, all ages received lower rates of return in 1980 than in 1960

Table 3. Regression of Log Earnings Model for Men within Economic Sector, 1960 and 1980[a,b]

| | Periphery | | | | Core | | | |
| | Transformative | | Service | | Transformative | | Service | |
Variables	1960	1980	1960	1980	1960	1980	1960	1980
Nonwhite	−0.414	−0.221	−0.315	[−0.201]	−0.342	−0.275	−0.288	−0.285
Contrast t	2.647[d]		3.236[d]		2.410[d]		0.081	
Education	0.065	0.071	0.056	0.040	0.061	0.057	0.040	0.049
Contrast t	0.707		3.771[d]		1.414		2.121[d]	
Professional/managerial	0.515	0.400	0.294	0.363	0.312	0.229	0.242	0.164
Contrast t	1.242		2.240[d]		3.256[d]		2.972[d]	
Age group[c]								
25–34	0.787	0.730	1.462	1.153	1.060	0.798	0.995	0.991
Contrast t	0.731		4.231[d]		10.277[d]		0.106	
35–44	0.980	0.960	1.700	1.488	1.246	1.061	1.176	1.299
Contrast t	0.244		5.851[d]		7.068[d]		3.212[d]	
45–54	1.027	1.091	1.671	1.521	1.265	1.135	1.183	1.314
Contrast t	0.748		3.985[d]		4.713[d]		3.300[d]	
55–64	0.975	1.089	1.511	1.401	1.229	1.054	1.116	1.179
Contrast t	1.194		2.618[d]		5.619[d]		1.434	
65+	0.539	0.481	0.884	0.479	0.654	[−0.049]	0.714	0.147
Contrast t	0.417		7.139[d]		12.859[d]		9.009[d]	
Intercept	6.607	6.638	5.969	6.443	6.632	7.018	6.932	6.930
Adjusted R^2	0.274	0.239	0.406	0.378	0.326	0.285	0.286	0.310
N	2,046	2,609	10,760	19,011	15,790	19,760	6,911	11,505

[a]Source: Tigges (1987), adapted from Table 6.5.
[b]Private sector workers in nonextractive industries with annual earnings greater than $0 (1959 constant dollars). Coefficients are unstandardized (metric) betas and are significant at the 0.05 level unless enclosed in brackets. The contrast t is the t statistic of the differences in the metric coefficients of 1960 and 1980.
[c]The excluded age group for 1960 is 14–24; for 1980, 16–24.
[d]Significant at the 0.05 level.

Table 4. Regression of Log Earnings Model for Women within Economic Sectors, 1960 and 1980[a,b]

	Periphery				Core			
	Transformative		Service		Transformative		Service	
Variables	1960	1980	1960	1980	1960	1980	1960	1980
Nonwhite	[0.084]	[−0.058]	−0.133	0.094	−0.358	[−0.033]	[−0.072]	[0.012]
Contrast t	9.823[d]		6.651[d]		4.352[d]		1.054	
Education	0.031	0.027	0.083	0.064	0.073	0.040	0.074	0.046
Contrast t	0.351		3.800[d]		3.579[d]		2.720[d]	
Professional/managerial	0.593	0.562	0.528	0.521	0.284	0.389	0.148	0.277
Contrast t	0.161		0.203		1.192		2.150[d]	
Age group[c]								
25–34	0.391	0.367	0.719	0.647	0.403	0.595	0.264	0.505
Contrast t	0.269		1.961[d]		3.343[d]		4.345[d]	
35–44	0.583	0.538	0.967	0.732	0.649	0.651	0.386	0.545
Contrast t	0.496		6.370[d]		0.034		2.767[d]	
45–54	0.722	0.488	1.176	0.909	0.704	0.758	0.602	0.649
Contrast t	2.427[d]		6.976[d]		0.841		0.743	
55–64	0.780	0.587	1.233	0.925	0.797	0.735	0.621	0.665
Contrast t	1.738[d]		6.984[d]		0.798		0.591	
65+	0.405	−0.245	0.782	0.309	0.331	0.194	[0.169]	[−0.012]
Contrast t	3.241[d]		7.034[d]		0.921		1.389	
Intercept	6.502	6.903	5.072	5.798	6.324	6.821	6.333	6.782
Adjusted R^2	0.079	0.079	0.222	0.199	0.091	0.107	0.057	0.105
N	1,683	2,393	12,969	27,658	3,961	6,751	3,934	9,651

[a]*Source:* Tigges (1987), adapted from Table 6.6
[b]Private sector workers in nonextractive industries with annual earnings greater than $0 (1959 constant dollars). Coefficients are unstandardized (metric) betas and are significant at the 0.05 level unless enclosed in brackets. The contrast t is the t statistic of the differences in the metric coefficients of 1960 and 1980.
[c]The excluded age group for 1960 is 14–24; for 1980, 16–24.
[d]Significant at the 0.05 level.

(Table 3). Further, men in periphery service industries also appeared to have lower mobility in 1980 than in 1960, though age received generally higher returns in core services. The Stanback and Noyelle argument that mobility in services is dependent on changing employers rather than jobs, and is therefore more limited, receives more support from periphery service than core service data.

Finally, the contention of postindustrial theory that a service economy is more meritocratic than an industrial one receives only limited support. Over time, being female or nonwhite had less influence on earnings, but education received lower rather than higher returns (Table 1). Furthermore, in 1980 men and women still had their earnings determined by quite different rules (compare Tables 3 and 4), and this was true even among full-time workers (Tigges, 1987). Others have shown that women still earn far less than comparable men within general occupational categories (Reskin and Hartmann, 1986).

More evidence against the meritocratic thesis comes from comparing the earnings determination process within service and transformative industries

(Tables 3 and 4). For men, service industries did not reward educational attainment more highly than transformative industries in either 1960 or 1980, and in core sector services, nonwhites continued to be penalized for their racial characteristics. For women, service employment is the norm, but this has not improved their position in the economy.

V. CONCLUSIONS: NEW BOUNDARIES FOR CAPITAL? OR FOR LABOR?

This chapter has focused upon the changes in the "what" and "how" of production. Compared to employment in transformative industries, service sector employment has grown but has not produced the meritocratic society envisioned by postindustrial theorists. Within service industries, the organization of production is key to understanding the earnings process, as new structuralists have argued. However, new structuralists have not expected differences to emerge within the core sector, nor have they predicted a reduction of the benefits of core sector employment. Dual economy theory has failed to predict these outcomes, partly because it has failed as a theory of social change. New segmentation theory considers the consequences for workers of the growth of services, as well as the new ways in which production is organized. The major forces behind the transformation of the post-World War II economy are the increasing size of the market, the rise of the large corporation, and the increased role of government and nonprofit institutions (Stanback and Noyelle, 1982).

Focusing specifically on changes in the dual economy (suggesting that the growth of services in the oligopolistic sector entails changes in the organization of production into smaller-size establishments, for example), I have conceptualized economic segmentation as consisting of transformative and service industries within core and periphery sectors. Looking at the earnings determination process within these economic sectors enables us to see different processes at work within the dual economy, and the ways in which these processes have changed between 1960 and 1980. In short, it allows us to assess whether new segmentation theorists are correct when they argue that sectoral boundaries are changing, and that the conventional dual economy interpretation is becoming out of step with empirical reality (Gordon et al., 1982; Stanback and Noyelle, 1982).

The analyses of the effects of sectors on earnings in 1960 and in 1980 for the labor force as a whole, and for men and women considered separately, support the new segmentation theory. The decline in the net effect of core sector employment between 1960 and 1980 and the significant differences between transformative and service industries within the core in 1980 suggest that the industry shift may be affecting the organization of production. The measures used to empirically define dual economy sectors may not tap all the important organizational dimensions of industrial activity. The change in *what* is produced in the postwar economy is leading to changes in *how* production is organized, even in oligopolistic markets.

The new segmentation theory advanced here is also a theory of occupational changes. The argument that being in a professional, technical, or managerial occupation is increasingly important for earnings was not strongly supported by my analyses. Only when the organizational dimensions of industries were not included in the regression model was there evidence of a bifurcation of earnings along occupational lines. This suggests that it is not service employment *per se* that accounts for increased inequality by occupation. However, within service industries, occupational differences in earnings have increased for men in the periphery and for women in the core. The way in which production is organized in service industries has enhanced the importance of occupation for some workers.

The sex and sector differences in the effects of occupation and age reinforce the new segmentation argument. The important dimensions of segmentation are organizational and compositional, defined by sex, industry type, and occupation. The organizational dimensions remain important (consider the magnitude of the differences between core and periphery employment in service industries), but here too changes are occurring. Within the core and the periphery, the organization of work, the geographic mobility of firms, the ability to utilize economies of scale may not differ dramatically by type of industry. However, the resources available to workers to ensure a high rate of return to their characteristics under these conditions appear to be increasingly dependent on whether they are involved in service or transformative production. Pfeffer (1977) provides a possible explanation of the industrial differences within the core. He argues that in work settings where productivity is difficult to assess, such as core service firms, social status background and contact networks have more influence on wages than in settings where objective measures of performance are readily available.

The differences in the earnings determination processes among the sectors and the changes over time illustrate the need to incorporate theorizing about the effects of changes in the "what" of production into the literature on the "how" of production. We need to recognize the role that service industries play in providing employment opportunities and income, and the diversity of those services. We need to see monopoly capitalism and its "dual economy" as a form of production that emerged from class struggle but is continually in the process of being transformed by changes in the resources of class actors. The relative decline in core sector employment, and the relatively large decrease in the share of employment in core transformative industries are part of this process of change. The parallelism between labor market outcomes and economic segmentation, which Gordon *et al.* (1982) saw as emerging in monopoly capitalism, appears to be breaking down. We need to work harder to understand the role of services in this breakdown.

Acknowledgments

The author acknowledges the helpful comments of Gary Green, Paula England, George Farkas, Arne Kalleberg, Thomas Steiger, and Rachel Rosenfeld. This research was supported by NICHD, National Research Service Award No. 5 T32 HD07168 from the Center for Population Research.

APPENDIX

Distribution of Labor Force in Each Economic Sector by Selected Characteristics, 1960 and 1980[a]

	Periphery		Core		All
	Transformative	Service	Transformative	Service	sectors
Race					
White					
1960	87.9	85.9	92.3	92.9	89.5
1980	80.2	84.8	86.2	85.9	85.2
Sex					
Male					
1960	55.3	45.4	80.0	63.8	61.2
1980	52.2	40.7	74.5	54.4	53.2
Occupation					
Professional, technical, managerial					
1960	5.1	23.2	11.9	20.2	17.7
1980	9.3	31.7	17.0	30.5	26.4
Age group					
< 25					
1960	19.1	24.1	15.4	16.8	19.5
1980	23.5	31.0	21.8	19.8	25.8
25–34					
1960	20.7	19.5	23.9	23.4	21.8
1980	27.0	25.3	28.4	30.9	27.4
35–44					
1960	23.3	20.4	25.6	24.3	23.1
1980	19.3	16.4	19.4	19.9	18.1
45–54					
1960	20.1	18.3	20.1	18.4	19.0
1980	15.2	13.1	16.5	15.8	14.7
55–64					
1960	12.5	12.3	11.7	12.7	12.2
1980	11.8	10.2	11.8	10.7	10.8
65+					
1960	4.3	5.4	3.2	4.3	4.4
1980	3.3	3.9	2.1	2.9	3.2
Education					
0–7					
1960	22.2	10.6	13.8	6.8	11.7
1980	9.8	3.3	4.6	1.8	3.6

(*continued*)

Appendix (*Continued*)

	Periphery		Core		All
	Transformative	Service	Transformative	Service	sectors
Education (*continued*)					
8					
1960	20.0	12.1	16.5	9.5	13.6
1980	7.3	2.9	4.6	2.0	3.4
9–11					
1960	26.4	22.7	23.9	17.2	22.3
1980	22.5	14.4	16.4	8.2	14.0
12					
1960	23.6	27.8	29.3	39.1	30.1
1980	41.1	34.1	42.9	39.2	37.9
13–15					
1960	5.8	13.4	10.2	17.0	12.5
1980	13.1	22.8	19.0	27.2	22.3
16					
1960	1.6	7.1	4.6	6.8	5.9
1980	4.2	10.7	7.8	12.3	10.0
17+					
1960	0.6	6.4	1.8	3.6	4.0
1980	2.1	11.9	4.6	9.4	8.9
Total					
1960	6.4	41.2	33.8	18.6	100
1980	5.0	47.0	26.7	21.3	100

[a]*Source:* Tigges (1987), adapted from Table 6.1.

REFERENCES

Averitt, Robert T. 1968. *The Dual Economy: The Dynamics of American Industry Structure.* New York: W. W. Norton.

Baran, Paul A., and Paul M. Sweezy. 1966. *Monopoly Capital: An Essay on the American Economic and Social Order.* New York: Monthly Review Press.

Baron, James, and William Bielby. 1980. "Bringing the Firms Back In: Stratification and the Organization of Work." *American Sociological Review* 45:737–765.

Beck, E. M., Patrick M. Horan, and Charles M. Tolbert. 1978. "Stratification in a Dual Economy: A Sectoral Model of Earnings Determination." *American Sociological Review* 43:704–720.

Bell, Daniel. 1976. *The Coming of Post-Industrial Society: A Venture in Social Forecasting,* 2nd ed. New York: Basic Books.

Blauner, Robert. 1964. *Alienation and Freedom: The Factory Worker and His Industry.* Chicago: University of Chicago Press.

Bluestone, Barry, and Bennett Harrison. 1982. *The Deindustrialization of America: Plant Closings, Community Abandonment, and the Dismantling of Basic Industry.* New York: Basic Books.

Braverman, Harry. 1974. *Labor and Monopoly Capital: The Degradation of Work in the Twentieth Century.* New York: Monthly Review Press.

Brooks, Geraldine. 1983. "Faced with a Changing Work Force, TRW Pushes to Raise White-Collar Productivity." *Wall Street Journal*, September 22, p. 33.

Browning, H. L., and Joachim Singelmann. 1978. "The Transformation of the U.S. Labor Force: The Interaction of Industry and Occupation." *Politics and Society* 8:481–509.

Burawoy, Michael. 1983. "Between the Labor Process and the State: The Changing Face of Factory Regimes under Advanced Capitalism." *American Sociological Review* 48:587–605.

Business Week. 1986. "Special Report: The Hollow Corporation." March 3:57–85.

Carey, Max L. 1981. "Occupational Employment Growth through 1990." *Monthly Labor Review* 104(8):42–55.

Davis, Kingsley, and Wilbert Moore. 1945. "Some Principles of Stratification." *American Sociological Review* 10:242–249.

Fuchs, Victor R. 1968. *The Service Economy.* National Bureau of Economic Research General Series, No. 87. New York: National Bureau of Economic Research.

Gordon, David M., Richard Edwards, and Michael Reich. 1982. *Segmented Work, Divided Workers: The Historical Transformation of Labor in the United States.* New York: Cambridge University Press.

Granovetter, Mark. 1984. "Small is Bountiful: Labor Markets and Establishment Size." *American Sociological Review* 49:323–334.

Hodson, Randy. 1978. "Labor in the Monopoly, Competitive and State Sectors of Production." *Politics and Society* 8:429–480.

Hodson, Randy. 1983. *Workers' Earnings and Corporate Economic Structure.* New York: Academic Press.

Hodson, Randy, and Robert Kaufman. 1982. "Economic Dualism: A Critical Review." *American Sociological Review* 47:727–739.

Kalleberg, Arne L., and Aage B. Sørensen. 1979. "The Sociology of Labor Markets." *Annual Review of Sociology* 5:351–379.

O'Connor, James. 1973. *The Fiscal Crisis of the State.* New York: St. Martin's Press.

Pfeffer, Jeffrey. 1977. "Toward an Examination of Stratification in Organizations." *Administrative Science Quarterly* 22:553–567.

Reskin, Barbara F., and Heidi I. Hartmann. 1986. *Women's Work, Men's Work: Sex Segregation on the Job.* Washington, D.C.: National Academy Press.

Shepherd, William G. 1982. "Causes of Increased Competition in the U.S. Economy, 1939–1980." *Review of Economics and Statistics* 64:613–626.

Singelmann, Joachim. 1978. *From Agriculture to Services: The Transformation of Industrial Employment.* Sage Library of Social Research, vol. 69. Beverly Hills: Sage.

Spaeth, Joe L. 1985. "Job Power and Earnings." *American Sociological Review* 50:603–617.

Stanback, Thomas M., Jr., and Thierry J. Noyelle. 1982. *Cities in Transition: Changing Job Structures in Atlanta, Denver, Buffalo, Phoenix, Columbus (Ohio), Nashville, Charlotte.* Totowa, NJ: Allanheld, Osmun.

Sullivan, Teresa A. 1981. "Sociological Views on Labor Markets: Some Missed Opportunities and Neglected Directions." Pp. 329–346 in *Sociological Perspectives on Labor Markets,* edited by Ivar Berg. New York: Academic Press.

Tigges, Leann M. 1987. *Changing Fortunes: Industrial Sectors and Workers' Earnings.* New York: Praeger.

Tolbert, Charles, Patrick Horan, and E. M. Beck. 1980. "The Structure of Economic Segmentation: A Dual Economy Approach." *American Journal of Sociology* 85:1095–1116.

U.S. Department of Labor Bureau of Labor Statistics. 1980. *Handbook of Labor Statistics.* Bulletin 2070. Washington, D.C.: U.S. Government Printing Office.

Wilkinson, Frank. 1981. "Preface." Pp. vii–xii in *The Dynamics of Labour Market Segmentation,* edited by Frank Wilkinson. London: Academic Press.

Wright, Erik O. 1978. "Race, Class, and Income Inequality." *American Journal of Sociology* 83:1368–1397.

Wright, Erik O., and Joachim Singelmann. 1982. "Proletarianization in the Changing American Class Structure." Pp. 176–209 in *Marxist Inquiries: Studies of Labor, Class, and States,* edited by Michael Burawoy and Theda Skocpol. Chicago: University of Chicago Press.

Young, Anne McDougall, and Howard Hayghe. 1984. "More U.S. Workers are College Graduates." *Monthly Labor Review* 107(3):46–49.

13

The Impact of Technology on Work Organization and Work Outcomes

A Conceptual Framework and Research Agenda

William Form, Robert L. Kaufman, Toby L. Parcel, and Michael Wallace

I. INTRODUCTION

It is a virtual cliche that American society is in the midst of an unprecedented technological transformation in all aspects of social and economic life. Nowhere is technological restructuring of society more apparent than in business and industry. One might expect that knowledge on the effects of technological change would be highly developed. Yet opinions differ radically on whether technological change has positive or negative effects on workers, managers, business, or society at large.

Below, we describe the alternative scenarios that theorists and researchers see as outcomes of technological change. With some risk of oversimplification we see three competing perspectives: (1) the "pessimistic" view of Braverman (1974) and his followers, who insist that work is becoming deskilled and that the quality of work is being degraded by management's strategy of technological rationalization; (2) the "optimistic" view of Bell (1973) and others, who assert that technology has upgraded the quality of work, leading to greater responsibility and professionalization among workers at all levels of responsibility; and (3) the "mixed-effects" model of Spenner

William Form, Robert L. Kaufman, Toby L. Parcel, and Michael Wallace • Department of Sociology, Ohio State University, Columbus, Ohio 43210.

(1979, 1983) and others who maintain that upgrading and downgrading effects occur at different points of the occupational and industrial structure, with the result of little net change in skill and other dimensions of work. Other research suggests the plausibility of developing an alternative approach—a "contingency" model that specifies how upgrading or downgrading are contingent upon a complex array of organizational and societal factors.

This chapter has two major goals. First, we review the sociological and economic literature on technology's effect on work organization and worker outcomes. This review is organized around the optimistic, pessimistic, and mixed-effects views as noted above. Evaluating this literature, we argue that the case study emphasis has resulted in conflicting and unrepresentative findings. Our second goal uses this review as the basis for sketching the idea of a contingency approach and a research agenda for social scientists interested in technological change. Given the limitations of previous research, we suggest several types of studies that address the issues under debate.

The scope of our review will be confined to the most central outcomes of technological change at several levels of social organization. The pessimistic and optimistic theories hypothesize uniform but opposite outcomes for workers; the mixed-effects school leaves open the possibility that changes in one work outcome may not be associated with changes in another (e.g., a single technological change may *lower* skill requirements, *raise* the level of job autonomy, and exert *no net change* on authority structures and work-related values). Our contingency approach argues that changes in work outcomes depend upon the organizational and market characteristics of an establishment, its current technology, and the new technology.

We believe that the development of the contingency approach is best served by a focus on three levels of an organization: the individual, the department, and the establishment. We use establishments, rather than firms or organizations, in order to focus on the level at which change is implemented. At each level several critical outcomes merit attention. In analyzing individuals, we want to understand the effects of technological change on job skills, job autonomy, and work-related values (e.g., job satisfaction, work commitment, and alienation from work). At the departmental level we focus on authority and supervisory relations. In establishments we study employment levels, aggregate changes in work force characteristics, changes in use of technology, and the decisions regarding implementation of technology. As we argue below, all of these relationships must be viewed in interaction with other characteristics of the establishment and with characteristics of the markets and the firm in which the establishment operates. We recognize that a focus on these three levels produces an incomplete picture because it does not fully incorporate all important macrolevel forces. Future models must integrate these forces with the model we articulate.

II. OPTIMISTIC, PESSIMISTIC, AND MIXED-EFFECTS SCENARIOS: SOCIOLOGICAL AND ECONOMIC LITERATURE

A. Sociological Literature

Scholars disagree on how technological change affects occupational skill, work autonomy, job satisfaction, and supervisory relations. Below, we briefly sketch the three major perspectives and then outline our preferred "contingency" perspective. Since Adam Smith (1776/1937), conventional social science wisdom has endorsed the *pessimistic* view that technological change (mechanization) speeds up the division of labor, erodes workers' skills, reduces their independence and autonomy, and makes them increasingly resemble the machines they are operating. Marx (1844/1963) thought that workers naturally resist this degradation of their work and that they would eventually rebel against capitalists to restore their lost independence. Marglin (1974) concluded from his study of the beginning of the industrial revolution that skill simplification was not technologically inevitable, nor was it necessarily more efficient or profitable than craft production (see also Piore and Sabel, 1984). He argued that managers' decisions to adopt new technologies were largely class-based: mechanization was introduced in order to reduce workers' skills, thereby reducing their control over production and fostering management's monopoly over skill and production knowledge. Thus, under capitalism, the growth of large-scale industrial organizations and worker deskilling, loss of work autonomy, reduced job satisfaction, increasing work alienation, and increasing supervision were integrally related (Simpson, 1985). Researchers from Adam Smith in 1776 to Braverman (1974) found that continuing technological advances eroded the skills and autonomy of many crafts, especially in the steel, automobile, printing, machine, and other industries (Noble, 1984; Stone, 1974; Walker and Guest, 1952; Wallace and Kalleberg, 1982).

During the long economic depression of the 1930s, mechanization, work simplification, and large-scale industrial organization continued to expand in the United States. Growing industrial strife convinced some observers that mechanization was homogenizing the interests of workers and increasing their discontent, thereby threatening capitalism itself (Briefs, 1937; Jones, 1941; Lynd and Lynd, 1937). Economic expansion during World War II temporarily submerged this pessimistic outlook, but soon after the war a spate of studies, especially in the automobile industry (Chinoy, 1955; Walker and Guest, 1952), showed that mechanization still deskilled workers, reduced their autonomy, diminished job satisfaction, and increased supervisory control. Though continuing prosperity forced some scholars to reexamine the discontents of technology (Bell, 1956), many scholars became even more alarmed when electronic controls (automation) were introduced in production. They thought that the new automation technology would accelerate the destructive effects of the old mechanical technology. A rash of studies in manufacturing and in white-collar bureaucracies such as banks and insurance companies (Hardin, Shepard, and Spier, 1965) allayed some fears. Apparently, workers' skills were being upgraded, work autonomy grew (Blauner, 1964), and, though supervision increased, it was not onerous (Shepard, 1971). Workers liked automation, and unemployment was not a problem.

Therefore, some scholars proposed an *optimistic* scenario: automation would eliminate low-skilled manual jobs and replace them with technical occupations that required more education. In large, growing, technologically dynamic firms, workers were building true careers, constantly upgrading their skills and spans of responsibility (Foote, 1965). America was becoming a society where "bad" jobs would become either obsolete or professionalized (Parsons, 1968). This process, originating primarily in manufacturing (Faunce, 1965), signaled a transition to a postindustrial society where manual skills were becoming obsolete. Bell (1973) and his followers leaped to the conclusion that everyone would become a professional. Workers would gain more work autonomy and job satisfaction and supervisory controls would be relaxed (Tracy and Azumi, 1976). Task uncertainty, which is typical of professional work, would lead to organizational decentralization, interoccupational consultation, and flexible organization rather than close and hierarchical supervision as predicted by pessimists (Hirschhorn, 1984).

Both the optimistic and pessimistic proponents of technological change typically based their predictions on case studies probably selected to demonstrate the desired results. An ideological axis emerged in the argument. The technological pessimists tended to be radicals who had a dim view of capitalism's future, while technological optimists tended to support the *status quo*. Both views attracted dedicated adherents. Bright's (1966) survey of automated industries suggested that automation only temporarily raised skills; in the long run it deskilled workers. Harry Braverman (1974) then provided the technological pessimists with an elegant theoretical restatement of Marx's (1844/1963) earlier speculations on deskilling. A rash of supporting case studies (see Zimbalist's 1979 collection) of automated industries quickly showed that automation's effects were similar to those of mechanization. Braverman's supporters then refined his position by demonstrating, for example, that some workers successfully resisted deskilling and supervisory tyranny (Burawoy, 1979), that deskilling has several dimensions (Wood, 1982), and that work can be degraded as much by organizational as by technological change (Spangler, 1984). But the optimists were comforted by the first truly national survey of technological change. Economist Eva Mueller and her colleagues (Mueller, Hybels, Schmiedeskamp, Sonquist, and Staelin, 1969) asked a cross section of U.S. workers whether they had recently experienced equipment change and what they thought about it. The great majority who experienced change said it improved their jobs and they liked the new technology.

Contentious social science had gone through a salutary stage: the technological pessimists had demonstrated that automation could reduce workers' skill, autonomy, and job satisfaction, while the technological optimists had shown that representative studies tempered the generalizations of the pessimists. But a third group of sociologists, whom we label the *mixed-effects proponents,* suggested that downgrading/upgrading trends cancel each other out, that specific work outcomes change at different rates (and maybe in different directions), and that the long-run effects of technology support neither the pessimistic nor the optimistic view. Typically, these theorists (Rumberger, 1981; Spenner, 1979, 1983) relied on longitudinal studies of the *Dictionary of Occupational Titles* to document that downgrading effects in one sector are offset by upgrading effects in another, culminating in "little net change" in the skills of the labor force. Similarly, Parcel and Benefo (1987) found that while the dimensions of occupational differentiation in the DOT (e.g., occupational complexity, unpleasantness of work) remained relatively constant between 1965 and 1977, some upgrading in the physical skill variables also occurred.

B. Economic Literature

Economists have also investigated the effects of technological change on work organization and worker adaptation, and their views may be grouped into the same three theoretical perspectives. Labor economists studied the impact of technological change on workers' skill by examining its labor market effects and labor unions' responses. Since the inception of institutional economics (Commons, 1918), labor economists have studied the effects of technological change on the demand and supply of labor at various skill levels. This tradition continues to be inspired more by a desire to explain the price of labor than to explain its changing skill composition. Yet, in explaining wage differentials, labor economists have studied how technological innovation changes the relative supply of skilled and unskilled labor. Many assumed that management first weighs the long-term and short-term costs of labor and equipment change and then decides on a strategy to increase profits. Historical studies of the industrial revolution (Kuczynski, 1967) supported the pessimistic scenario that the introduction of machinery destroyed many artisan skills and created a large unskilled industrial proletariat.

Labor economists have also examined the employment effects of technological change. In one sense, unemployment represents the ultimate deskilling effect. It announces that society has no use for the unemployed worker's skill. While we cannot review the vast literature on unemployment, we observe that it supports the pessimistic scenario of technological change. With risk of oversimplification, we note that labor economists have shifted their concern over time from cyclical and frictional unemployment to hidden and especially structural unemployment (Gillpatarick, 1966; Gordon, 1972; Killingsworth, 1963). While the debate continues on the size of structural unemployment, some observers see a rising residue after each economic cycle or recession (Hall, 1970). Piore (1979) argues that the demographic groups most prone to unemployment work in low-skill, secondary labor market jobs that do not provide workers secure employment over time.

Investigations of the relationship between technological change and union composition tend to support the pessimistic deskilling hypothesis.

First, after the Great Depression, industrial unions grew faster than craft unions, perhaps signaling that manufacturing workers were becoming increasingly deskilled. Second, students of industrial unions agree that industrial unions generally resisted deskilling effects of technological change less than craft unions (Somers, 1963). Increasingly, both historical (More, 1980) and contemporary (Sabel, 1982) studies show that unions respond to skill threats by accepting technological innovation (partly in exchange for economic benefits) but try to control how the new technology will be utilized.

Third, labor economists agree that long-term wage differentials among skills levels have declined (Douglas, 1930; Rothbaum, 1957). This condition can result from a decline in the supply of unskilled labor, leading to higher wages for unskilled workers (probably the more popular view), or an increasing supply of skilled workers (technological upgrading), leading to their lower relative wages. Both interpretations support the thesis that technological change homogenized skills and reduced wage differentials. Of course, an increase in aggregate investment in schooling can also increase the supply of skilled workers (Schultz, 1981). Freeman (1976) argues that overeducation produces similar effects. Dresch (1975) echoes the optimistic scenario on employment effects by suggesting that technological advance widens the role for educated labor, but he also admits that wage levels for educated labor can decline relatively under these conditions.

Roberts (1984) also supports a pessimistic scenario. He argues that as computers and robots perform more tasks, a two-tiered work force develops. Executives will decide how the new technology will be used, while scientists and engineers will develop the new technologies. Unskilled workers will perform dull and routine tasks in poor work environments. Their employment will be part time, dead end, and lacking in security. Permanent, well-paid jobs in skilled and semiskilled production and maintenance will shrink, thus resulting in a smaller middle class. Office automation will also slow down the growth of the clerical sector, and even middle-management jobs will be jeopardized.

Economists who adhere to the optimistic scenario assume that the free market will overcome temporary dislocations associated with technological change. Though some workers may need retraining, most workers will profit from an unfettered economic system that quickly reaches an equilibrium. Optimists point to studies of the late 19th- and early 20th-century industrialization in Europe and the United States that show that machinery replaced unskilled labor more rapidly than skilled labor, that most industrial workers are at least semiskilled machine operatives (Knapp, 1976; Reynolds, 1974), and that higher wages accompanied this upgrading of the labor force because of the increased productivity afforded by the new technology.

Several contemporary analysts also support the optimistic scenario. McLennan (1984) summarizes the views of businesses on the effects of technology. They point to recent declining productivity in the United States relative to other countries and the lagging pace of technological innovation and productivity. They argue that, to increase productivity, more investments in technology must be made and that these investments must be allowed time to pay off. In their view, government should provide an economic atmosphere where investments can flourish by keeping inflation low, pursuing deregulation, and promoting tax policies favoring investment. In addition, schools should prepare students for the high-technology jobs by emphasizing scientific and technical skills. Labor should cooperate by not pushing wages beyond productivity gains. With this strategy, technological innovation creates a net increase in jobs and a demand for highly skilled and technical workers. Although workers permanently dislocated by technological change should be helped, such help should not impede labor-market adjustments.

Levy, Bowes, and Jondrow (1984) present results from an econometric analysis that bolster the optimistic scenario. They conducted a disaggregated analysis of employment effects in five basic industries: steel, automobiles, aluminum, coal, and iron. They point to three types of effects: (1) a direct effect of decreasing total inputs into production; (2) a direct effect of shifting demand among inputs, e.g., away from labor and toward capital; and (3) indirect output enhancement effects such that technology causes product price declines, increased sales, and, therefore, an increase in labor demand. They found that although technological advance substituted other inputs for labor, this shift was gradual. The impact of technological change on employment was noticeably smaller than the effects of wage rate changes and declines in output due to recession. Their evidence also supports the contention that output enhancement effects lead to employment growth. Moreover, industry quit rates far exceeded employment declines due to technological change, although there were layoffs when the substitution effects were concentrated within a limited area.

Even more optimistic is Lawrence's (1984) neoclassic approach to technology-producing industries. He argues that even though new technologies (including information technology) may be labor-saving, they do not necessarily suppress labor demand. Offsetting factors include (1) increasing direct demand within the industry due to the lower costs of using new technology; (2) increasing indirect demand in industries producing inputs for firms that adopt new technology; and (3) labor market clearing mechanisms that drop wages (and therefore increase employment) as workers are displaced. Like Levy *et al.* (1984), Lawrence assumes that compensating forces allow relevant markets to regain equilibrium over time.

Finally, Kerr and others (Kerr, Dunlop, Harbison, and Myers, 1960) call attention to exogenous factors that can increase the supply of skilled workers. They contend that advanced industrial societies upgrade the quality and the skills of the labor force by increasing its education and human capital. Thus, employers can increasingly shift workers from one job to another with relatively little specialized training; that is, the substitutability of workers for one another increases over time. Though skill upgrading is directly achieved by technological change in industry, it may also be indirectly achieved through the growth of the educated labor force. Such exogenous sources of change must be controlled in evaluating the effects of technological change.

The mixed-effects model is also represented in the economics literature. For example, although labor economists agree on the long-term secular trend, they have shown that the market and skill composition effects of technological change may vary within the secular trend. Thus, Ozanne (1962) and others have shown that the skill mix even in the same industry varied over the century and that labor unions changed their position and tactics with respect to technological change and pay for different skills. Perlman (1958) and Schoeplein (1977) have shown that in the post-World War II era of rapid technological change, the proportion of skilled workers stabilized or increased and that wage differentials widened in various industries, occupations, and regions. They called for a revision of economic theory to consider the mixed effects of technological and market changes on skill and wage differentials.

C. Overview

We conclude that studies remain inconclusive on the effects of technological change on skill requirements, employment levels, wages, worker autonomy, and supervision in the workplace. Depending on the time frame and other parameters, studies reveal optimistic, pessimistic, or mixed effects. In part, this can be traced to an overreliance on case studies by economists and sociologists alike. Proponents of each theoretical perspective have been able to find cases that support their view. With the exception of Rumberger (1981) and Spenner (1979, 1983), researchers have tended to avoid representative studies of the industrial and occupational structure. In addition, the reliance on case studies has contributed to three biases. First, many studies have focused on manual workers and neglected the growing white-collar segment of technical, supervisory, professional, and administrative workers. While this bias was compatible with the historic concerns of economists with collective bargaining, it deals inadequately with technology's impact in a changing economy. Second, case studies have had a large-industry bias, reflecting economists' interest with labor–management relations and sociologists' interest in corporate capitalism. Third, case studies of industries have resulted in an insufficient range of local labor market studies needed to specify the technological, industrial, and market characteristics that produce different effects. Neither discipline has launched studies that are sufficiently broad in scope to take cognizance of community labor markets as organic economic and social entities.

We also noted different disciplinary orientations to studies of technological change. Economic models are often narrow in scope and designed to check whether markets operate as theory would predict. On the other hand, sociological models tend to be broad, exploratory, and searching for a variety of factors relevant to what is being studied. Sociological studies have not focused simply on skill or employment effects but have also paid attention to issues of autonomy, supervision, and work-related values. Labor economists have emphasized the product markets in which firms buy and sell more than the strategies of labor and management, while sociologists have concentrated on labor's resistance to management's technological innovations. Clearly, the question of the effects of technological change cannot be resolved without considering the interaction between economic conditions involved and long- and short-term strategies of labor and management to deal with technological change in different industries. Understandably, the sociological bias of inclusiveness is reflected in the research agenda we advocate. At this stage, the research design of our study lacks the parsimony of economic models that make some assumptions that we, as sociologists, would not adopt.

III. THE CONTINGENCY APPROACH

It should be obvious that we are not comfortable with any current perspective that deals with the effects of technological change because they all overgeneralize from a limited range of evidence. More important, they pay insufficient attention to the organizational context in which technological changes occur and the organizational and personal consequences of such change. We prefer what we label the *contingency* view, which posits that the effects of technology on skill, authority relations, job autonomy, and work-related values are contingent on a set of organizational and societal variables that have not yet been adequately specified.

Our contingency view is suggested, though not clearly articulated, in the work of several scholars. Edwards (1979) showed that the relations between workers and their supervisors varied according to an enterprise's technology. Small enterprises that had simple technologies exhibited strict personal authority. In large mass-production firms, the assembly line rather than supervisors controlled the work of assemblers; in white-collar bureaucracies, bureaucratic rules controlled the employees. Earlier evidence blending with this perspective was provided by Woodward's (1965) classic study of technology and industrial organization, Burns and Stalker's (1966) study of technological change in transportation, manufacturing, and chemical process industries, and Blauner's (1964) study of technology, autonomy, and alienation in four types of manufacturing industries. Piore and Sabel (1984) argue that such relationships between technology and organizational structure are not inevitable. They argue that advanced industrial societies are at a "second industrial divide" in which technological advances have made possible fundamental changes in the established patterns of organizational structure and technology usage.

Our contingency view is thus premised on a disparate set of ideas and research findings that do not easily "fit" the pessimistic, optimistic, or mixed-effects scenarios. While there is a superficial resemblance to the mixed-effects argument, the contingency approach demands specification of the factors that create divergent workplace outcomes. This approach requires rigorous methods of design and analysis in order to tap the underlying organizational processes.

Several analyses acknowledge the possibility that both the optimistic and pessimistic scenarios may be correct, each under different conditions. Representative of this contingency group is Vrooman's (1984) analysis of technology's effect on the distribution of labor income. He argued that the effect of technology depends upon whether the worker is employed in the primary or the secondary labor market. Using data for young men and young women surveyed in the National Longitudinal Surveys, he found that returns to work experience were nonexistent in the secondary labor market, regardless of the industry's level of technology (measured by productivity-related indicators). For workers in lower-tier primary labor-market jobs, returns to experience were significant in high-technology (productivity) industries. Upper-tier primary labor-market workers also obtained returns to experience, but they were not related to the technology levels of their industries.

Applebaum (1984) also acknowledged that technological change may follow either the optimistic or the pessimistic scenarios. If the optimistic scenario is correct, the introduction of technology could promote economic growth both by increasing the rate of labor productivity and total output. She notes that periods of technological advance have not been periods of high unemployment but, rather, periods of expanding employment. If the pessimistic scenario is correct, perhaps the savings needed to finance technological innovation come from slower growth in the compensation of production workers, not from voluntary savings. Workers displaced from traditional smokestack industries could find it difficult to become reintegrated into an economic system that demands different skills. Black males may be the hardest hit in this transition, a function of their disproportionate participation in the contracting industries. Here Applebaum echoes Roberts's (1984) concern regarding the two-tiered job system that has grown in response to the expansion of high-technology work. Applebaum emphasizes that many jobs in the high-technology sector are not high-tech jobs, nor are they even good jobs.

Theories of a dual economy or a dual labor market (Doeringer and Piore, 1971; Gordon, 1972; Tolbert, Horan, and Beck, 1980) are broadly consistent with the contingency approach. Such theorists argue that the market context of firms establishes major contingencies for the structure and operation of the labor process within firms. Firms in the economic core, where rapid technological change is normal, develop internal labor markets where workers continue to improve their skills throughout their careers. Thus, even where industrial unions predominate, skill upgrading can become the norm. On the other hand, in labor-intensive firms in the economic periphery, deskilling is probably the norm. The implications of dual market theory are that skill differentiation of workers varies by economic sector and that workers in some sectors are experiencing skill upgrading while others experience skill downgrading.

Theories of economic segmentation also imply that the impact of technological change on skill and unemployment is contingent on particular industry and organizational characteristics. For example, Berger and Piore (1980) use dual labor market theory to suggest that some firms retain and upgrade their pool of skilled talent and export the deskilled work to the economy's periphery. To our knowledge, no one has surveyed submarket studies to ascertain which industry and organizational characteristics lead to skill upgrading. skill downgrading, and/or unemployment effects.

Dual economy and dual labor market approaches have recently been criticized as oversimplified accounts of economic and labor market segmentation and of the organization of work within segments (Baron and Bielby, 1984; Hodson and Kaufman, 1982; Wallace and Kalleberg, 1981; Zucker and Rosenstein, 1981). As Piore and Sabel (1984) note, skill upgrading can occur in the economic periphery, not just in the core, depending upon the characteristics of the markets in which firms operate, and upon labor and management choices. For example, in the labor-intensive longshore industry, Kahn (1976) found that aggressive labor unions' demands sped up management's decisions to institute technological change that called for higher and more specialized skills, leading to the formation of internal labor markets similar to those found in core firms. Geschwender and Levine (1983) showed that the displacement of unskilled manual agricultural labor in the sugar industry of Hawaii was achieved by mechanization and skill upgrading.

In reaction to this, scholars have begun to adopt a "resource approach" that specifies how the different dimensions of economic organizations (e.g., size, market power, capital intensity) provide resources and vulnerabilities to workers and management in their struggles to control work organization (Baron and Bielby, 1984; Hodson, 1983; Hodson and Kaufman, 1982; Parcel and Mueller, 1983; Schervish, 1983). In line with this emergent perspective, a primary aim of our research agenda is to specify the characteristics of organizational, economic, and labor market structure that create contingent relationships between technology and the labor process.

IV. DEVELOPING A RESEARCH AGENDA

We believe that the establishment provides the most appropriate level at which to begin studying the workplace impacts of technological change for two reasons. First, a focus on establishments permits the evaluation of the different theoretical perspectives at several levels simultaneously. Individuals, work units or departments, and establishments can each be analyzed. It is important to study such a variety of levels since some hypothesized consequences apply at only certain levels. While skill and labor utilization as dependent variables can be studied at all levels, autonomy and work-related values can only be individual level variables, and supervisory and authority structures as dependent variables can best be studied at the department and establishment levels. Second, establishments can be linked to the firms, industries, and markets in which they operate. Data on each of these higher levels can then be used to explore the contingencies that these characteristics establish for relationships at the individual, department, and establishment levels. In the Appendix we provide an illustrative list of the variables that could be measured and used at each level of analysis.

In the next section we describe the specific hypotheses, at each of the three levels within establishments, that should be used to evaluate the three theoretical perspectives. In the following section we briefly review and evaluate research designs that have been used to study the impact of technology. In light of this assessment, we propose a new design that captures the representativeness of surveys and yet provides some of the contextual understanding offered by case studies. We conclude with a discussion of how the proposed study design will provide data that will enable us to evaluate the optimistic and pessimistic approaches and to elaborate the mixed-effects model into a contingency approach.

A. Research Questions

At the *worker level,* the main research questions of interest are (1) the relationships involving the three central dependent variables of skill, autonomy, work-related values, and the type of surrounding technology, and (2) the relationship between changes in the three dependent variables to changes in workplace technology. More specifically:

The *pessimistic* orientation predicts that technological innovation will result in lower skills, a narrowing scope of task contents, a decrease in cognitive skill requirements, higher levels of unemployment resulting from machine displacement, closer supervision, a loss of autonomy, lowering of intrinsic job satisfaction, and higher work alienation.

The *optimistic* orientation predicts that technological innovation will result in higher skills, an increase in task uncertainty, an increase in cognitive skill requirements, a lowering of unemployment risks owing to the shift in the skill mix, looser supervision of the worker, an increase in autonomy, more interoccupational consultation, an increase of intrinsic job satisfaction, and lower work alienation.

In contrast, our *contingency* approach predicts that the effects of technological innovation would vary according to the type of technological innovation, the characteristics of the establishment (size, capital intensity, market position, unionization), and type of organizational structure in which the technological innovation is embedded. Moreover, a major contention of this approach is that changes in skill, labor utilization, authority relations, autonomy, job satisfaction, and alienation will occur not only by technological innovation but equally by accompanying changes in organizational structures.

At the *department* level, we see a need to probe two different sets of concerns. First, we assess the key individual level variables (worker skill, autonomy, job satisfaction) from the point of view of departmental managers. This allows us to evaluate the fit between *worker perceptions* of key variables and *management's specification* of these variables. How does technological innovation affect employee demand? What happens to redundant and displaced workers (firing, retraining, attrition)? How does technological innovation change the departmental division of labor? Do changes in job content and skill mix permeate the entire department or just a few specific jobs? How does the supervisory structure as a whole change as opposed to the supervision of a particular worker? Such questions cannot be answered by analyzing individual-level data since the individuals are drawn from disparate departments and establishments. The specific predictions of each orientation follow:

The *pessimistic* orientation predicts that technological change skews the skill mix toward low-skilled jobs, that jobs become more narrow and specialized as a result of the greater division of labor, that worker demand declines resulting in a smaller work force and more unemployment, that supervision becomes more intensive with closer control over worker activities, and that the cognitive skill requirements of supervisors increase. A secondary prediction is that work that has been deskilled will become feminized or assigned to deprived ethnic and racial groups.

The *optimistic* orientation predicts that the departmental skill mix shifts more toward highly skilled workers, that work tasks become broader in scope, that new jobs with new skills are created, that worker demand will be stable, that the supervisory structure becomes more decentralized, and that the supervisory style becomes more consultative.

Our *contingency* approach predicts that the effects at the department level will vary with a variety of factors including size of department, type of technology chosen, place of the department in the establishment (line, staff, sales, echelon), and the previous establishment structure. Moreover, the skill downgrading of, or declining demand for, some jobs could be counteracted by skill upgrading and increased demand for other jobs.

At the *establishment* level, the issues resemble those described at the department level, but at a higher level of aggregation. For example, are changes in employee demand or supervisory structures within a single department accompanied by equivalent changes in other departments or not?

The *pessimistic* approach predicts that the establishment-wide demand for workers declines, that the establishment's division of labor becomes more complex, and that the supervisory structure becomes more hierarchical.

The *optimistic* approach predicts that there will be no change in total demand for workers, that the supervisory structure becomes more decentralized, and that the staff specialists increase in number.

Our *contingency* approach predicts that the effects at the establishment level vary depending upon whether or not an establishment is a subsidiary or part of a larger firm, the type of technology chosen, the establishment's characteristics and structure, and characteristics of the market in which the establishment operates. Moreover, it argues that the declining demand and position of some departments may be counteracted by increased growth and power of other departments.

Establishment-level data permit us to assess some implicit assumptions in the pessimistic and optimistic theories. For example, both theories assume that the technological level of large and growing firms is high and that such firms are engaged in more technological innovation than small or stagnant firms (Sabel, 1982). It is important to evaluate these assumptions empirically. Establishment-level data are also critical for identifying the organizational factors that are important in the contingency approach, e.g., how establishment characteristics affect the level of technology and frequency of technological innovation.

B. Previously Used Designs for the Study of Technological Impacts

Past studies of technology's impact on the organization of work have clear design limitations. At one extreme, case studies of occupations or industries have provided rich information on the dynamics of technological change, but they lacked generalizability to other settings. At the other extreme, studies that use representative national or subnational surveys of the labor force have provided broad pictures of technological trends, but have slighted the causes of change suggested by case studies. And both approaches have failed to incorporate a systematic view of how organizations' characteristics and structure affect the adoption and implementation of technological change in the workplace.

The case study at its best examines the interplay of technology, organizational structure, and work conditions in a wealth of detail and a depth of understanding. Especially useful are case studies that compare different work settings (e.g., Horowitz and Herrenstadt's (1966) collection of case studies). Blauner's (1964) study of four industries (textile, chemical, automobile, and printing) demonstrated that much can be accomplished by judiciously selecting the settings, although his approach slighted the role that organizations play in the technological change process. Burns and Stalker's (1966) research on technological change in three industries (transporation, manufacturing, and chemical process) also provided a classic example of the power of this approach. Even so, only a few case studies live up to such standards (Perrow, 1984); most fail to take full advantage of their ability to incorporate an organizational perspective (e.g., Denny and Fuss, 1983). Many case studies omit consideration of the organizations in which changes occur and concentrate on a few industries or occupations (Carter, 1984; Glenn and Feldberg, 1977; Levy *et al.*, 1984; Noble, 1984; Stone, 1974). Moreover, all case studies share a fundamental weakness. However ingeniously designed, their results are not generalizable much beyond the specific work settings studied.

In sharp contrast is the research design that incorporates a representative array of occupational and industrial settings. One variant uses archival data, often in longitudinal analyses, to study skill changes resulting from the impact of technological change. For example, Spenner (1979, 1983) and Rumberger (1981) used the *Dictionary of Occupational Titles* and Wright and Singelmann (1982) and Kasarda (1985) used census data (the *Census of Manufacturing,* the *Census of Business,* and the *County Business Patterns*) to assess the consequences of technological change on working conditions. Many conventional surveys of working conditions, such as the Quality of Employment Survey (QES), have relied on a *random household design*. Such data are generally representative of the labor force because they ensure that persons in diverse occupations and industries will be chosen in proportion to their distribution in the labor force. In 1969 Mueller and her colleagues utilized a random household design that provided a classic benchmark for studies of technology's impact. But they retrieved little organizational data. Indeed, the organizational data that can be gathered from individual respondents are very limited. And the quality of such data is highly suspect because it relies on respondents' subjective impressions of organizational characteristics. For instance, even workers' reports of such simple organizational data as the number of persons employed are notoriously unreliable. This shortcoming of simple household designs prevents researchers from gathering data that connect organizational processes to individual outcomes.

In short, both case studies and surveys have limitations with respect to the organizational data they produce. But, as we have argued, an organizational perspective is critical for understanding technological change in the workplace because organizations link macro- and microlevel issues in technological change. At the macrolevel, for instance, an organizational focus provides insight into how technological decisions made *in the aggregate* can transform the technological face of American industry. Currently, deindustrialization and robotization are examples of such macrolevel outcomes that confront managers, workers, and society at large. At the microlevel, the organizational focus provides contextual information on how workers respond to technological changes in the establishment. Since an organization's structure, characteristics, and environment affect the parameters of technological choices, a research design is needed that incorporates these considerations in assessing how workers and establishments respond to equipment and organizational changes.

C. Alternative Designs

Several studies have experimented with *organizationally based designs* that also have large samples of individual workers. Such a design is under consideration in an update of the University of Michigan's Quality of Employment Survey, perhaps in conjunction with a separate household-based sample. An organizational design was utilized by Lincoln and Kalleberg (1985) in their Indianapolis-Tokyo Work Commitment Project. In each city, they distributed questionnaires to workers in 50 manufacturing firms and also to a sample of managerial personnel at various levels of these firms. In addition, interviews and mail-back questionnaires were conducted with key firm informants, such as the chief executive officer (CEO) and the personnel manager. Though this design provided rich organizational data, it lacked the representativeness of the household design. Kalleberg and Lincoln sampled firms in only seven manufacturing industries. Selection criteria within that subsample further limited the representativeness of the data. As a result, even though data were collected from over 4,000 respondents in each country, the study's findings cannot be generalized to the entire occupational and industrial structure.

This is a serious defect for illuminating the issues discussed above. For example, assuming that different types of technological change lead to different unemployment effects, this organizationally based design would not fully uncover this relationship since only workers who are currently employed and only those in certain industries are interviewed. Moreover, incomplete coverage of the occupational and industrial structure makes it impossible to determine the counteracting trends in different segments of the economic structure. An added statistical liability is the limited between-firm variance that can be explained with data from only a few firms. In the Kalleberg-Lincoln study, the limited number of firms (50) studied may account for the low explanatory power of firm characteristics.

Despite such limitations, organizationally based designs are a step in the right direction since such designs link individual and organizational data. One research design of this type, which has not yet been used to study technological change, links a representative sample of organizations to a representative sample of workers. The *three-stage hierarchical design* that we have been exploring integrates the best features of both the household and organizationally based designs. It ensures representativeness of the entire labor force, while it also provides organizational data needed to understand technological change in the workplace. Further, it virtually ensures that each respondent is matched with unique organizational data, thus maximizing the potential explanatory power of organizational variables. In the Appendix we provide an illustrative list of variables that would be of primary interest at each level of this design.

The first stage involves a household survey akin to the conventional household design. In this stage respondents constitute the representative sample of the work force, which we label the "target workers." Standard survey design and interviewing techniques would be used to secure information on the respondents' work situation: the relevance of technological and organizational change for skill demands, work autonomy, work adaptation, and organizational environment. Workers would also be asked to identify their establishment, department, and supervisor. These data would be used in the two subsequent stages of the design to gather needed departmental and establishment data.

The second stage involves an interview with the department-level managers identified by the target workers. This instrument would focus on issues that managers confront in implementing technological change in their work units, and how it affected the overall organization of work, employee skill requirements, and the structure of departmental authority. The manager would also be asked to provide the name of the chief executive officer (CEO) or other person responsible for planning the establishment's technological innovation strategy. This stage of the design simultaneously provides a weighted-representative sample of managers' responses to technological change, as well as contextual (department-level) data that can be mapped onto the target worker data base.

Finally, the third stage of the design focuses on establishment-level data retrieved from the CEO, or the top management representative at the physical location where the target worker is employed. Data from the CEO could be collected through a short interview supplemented by a mail-back questionnaire that concentrates on more detailed economic and technical data that may not be immediately at hand during the interview. These data would provide (a) economic information on the rationale for technological change, and (b) data on the employment effects that are so conspicuously absent in most sociological research. They would also provide rarely available data on organizational factors that shape the establishment's decisions in making technological choices (or nonchoices). These establishment-level data would constitute contextual materials to interpret what is going on at the two lower stages of the analysis (i.e., worker and department).

This third stage of the design is particularly critical for linking the establishment to higher-level contextual factors. The CEOs transmit industry and market forces relevant to technology into enterprise policies regarding the rate of technological change. While others may develop plans for implementing change, the executive level must respond to external forces to initiate change and has authority to institute change. Data obtained from this level will provide a bridge for analyses dealing with variations in local responses to macrolevel factors affecting technological change.

Obviously, modifications of this design would be required in some circumstances. For example, in the case of the self-employed, the department-level and establishment-level stages of the design would be dropped. Also, the inclusion of state or federal government employees creates special but not insurmountable problems. However, since over 90% of American urban workers are employed in moderate or large-scale business or government enterprises, the research design is generally applicable. The major disadvantages of this design are: (a) the labor-intensive costs of conducting three interviews to complete a single case, (b) the possibility of lower response rates at the department and establishment levels, and (c) limits on the amount of organizational data that can be gathered (even though this design permits the collection of more such data than do most designs).

Two recent studies suggest that a multistage design is feasible. First, in a study of the Chicago labor market, Bridges and Villemez (1985, 1986) successfully asked respondents to identify the name and location of their employers. Follow-up interviews with employers successfully obtained establishment data for an 80% response rate. Somewhat lower response rates resulted when establishments preferred to respond to questionnaires rather than answer questions over the phone. Second, a study of authority structures in the workplace by Spaeth (1985) started with a random sample of Illinois workers and proceeded up the authority chain by asking successive waves of respondents to identify their direct supervisors. Spaeth reported surprising success in securing respondent cooperation at all levels of supervision, in some cases six levels removed from the original worker.

The advantages of the data retrieved through this three-stage hierarchical design are numerous. The main advantage for research and analysis is the acquisition of contextual work-unit and establishment-level data that can be mapped onto a data base of target workers. But many researchers (ourselves included) would also use such data to study the mechanisms by which *establishments* make decisions about technology and the consequences of the decisions for the changing industrial base. Researchers can also use the *department-level* data to study how managers implement technological changes. In short, the three-stage hierarchical design provides organizational data that can be analyzed at any of the three levels or in any combination of levels.

The fact that this design produces a representative sample of respondents is an advantage that cannot be overemphasized. This design makes it possible to determine whether people are unemployed or have changed jobs as a result of technological change. For the unemployed, information obtained regarding their most recent job can be identified and would parallel the data for other respondents who are currently employed. A sufficient sample size would allow for estimates regarding the proportion of the work force unemployed as a function of technological change as well as for analysis regarding the characteristics of these individuals. Comparable data on recent job changes would also be of interest.

As the above discussion suggests, there are a number of complex issues that must be considered in implementing this three-stage hierarchical design. We are currently wrestling with these questions in a pilot study of a single metropolitan labor market. This study will provide insights regarding design decisions and will suggest the feasibility of the design for larger-scale projects, such as state or regional labor market studies.

D. Issues for Future Research

The above discussion has not addressed the measurement issues that are so critical to the success of the research program. A central concern is how to measure technological innovation. It is easier to note whether technological change has occurred in a work setting than to gauge the extent of technological innovation. Using an ordinal scale, such as those developed by Bright (1966) and Mueller *et al.* (1969), one could argue that introducing a major computer system that all workers use either directly and indirectly is a greater innovation than replacing a single copying machine used by one department. On the other hand, the products of this new copying machine may affect other departments in the organization. Clearly, establishing an interval scale of technological innovation is hazardous and difficult. For some purposes, a monetary scale might suffice; the more costly the innovation, the more far-reaching its effects on the organization. The issue of time lags is also fundamental. Many researchers assume that the introduction of a new machine has immediate effects. This may not be entirely true even for batch production, but it is less the case for service industries that introduce information-processing technology. While the aim is to increase future productivity, existing functions must be maintained during the long period of change. Researchers must grapple with these critical considerations as work on this research agenda unfolds.

We recognize that both technological and nontechnological factors affect the outcomes we seek to explain. Organizational changes, for example, dictated by cost-saving measures designed to make a firm more competitive, could easily affect job satisfaction, employment levels, and job composition in the absence of any technological change. Corporate mergers and reorganizations may have the same effects. Work-related values can also be affected by changes in personnel policies. Therefore, an adequate research design must incorporate controls, either physical or statistical, for factors that, if absent, would not allow appropriate causal inferences. As discussed above, one strategy that may help to provide macrolevel controls is to attach firm, industry, and market data to establishment cases, thus enlarging the scope of the contextual file. In this way individual or department level outcomes could be explained, in part, as a function of these larger concerns.

In the next decade, technological change will revamp work, transform worker organizations, and restructure the industrial landscape of cities and entire regions. Already these changes are being felt in major metropolitan areas in a number of ways. In some cities the pessimistic scenario is being played out: technological change is seen as eliminating jobs, downgrading skills, and enlarging disparities in income and other job rewards. In other cities, technological change is creating new jobs, upgrading skills, and elevating the standard of living for the community as a whole, providing support for the optimistic view. Most cities are caught somewhere in the middle, experiencing a unique blend of these outcomes and forced to make difficult choices that will have a lasting and perhaps irreversible impact on their social, economic, and demographic structures. Inadequate research and planning for technological change may adversely affect institutions that interface with the workplace, creating pressures on business leaders and metropolitan administrators to respond. The exacerbation of urban poverty, the erosion of the metropolitan tax base, changing demands on educational institutions, demands for job retraining services, the breakdown or recomposition of family structures, and a general deterioration of the quality of urban life are likely outcomes for cities that make the wrong choices.

Research is also needed to evaluate the consequences of technological change for different sociodemographic groups. From the individual to the societal level, technological change may differentially benefit or harm minority and majority populations in the United States. For example, the central theme of a recent Brookings Institute edited symposium (Peterson, 1985) was that urban life and work is being fundamentally reshaped by technological change in an advantageous way for the majority of the labor force. But at the same time, "the deleterious side effects of technological change are exacerbated in perverse ways by continuing racial tension and conflict. . ." (Peterson, 1985:3). In particular, Kasarda (1985) argues that urban technological change widened the gap between urban job opportunity structures and the available skills of disadvantaged residents. As entry-level jobs are being replaced by knowledge-intensive jobs, the white majority prospers and enjoys higher employment levels and other rewards, while some racial and ethnic minorities suffer from lower employment and rewards due to skill mismatch.

Such pronouncements, with their corresponding policy recommendations, imply that knowledge is highly developed about the effects of technological change on work outcomes, work organizations, and the demand for types of labor within urban locales. Yet, as we have argued above, opinions among academicians and lay people differ greatly on whether technological change is "good" or "bad" for workers, managers, cities, or the society at large. Clearly, knowledge about changes in skill requirements and labor utilization brought about by technological change is important for cities in planning their growth. It is especially important in planning for quality growth, for growth of low-skilled jobs is of dubious value. Employers also need to know what organizational problems they will encounter when they introduce technological changes, what changes in skill mix they will require, what changes in the supervisory structure are necessary, and what consequences change will have on employee morale and satisfaction. Last, workers need to know what technological changes will do to their skills, their autonomy, and their work environment, as well as what retraining opportunities they will have. We look forward to the construction of additional research agendas that, in conjunction with the one we have sketched out here, will address these vital issues.

ACKNOWLEDGMENTS

Owing to equal contributions, the authors' names are listed alphabetically. Our ideas and their expression have been improved by comments from Robert Averitt, Randy Hodson, and the book's editors, Paula England and George Farkas. A version of this chapter was presented at the November 1986 meetings of the Regional Science Association in Columbus, Ohio.

APPENDIX

Illustration of Variables to Be Collected at Each Level of the Study

Level One: Target Worker

Dependent variables

Job description, including skill and autonomy
Is target worker a supervisor and if so then supervisory duties: span of control, span of responsibility, number of levels of supervision above, number of levels of supervision below
Informal supervisory responsibilities
Resources controlled
Skill training acquired: type, length of time, source of training
Job satisfaction
Reactions to current technology and to change in technology
Change of job (promotion/demotion/transfer) over last x years
Change in interactions with other workers over last x years
Change in job description over last x years

Change in job satisfaction over last x years
Change in who supervises target worker and/or how supervision is done

Independent variables

Technology utilized/confronted in work process
Other organizational changes
Change in technology over last x years

Control or informational variables

Sociodemographic standards: age, race/ethnicity, gender, family composition, personal earnings, family income, education, hours worked, weeks worked, tenure, seniority, employment status
Knowledge and opinions about community training programs
Interactions with other workers
Mobility expectations, intra- and interfirm
Member of union?
Work unit covered by collective bargaining agreement?
Questions about other household workers: number of employment statuses
Name and address of place of work
Name and title of department head
Name of department (administrative unit) in which work

Level Two: Department of Target Worker

Data on department head as a worker

Dependent variables

Job description of department head, including skill and autonomy
Skill training acquired: type, length of time, source of training
Span of control and span of responsibility
Informal supervisory responsibilities
Resources controlled
Change in supervisory duties over last x years
Change in job description of department head over last x years

Independent variables

Technology utilized/confronted in work process by department head

Control or informational variables

Subset of sociodemographic questions from above about department head
Name and phone number of chief executive officer (CEO) of establishment

Data on target worker from department head

Dependent variables

Change in job description of target worker over last x years
Change in supervision of target worker over last x years

Independent variables

Type of technology used by target worker
Change in technology used by target worker over last x years

Department level data from department head

Dependent variables

List of job titles in department; for each job title: gender and race composition, skill requirements
Change in list of job titles and characteristics over last x years
Number of supervisors in department
Number of employees in department
Number of levels of supervision in department
Number of levels of supervision above department
Change in supervisory system in department over last x years
Change in number of employees in department over last x years

Independent variables

Types of technologies used in department
Change in technology over last x years

Control or informational variables

"Product" produced in department
Department budget (capital and expenses) and budget change in last x years
Name and phone number of CEO of establishment

Level Three: Establishment Data

Dependent variables

Number of employees
Worker displacement or growth in department over last x years
Growth or decline in total number of employees over last x years
Number of departments
Number of levels of supervision
Assessments of local economic policies and work force adaptability

Independent variables

Assets, liabilities, and sales
Market position/share in local, regional, and national markets
Capitalization rate
Profitability or net income
Growth or decline in assets over last x years
Growth or decline in sales over last x years
Compared to other enterprises in industry is firm leader, follower, or unchanging with respect to use of technology?
Unionization of establishment

Control or informational variables

How does target department fit into grand scheme of establishment's use of technology?

Budget (capital and expenses) and change in budget over last *x* years

"Product" produced by establishment

Changes in product over last *x* years

Branch or subsidiary of parent company?

Name of parent company

REFERENCES

Applebaum, Eileen. 1984. "High Tech and the Structural Employment Problems of the 1980s." Pp. 23–48 in *American Jobs and the Changing Industrial Base,* edited by Eileen L. Collins and Lucretia Tanner. Cambridge, MA: Ballinger.

Baron, James N., and William T. Bielby. 1984. "The Organization of Work in a Segmented Economy." *American Sociological Review* 49:454–473.

Bell, Daniel. 1956. *Work and Its Discontents.* Boston: Beacon Press.

Bell, Daniel. 1973. *The Coming of Post Industrial Society.* New York: Basic Books.

Berger, Suzanne, and Michael J. Piore. 1980. *Dualism and Discontinuity in Industrial Societies.* Cambridge: Cambridge University Press.

Blauner, Robert. 1964. *Alienation and Freedom: The Factory Worker and His Industry.* Chicago: University of Chicago Press.

Braverman, Harry. 1974. *Labor and Monopoly Capitalism: The Degradation of Work in the Twentieth Century.* New York: Monthly Review Press.

Bridges, William, and Wayne Villemez. 1985. Informal Hiring and Ascription in the Labor Market: Are Weak Ties Just for Guys? Paper presented at the Annual Meetings of the American Sociological Association, Washington, D.C.

Bridges, William, and Wayne Villemez. 1986. "Informal Hiring and Income in the Labor Market." *American Sociological Review* 51:574–582.

Briefs, Goetz. 1937. *The Proletariat.* New York: McGraw-Hill.

Bright, James. 1966. "The Relationship of Increasing Automation and Skill Requirements." Appendix of Vol. II, *The Employment Impact of Technological Change, Technology and the American Economy.* National Commission on Technology, Automation and Economic Progress. Washington, D.C.: U.S. Government Printing Office.

Burawoy, Michael. 1979. *Manufacturing Consent: Changes in the Labor Process under Monopoly Capitalism.* Chicago: University of Chicago Press.

Burns, Thomas, and G. M. Stalker. 1966. *The Management of Innovation.* London: Tavistock.

Carter, Nancy M. 1984. "Computerization as a Predominate Technology: Its Influence on the Structure of Newspaper Organizations." *Academy of Management Journal* 27:247–270.

Chinoy, Eli. 1955. *Automobile Workers and the American Dream.* Garden City, NY: Doubleday.

Commons, John R. 1918. *History of Labor in the United States,* vol. 1. New York: Macmillan.

Denny, Michael, and Melvyn Fuss. 1983. "The Effects of Factor Prices and Technological Change on the Occupational Demand for Labor: Evidence from Canadian Telecommunications." *Journal of Human Resources* 17:161–176.

Doeringer, Peter B., and Michael Piore. 1971. *Internal Labor Markets and Manpower Analysis.* Lexington, MA: D. C. Heath.

Douglas, Paul H. 1930. *Real Wages in the United States—1890–1926.* Boston: Houghlin Mifflin.

Dresch, Stephen P. 1975. "Demography, Technology, and Higher Education: Toward a Formal Model of Educational Adaptation." *Journal of Political Economy* 83:535–569.

Edwards, Richard C. 1979. *Contested Terrain: The Transformation of the Workplace in the Twentieth Century.* New York: Basic Books.

Faunce, William A. 1965. "Automation in the Automobile Industry." *American Sociological Review* 24:401–407.

Foote, Nelson. 1965. "The Professionalization of Labor in Detroit." *American Journal of Sociolgoy* 58:371–380.

Freeman, Richard B. 1976. *The Over-Educated American.* New York: Academic Press.

Geschwender, James A., and Rhonda F. Levine, 1983. "Rationalization of Sugar Production in Hawaii, 1946–60: A Dimension of Class Struggle." *Social Problems* 30:352–368.

Gillpatrick, Eleanor. 1966. "On the Classification of Unemployment: A View of the Structural-Inadequate Demand Debate." *Industrial and Labor Relations Review* 20:201–212.

Glenn, Evelyn, and Roslyn L. Feldberg. 1977. "Degraded and Deskilled: The Proletarianization of Clerical Work." *Social Problems* 25:52–64.

Gordon, David M. 1972. *Theories of Poverty and Underemployment.* Lexington, MA: D. C. Heath.

Hall, Robert E. 1970. "Why Is the Unemployment Rate so High at Full Employment?" *Brookings Papers on Economic Activity* 3:369–402.

Hardin, Einar, Jon M. Shepard, and Morris S. Spier. 1965. *Economic and Social Implications of Automation: Abstracts of Recent Literature.* East Lansing: Michigan State University Press.

Hirschhorn, Larry. 1984. *Beyond Mechanization.* Cambridge, MA: M.I.T. Press.

Hodson, Randy. 1983. *Workers' Earnings and Corporate Economic Structure.* New York: Academic Press.

Hodson, Randy, and Robert L. Kaufman. 1982. "Economic Dualism: A Critical Review." *American Sociological Review* 47:727–739.

Horowitz, Morris, and Irwin Herrenstadt. 1966. "Change in the Skill Requirements of Occupations in Selected Industries." Pp. 227–287 in Appendix of Vol. II, *The Employment Impact of Technological Change, Technology and the American Economy.* National Commission on Technology, Automation, and Economic Progress. Washington, D.C.: U.S. Government Printing Office.

Jones, Alfred Winslow. 1941. *Life, Liberty, and Property.* Philadelphia: Lippincott.

Kahn, Lawrence M. 1976. "Internal Labor Markets: San Francisco Longshoremen." *Industrial Relations* 15:333–337.

Kasarda, John D. 1985. "Urban Change and Minority Opportunities." Pp. 33–67 in *The New Urban Reality,* edited by Paul E. Peterson. Washington, D.C.: Brookings Institute.

Kerr, Clark, John T. Dunlop, Frederick H. Harbison, and Charles A. Myers. 1960. *Industrialism and Industrial Man.* Cambridge, MA: Harvard University Press.

Killingsworth, Charles. 1963. "Cooperative Approaches to Problems of Technological Change." Pp. 80–93 in *Adjusting to Technological Change,* edited by Gerald G. Somers. New York: Harper & Row.

Knapp, Vincent J. 1976. *Europe in the Era of Social Transformation: 1700–Present.* Englewood Cliffs, NJ: Prentice-Hall.

Kuczynski, Jurgen. 1967. *The Rise of the Working Class,* translated by C. T. A. Ray. New York: McGraw-Hill.

Lawrence, Robert Z. 1984. "The Employment Effects of the New Information Technologies: An Optimistic View." *Brookings Discussion Papers in International Economics, No. 20.* Washington, D.C.: Brookings Institute.

Levy, Robert A., Marianne Bowes, and James M. Jondrow. 1984. "Technical Advance and Other Sources of Employment Change in Basic Industry." Pp. 77–95 in *American Jobs and the Changing Industrial Base,* edited by Eileen L. Collins and Lucretia Tanner. Cambridge, MA: Ballinger.

Lincoln, James R., and Arne L. Kalleberg. 1985. "Work Organization and Workforce Commitment: A Study of Plants and Employees in the U.S. and Japan." *American Sociological Review* 50:738–760.

Lynd, Robert S., and Helen M. Lynd. 1937. *Middletown in Transition: A Study in Cultural Conflicts.* New York: Harcourt Brace.

Marglin, Steven. 1974. "What Do Bosses Do?" *Review of Labor Economics* 6:33–60.

Marx, Karl. 1963. *Early Writings,* edited and translated by T. B. Bottomore. New York: McGraw-Hill. (Originally published 1844)

McLennan, Kenneth. 1984. "Industry Perspectives on Adjustment to Economic Change." Pp. 163–182 in *American Jobs and the Changing Industrial Base*, edited by Eileen L. Collins and Lucretia Tanner. Cambridge, MA: Ballinger.

More, C. 1980. *Skill and the English Working Class: 1870–1914*. London: Croom Helm.

Mueller, Eva, Judith Hybels, Jay Schmiedeskamp, John Sonquist, and Charles Staelin. 1969. *Technological Advance in an Expanding Economy: Its Impact on a Cross-Section of the Labor Force*. Ann Arbor, MI: Survey Research Center.

Noble, David F. 1984. *Forces of Production: A Social History of Industrial Automation*. New York: Knopf.

Ozanne, Robert A. 1962. "A Century of Occupational Differentiation in Manufacturing." *Review of Economics and Statistics* 44:292–299.

Parcel, Toby L., and Kofi Benefo. 1987. "Temporal Change in Occupational Differentiation." *Work and Occupations*. 14:514–532.

Parcel, Toby L., and Charles W. Mueller. 1983. *Ascription and Labor Markets: Race and Sex Differences in Earnings*. New York: Academic Press.

Parsons, Talcott. 1968. "Professions." *International Encyclopedia of the Social Sciences*. New York: Macmillan and Free Press.

Perlman, Richard. 1958. "Forces Widening Occupational Wage Differentials." *Review of Economics and Statistics* 40:107–115.

Perrow, Charles. 1984. *Normal Accidents: Living with High Risks*. New York: Basic Books.

Peterson, Paul E. 1985. "Introduction: Technology, Race, and Urban Policy." Pp. 1–32 in *The New Urban Reality*, edited by Paul E. Peterson. Washington, D.C.: Brookings Institute.

Piore, Michael J. 1979. *Inflation and Unemployment: Institutionalist and Structuralist Views*. White Plains, NY: M. E. Sharpe.

Piore, Michael J., and Charles F. Sabel. 1984. *The Second Industrial Divide*. New York: Basic Books.

Reynolds, Lloyd G. 1974. *Labor Economics and Labor Relations*. Englewood Cliffs, NJ: Prentice-Hall.

Roberts, Markley. 1984. "A Labor Perspective on Technological Change." Pp. 183–205 in *American Jobs and the Changing Industrial Base*, edited by Eileen L. Collins and Lucretia Tanner. Cambridge, MA: Ballinger.

Rothbaum, Melvin. 1957. "National Wage Structure Comparisons." Pp. 299–327 in *New Concepts in Wage Determination*, edited by George W. Taylor and Frank C. Pierson. New York: McGraw-Hill.

Rumberger, Russel W. 1981. "The Changing Skill Requirements of the Jobs in the U.S. Economy." *Industrial and Labor Relations Review* 34:578–591.

Sabel, C. F. 1982. *Work and Politics*. Cambridge: Cambridge University Press.

Schervish, Paul G. 1983. *Vulnerability and Power in Market Relations: The Structural Determinants of Unemployment*. New York: Academic Press.

Schoeplein, Robert N. 1977. "Secular Changes in the Skill Differentials in Manufacturing: 1952–1973." *Industrial and Labor Relations Review* 30:314–324.

Schultz, Theodore W. 1981. *Investing in People: The Economics of Population Quality*. Berkeley: University of California Press.

Shepard, Jon M. 1971. *Automation and Alienation*. Cambridge, MA: M.I.T. Press.

Simpson, Richard L. 1985. "Social Control of Occupations and Work." *Annual Review of Sociology* 11:415–436.

Smith, Adam. 1937. *An Inquiry into the Nature and Causes of the Wealth of Nations*. New York: Modern Library. (Originally published 1776)

Somers, Gerald. G. (ed.). 1963. *Adjusting to Technological Change*. New York: Harper & Row.

Spaeth, Joe L. 1985. "Job Power and Earnings." *American Sociological Review* 50:603–617.

Spangler, Eve. 1984. Contested Terrain: The Changing Division of Labor among Salaried Attorneys. Unpublished manuscript, Department of Sociology, Boston College.

Spenner, Kenneth I. 1979. "Temporal Changes in Work Content." *American Sociological Review* 44:968–975.

Spenner. Kenneth I. 1983. "Deciphering Prometheus: Temporal Changes in the Skill Level of Work." *American Sociological Review* 48:824–837.

Stone, Katherine. 1974. "The Origins of Job Structures in the Steel Industry." *Review of Radical Political Economics* 6:113–173.

Tolbert, Charles M., II, Patrick M. Horan, and E. M. Beck. 1980. "The Structure of Economic Segmentation: A Dual Economy Approach." *American Journal of Sociology* 85:1095–1116.

Tracy, P., and K. Azumi. 1976. "Determinants of Administrative Control: A Test of a Theory with Japanese Factories." *American Sociological Review* 41:80–94.

Vrooman, John. 1984. "Effects of Technology on the Distribution of Labor Income." Pp. 115–123 in *American Jobs and the Changing Industrial Base,* edited by Eileen L. Collins and Lucretia Tanner. Cambridge, MA: Ballinger.

Walker, Charles R., and Robert Guest. 1952. *The Man on the Assembly Line.* Cambridge, MA: Harvard University Press.

Wallace, Michael, and Arne L. Kalleberg. 1981. "Economic Organization, Occupations, and Labor Force Consequences: Toward a Specification of Dual Economy Theory." Pp. 77–117 in *Sociological Perspectives on Labor Markets,* edited by Ivar Berg. New York: Academic Press.

Wallace, Michael, and Arne L. Kalleberg. 1982. "Industrial Transformation and the Decline of Craft: The Decomposition of Skill in the Printing Industry." *American Sociological Review* 47:307–324.

Wood, Stephen (ed.). 1982. *The Degradation of Work?: Skill, Deskilling, and the Labour Process.* London: Hutchinson.

Woodward, Joan. 1965. *Industrial Organization: Theory and Practice.* London: Oxford University Press.

Wright, Erik Olin, and Joachim Singelmann. 1982. "Proletarianization in the Changing Class Structure." *American Journal of Sociology (Suppl.)* 88:176–209.

Zimbalist, Andrew (ed.). 1979. *Case Studies on the Labor Process.* New York: Monthly Review Press.

Zucker, Lynne G., and Carolyn Rosenstein. 1981. "Taxonomies of Institutional Structure: Dual Economy Reconsidered." *American Sociological Review* 46:884–889.

VI

SOCIOLOGICAL AND ECONOMIC APPROACHES TO THE STUDY OF INDUSTRIES, FIRMS, AND JOBS

Economic and Sociological Views of Industries, Firms, and Jobs

Paula England and George Farkas

> . . . at some point economic conditions tend to become
> causally important, and often decisive, for almost all social
> groups, at least those which have major cultural significance;
> conversely, the economy is usually also influenced by the
> autonomous structure of social action within which it exists.
> —Max Weber (1922/1968:341)

I. INTRODUCTION

At least since Weber, some sociologists have focused on topics lying on the border between their field and economics. Of the 13 chapters in this volume, 10 may be classified this way. The remaining 3—the chapters by Averitt, Lang and Dickens, and Williamson—represent a more unusual genre: economists working the other side of the border. However, such efforts also have a history that dates back more than 50 years, to the work of John Commons and the institutional economists (see Williamson, Chapter 8).

What, then, is new? To a small but unprecedented degree, sociologists and economists are each aware of, and responding to, work in the other discipline and are seeing possibilities for cross-fertilization across a wide set of topics. While sociology and institutional economics have long had much in common, mainstream economics has recently changed in ways that make cross-fertilization with sociology more likely. This is particularly the case for the subject matter of this volume: the structure and behavior of industries, firms, and jobs, and their consequences for the lives of workers. Yet the fundamental viewpoints of the two disciplines still diverge sharply. Our purpose here is to review the major theoretical themes that are central to each discipline's treatment of the topic of this volume, with an eye toward their consistency or inconsistency with one another and with empirical evidence.

This chapter is organized as follows. Section II summarizes the tradi-

Paula England and George Farkas • School of Social Sciences, University of Texas-Dallas, Richardson, Texas 75083-0688.

tional economic perspective; Section III undertakes the same task for sociology. The result is a focus on the fundamental divergence between the two perspectives: Economists emphasize rational (economizing) action by atomistic individuals, while sociologists emphasize groups and positions in society, and their consequences for individual action and outcomes. Section IV explores how these divergent perspectives are treated by the chapters in this volume. The discussion is organized around three themes: (a) the endogeneity or exogeneity of preferences, (b) market price equilibration and the logic of evolutionary change, and (c) inequality and power. The chapter concludes with a brief consideration of the features that an integration of sociological and economic views should contain.

II. THE ECONOMIC VIEW

Economics is about rational ("economizing") behavior of individuals in the presence of scarcity. Such "optimization" or "maximization" is seen as an attempt to make those choices yielding the greatest amount of personal "utility," given one's constraints. Neoclassical economists traditionally studied such behavior while assuming perfect and costless information, and many economic models still make this assumption. Recently, however, economists have emphasized the importance of the costs of gathering and disseminating information and of other transactions. The notion of "optimization" now includes calculating what resources it is worthwhile to spend collecting information, and what "governance structures" best economize on transaction costs (Williamson, Chapter 8). The "new institutional economics" attempts to explain the emergence of institutional structures as a result of optimizing behavior by firms and individuals facing such costs.

Each individual's preferences or tastes determine the amount of utility provided by different combinations of leisure, job conditions, consumer goods, household arrangements, friendship, and similar factors. Economists do not attempt to explain the origin of these tastes. Stigler and Becker (1977) have argued that there is little variation in tastes, and thus that most behavior can be explained by variations in (a) the economic constraints of prices or (b) the resources one is endowed with by biology, by one's family of origin, or by gifts (Becker, 1976, 1981:ix–x). Other economists assume that tastes vary across individuals and see a role for disciplines such as sociology in explaining variation in preferences (Hirschleifer, 1984:9). As observed by Lang and Dickens (Chapter 4, this volume), neoclassical economists assume that preferences are exogenous to economic models (see also Schultz, 1981:152). This view is related to the focus on the atomistic individual. By assuming that tastes are exogenous to economic processes, economists ignore the likelihood that individuals have their tastes affected by group culture, networks of social communication, and structures of position and power centered in economic institutions. This atomism contrasts with the sociological emphasis on social structural effects on individual preferences and habits.

It is commonly believed that economics deals with behavior oriented toward materialistic ("pecuniary") goals, whereas sociology deals with behavior in which nonpecuniary tastes such as "social" motivations are prominent. This is often but not always true, and certainly it is not true in principle. Indeed, scholars within each field have been at pains to define a much wider scope for their activities. Sociologists have long been concerned with the study of social stratification, work, occupations, labor markets, and industries, all subjects involving "pecuniary" matters such as earnings, commodities, and economic exchange. The discussions by sociologists in this volume are examples of such work. Thus, sociology cannot be defined in terms of its concern with nonpecuniary values. Nor can economics be defined in terms of behavior directed at pecuniary ends, since economists assume that economizing behavior pervades all forms of human action. They recognize that individuals often trade off pecuniary compensation for interesting or safe work, leisure, or more satisfactory family arrangements. This is embodied in the notion of compensating differentials in labor markets (Flanagan, Smith, and Ehrenberg, 1984: 179–196; Hamermesh and Rees, 1984:279–194), and in the contention that individuals maximize utility or full income, not merely net monetary gain (Schultz, 1981: Chap. 4).

Yet, despite their formal recognition that individuals have both pecuniary and nonpecuniary goals, economists seeking empirical predictions often assume that actors simply seek to maximize pecuniary gain. By contrast, economists are most likely to invoke nonpecuniary tastes when these can be used to explain a discrepancy between empirical evidence and the neoclassical paradigm. Thus, for example, the seeming anomaly presented by dual labor markets (that workers of equal human capital have different earnings depending on the sector they are employed in) is rendered consistent with neoclassical theory by positing that jobs in the secondary sector offer nonpecuniary benefits that lead workers with certain tastes to choose such jobs over those that pay more in the primary sector. (See Lang and Dickens, Chapter 4, and Farkas *et al.*, Chapter 5.)

Economics is also concerned with the relations of exchange within markets. An individual is seen to voluntarily undertake an exchange when the outcome is better than that from any other available option (Hirschleifer, 1984:12). Competitive markets are those in which there are many potential buyers for each seller, and vice versa. This situation generates constant pressure toward equilibrium via price adjustment. Thus, when the price for a good or service is such that the amount supplied exceeds the amount demanded, the competition between sellers will cause prices to fall. The lower price will cause sellers to produce and sell less and buyers to buy more. In theory, the price will stabilize at precisely that point where the amount supplied just equals the amount demanded. In the absence of further shifts in the location of supply or demand curves, the price will remain constant at this "market-clearing equilibrium."

Exchanges are defined as "pareto-optimal" if someone's utility is increased by the exchange while no party to the exchange thereby loses utility.

That is, exchange is pareto-optimal if it is voluntary in the sense that individuals participate only when so doing will make them better off. Economists do not analyze which of the two parties "got more" from the exchange because of their assumption that interpersonal utility comparisons are impossible (Hirschleifer, 1984:476–477). Thus, pareto-optimality rather than equity or equality is the criterion by which economists typically judge outcomes.

Another area of difference between economists and sociologists concerns group power differentials and inequality. When sociologists speak of power within a social interaction, they mean that one party receives more of what he or she wants (more "utility," in economists' terms) from the interaction than the other one does. But economists avoid such assertions since, as mentioned above, they believe that interpersonal utility comparisons are meaningless. For example, there is no evidence that would convince most economists that employers have more power than employees, or husbands more power than wives.

When economists speak of power, they refer to market power, defined as the ability to sell or buy at a more favorable price than would obtain under competition. In their view, this can occur only where there is either one or only a few sellers (monopoly or oligopoly) or one or only a few buyers (monopsony or oligopsony). In the case of oligopoly or oligopsony, collusion is also required to achieve market power. Yet market power is not defined in terms of an interpersonal utility comparison. Rather, power is said to exist when the market price is different from what it would be under competition.

Economists make little use of the notion of coercion within market relations. For them, coercion involves appropriating something owned by someone else without compensation agreed to by both parties (Hirschleifer, 1984:12). Theft is an example. But capitalist property rights do not qualify as an example, no matter what the political or social consequences of such rights, and no matter how great the resulting inequality. For economists, market relations can never be coercive; rather, the essence of coercion and power lies in barriers to competition and free exchange. Even the actions of democratically elected governments in taxing and regulating the economy are viewed as non-pareto-optimal. When economists do advocate such policies, they are defended on the basis of equity or some special circumstance of "market failure" having no natural place, or at best a modest place, within the neoclassical paradigm. (See Thurow, 1983; Averitt, Chapter 2, this volume.)

Though economists do not believe that ordinary market phenomena can be defined as "coercive," they do have a concept of discrimination. If it can be shown that one group of workers is paid more than another group that is equally productive under the same conditions, economists define this as discrimination (Arrow, 1973). Yet this is not necessarily interpreted as a matter of power or coercion. And economists believe that discrimination should eventually erode in competitive labor markets. The argument proceeds as follows: Consider a situation where some employers will not hire women in "male" jobs, or will hire them only at a wage rate lower than that paid to the males in these jobs. If this discrimination is based on employers' tastes, and there is some dispersion in tastes, then those employers with the least discriminatory tastes will begin to hire women. These employers will find that women are a bargain because other employers' discriminatory acts have lowered the wage that women can command. Thus, by hiring women they are able to cut their labor costs and increase their profit above that earned by discriminating employers. As employers who will not hire women lose market share or go out of business, women's job distributions should eventually converge with men's. In addition, since only those employers with little or no taste for discrimination will remain, women will be able to command the same wage as men. A similar logic argues for the erosion of discrimination arising from reasons other than tastes. Thus, in the example of monopolistic collusion between male workers and employers to keep women out of "male jobs," discrimination should erode because of the temptation of individual employers to break out of the "cartel" and take advantage of cheaper labor. Economists' belief that such "free rider" behavior is pervasive represents another example of their view of individuals as nonsocial atoms without compelling group loyalties.

III. THE SOCIOLOGICAL VIEW

The greatest distinction between the sociological and economic viewpoints is that sociologists go beyond the individual as atomistic optimizer to focus on the structure of groups and positions within society. Thus, sociologists see individual action occurring within a context in which job positions, material interests, cultural values, and personal networks create social solidarity within groups and social cleavages between groups. An individual's position within the societal structure has profound implications for his or her preferences, strategies, habits, and outcomes. Like economics, sociology contains micro- and macrotheories. But, whereas economists believe that macroeconomics should flow from microeconomics, most sociologists see micro- and macroprocesses as reciprocally influencing one another.

Sociologists examine causal links between all sectors of society. As indicated by the quotation from Weber at the beginning of this chapter, sociologists view "the economy" as the formal markets that are but one part of society. But economists are increasingly extending their studies beyond formal markets to include institutions such as the family and government. Thus, the distinction between sociology and economics will be increasingly defined by what causal processes are asserted to operate, not what topic is under analysis.

There is much greater variation in the causal processes posited by sociologists than by economists. Thus, to summarize "the sociological view" is to be selective. The view we present draws on the microtraditions of exchange theory (Wilson, 1983:19–39) and symbolic interactionism (Shibutani, 1986; Wilson, 1983:122–144), and the macrotraditions of structuralism (Kohn,

Schooler, Miller, Miller, and Schoenberg, 1983; Wilson, 1983:40–62) and conflict theory (Collins, 1975, 1986). (For a synthetic treatment, see Collins, 1985.)

Microsociology takes the structural and distributional realities that constrain individuals for granted. It focuses on the consequences of interactions
between individuals. Sociological exchange theory is similar to microeconomics in its emphasis on rational action by individuals who engage in exchanges
(Wilson, 1983:19–39). The focus is on how patterns of interaction and distribution flow from exchanges between rational individuals. Yet, unlike economists, exchange theorists do make interpersonal utility comparisons and
speak of which party has more power than another, drawing conclusions
about who is getting more from relationships. Sociologists support such conclusions with research showing that individuals judge equity by comparing
the ratio of benefits to effort expended by each of the parties to an exchange.
Exchange theory has also been influenced by notions of conditioning imported from behavioral psychology. In one sense, behaviorists' notion that individuals respond to rewards and punishments is perfectly compatible with the
microeconomic assumption that individuals rationally pursue their self-interest. But psychologists' empirical work has shown that behavior may persist
unchanged even in the face of only intermittent reinforcement. There is thus a
tension between the economic view of an individual's continually choosing
optimal behavior and the behavioral view that individuals are "conditioned"
to habits that persist even after the reward structure has changed. Sociologists
accept the importance of habits more easily than economists do since habit
implies that rationality is not fully in force at all times. (For a sociological
discussion of habit, see Camic, 1986. Note that, by contrast, Williamson
[Chapter 8, this volume] refers to habit as the "tosh" that theories should de-
emphasize.)

A second microtradition in sociology is symbolic interactionism. Here the
focus is on communication between individuals as they create and negotiate
symbols and definitions of the situation that lead to role definitions and
cultural worldviews. It is through such interactions that events and objects
take on their meanings. One result of the individual's interaction with others
is the creation of his or her notion of a "generalized other," that is, the general
expectations of the group or groups to which one belongs. It is the ongoing
negotiation within the self between one's spontaneous desires and the generalized other that creates meanings and guides behavior. This process also
creates a sense of self, including the demeanor appropriate to one's role, and
the deference and status honor due oneself and others. Rituals and rules of
conduct flow from these meanings. In this view, actors do not passively
respond to roles imposed on them by the social structure, but rather help to
define and create culture and the expectations that go with various positions
or roles. It is the microprocesses of transactions, either instrumental or expressive, that concern symbolic interactionists.

Many sociologists not formally part of the "symbolic interactionist
school" share some of these ideas. For example, most sociologists believe that
group norms are internalized to the point that they are experienced as a

constraint capable of overriding individual preferences because of a feeling of morality and group loyalty, even where the possibility of detection or punishment is minimal (Collins, 1982:3–29). Often the notion of the "generalized other" is invoked to explain this process of internalization. Collins's integration of the microinteractionist tradition with a general conflict theory is an example of borrowing from symbolic interactionism (Collins, 1975, 1981). This builds on Weber's notion that "status groups" develop a common life-style and viewpoint through interaction, and is consistent with the emphasis on communication developed by symbolic interactionists. (For a general treatment of communication processes and group structure, see Shibutani, 1986. For a sociologist's quasi-economic discussion of the determinants of group solidarity, see Hechter, 1983.)

Structuralism is a macrotradition in sociology that examines how systems of positions and networks condition and limit individual behavior. This view encompasses several different perspectives. One holds that networks of personal relationships are structures that affect loyalties, preferences, and resources (Granovetter, 1985, and Chapter 9, this volume). A second is the school of social psychology referred to as "social structure and personality." In this perspective, the psychology (including preferences and habits) of individuals is shaped by their "structural position," e.g., attributes of their job or role (House, 1977; Kohn et al., 1983). Finally, "new structuralist" studies of stratification examine how the characteristics of one's job affect wages and other rewards, net of individual characteristics. (See Kalleberg and Berg, Chapter 1, and Farkas et al., Chapter 5.)

Sociologists often identify undesirable outcomes with residence in particular structural positions. Examples include psychological distress, restricted mobility, lack of opportunity for useful network connections, and low wages. Consider the common structural finding that differences in measured human capital between people holding "disadvantageous" and "advantageous" jobs are not sufficient to explain the differential in rewards. We also observe that females, minorities, and individuals from lower social class backgrounds are more likely to occupy such jobs, even after adjustment for measurable human capital. Economists typically explain such findings by one of two assertions. Either the groups in the lower-paying jobs have lower levels of unmeasured human capital, or the lower-paying jobs have nonpecuniary characteristics sufficiently attractive to compensate for their lower wage. How do these differ from sociologists' explanation of such structural findings?

Sociologists might posit that the placement of a group in disadvantageous jobs arises through socialization or restricted information and planning. Thus, females often choose sex-typical jobs long before learning that such jobs pay badly. While economists acknowledge that individuals have imperfect information because of both search costs and bounded rationality, they de-emphasize such factors by comparison with sociologists.

Sociologists also posit that discrimination has limited the options of those in the less desirable jobs. Many economists are skeptical of this because they believe that discrimination should erode in competitive labor markets, as discussed above. Yet sociologists argue that group loyalty leads to individually irrational discriminatory action whose consequences are materially advantageous for a group (e.g., of white males) as a whole. Sociologists also emphasize the effects of discriminatory job assignments that perpetuate group differences and create new discrimination. The social-psychological effects may be due to habituation in counterproductive work or reward patterns (such as learning that investment is futile), or be a consequence of leading to new discrimination (England and Farkas, 1986). These behavioral effects may be due to habituation in counterproductive work or reward patterns (such as learning that investment is futile), or as a consequence of interaction with others who have been socialized in this way. This mechanism is typical of sociologists' belief that the social psychology of preferences or habits is (jointly) endogenous with economic outcomes. By contrast, economists assume that preferences are exogenous.

Sociological conflict theory (Collins, 1985:47–117) emphasizes the constraining effects of the distribution of power and other rewards. (Some sociologists think of such distributions as "structures" and thus would see this view as another strand of structuralism.) Individuals are born into a world with a particular and unequal distribution of resources. Those with more resources have more power to perpetuate their advantage because they have more ability to withhold things others want, and because they can promote the "false consciousness" of cultural belief systems legitimating the distributional *status quo*. Common applications of this view are to the dominance of groups defined by gender, race, class, and cultural life-style. Once a group has a power advantage, it keeps it until another group becomes sufficiently mobilized and amasses sufficient resources to wage and win a conflict.

Economists would object if this line of reasoning were to conclude that certain groups are more advantaged, all things considered, than others. While they agree that certain individuals are born with greater "endowments" than others (e.g., more intelligence), they would not conclude from this that such groups have power or advantage in the sense of "greater utility" than others because of their assumption that interpersonal utility comparisons cannot be made.

IV. DIVERGENCES BETWEEN SOCIOLOGY AND ECONOMICS: THREE THEMES

The discussion above has contrasted the views of sociology and economics. Below, these divergences are placed in sharper relief by focusing on three recurrent themes in the chapters of this volume.

A. The Endogeneity or Exogeneity of Preferences

As noted above, economists traditionally assume that preferences are exogenous to economic behavior. Indeed, Lang and Dickens (Chapter 4) state that exogenous tastes and rational action are the two basic assumptions of neoclassical economics. In their view, the most significant departure of dual labor market theory from the neoclassical paradigm lies in its relaxation of the assumption of exogenous tastes in favor of the view that tastes are affected by the sector in which one is employed. Lang and Dickens identify such social-psychological feedback effects as the area where sociologists and economists, working together, can most effectively challenge and transform neoclassical economics. (See also England and Farkas, 1986; Farkas and England, 1985; Farkas *et al.*, Chapter 5.)

Granovetter (Chapter 9) also deals with the issue of endogeneity in his discussion of how social networks relate to the statistical distinction between "heterogeneity" and "state dependence." This distinction has arisen in research on unemployment but is applicable to the effects of occupying any status or position. If earlier unemployment is observed to predict later unemployment, this may be because there is some personal characteristic of the unemployed that leads them to have a greater chance of unemployment in all time periods. This is called "population heterogeneity" since it is differences in the underlying characteristics of individuals that lead to differential unemployment. Alternatively, the intertemporal correlation may arise because unemployment has an enduring negative effect on one's chances of later employment. This is "state dependence." When differences in outcomes are due to initial heterogeneity, this is consistent with seeing preferences, culture, and habits as exogenous rather than endogenous to the structural position one holds. By contrast, state dependence suggests the endogeneity of preferences, culture, and habits. The existence of "state dependence" is a principle claim of the structural view within sociology.

Yet, as Granovetter points out, even when economists posit the operation of state dependence, they typically proceed from atomistic assumptions. It is as if the individual "catches something" from the state occupied, and then carries this new characteristic inside a nonsocial self. By contrast, the sociological view advanced by Granovetter argues that what is endogenous to an individual's social position is the network of interpersonal relationships accompanying it. This network of associations will affect tastes, resources, and thus behavior in an ongoing way.

The notion that structural positions have their effects in an ongoing, social world is also at the root of Granovetter's hostility toward "culture" used as a *deus ex machina*. When economists (and some sociologists) treat culture as something imbibed in childhood and henceforth unchanging, culture becomes an exogenous input into economic models for the explanation of unequal individual outcomes. By contrast, the sociological perspective sees culture as being formed and sustained through ongoing processes of social communication (Shibutani, 1986). These processes are themselves affected by the rewards and network linkages provided by the positions one occupies. Thus, economic outcomes cannot be explained by a notion of culture that doesn't include ongoing as opposed to merely one-time social effects.

The issue of endogeneity also underlies the Lang and Dickens contention (in Chapter 4) that the absence or presence of "efficiency wages" determines wage differences between the primary and secondary labor markets. They argue that industrial differences in technology and production processes determine whether it is economic to pay above-market wages. For example, if the production process is such that turnover is especially expensive, or shirking by workers particularly damaging or difficult to detect, profits can be increased by offering above-market wages. Such wages will lower shirking, malfeasance, and turnover by improving morale and/or giving employees an incentive to avoid quitting or being fired. This contrasts with the usual neoclassical assumption that, given a particular technology of production, workers' productivity is exogenous to the wage rate.

Yet, despite seeing workers' productivity as endogenous to the wage rate, Lang and Dickens believe that the theory of efficiency wages can be integrated back into neoclassical economics. At first glance, this appears to contradict their view that exogenous preferences are a defining assumption of neoclassical theory. Yet the two can be reconciled by distinguishing between endogenous ultimate preferences, which would be antineoclassical, and endogenous behavioral patterns resulting from changed incentives, which the neoclassical paradigm can possibly absorb. This distinction would benefit from further elaboration. A potential difficulty is that "behavioral patterns" may be difficult to distinguish empirically from "preferences." Indeed, as a consequence of the role played by habit in the persistence of behavioral routines over time (Camic, 1986; Nelson and Winter, 1982; Thurow, 1983: Chap. 8), preferences and behavioral patterns may be subjectively indistinguishable even to the individuals holding them.

The endogeneity of preferences and behavioral proclivities are one of the explanations that Farkas *et al.* (Chapter 5) provide for the failure of discrimination to erode completely in competitive markets, and for the failure of (human-capital-adjusted) wage differences between industrial sectors to erode completely under competition. If individuals whose first job is disadvantageous have their work orientation thereby affected, their chances of moving to a better job may be permanently damaged. Yet it is just such mobility that is expected to facilitate those market forces able to erode discrimination and uncompensated wage differences between structural positions. This failure of uncompensated wage differences to erode is consistent with the structural effects on wages found by DiTomaso's case studies (Chapter 10), as well as the suggestions of discrimination against women and minorities found by both DiTomaso (Chapter 10) and Hodson (Chapter 11).

In sum, neoclassical models would greatly profit from revision admitting the possibility of endogenous tastes and habits. Unfortunately, this leads to theoretical complication and indeterminacy. To take but one example, we can no longer be assured of a unique and stable market equilibrium, reached relatively quickly via price adjustment. It is to this basic feature of the neoclassical model that we now turn.

B. Market Price Equilibration and Evolutionary Logic

The economic theory of general equilibrium proves mathematically that neoclassical assumptions imply market equilibrium (Arrow and Hahn, 1971; Hildenbrand, 1982; Weintraub, 1985). Yet, even in the absence of the full set of neoclassical assumptions, most economists see strong forces pushing market participants toward economic efficiency. Thus, Williamson (Chapter 8) recognizes that rationality is bounded. Yet he still believes that evolutionary "natural selection," the market competition between more and less efficient firms, guarantees the continual reduction of inefficient behavior. The claim is that even if owners and managers aren't always fully rational, those who are less efficient will go out of ·business. Some version of this belief pervades economists' approach to nearly all issues. Whether the assertion is that cartels will dissolve, that discrimination will erode under competition, or that firms will choose governance structures and degrees of vertical integration that improve productivity, economists evince great faith in the ineluctable power of market forces to push toward, if not actually to, a more efficient equilibrium.

Sociologists all too often ignore market forces, the logic of which many do not understand. This is a defect they would do well to correct. Nonetheless, it is wise for sociologists, while recognizing market forces, to question their strength, and the resulting speed of adjustment. Group membership, social network ties, institutional practices, and endogenous preferences and habits may blunt, eliminate, or even reverse the expected effect of these market forces. Indeed, this is the best explanation for the long-term post-Civil War persistence of racial discrimination in employment (Wright, 1986). For Southern labor markets, this ineffectiveness of market forces was at least partly due to the geographical immobility of firms and workers. These high costs of geographical mobility are important determinants of the persistence of regional differentials in returns to human capital reported by Beck and Colclough (Chapter 6).

A further argument for the slow speed of market adjustment concerns the empirical importance of rationality. Williamson is surely correct in believing that evolutionary changes can occur even when rationality is bounded. But the evolutionary process will proceed more quickly if firms respond to market pressures by changing and improving their techniques; a slower rate of change results when relatively unchanging firms must be replaced by more efficient newcomers. Hodson (Chapter 11) finds what he judges to be irrational personnel policies in high-tech industries. He observes neither efficiency wages (Lang and Dickens, Chapter 4) nor implicit contracts (England and Farkas, 1986: Chapter 6), despite economists' belief that these are rational when firm-specific training is involved. Hodson's observation supports the view that individual firms follow habits in a relatively unchanging way so that market forces operate only via the "deaths" of inefficient firms; it is consistent with the sociological "population ecology" theory of organizations (Aldrich, 1979; Hannan and Freeman, 1977).

In labor markets, competitive forces operate largely through the mobility of workers between jobs, firms, and industries. Thus, the demonstration of barriers to mobility between core and peripheral sectors is a key element in explaining the failure of intersectoral wage differentials to erode. Jacobs and Breiger (Chapter 3) show that mobility between sectors is limited. Yet most of the observed immobility between the two sectors among white males results from staying in the same occupation or detailed industry rather than from any special difficulty in crossing sectoral boundaries. The interpretation of these facts cuts two ways. Jacobs and Breiger emphasize the mobility that does exist across sectoral boundaries, and the fact that immobility is as great within as between sectors. Thus, they conclude that intersectoral immobility cannot explain intersectoral wage differences. Our interpretation differs from theirs as a matter of degree. The wage differences between sectors come into existence because various structural locations provide different levels of bargaining power and other resources to workers for reasons quite unrelated to mobility (Farkas *et al.*, Chapter 5). However, as Jacobs and Breiger correctly point out, a degree of intersectoral immobility is necessary for these wage differences to persist. To the extent that they find some intersectoral mobility, we agree that these are forces that militate toward the erosion of sectoral wage differences. But our interpretation emphasizes that forces discouraging any kind of mobility (Farkas *et al.*, Chapter 5) act to preserve a wage differential between sectors even if mobility is as sluggish within as between sectors. The sluggishness of mobility means that market forces act more slowly than would otherwise be the case.

The Jacobs and Breiger finding that there is no special salience of sectoral boundaries in mobility patterns leads them to support the recent trend of "new structuralist" studies toward the firm and away from the industrial or "industry-sector" level of analysis. This trend receives support from Averitt (Chapter 2), who argues that the large firms in the core of the economy generally operate in a number of different industries.

As for the overall validity of an economic paradigm that sees constant evolutionary improvement, Granovetter (Chapter 9) considers it to be similar to Parsonian functionalism in its Panglossian bias. Both functionalist sociology and economic arguments about natural selection assume that existing arrangements must be serving a useful purpose or they would have vanished. Williamson (Chapter 8) agrees that his argument is functionalist but defends it by claiming that it satisfies Elster's criterion for "full functionalism." That is, he presents an explicit causal mechanism to make the model's assertions testable. This argument will be resolved only after further work with the transactions cost/evolutionary economics model provides more detailed empirical tests. However, there is another divergence between economists and sociologists, even those of the functionalist persuasion: The two groups mean different things when they speak of evolution toward the "best" arrangements. The issue is, best for whom?

For sociological functionalism, "best" means "functional" for everyone under consensual norms in which all agree that existing hierarchies and inequalities are "functionally necessary." For economic natural selection "best for everyone" refers to pareto-optimality. That is, market economies and institutional governance structures in the private sector achieve efficiency via a sequence of moves each of which makes at least one party better off without taking from anyone something already owned. Yet this economic view takes initial "endowments," including behavioral proclivities as well as material resources, to be exogenous, raising the issue of endogeneity once again. This view also generates a ready acceptance of any resulting inequality, a view not generally shared by sociologists. This disciplinary divergence provides our final theme.

C. Inequality and Power

Neoclassical economists have long minimized issues of inequality and power. In part this is because they believe that interpersonal utility comparisons are meaningless, so that we can never infer from the distributional consequences of transactions that one party or group received a "better deal" overall. Economists speak of "power" only in reference to a lack of competition, and even here they believe monopoly and oligopoly to be transitory. This belief follows from their tendency to see atomistic individuals rather than the group structure of society. By contrast, if individuals strongly experience group identities and loyalties, collusive action will be easier, and "free riders" rare. (For evidence that free ridership may be less of a problem than economists usually suppose, see Marwell and Ames, 1979, 1980.)

Averitt (1968) was leaning against neoclassical winds when he argued that "core" firms gain their higher profits at least partly as a consequence of market power achieved by persistent oligopoly. (He also saw technology as a key factor.) Averitt (Chapter 2) argues that the neoclassical view we take for granted as "objective truth" is itself an ideology that uses "efficiency" to justify a hierarchical world order dominated by its proponents. As U.S. firms become subordinate to Japanese and other world producers, American economists may begin to see hierarchy as dysfunctional, even where it results from market forces.

The chapters by Farkas *et al.* (5), Beck and Colclough (6), Tomaskovic-Devey (7), DiTomaso (10), Hodson (11), Tigges (12), and Form *et al.* (13) illustrate the interest sociologists take in inequality, and the disinclination of sociologists to assume that the distributional shares generated by markets are always either "functional" or "optimal." Thus, sociologists have recently questioned whether the evolution of the U.S. economy toward services and "high-technology" production is generating an occupational distribution with increased inequality and less mobility. Hodson (Chapter 11) and Tigges (Chapter 12) claim that this is the case, while Form *et al.* (Chapter 13) are more tentative, arguing for a view in which the effects of technology are contingent upon social and organizational variables. Tigges finds that the advantages of employment in the "core" sector fell between 1960 and 1980, partly owing to increased wage differentials between service and manufacturing industries within the core. Whatever the ultimate resolution of these issues, it is useful to observe that the neoclassical paradigm is incompatible with the notion that market shake-outs or the pursuit of comparative advantage by U.S. firms can be other than efficient for the U.S. economy, even if it were to make the distribution of wages more unequal. One exception to this view is the work (cited by Averitt, Chapter 2) by Bulow and Summers, using efficiency wages to argue that industrial policy may sometimes be efficient. But this is a novel view, and it is foreign to most neoclassical economists. Sociologists, with their concept of the group structure of society and the unequal power of these groups to shape goals and agendas, are more accustomed to asking how economic evolution and social change may be disadvantageous to particular minority groups, class groups, or even a majority of U.S. workers. Since such an outcome may well be pareto-optimal, economists are more likely than sociologists to see it as an unfortunate but necessary consequence of competitive processes.

Sociologists and economists also have differing views of the possibilities for egalitarian "social engineering." Hodson (Chapter 11) stresses the positive effects for productivity and workers' satisfaction that might arise from allowing shop-floor workers in high-tech industries greater decision-making power. In contrast, Williamson (Chapter 8) argues that if such arrangements were realistic for "human nature as we know it," they would already exist. Of course, this view once again rests on the economists' evolutionary logic that takes as given or optimal the differential power of groups to determine the governance structures in firms, and thus to determine the amount of worker participation in decisions.

V. CONCLUSION

Economic and sociological approaches to industries, firms, and jobs exemplify the differences between the disciplines of sociology and economics. Economists see an atomistic world of optimizing individuals with exogenous tastes and endowments. The results of market transactions are seen as efficient in the pareto-optimal sense. This generates an elegant body of mathematizable deductive theory with determinate predictions. But rigid assumptions lead economists to ignore evidence inconsistent with their theory. We believe that economists are empirically in error to assume that preferences and behavioral proclivities are exogenous to economic models. It is also unrealistic to assume that optimal equilibria will result from the natural selection of competition. Instead, strong inertial tendencies are caused by the costs of search and adjustments, bounded rationality, the role of habit in behavior, and feedback effects from market outcomes to behavioral proclivities. These cause many predicted changes to occur only slowly, sporadically, and reversibly. It is also unrealistic to assume that interpersonal utility comparisons are impossible. Although they raise difficult measurement issues, generalizations about which groups and positions are advantaged are certainly possible. If economists were to revise these assumptions, they would be less sanguine about inequality.

Being free of these assumptions, sociologists observe that the structural roles in which individuals find themselves affect their tastes, outlooks, power, social networks, and group loyalties in ways that could not have been anticipated in advance. Tracing out such effects gives sociology a somewhat deterministic view of the effects of social positions on the individual, a view that contrasts with the free-choice emphasis among economists. Thus, there is a paradox that the sociological view is more deterministic than the economic model, while its predictions are less deductively determinate. Consequently, sociologists are often guilty of the opposite error, looking only to empirical induction with little theoretical guidance. In particular, sociologists are too little aware of the widespread, powerful, and theoretically predictable consequences of the equilibration mechanism of markets.

The best hope for improved understanding of industries, firms, and jobs lies with a hybrid model that is more alert to endogenous preferences, disequilibria, and power inequalities than is current within economics, yet more alert to market forces than is current within sociology. Implementation and testing of this model will require a balance between deductive reasoning and fidelity to empirical evidence somewhere between the current practices of the two disciplines.

REFERENCES

Aldrich, Howard. 1979. *Organizations and Environments.* Englewood Cliffs, NJ: Prentice-Hall.

Arrow, Kenneth. 1973. "The Theory of Discrimination." Pp. 3–33 in *Discrimination in Labor Markets,* edited by O. Ashenfelter and A. Rees. Princeton: Princeton University Press.

Arrow, Kenneth, and Frank Hahn. 1971. *General Competitive Analysis.* San Francisco: Holden-Day.

Averitt, Robert T. 1968. *The Dual Economy: The Dynamics of American Industry Structure.* New York: W. W. Norton.

Becker, Gary. 1976. *The Economic Approach to Human Behavior.* Chicago: University of Chicago Press.

Becker, Gary. 1981. *A Treatise on the Family.* Cambridge, MA.: Harvard University Press.

Camic, Charles. 1986. "The Matter of Habit." *American Journal of Sociology* 91:1039–1087.

Collins, Randall. 1975. *Conflict Sociology: Toward An Explanatory Science.* New York: Academic Press.

Collins, Randall. 1981. "On the Micro-foundations of Macro-sociology." *American Journal of Sociology* 86:984–1014.

Collins, Randall. 1982. *Sociological Insight.* New York: Oxford University Press.

Collins, Randall. 1985. *Three Sociological Traditions.* New York: Oxford University Press.

Collins, Randall. 1986. *Weberian Sociology.* Cambridge: Cambridge University Press.

England, Paula, and George Farkas. 1986. *Households, Employment, and Gender: A Social, Economic, and Demographic View.* New York: Aldine.

Farkas, George, and Paula England. 1985. "Integrating the Sociology and Economics of Employment, Compensation, and Unemployment." Pp. 119–146 in *Research in the Sociology of Work,* vol 3, edited by R. Simpson and I. H. Simpson. Greenwich, CT: JAI Press.

Flanagan, R., R. S. Smith, and R. G. Ehrenberg. 1984. *Labor Economics and Labor Relations.* Glenview, IL: Scott, Foresman.

Granovetter, Mark. 1985. "Economic Action and Social Structure: The Problem of Embeddedness." *American Journal of Sociology* 91:481–510.

Hamermesh, Daniel S., and Albert Rees. 1984. *The Economics of Work and Pay*. New York: Harper & Row.

Hannan, Michael, and John Freeman. 1977. "The Population Ecology of Organizations." *American Journal of Sociology* 82:929–964.

Hechter, Michael. 1983. "A Theory of Group Solidarity." Pp. 16–57 in *The Microfoundations of Macrosociology*, edited by M. Hechter. Philadelphia: Temple University Press.

Hildenbrand, Werner (ed.). 1982. *Advances in Economic Theory*. Cambridge: Cambridge University Press.

Hirschleifer, Jack. 1984. *Price Theory and Applications*. Englewood-Cliffs, NJ: Prentice-Hall.

House, J. S. 1977. "The Three Faces of Social Psychology." *Sociometry* 40:161–177.

Kohn, Melvin, Carmi Schooler, J. Miller, K. Miller, and R. Schoenberg. 1983. *Work and Personality: An Inquiry into the Impact of Social Stratification*. Norwood, NJ: Ablex.

Marwell, Gerald, and Ruth E. Ames. 1979. "Experiments on the Provision of Public Goods, I: Resources, Interest, Group Size, and the Free-Rider Problem." *American Journal of Sociology* 84:1335–1360.

Marwell, Gerald, and Ruth E. Ames. 1980. "Experiments on the Provision of Public Goods, II: Provision Points, Stakes, Experience, and the Free-Rider Problem." *American Journal of Sociology* 85:926–937.

Nelson, Richard R., and Sidney Winter. 1982. *An Evolutionary Theory of Economic Change*. Cambridge, MA: Harvard University Press.

Schultz, T. P. 1981. *The Economics of Population*. Reading, MA: Addison-Wesley.

Shibutani, Tomatsu. 1986. *Social Processes*. Berkeley: University of California Press.

Stigler, George, and Gary Becker. 1977. "De Gustibus Non Est Disputandum." *American Economic Review* 67:76–90.

Thurow, Lester. 1983. *Dangerous Currents: The State of Economics*. New York: Random House.

Weber, Max. 1968. *Economy and Society*, edited by G. Roth and K. Wittich. Berkeley: University of California Press. (Originally published 1922)

Weintraub, E. Roy. 1985. *General Equilibrium Analysis*. Cambridge: Cambridge University Press.

Wilson, John. 1983. *Social Theory*. Englewood Cliffs, NJ: Prentice-Hall.

Wright, Gavin. 1986. *Old South, New South*. New York: Basic Books.

Index

WITHDRAWN

3 1542 00116 2761

WITHDRAWN

331.12
I42f

DATE DUE

Trexler Library
Muhlenberg College
Allentown, PA 18104

DEMCO